THE PENTATEUCH

IN THE

PROGRESSIVE REVELATIONS OF GOD TO MEN

By REV. HENRY COWLES, D.D

WIPF & STOCK · Eugene, Oregon

Wipf and Stock Publishers
199 W 8th Ave, Suite 3
Eugene, OR 97401

The Pentateuch in its Progressive Revelations of God to Men
By Cowles, Henry
Softcover ISBN-13: 978-1-7252-9097-6
Hardcover ISBN-13: 978-1-7252-9098-3
eBook ISBN-13: 978-1-7252-9099-0
Publication date 11/2/2020
Previously published by D. Appleton & Co., 1879

This edition is a scanned facsimile of the original edition published in 1879.

PREFACE.

My reasons for treating the Pentateuch topically rather than textually will be obvious. Criticism on the original text is rarely needed. There is seldom the least occasion to aid the reader in following the line of thought or the course of argument. The demand here is rather for the discussion and due presentation of the great themes of the book. My plan has therefore aimed to meet this demand, discussing these themes *critically* so far as seemed necessary either because of their intrinsic nature or because of popular objections or misconceptions; and always *practically* so far forth as to show the important moral bearings of these themes as revelations of God to man. It has been, however, my purpose to explain all the difficult, doubtful, or controverted passages.

The modern objections to Genesis, more or less related to true science, have been brought under special examination because they are at present eliciting so much public attention. Let all real truth be welcomed and held in honor, whether revealed in the works of God or in his word. It is *knowledge of God* that we seek; some of which we learn through his works of creation or of providence; more through his revealed word. It behooves us to dismiss all apprehensions lest these diverse forms of divine revelation may come into real conflict, and equally, all fear lest the Bible should be compelled to recede as Science advances.

The points of contact between sacred and profane history and antiquities have been carefully examined, both for their own intrinsic interest and for the incidental confirmation which they bring to the sacred volume.

PREFACE.

As will appear in the Introduction I have had an eye somewhat to the idea of *progress* in these successive steps of divine revelation—yet with an aim not so much to prove a point disputed as to illustrate a fact sometimes overlooked; hoping thus to heighten the reader's interest.

This wonderful grouping of those events of the earliest ages of time, given us of God through the masterly hand of Moses, is for every reason worthy of profoundest study. In the humble hope that these pages may serve to obviate old difficulties; suggest new aspects of truth; inspire fresh zeal in this study; and enhance the spiritual profit of every reader—this volume is submitted to the Christian public. HENRY COWLES.

OBERLIN, O., October, 1873.

CONTENTS.

INTRODUCTION, p. 1.

CHAPTER I.

CREATION, p. 9.
    Naturally the first fact revealed; Its moral lessons, 9;
    The origin of this record and the manner of its revelation to men, 12;
    Nature and the supernatural, 13; Theories on the origin of life, 14;
    The sense of the word "day" in Gen. 1:16;
    Argued (1) From the laws of language, 17; (2) From the narrative itself, 18;
    Objection from the law of the Sabbath, 21;
    (3) From Geological facts and their bearings on the question, 22;
    Prominent points of harmony between Genesis and Geology, 25;
    Does "Create" (Gen. 1:1) refer to the original production of matter? 26;
    The relation of v. 1 to v. 2, and to the rest of the chapter, 29;
    The work of the fourth day, 31;
    The sense of the record as to the *origin of life*, vegetable and animal, 32;
    On God's "making man in his own image," 33;
    The relation of Gen. 2: 4-25 to Gen. 1: 35.

CHAPTER II.

INVARIABILITY OF "KIND" IN THE VEGETABLE AND ANIMAL KINGDOM, 37;
    The theory of Mr. Darwin, 38; The issue between Darwin and Moses, 38;
    Darwin's five main arguments, 39; Brief replies, 40;
    Objections bearing generally against Darwin's scheme, 43;
    (1) It requires almost infinite time back of the earliest traces or possibilities of life, 43;
    (2) Requires what Nature does not give—a close succession of animal races, differing but infinitesimally from each other, 43;
    (3) His argument is essentially *materialistic* and is therefore false, 45;
    (4) It ignores man's intellectual and moral nature, 46;
    (5) It ignores or overrides the law of nature by which hybrids are infertile, 46;
    (6) This scheme is in many points revolting to the common sense of mankind, 46;
    (7) It is recklesss of the authority of revelation, 48.

THE ANTIQUITY OF MAN.

Two main questions: (1) Is the human family older than Adam? 49; (2) How far back was Adam?

The argument for man's high antiquity, (1) From traces of his skeleton, 50; (2) From his tools and works, 52; (3) From the traditions and chronologies of the old nations, 59.

CHAPTER III.

HEBREW CHRONOLOGY, 60;
 From birth of Christ back to the founding of Solomon's Temple, 60;
 First disputed period—that of the Judges, 60; second do. that of the sojourn in Egypt, 62; third do.; between Terah and Abraham, 64; fourth do.; from the creation to the flood, 66; fifth do.; from the flood to the call of Abraham, 68.

CHAPTER IV.

ANTIQUITY OF MAN RESUMED, 72;
 On the Antiquity of Egypt, 72;
 The date of Menes, its first king, and of the pyramids, 74;
 Unity of the human race: Were there races of pre-Adamic men, now extinct? 75;
 Are the present living races descendants of the same first pair? 75;

CHAPTER V.

THE SABBATH, 77;
 As old as Eden; made for man as a race.

CHAPTER VI.

THE EVENTS OF EDEN, 81;
 Is the description of man's fall symbolic or historic? 81;
 The moral trial, 84; The temptation, 87; The fall, 88.
 The curse; the first installment of the penalty for transgression, 89;
 The first promise, 90.

CHAPTER VII.

FROM THE FALL TO THE FLOOD, 92.
 Notes on special passages, Gen. 4: 1, "I have gotten a man—the Lord," 92; Gen. 4: 6, 7—words of the Lord to Cain, 92; Gen. 4: 23, 24, the song of Lamech, 92; Abel's offering and the origin of sacrifices, 93; The great moral lessons of the antediluvian age, 95.

CHAPTER VIII.

THE FLOOD, 99;
 Its moral causes, 99; Its physical causes, 101; Was this flood universal? 102; (*a*) as to the earth's surface, (*b*) as to its population; Traditions of a great deluge, 105.

CONTENTS. vii

CHAPTER IX.

FROM THE FLOOD TO THE CALL OF ABRAHAM, 107;
  The law against murder and its death-penalty, 107; The prophecy of Noah, 108; The genealogy of the historic nations, 110; Babel and the confusion of tongues, 112.

CHAPTER X.

ABRAHAM, 114;
  His personal history; the divine purposes in the new system inaugurated with him;
  Concentration of moral forces; a more definite *covenant* between God and his people;
  Utilizing the family relation, 116;
  Developing a great example of the obedience of faith, 120; (*a*) In leaving his country at God's call, 120; (*b*) In waiting long but hopefully for his one son of promise, 120; (*c*) In obeying the command to offer this son a sacrifice, 121;
  God's revelations to Abraham *progressive*, 122;
  The missionary idea in this system—blessings to all the nations, 125;
  The Messiah included in these promises, 126;
  Sodom and Gomorrah, 128;
  The angel of the Lord, 130.

CHAPTER XI.

THE PATRIARCHS, ISAAC, JACOB, JOSEPH, 132;
  Isaac, 132; Jacob and Bethel, 133; Jacob at Mahanaim, 137; The struggle of prayer; The points and grounds of this conflict; The law of prevailing prayer, 140;
  Jacob and Joseph, 143; Developments of personal character, 144; Joseph in Egypt, 146; The hand of God in this history—seen in the sufferings of the innocent, 155;
  The hand of God in overruling sin for good, 158;
  The purposes of God in locating Israel in Egypt, 160;
  Ancient Egyptian history and life confirms Moses, 162;
  Special passages considered:
  Going down into Sheol, Gen. 37: 35; Jacob's benedictions upon his sons, Gen. 49, 168; The Scepter of Judah, Gen. 49: 10, 169;
  The less readable portions of Genesis, 171; Close of Genesis, 172.

CHAPTER XII.

EXODUS—
  The oppression, 173; Moses, 175; His great mission, 179;
  The ten plagues, 185:
  These plagues supernatural, 187; Several of them specially adapted to Egypt, 189; The case of the magicians, 190; The shape of the demand upon Pharaoh to let the people go, 193;
  The hardening of Pharaoh's heart, 194;
  History of the case 195; What is said of God's purpose in it, 203; Light on this case from God's revealed character, 204.

CHAPTER XIII.

THE PASSOVER, 206;
    Consecration of all first-born, 208;
    The long route to Canaan, 210; The march and the pursuit, 211; The guiding pillar of cloud and of fire, 212; The locality of the Red Sea crossing, 216.

CHAPTER XIV.

THE HISTORIC CONNECTIONS OF MOSES WITH PHARAOH AND EGYPT, 217.

CHAPTER XV.

THE EVENTS NEAR AND AT SINAI, 223;
    The manna, 223; Rephidim; water by miracle, 226; The battle with Amalek, 229; *Jethro*, 230;
    The Scenes at Sinai, 232;
    The national covenant; The giving of the law, 234;
    The moral law, given from Sinai, 236;
    To be distinguished from "the statutes and judgments," 237;
    The commandments considered severally; (1) 238; (2) 239; (3) 241; (4) 241; (5) 243; (6–9) 243; (10) 245;
    Progress in the revelations of God to man, 246.

CHAPTER XVI.

THE HEBREW THEOCRACY:
    The supreme power, 251; The powers of Jehovah's Vicegerent, 253; The General Assembly and their Elders, 254; The scope afforded for self-government, democracy, 255; The fundamental principles of this system, 258; Its union of Church and State, 259; Its principles and usages in regard to war, with notice of the war-commission against the doomed Canaanites, 261; The grant of Canaan, and the command to extirpate the Canaanites, 262.

CHAPTER XVII.

THE CIVIL INSTITUTES OF MOSES, OR THE HEBREW CODE OF CIVIL LAW:
    General view of it, 270; Analysis of the crimes condemned, 273;
    Crimes against God:
    Idolatry, 273; Perjury, 274; Presumptuous sins, 275; Violations of the Sabbath, 276; Magic arts, 276;
    Crimes against parents and rulers, 279;
    Crimes against person and life, i. e. crimes of blood, 280;
    Cities of refuge, 282; Murder by unknown hands, 284;
    Crimes against chastity, 285;
    Statutes to protect rights of property, 286;
    Statutes against usury, 288; Statutes for the relief of the poor, 289;
    Crimes against reputation, 292.

CHAPTER XVIII.

CIVIL INSTITUTES OF MOSES CONCLUDED:
Hebrew servitude, 294;
Man-stealing, 294; No rendition of fugitives, 295; Severe personal injuries entitled to freedom, 295; Periodical emancipation, 296; Religious privileges of servants, 298; The slavery that existed before Moses, 299; The condition of Israel in bondage in Egypt, 299;
The Jubilee, 300;
Its bearing upon foreign servants, 301; Meaning of "bond-servant," 302; Servants of foreign birth, 302;
Judicial Procedure, 304;
Judges; The seat of justice, 305; The processes of prosecution, 305; Advocates; of witnesses, 305;
Punishments, 306;
Fines, 306; Sin and trespass offerings, 307; Stripes, 307; Excommunication, 308; Modes of capital punishment, 308; Disgrace after death, 308; Judicial procedure and punishment summary, 308; Statutes without penalties, 309;
Two Historic Questions:
(*a*) How far is this system indebted to Egypt? 311;
(*b*) How far have the best civil codes of the most civilized nations been indebted to this Hebrew code? 314;
Progressive revelations of God in this code, 319.

CHAPTER XIX.

THE RELIGIOUS SYSTEM OF THE HEBREWS, 321;
Classification of sacrifices, 322; Choice of animals for sacrifice, 323; The scenes of sacrifice, 324; The significance of sacrifices, 325; Of the portion taken as food, 326; Special sacrifices, 327;
Sacred times and seasons, 327;
The three great festivals, 328; The Feast of Pentecost, 328; The Feast of Tabernacles, 329; The great day of Atonement, 331;
Sacred Edifices and Apparatus, 334;
The Sacred Orders, 335; Present value of the Mosaic ritual, 336; Its lessons on the blood of atonement, 338; That these lessons are steps of *progress* in the revelation of God to men, 340.

CHAPTER XX.

HISTORIC EVENTS OF HEBREW HISTORY FROM SINAI TO THE JORDAN, 342;
The golden calf, 342; The intercession of Moses, 344; The Lord reveals his name and glory, 346; Incidents connected with this idol-worship, 350; Lessons from Moses on prayer, 353; Taberah and Kibroth-hataavah, 354; Miriam and Aaron envious of Moses, 355; Kadesh-barnea and the unbelieving spies, 356; Rebellion of Korah and his company, 360; The fiery serpent and the brazen one, 363; Balak and Balaam, 364; Balaam's prophecies, 367; His prayer, 368.

CHAPTER XXI.

ON THE LAST FOUR BOOKS OF THE PENTATEUCH:
Their *method* and *subject-matter*, 375; *Leviticus*, 376; Numbers, 876; Deuteronomy, 377; Deut. 26, 378; The prophet like Moses, Deut. 18, 380; The blessings and the curses, 383; The last words of Moses, 384; Deut. 32, 385; Moses blesses the tribes, Deut. 33, 394; Death and character of Moses, 401;
The Mosaic system and the future life, 403;
Progressive developments of truth and of God, 412.

INTRODUCTION.

THE REVELATIONS OF GOD TO MEN PROGRESSIVE.

It is supposable that God might have made his entire written revelation of himself to men *at once*, through one inspired prophet and one only; in one definite locality (Eden or Jerusalem), and all brought within a twelve-month. But he did not deem this the wisest way. He preferred to speak at considerable intervals of time—through a long succession of "holy men of old;" "at sundry times and in diverse manners" (Heb. i: 1). Among the choice results of this progressive method we may name the following: (1.) That by means of it God made large and admirable use of *history*. This was revealing himself to men, not simply by his *words* but by his *works*. In ways which men could not well mistake, he was thus able to manifest himself as the God of nations; also as the God of families; and not least, as the God of individual men. It was vital to human welfare that he should place himself before men as being not a heathen Brumha, sunk in unconscious sleep for ages, but as the All-seeing, ever-active One, exercising a real government over men, ruling in equity and yet with loving-kindness; ever present amid all their activities and impressing himself upon the thought and the heart of the race. In this line of policy how admirably did he give promises to his servants to inspire their faith in himself; then prove that faith through years and ages of trial and delay; but at last confirm his word by its signal fulfillment! By what other method could He so effectually reveal himself as a *personal God*—the personal Friend of his trustful children—evermore worthy of their supreme confidence, whether they could or could not see at once all the reasons of his ways?

His providential rule over nations as such found in this method ample scope for the fullest illustration. The record of this ruling in the ministrations of prosperity and adversity; in the rise and the ruin of great nations through the lapse of the world's early centuries, constitute a marvelously rich portion of this progressive revelation of God to man.——A Bible made up of words from God without any *deeds* of God would be open to dangerous misunderstanding and thus might in great measure fail of its purpose. At best it would be tame and unimpressive compared with the method God has chosen of revealing himself largely in actual works at innumerable points along the ages for more than four thousand years.

(2.) Again; no small gain accrued from the large number and various qualities of the holy men through whom God spake. The personal blessing to themselves was too rich to be limited to any one man. Rather let it be shared by many scores of men, standing forth before their respective generations age after age from Adam down to him of Patmos.——We may also note the large range of diversity in their personal character and in their endowments as authors. How varied were the circumstances of their lives and the moral trials which were the refiner's fire to their spiritual life! How abundantly by this means did their personal experiences illustrate the ways of God with those who come nearest to him in the fullness of heart communion! How many chapters are thus provided of the most reliable most varied and easily applied Christian experience!

By means of the diversity of inspired writers, the Bible is enriched with the charms of a large variety in style, as well as in the experiences of the Christian life. Among all the sacred penmen, no two minds are cast in the same mold. Poetry, eloquence, imagination, logic, sublimity, pathos—in what endless combinations do we find these gifts apportioned and manifested! How should we admire the wisdom which chose out men of gifts so diversified, and then adopted a method of inspiration which left each writer's mind to the unrestrained development of its own peculiar genius.

(3.) Yet farther; the progressive historical method of making up the Bible opened the door widely for miracles and prophecy. The occasions for miracles were multiplied. They could be introduced naturally where manifold and not single results should accrue. In this way there was no need to manufacture opportunities for miraculous interposition. Abundant occasions arose to demand them, when consequently they had a most thrilling effect. We may see this in the scenes of the Exodus, the conquest of Canaan, the rescue of Hezekiah and his people.

So also of prophecy. It asks for *time*. On the supposition that the fulfillment is to appear in the Scriptures, an interval of some duration must come between the utterance and the fulfillment. It was also wise that prophecy should subserve the superadded purpose of spiritual comfort to God's people during the ages between comparative darkness and forth-breaking light. In fact it gave to God's people the first single beams of morning twilight, bearing the grateful assurance that the Sun of Righteousness would surely rise on the nations in the fullness of gospel times.

(4.) Still again; by this method of making up inspired history it is placed side by side with profane history and the most ancient monuments of the race, and thus invites investigation on the point of its truthfulness. Is this progressive history of God's ways toward men confirmed by whatever reliable history of the same period has come down to us through other sources? This point well deserves and richly rewards a careful examination.

(5.) Moreover, it is to be presumed that God would commence his revelation of himself to our race in the very infancy of their existence. The Bible shows us that he did. Assuming that at this point they had every thing to learn, we ought to expect that their first Bible lessons would turn their thought to the great truths of *natural religion*—the manifestations of God in his *works of creation and providence*. In harmony with this reasonable expectation, we read—"In the beginning God created the heavens and the earth." In that opening chapter of revelation, God said, "Let there be light," and it was; also "a firmament" above, and it was; "Let the dry land appear," and it appeared; "let there be light-bearers in the heavens," and they shine forth; let grass and herbs grow; let creatures live in the waters, in the air, and on the dry land, and it was so; and finally, "let us make *man*," far unlike all the rest—"in our own image and likeness"—and god-like man sprang into being. So onward the narrative witnesses to the ever-present hand of God in the mists, the rains, and the teeming vegetation of the new-made world. God, the great Author of nature; God in nature and evermore over all nature, was the first lesson recorded in God's revelation of himself to men.

In natural order, the next lesson like this, is *God in providence*—God administering the agencies of earthly good or ill, making his presence manifest among his intelligent and moral offspring, and even "coming down to see" (as the early record has it) what men were doing and whether the cry coming up to him told truthfully of the guilty violence perpetrated by man upon his fellows. This idea—God ruling over the race in righteous retribution for their good or evil deeds—was obviously one of the first great moral lessons to be illustrated, enforced, impressed. So vital is this conviction to the ends of a moral government that it should not surprise us if the actual administration of present rewards and punishments in the common course of human life in this world should be made far more prominent and palpable in the early than in the later ages of the race, so much so as to force itself upon the dullest eyes and compel the attention of the most stupid and reluctant observers.——Such (we shall have occasion to notice) was unquestionably the divine policy throughout the earlier stages of human history, abundantly apparent in the records of the Bible. In later times, the exigencies of a system of probation, and especially the importance of giving large scope to *faith*, after sufficient evidence has been afforded, served to impose narrower limits upon present retribution, reserving the larger share to the perfect adjustments of the great future. In the earlier stages of human history, it would obviously be vital to give men sufficient demonstration that God *does rule*, and therefore is to be believed when he threatens to punish either here or hereafter, and consequently is evermore to be *feared* as the certain avenger of crime. Hence the imperative need in those early ages of such manifestations of God's justice as would impress the *fear* of his name. With our eye open to the native pride of depraved souls and to their appalling tendency to disown God and bid him "depart" and not trouble them with his "ways," it will not surprise us that God should shape his earliest agencies of providence to inspire fear rather than love. It needs but the least thought to see that this policy was a simple necessity—the most obvious dictate of wisdom. In this point revelation might naturally be *progressive,* advancing as soon as was safe and wise from manifestations inspiring fear to those which would reveal his love.

The doctrine of divine providence in regard to the sufferings of good men—one of the hardest problems of human life—might be expected to unfold itself gradually. It would be quite too much for the infancy of human thought and knowledge to grasp this problem and master all its intricacies. Hence the scope for a gradual unfolding (as we may see) all the way from the discussions in Job and the Psalms to the clearer light which shines in the epistle to the Hebrews, as also in Peter and Paul. This beautiful illustration of progress in divine revelation will well reward attention in its place.

(6.) On the supposition that God's scheme for the recovery of our lost race contemplated some atonement for sin—a provision in its very nature and relations toward both God and man exceedingly delicate and critical—it is at least presumable beforehand that God would bring out this idea *with great care*—with the wisest precaution against misconception, and not improbably with some foregoing illustrations of its significance and of its intended application. Precisely this we see in the great sacrificial system of the Mosaic economy. We only put essentially the same idea into other and more general terms when we say that a protracted course of successive revelations provides for making an antecedent economy pave the way for a subsequent one—a first revelation preparatory to a second—one set of ideas imprinted and impressed upon the human mind, made conducive to other and higher revelations yet to follow. The wisdom of such progressions can not fail to impress itself upon all thoughtful minds.——Thus God's revelations of himself from age to age were adjusted to the advance in spiritual development which he had provided for in the human mind. As training and culture developed higher capacities, new lessons were in order and higher attainments were made. "Whoso is wise and will observe these things, even they shall understand" the loving-kindness and matchless wisdom of the Lord.

To forestall misapprehensions (possible and sometimes actual), let it be noted that progress in the revealed science of God by no means supersedes what has gone before. Naturally it only serves to place old truths in new and richer light. No one fact affirmed concerning God in the earlier ages is denied in the later. Certain features of his character may be brought out more prominently in the later lessons, but there is no unsaying of the things said before. Nothing can conflict with this axiom of divine science—"I am the Lord; I change not." Prominence may be given in the early ages to such manifestations as impress men with fear and as set forth God's righteous justice toward transgressors; while later revelations may disclose more fully the depths of divine love and compassion. Yet let none infer that God is less just in the New Testament than in the Old, or that the earlier policy of God's throne has been modified to a larger leniency toward persistent criminals. The men who flippantly talk of throwing aside the older revelation "as they do an old almanac" mistake most egregiously. God has written nothing to be thrown aside. The oldest records still give us lessons of God shining with unfading freshness and undimmed glory. The statutes binding on Israel in the wilderness and in Canaan may not be in the same sense binding on our age, but they have not for this reason become valueless. They made revelations of God then, truthful and rich; they make revelations of God still which it were but small indication of wisdom or good sense to ignore.

CHAPTER I.

CREATION.

FITLY the written word of God to the race begins with the *creation*. In every reflecting mind the first inquiry must be this: Whence am I? Whence came my being—this wonderful existence; these active powers? It must be that I am indebted for all these gifts to some higher Being; how earnestly then do I ask—*To whom?*——No other question can claim priority to this. Every thing in its nature and relations gives it precedence above all other questions. Inasmuch as my reason affirms to me that I owe my existence to some great Maker, I feel that I must know Him and must know my responsibilities to Him. I need to learn also how the further question—my future destiny—may link itself with my relations to Him who brought me into being.

Of secondary yet similar interest are the corresponding questions as to the world we live in. Who made it? Does its Maker hold it under his own control? Does He still operate its forces and wield its agencies? Have I any obligations and duties toward Him who made the earth and all that is therein? Verily I must assume that if there be a God, at once Creator and Upholder of the earth and Father of his rational offspring, his written word will hasten to throw light on the otherwise dark minds of his children—will let them know that "in the beginning God made the heavens and the earth" and man.

The *moral lessons* of this great fact—God our Creator—are forcibly brought out in later scriptures. Listen to the Psalmist: "O come, let us sing unto the Lord ..... for he is a great God and a great King above all gods. In his hands are the deep places of the earth; the strength of the hills is his also. The sea is his and he made it, and his hands formed the dry land. O come, let us worship and bow down; let us kneel before the Lord our Maker, for he is our God and we are the people of his pasture and the sheep of his hand." (Ps. 95: 1–7.) Note also the blended sublimity and beauty of David's appeal: "Praise the Lord; sing unto him a new song, for the earth is full of the goodness of the Lord. By the word of the Lord were the heavens made and all the host of them by the breath of his mouth. He gathereth the waters of the sea together as an heap; he layeth up the depth in store-houses. Let all the earth fear the Lord; let the inhabitants of the world stand in awe of him, for he spake and it was: he commanded, and it stood fast." (Ps. 33: 1–9.) Still higher if possible rises the lofty strain of Isaiah when he would set forth the unequalled power of the great Creator as the Refuge and Salvation of his trustful children:—"Who hath measured the waters in the hollow of his hand and meted out heaven with a span, and comprehended the dust of the earth in a measure, and weighed the mountains in scales and the hills in a balance? To whom then will ye liken God"? etc. (Isa. 40: 12, 18).——So when Job had indulged himself too far in questioning the ways of God in providence, the Lord replied out of the whirlwind, demanding of him—"Where wert thou when I laid the foundations of the earth? Declare if thou hast understanding. Who hath laid the measures thereof if thou knowest—who hath stretched the line upon it? Whereupon were the foundations thereof fastened, or who laid the cornerstone thereof when the morning stars sang together and all the sons of God shouted for joy"? ..... "Canst thou lift up thy voice to the clouds that abundance of waters may cover thee? Canst thou send lightnings that they may go and say unto thee, Here are we"? (Job 38: 4–7, 34, 35.)

In that great conflict of ages against idolatry, the one final appeal was wont to be made to this great fact of God's Creatorship. We have examples in Ps. 115: 2–8 and Jer 10: 1–16 and elsewhere.——Thus throughout the sacred word this great fact that God is our Creator, involving the whole sphere of God in nature, stands as the first witness to his true divinity, the first proof that in him we live and have our being—the ground of the first claim upon us for supreme homage, worship, trust, love and obedience. The first lessons taught in Eden were taken from this great and open volume of natural religion. The first lessons which God's people were to place before the heathen in their mission work of the early ages were drawn from the visible worlds and from their testimony to the Great Creator. These manifestations are the alphabet of God; the point therefore from which progressive revelations begin.

Noticeably the record of the creation (Gen. 1 and 2) rests not with simply giving the general statement that God made all things, but enters somewhat into the particulars, reciting in certain points the *steps of the process and the order of its details.* First the heavens and the earth had a beginning and this beginning was *from God.* At some stage in the process, perhaps the next in order after the heavens and the earth could be said to be, the earth was chaotic, *i. e.* formless and desolate; then God brought forth light; then to clear the atmosphere somewhat of mists and vapors, he caused some of its waters to rise into the expanse, and some to descend to the earth below; then gathered the waters below into seas, leaving portions of the earth's surface dry land. Then he brought forth grass and herbage; next, the light-bearers in the heavens appeared—the sun, moon and stars; then came into being fish, reptiles and fowl; and on the sixth day land animals and man. Thus in six successive periods of time, through steps of gradation easily traced by the witnessing "sons of God" (Job 38: 7), the processes of this creative work were finished. The Great Father would have his first-born unfallen "sons" as well as his later-born and redeemed children enjoy these works of his creative hand, and therefore he developed them slowly and in the order of naturally successive steps that they might see that all was truly "good," "very good."

Partly because of advances made within recent times in physical science, partly because of speculations not always friendly in tone to the inspired record, and partly because of the intrinsic interest and importance of the subject, some special points in this narrative demand very particular attention.

1. *The origin of the written record and the manner of its revelation to men.*

The entire book of Genesis is ascribed to Moses on most valid grounds; whether as compiler only or as original author, is, therefore, the first question.——I do not see how this point can be determined with absolute certainty. The probabilities in my view favor the supposition of previously written documents, these probabilities arising, not to any considerable extent from manifest differences of style in its various portions, and not at all from diversities in the use of the names of God, Jehovah and Elohim; but mainly from the strong presumption that such genealogical records as abound in Genesis, coupled so largely with numbers, would be put in writing before the age of Moses. Men who had the knowledge of writing would certainly appreciate its utility for the preservation of such facts as these.—— And further; the very use of the word "generations"* (Gen. 2: 4) in the sense of history, and much more still the statement (Gen. 5: 1), "This is the *book* of the generations of Adam," raise this presumption nearly or quite to a certainty.——In making up the historical portions of the Scriptures it seems rational to assume that the Lord moved "holy men of old" to put in writing such facts falling under their personal observation and immediate knowledge as he deemed useful for these sacred records. In some cases the writer might be (as was Luke) just one remove from the original eye-witnesses, yet in a position to learn the facts with "perfect understanding" and "certainty." We should not doubt the *power* of God to give to holy men these historic facts by immediate revelation; but the question is not one of power, but of wisdom, of divine policy, and of fact. The divine policy seems to have been (in this case as in miracles) never to introduce the supernatural, the miraculous, to do what the natural might accomplish equally well. On this principle inspired men were moved of God to use their own eyes and minds in writing Scripture history in all cases when the facts came within their certain knowledge. There were facts, like these of the creation, which fell under no human eye, and which therefore do not come under this

*הולדות

principle. Some form of direct revelation from God is, therefore, to be assumed here. Though the supposition of a revealing angel might find some support from subsequent prophetic Scriptures, yet a direct revelation from God to some inspired writer is the more obvious supposition.——It has been asked—Was this creation in its processes and announcements shown in a manner analogous to prophetic vision—the writer then recording in his own phrase what he saw and heard?—— There being no testimony on this point from either of the two parties—the divine Revealer or the human writer—we must leave it undecided. Fortunately it is of no particular importance to us.——It is, however, of some importance that we consider the question whether in this account of the creation we are to look for statements adjusted to science—not merely to the stage of its progress in this present year of the nineteeth century, but to the perfect science of ultimate fact; or, on the other hand, for statements adapted to the average mind of Hebrew readers in the age of Moses, written for their comprehension, instruction and spiritual culture. I answer unhesitatingly, the latter. "All Scripture, given by inspiration of God, is profitable for doctrine . . . . . and for instruction in righteousness" (2 Tim. 3: 16), and was of God designed and shaped for these ends.—— Yet let it be borne in mind; these statements respecting the processes of creation, being in the sense intended, actually true, will not conflict with any true science. They may omit processes which human analysis and research may render probable, passing them as not germain to the scope of a moral revelation and as not likely to be intelligible to the masses of mankind.——Finally—that the assumed stand-point of view from which these processes of creation are contemplated is on this earth and not elsewhere in the universe is certain from the fact that it was written to be read and understood by men and not by angels. Hence we must expect the facts to be presented *as they would have appeared to a supposed observer upon our globe.*

2. *What is the true idea of nature, and what the line between nature and the supernatural?*

A reference to familiar facts will best set forth the case. Thus; it is in and by nature that at a certain temperature water becomes vapor; at another temperature, ice; that vapor rises in the atmosphere, water runs downward, and ice abides under the laws of solids. On the other hand it is *not* in nature that water in any of its forms creates itself. Its elements can not begin to be, save by some power above nature.——Again, by nature plants and animals reproduce their kind, but never can of themselves *begin* their own existence. Hence some of the processes brought before us in this record of creation come under the head of nature; others are as obviously supernatural—from the immediate hand of God. The work of the second day—the mists of the atmosphere, in part ascending in vapor, in part precipitated upon the earth in water—seems to have followed natural law. In the work of the third, the waters on higher portions of the earth's surface subsiding into the seas, follow the law of flowing water. But the original creation of matter and the beginnings of life, both vegetable and animal, must have been supernatural—from the immediate fiat of the Almighty.

This point would scarcely need special definition had not extreme views been put forth in our times; as (*e. g.*) that nature is virtually a second-rate deity—indebted to God, indeed, for the original gift of its powers, but thenceforward working those powers independently of God—made to run without God after he has once wound it up as the mechanic makes and winds up his watch. But the Scriptures recognize no such semi-deification of nature. According to their teaching, God still "*upholds* all things by the word of his power" (Heb. 1: 3); "By him all things consist" (Col. 1: 17)—*i. e.*, are maintained in their existence—are held to system and order under natural law. It is precisely God himself who gives or withholds the rain; who calls to the lightnings and they answer, "Here we are"—(Job 38: 35); and it is none the less God who wields these agencies because he does it in harmony with principles which are just as fixed as he pleases to have them. Therefore true science will take no exception to the doctrine that nature is nothing more or less than *God's established mode of operation*. We may call these modes of operations "laws" or "powers," and may think and speak of them as constituting "Nature;" but if we come to regard Nature as a maker and a doer,

CREATION: ON THE ORIGIN OF LIFE. 15

working independently of God, we have (inadvertently perhaps, but none the less really) ruled God out of his own universe. Both Scripture and reason hold that "in him we live and move and have our being." (Acts 17: 28.) The broad fact that God's intelligent creatures must live in this material world and be constantly acting upon matter and acted upon by matter, suggests abundant reasons why God should ordain fixed laws for the changes and states of all material things. But why should we think of God's hand as any the less present in all these changes of material states and forms because they follow fixed and ascertainable laws? In truth the divine wisdom is only the more abundantly manifested by means of this reliable uniformity.

Another doctrine yet more extreme severs all connection between nature and an intelligent Power above and over her, and thus makes her *supreme* in her domain. This is so far Atheism—ruling God out from at least the entire material universe.——Yet, again; to make nature herself intelligent—to ascribe to nature whatever traces of design appear in her operations, and to hold that nature is herself the universe, undistinguishable from any higher spiritual power, is Pantheism.——It is therefore important to define nature so that her true relations to the Supreme Intelligence—the very God—Creator and Lord of the universe—shall be distinctly seen and reverently recognized.

The advocates of extreme naturalism have labored faithfully to verify their doctrine by experiment. They have put Nature to task—not to say torture—to compel her to originate *life*. Pushing their chemical analysis of those forms of matter in which life is thought specially to reside, they flatter themselves that they have at last got their hands on the very elements which, brought together, make life, viz, carbonic acid, ammonia, and water, chemically combined. To this compound they give the name, "protoplasm." They have found, they say, that where life is there is protoplasm, its home and dwelling-place at least; and that life never appears lodging in any other home. They can not see that the presence of life adds any thing to this compound, or that its absence takes any thing away. Therefore they are sure they have found what makes life.

Now the skillful chemist in his laboratory has not the least difficulty in providing himself with carbonic acid, ammonia, and water. Why then does he not evolve the long-sought-for *life-force* and prove his doctrine, past all doubt? Let him bring out new beings, new forms of life, vegetable or animal or both, in ample diversity, for the range is unlimited. Let his laboratory push forth into being such troops of offspring as will forever confound gainsayers and prove that Nature, properly manipulated, is equal to the production of life-forces in endless variety and abundance.

Have any modern scientists done this? Not yet. Have they made any approximation toward it? Mr. Huxley thinks he has come so near to it that if he could only have at his service the favorable conditions of the very earliest state of matter, he should succeed. "If it were given me (says he) to look beyond the abyss of geologically-recorded time to the still more remote period when the earth was passing through physical and chemical conditions which it can no more see again than a man can recall his infancy, *I should expect to be a witness of the evolution of living protoplasm from not living matter*. That is the expectation to which analogical reasoning leads me."*——"Not living matter evolving living protoplasm" means that matter itself, dead matter, begets real life. Nature would thus become herself a creator, exercising the most decisive functions of the Infinite God. Mr. Huxley can not make Nature do this exploit in the present state of this world or of the universe; but he fully believes there was a time when he should have seen it if he had been there! This is his proof of the new doctrine. He will not presume to "call it any thing but an act of philosophic faith."

3. *The sense of the word "day" as used in Gen. I. of the six days of creation.*

To simplify the subject I make the single issue—Is it a period of twenty-four hours, or a period of special character, indefinitely long? The latter theory supposes the word to refer here not so much to *duration* as to *special character*—the sort of work done and the changes produced during the period contemplated.

---

*Lay sermons on spontaneous generation; pp. 364–366.

Turning our attention to this latter theory, we raise three leading inquiries:

(1.) Do the laws of language and, specially, does the usage of the word "day" permit it?

(2.) Apart from the bearing of geological facts, are there points in the narrative itself which demand or even favor this sense of the word?

(3.) What are the geological facts bearing on this question, and what weight may legitimately be accorded to them?

(1.) Beyond all question the word "day" is used abundantly, (and therefore admits of being used) to denote a period of special character, with no particular reference to its duration. We have a case in this immediate connection (Gen. 2: 4), where it is used of the whole creative period: "In the *day* that the Lord God made the earth and the heavens." Under the same usage we have "the *day* of the Lord (1 Thess. 5: 2) for the day of judgment; "the *day* of God," in the same sense (2 Pet. 3: 12); "the *day* of salvation" (2 Cor. 6: 2); "day of redemption" (Eph. 4: 30); a "day of darkness and of gloominess; a day of clouds and of thick darkness" (Joel 2: 2). "In the day of prosperity, be joyful; but in the day of adversity, consider" (Eccl. 7: 14). "If thou hadst known in this thy *day* the things," etc. (Luke 19: 42). So also Job 19: 25, and John 8: 56, etc.

To set aside this testimony from usage as being inapplicable to the present case, it has been said—
(a.) That here is a succession of days, "first day," "second day," "third day," etc., and that this requires the usual sense of days of the week.——To which the answer is that here are six special periods succeeding each other—a sufficient reason for using the word in the peculiar sense of a period of special character. Each of these periods is distinct from any and all the rest in the character of the work wrought in it.——The reason for dividing the creative work into six periods—"days"—rather than into more or fewer lies in the divine wisdom as to the best proportion of days of man's labor to the one day of his rest, the Sabbath. God's plan for his creative work contemplated his own example as suggestive of man's Sabbath and was shaped accordingly. This accounts for dividing the work of creation into six

special periods, correlated to God's day of rest from creative work.——(b.) It will also be urged that each of these days is said to be made up of evening and of morning—"The evening and the morning were the first day," etc. But the strength of this objection comes mainly from mistranslation and consequent misconception of the original. The precise thought is not that evening and morning composed or made up one full day; but rather this: There was evening and there was morning—day one, *i. e.*, day number one. There was darkness and then there was light, indicating one of the great creative periods.*

It is one thing to say—There were alternations of evening and morning—*i. e.* dark scenes and bright scenes—marking the successive periods of creation, first, second, third, etc.; and another thing to affirm that each of these evenings and mornings *made up* a day. The point specially affirmed in the two cases, though somewhat analogous, is not by any means identical.——Let it be considered moreover, that while in Hebrew as in English, *night* and *day* are often used for the average twelve-hour duration of darkness and of light respectively in each twenty-four hours, yet in neither language are the words *evening* and *morning* used in this sense, as synonymous with night and day. Indeed "evening" and "morning" are rather points than periods of time; certainly do not indicate any definite amount of time—any precise number of hours; but are used to denote the two great changes—*i. e.* from light to darkness and from darkness to light; in other words, from day to night and from night to day. Therefore to make evening and morning added together constitute one day is entirely without warrant in either Hebrew or English usage and can not be the meaning of these passages in Genesis.†

(2.) *The showing of the narrative itself,* considered apart from the bearing of geological facts.

(a.) Here vs. 3–5 demand special attention, this first

---

* Dr. A. M'Caul in "Aids to Faith," page 241 renders it—"And evening happened and morning happened—one day." Precisely this is the sense of the Septuagint and of the Syriac. See also Tayler Lewis in Lange's Genesis, pp. 132, 133.

† See the usage in David (Ps. 55: 17), "Evening and morning and at noon will I pray."

day being the model one.——I understand "evening" to be the chaotic state of v. 2, when "darkness was on the face of the deep," and "morning" to be that first "light" which God spake into being. The reason for using these words—"evening and morning"—in this sense I find in the universal sentiment of mankind that light is pleasant and darkness is not. This sentiment is indicated here; "God saw the light that it was good." The state of chaos was in contrast with this— dismal, dreary, awakening no sense of beauty or order; no emotions of joy. The light of day brings joy, and the freshest and best sensation of it comes with the morning. Hence these words were fitly and beautifully appropriate to the two great creative states—first chaos; secondly, light—which together marked off the first of the six creative days.——But we can not for a moment think of this chaotic state as being only twelve hours. We can not rationally think of the word "evening" applied to it as having any reference to time, duration. It was an evening only in the sense of being dark, desolate, any thing but joyous like the morning. The word "evening" may be chosen rather than night for the sake of a more perfect antithesis with "morning."

(b.) Throughout at least the first three of these creative epochs there was no sun-rising and setting to mark off the ordinary day. These therefore were not the common human day; but, as Augustine long ago said, these are the days of God—divine days—measuring off his great creative periods. God moved through these six great periods by successive stages of labor and of rest. Beginning with the long evening of chaos; then advancing to a glorious day of light; then, after a cessation analogous to man's rest by night, he proceeded to the work of the second day—the joyous and beautiful development of the firmament in the heavens. So onward by stages of repose and of activity, these figurative evenings and mornings continued through the six successive epochs of creation.

(c.) In some at least of these creative epochs, the work done demands more time than twenty-four hours. For example, the gathering of the waters from under the heavens into one place to constitute the seas or oceans and leave portions of the earth's surface dry land. Nothing short of absolute miracle could effect this in one human day. But miracle should not be assumed here, the rule of reason and the normal law of God's operations being never to work a miracle in a case where the ordinary course of nature will accomplish the same results equally well. We must the more surely exclude miracle and assume the action of natural law only throughout these processes of the creative work because the very purpose of a protracted rather than an instantaneous creation looked manifestly to the enlightenment, instruction, interest, and joy of those "morning stars," the "sons of God" who beheld the scene, then "sang together and shouted for joy" (Job 38: 7).——

The greatness of the work assigned to the fourth day stringently forbids our compressing it within the limits of one ordinary human day. Especially is this the case if we understand the verse to speak of the original creation of these light-bearers—the sun and the moon and the stars also, and of their adjustment in their spheres for their assigned work. Think of the vastness of the sun and of the numbers, magnitude, and immense distances of the stars; and ask how it is possible that the creation of these bodies could be either instructive or joyful to the beholding angels if it had been all rushed through within twenty-four hours of human time.—— This difficulty is in a measure relieved if we suppose the fourth day's work to have been, not the original creation of these heavenly bodies, but only the bringing of them into the view of a supposed spectator upon the earth—*i. e.* by clearing the atmosphere so as to make these heavenly bodies visible. The question at issue between these two constructions of the fourth day's work must be examined in its place.——The amount of creative and other work brought within the sixth day should be noticed. First, God created all the land animals; then Adam; then he brought "every beast of the field and every fowl of the air" to Adam to see what he would call them—which at least must assume that Adam had attained a somewhat full knowledge of language, and that he had time enough to study the special character of each animal so as to give each one its appropriate name, and time enough also to ascertain that there was not one among them all adapted to be a "helpmeet" for himself. Then the "deep sleep" of Adam—how long protracted, the record saith not; and finally the creation of Eve from one of his ribs—all to come within the sixth day; for the creation of Eve certainly falls within this day, being a part of the creative work, and accomplished, therefore, before God's seventh day of rest from all his work began. These labors of the sixth day, moreover, were precisely such as should not be rushed through in haste. The importance, not to say solemnity, of these transactions and the special interest they must be supposed to awaken in the first-born "sons of God" most stringently preclude precipitate haste. It is not easy to see how Moses or his intelligent readers of the early time could have supposed all this to have transpired within the twelve hours of light in a human day.——We may say, moreover, in regard to each and all of these six creative periods that if the holy angels were indeed spectators of these scenes and if God adjusted his methods of creation to the capacities of these pupils—these admiring students of his glorious works—then surely we must not think of his compressing them within the period of six human days. Divine days they certainly must have been, sufficiently protracted to afford finite minds scope for intelligent study, adoring contemplation, and as the Bible indicates, most rapturous shouts of joy.

Against the theory of indefinitely long periods, it is objected that *the law of the Sabbath demands the usual sense of the word "day."* The record in Gen. 2: 2, 3, is— "On the seventh day God ended his work which he had made; and he rested on the seventh day from all his work which he had made. And God blessed the seventh day and sanctified it, because that in it he had rested from all his work which he had created and made." The words of the fourth command are—"Six days shalt thou labor and do all thy work; but the seventh day is the Sabbath of the Lord thy God, etc.—for in six days the Lord made heaven and earth: wherefore the Lord blessed the Sabbath day and hallowed it."——The real argument here rests on the analogy between God's working and resting, and man's labor and rest. In each case the period of labor is six out of seven; of rest, one in seven. This argument does not require that God's six working days and one resting day should be of twenty-four hours each. If it did, we should be hard pressed to show that God's seventh day of rest from creation's work was a merely human day from sun to sun. No; it suffices if we make God's days of creative energy and of creative rest each and all *divine days*—all alike periods of indefinite length—all of the same sort; and on the other hand man's days of labor and his day of rest, all human days, of the same sort with each other, from sun to sun. As God's resting day is plainly of indefinite length—a period known by its character and not by its duration, so should his days of creative labor be: not only so *may* they be, but so they *ought* to be according to the analogy and argument in the case.——We come therefore to the conclusion that entirely apart from the demands of geological science, the creative days must be periods of indefinite length, called "days" with reference to the peculiar work done in them and to their peculiar character, and not as being the ordinary human day of twenty-four hours. It may be admitted, moreover, that the phraseology and the whole shaping of the narrative in respect to days may have contemplated the institution of the Sabbath—to be founded as shown above upon the analogy of God's labor and rest with man's permitted labor and enjoined rest in commemoration of God's work of creation.

(3.) We are to consider *the geological facts bearing on this point and the weight legitimately due to them.*

If the point last put has been sustained, it will be seen at the outset that even should geology make large demands for time, far beyond the ordinary human day, we shall have no occasion to strain the laws of interpretation to bring the record into harmony with such demands.——We open this inquiry therefore into the facts of geology, not so much to make out if possible a harmony between them and Genesis by toning down the facts of science or by toning up the inspired record, as to show how readily and how beautifully the facts just as they are (so far as known) accord with the legitimate sense of the sacred record.

Preliminary to the main inquiry before us is the question as to the primary original state of matter. Was it brought into existence in its primordial elements—those molecules which not only defy all human effort at analysis, but which seem to be in their nature the simplest forms of matter?——Chemistry has shown that many of the most familiar substances, long sup-

CREATION: ON THE WORD "DAY."

posed to be simple, are really compound. Were they brought into existence in the state in which we commonly see them, or in their ultimate, most simple elements? For example, did God originally create water, or the two gases (hydrogen and oxygen) of which it is composed, which were subsequently combined chemically into water?——On this point the Scriptures are silent. If Science has any thing to reveal about it, the field is open to her and she may proceed, nothing in the sacred Scriptures dissenting or restricting. If she succeeds in proving or half proving that the first state of matter was nebulous—a "fire-mist"—gaseous in form, very well. I do not see that the record of Moses contests this theory. It passes this point with no dogmatic statements whatever, not even a fact which necessarily implies either the affirmative or the negative. The record in Genesis does assume that at the point where the second day's work begins, the atmosphere was heavily charged with vapor, and that a part of this was precipitated upon the earth in water and a part borne upward into the higher strata of the atmosphere. The third day's work gathered the waters then upon the earth's surface into the ocean beds and left portions of the land dry. Consequently the state of the atmosphere, and in general the condition of the waters of our globe were not arranged at first just as we have them now. So much we are told.

There are yet other preliminary questions.

On the shores of lakes, seas, oceans, we find pebbles rounded and smooth, mineralogically of the same elements which are found in rock formations. Were they created in this rounded and worn state, or were they once portions of these rock strata, but subsequently broken up by natural agencies and worn by the action of flowing water?

Another case. Coal beds often contain what seem to be whole trees' and huge vegetables (ferns, etc.) apparently charred and converted into coal. Were they created just as we find them, or were they indeed trees and vegetables before they became coal?——Yet another case. The rocks nearest the surface contain almost universally more or less of what seem like fossilized plants and animals. They have the form of the plant or animal in wonderful perfection. Were these fossiliferous rocks, containing apparent fossils, created as we see them, or were these fossils once real plants and animals?——I see no reason whatever to hesitate over these questions. We can not suppose that God created these worn and rounded pebbles, these charred trees and ferns, these prints of animal footsteps—these *fac-similes* of his creative work in the vegetable and animal kingdom, for the sake of puzzling or misleading, or, in plainest words, deceiving his intelligent offspring. He never could have meant to baffle all scientific inquiry into his works of creation. Rather we must assume that he lays his works open to such inquiries, and invites men to study and learn his ways. If this be admitted, it follows that these stratified and fossil-bearing rocks open to us a great volume of Pre-Adamic history of our globe, revealing its processes of rock-formation; to some extent its climatic and various conditions for the support of life, vegetable and animal, and for its successive populations of plants and animals.

Grouping comprehensively some geological facts bearing on the duration of the great creative periods, I note (1.) Vast strata of rock-formations, widely diverse from each other, too diverse to have been formed under the same circumstances and conditions of our globe. Some—the lowest in relative position—appear to have been once in a state of fusion under intense heat, while others—in general all the higher rocks—seem to have been deposited under water. Mineralogically, these rocks differ from each other very widely and also from the fused rocks.——(2.) Again, some are manifestly composed of fragments of pre-existing rocks, broken off and worn by long-continued attrition and then compacted—known as pudding-stone—the breccias.—— (3.) Yet again; immense strata of these intermediate and higher rocks contain fossil organic remains, some of vegetables, others of animals or of both, and also in very great variety. More marvelous still; they are found occurring in groups, bearing a well defined relation to each other, so that one stratum of rock contains species of vegetables and also of animals in a measure adapted to each other, and adjusted to the condition of the earth's surface and climate at one and the same time. Another stratum shall contain a different group.

to some extent new and yet not altogether so, but lapping on with some of the earth's old inhabitants reproduced, and omitting other species.——(4.) Again, immense beds of coal are found, undoubtedly of vegetable origin, differing somewhat widely from each other as having been formed from diverse vegetable and forest material, and under various degrees of heat and pressure. No small amount of time must be given for the growth and deposition of these mountain piles of tree and fern.——The charring of these coal-pits of nature was provided for in the "fervent heat" of the earth just below the surface, coupled with pressure brought upon them it would seem by convulsions and upbreakings, to which the earth's crust has been many times subjected.——(5.) Limestone, largely of animal origin, demands in like manner time for the growth of the animals whose shelly incasements, accumulating age after age, have made such ample provision of limestone and of lime for the use of man.

This list of nature's facts as the practiced eye reads them from the crust of our earth does not claim to be exhaustive. If it were all, however, it would still be amply sufficient to sustain the demand for long creative periods as opposed to ordinary human days. It should not be forgotten that this demand, coming forth from the facts developed in the crust of the earth, falls in most fully with what we have seen to be the legitimate construction of the Mosaic record.

Prominent points of harmony between Genesis and Geology.

(1.) Creation was a *gradual process*, spanning from beginning to end long periods of time. I use the word "creation" to comprehend not only the original production of matter, but its subsequent changes and transformations till the earth was fully prepared for the abode of man.

(2.) *The earth was for a considerable time under water.* The record of Moses is decisive to this point. The current theory in respect to the formation of most if not all the rocky strata of the earth's crust is equally so.

(3.) *There was light on the earth before the appearance of the sun.* Genesis dates the light from the first day; the appearance of the sun, from the fourth.——The theory that the primitive state of created matter was gaseous (or nebulous) provides for this, since it is well known that the chemical combination of the two gases that form water (for instance)—a combination produced by electricity, evolves light. But we are not restricted to this hypothesis to account for light before the sun was visible. The state of the atmosphere may furnish all the causes needed. See below, page 32.

(4.) *Vegetables were created before animals.* So Moses, for he locates the former on the third day; the latter on the fifth and sixth. This is of course the order of nature since the animals are to subsist on vegetables. Geology finds vegetables in fossil state below the earliest animals.

(5.) Among the animal tribes, those of the water are before those of the land. Genesis gives us fish and reptiles and even fowl before the mammals—land animals—the former on the fifth day; the latter with man on the sixth. Geology indorses this order, showing that fish and reptiles lie in rocks lower and older than quadrupeds.

(6.) Man is last of all. The testimony of the rocks is here at one with that of Genesis—other animals and the vegetables also, long ages before man.

Now how has it happened that this record, coming to us through Moses, harmonizes so wonderfully with the main results of a science yet in its infancy—almost utterly unknown until the present century? Is it due to the scientific attainments of Moses? Is it not rather due to inspiration—"holy men of old"—Moses himself or the fathers before him—being taught by the same Being who "in the beginning created the heavens and the earth?" The marvel is that this record should be so constructed as to present a very intelligible view of the processes of the six days' work to the average mind of the race before geological science was born, and yet when this science begins to develop the constitution and composition of the earth's surface, the inspired record is found to harmonize with these developments in all important features. So it is wont to happen. Truth rejoices in the light. A truthful Bible and all true science meet in loving communion, evincing their common parentage—offspring of the same Infinite Father.

4. "In the beginning God created the heavens and the earth." Was this the original production of matter;

or was it only the modification of pre-existent matter into new forms? (1.) That this was the original production of matter is probable a priori *because it is true*, and because it is a truth very important to affirm in this first revelation. Matter is *not* eternal and self-existent. Those who intelligently believe in one Supreme God—an Infinite, Intelligent Spirit, will need no words wasted to disprove the assumption that matter existed from eternity, the Author of itself; for this assumption ascribes to matter the distinctive qualities of God himself.——It is moreover important that God should declare himself to be the author of all existing matter in the universe. This is one of his great and distinctive works—one which human speculation has been prone to deny him, and which therefore it is of the utmost consequence that he should affirm. (2.) The passage (Ps. 90: 2) ascribed to Moses, expressly declares that God existed "*before the mountains.*" "Before the mountains were brought forth, even from everlasting to everlasting thou art God." Moses did not think matter to be eternal. He knew and taught that God existed from eternity and that matter did not. The obvious sense of his words is that God "brought forth" (*i. e.* into existence) the mountains of this earthly globe.

(3.) The writer to the Hebrews affirms that this doctrine—God the original Creator of matter—is accepted *by faith, i. e.* upon the credit of God's own testimony. "By faith we understand that the worlds were framed by the word of God so that things which are seen were not made of things that do appear" (Heb. 11: 3). Not being constructed out of matter previously apparent, they must have been made by the direct production of matter not before existing.

(4.) This is the natural and obvious sense of the words and this the place to affirm this first fact in the work of creation. This is the point to start with. How came the matter of the universe into being at all? Whence came this material substance composing the heavens and the earth? In the beginning God created it.——It may be said truthfully that if God had purposed to reveal himself as the Author of matter—the real Maker of it all—he could have found no words more fitted to his purpose than these. Hence to deny that this is their sense is the next thing to denying to God the right or the power to reveal this fact at all.

(5.) It is objected that the primary sense of the word bara * (used here) is not to bring into existence what had no existence before, but "to cut, to cut out, to carve" (Gesenius); "to cut, form, fashion" (Fuerst). But this objection, though plausible to a merely superficial view, is really of very little force. Usage, not etymological relation, gives law to language. The etymological, primary sense of *barak*, the common Hebrew word for *bless*, is to break; then to bend as the knee, to kneel and to cause one to kneel; and then, perhaps from the custom of kneeling to receive the patriarchal benediction, or to implore blessings from God, comes the ultimate and by far the most common significance—to bless. Usage in every case must determine the most common and therefore most probable sense; then the context and the known opinions of the writer come in to aid toward the true sense in any given instance.

In the Hebrew verb regard must be had to its form, technically called its "conjugation," since the sense of the several conjugations from the same root may vary widely. In this verb (bara) the sense of Hiphil conjugation is to *fatten*—which is very remote from the sense of "Kal" and of its passive "Niphal." In Piel only do we find the etymological sense to cut, to carve out (five times only) and these spoken of human operations exclusively (Josh. 17: 15, 18 and Ezek. 23: 47 and 21: 19). But in Kal and its passive Niphal, we find the word used forty-eight times, and *always of divine operations*—always of some form of creative work wrought by God himself and never by man.†

* ברא

† The following synoptical view of the passages in which ברא or בכרא occurs is given in the Bibliotheca Sacra (Oct. 1856, pp. 763, 764) by Prof. E. P. Barrows.——"It is used,

I. *Of the original creation:* 1. Of the world generally, or parts of it: Gen. 1: 1 and 1: 21 and 2: 3, 4 and Ps. 89: 12 and 148: 5 and Isa. 40: 26 and 40: 28 and 42: 5 and 45: 18 (twice), Amos 4: 13. Also Isa. 45: 7 (twice); making fourteen times in all.——2. Of rational man: Gen. 1: 27 (thrice) and 5: 1, 2 (twice) and 6: 7 and Deut. 4: 32 and Isa. 45: 12 and Eccl. 12: 1 and Mal. 2: 10. Here also we may conveniently place Ps. 89: 47; twelve times.

II. *Of a subsequent creation:* 1. Of the successive generations of men, Ps. 102: 18 and of animal beings, Ps. 104: 30.——2. Of nations

The testimony therefore from usage is entirely conclusive to the point that this word in this form of it was specially appropriated to signify God's creative acts—the exertion of his creative power.——There are two other Hebrew words having the sense to make, to form, [asah and yatsar], which are sometimes used of God as creating but by far most often of *man's* work in forming and molding material things. Now note the argument. The Hebrews had these three words for *making*, out of which one only is used exclusively of God—never of man—as a maker. Now there is one special sense in which God can make and man can not, viz. that of bringing into existence what had no existence before. Over against this, place the fact that their word "bara" is used of God's making forty-eight times and of man's making never, and we must conclude that they expressed by this word that distinctive power of God which man never can even approach—viz. the power to *give existence to matter, to mind and to life.* In passages where this sense of "bara" is appropriate, there can be no question that it is the real meaning.

5. *The relation of v. 1 to v. 2 and to the rest of the chapter.*

Some have maintained that v. 1 is only a statement in general terms of the contents of the chapter, a heading, stating no particular fact distinct from what follows.——Others take it to be one fact in the series—the first step in the process of the creative work—the successive steps then following in due order. This latter construction I accept; and urge in its support,

(1.) That this is the most obvious sense of the words. The word "And" (v. 2) "*And* the earth was without

under the figure of individuals, Ezek. 21: 35 (Eng. version v. 30) and 28: 13, 15; three times in Ezekiel only.——3. Of particular men as the instruments of God's purposes; Isa. 54: 16 (twice).——4. Of miraculous events; Ex. 34: 10 and Num. 16: 30 and Jer. 31: 22.——5. Of events foretold in prophecy; Isa. 48: 7.

III. *Of creation in a moral sense:* 1. Of a clean heart and holy affections and actions; Ps. 51: 10 and Isa. 45: 8 and 57: 19.——2. Of Israel as God's covenant people, or of a member of Israel; Isa. 43: 1, 7, 15.——3. Of a new and glorious order of things for Israel and in Israel; Isa. 4: 5 and 41: 20 and 65: 17, 18 (twice).

An examination of these passages (half of which relate to the original creation) will show that in every instance the idea is that of bringing into being by divine power. Whether that which is created is new matter, or something else that is new, must be determined by the context."

form," etc., must be taken as *continuing* the subject—not as *commencing* it. It should give us another and succeeding fact, and not be taken to *begin* a detailed history.

(2.) This is the natural order of the facts. First, matter must be brought into existence. Nothing can be done with it, nothing can be said about it, until it *is*. The first verse therefore is the natural beginning of the narrative—the first fact to be stated. The second verse gives naturally the next fact, viz. the condition of this matter immediately prior to the six days' creative work upon it. Deferring the little he has to say upon the "heavens," he calls our attention to the earth as being of chief interest to man, and makes this the main theme of the chapter.——An observer would have seen the earth mantled in darkness, its atmosphere laden with murky vapors and dense mists; the surface (if indeed the waters below could be distinguished from the waters above) one wide waste of waters, all formless, vast, dismal; with nothing of order or beauty on which the eye could rest. Above and upon this shapeless mass the Spirit of God was hovering, or shall we say *incubating*, for such may be the figure involved in the Hebrew verb. Moreover it seems to be implied that this action of the creative Spirit was protracted. The Hebrew participle (used here) expresses continued action—was brooding over, incubating, this wild, waste, desolate mass.

Some scientific men suppose they find in this second verse, not water, but the gaseous matter which ultimately became water and solid earth. This construction originates in a theory in regard to the primal form in which the matter of our world came from the Creator's hand, which theory may or may not be true, but if true is too remote from the common mind and too foreign from the scope of divine revelation to allow us to suppose that God would refer to it in his revelation. ——Carrying out this scientific theory, some have held* that not only the "waters" of v. 2 but those of vs. 6, 7, were gases, not waters. The fatal objections to this theory are—that these "waters" are the same which in vs. 9, 10, are "gathered into one place" and "called seas;" also that the common people for several thousand

* See Bib. Sacra, April, 1855, pp. 325, 326.

years could not have understood Moses if he had spoken of gases—certainly could not have understood their common word for waters to mean gases.——It is not well to strain and force this simple narrative to speak so scientifically as to be unintelligible to those for whom it was primarily written.——The first state of created matter may have been gaseous. The record in Genesis has said nothing to forbid this. It certainly could not come within its province to teach it. Suffice it that time enough may be found between verses 1 and 2 for a portion of this gaseous matter to form water—not to say also to form the more solid portions of this globe.

The connection of v. 2 with v. 1 is such that an indefinitely long period may have intervened. The first verb of v. 2 implies no close connection with v. 1. But in v. 3 the form of the first verb—" And *then* God said"—does make a close historical connection with v. 2.

6. The work of the fourth day. Were the light-bearers ("lights" in the sense of luminaries) in the heavens, viz. the sun, moon, and stars also, "made," created, on this day, or simply brought forth to the view of a supposed observer upon the earth?——The latter theory that they were not first brought into being then, but only brought into view from the earth—seems to me most probable, because—(1.) To suppose them created then would be out of all proportion for one day's work among the six. Throughout the other five days' work a beautiful proportion obtains: it should therefore be expected in this.——If it be said that this consideration draws its great strength from our astronomical knowledge of those heavenly bodies—much more enlarged than those of the age of Moses, I answer (a.) Moses, "learned in all the wisdom of the Egyptians," was not altogether a novice in astronomy—(b.) Modern astronomy is essentially true, not overrating the relative magnitude of the heavenly bodies; and this record in Genesis comes from one who knew all the truth.

(2.) If these verses be understood to speak of their original creation, it would seem to be out of place here between the creation of vegetables (third day) and of the earliest born animals (the fifth). But in the sense of bringing these heavenly bodies to view and the sun into its normal action upon vegetables and upon animal comfort, it is precisely in place.

(3.) According to the interpretation given to v. 1 (above) the matter composing these heavenly bodies was brought into existence "in the beginning" when "God created the heavens" as well as "the earth" and before the six days' work began. If so, then the intervening processes of modification must naturally have been going on from that time until this fourth day.

(4.) Some expositors and scientists account for the light on the first day without the sun by means of electricity or other chemical agents; but it is scarcely possible that Moses and his first readers could have thought of any thing but the sun as the source of that light, especially because "God called it Day," and the darkness alternating with it then (as ever since the earth began its diurnal revolutions) "he called Night." This reference to day and night must naturally carry every Hebrew mind to the *sun* as the source of that light and to its well-known withdrawal at evening as the reason for the darkness and the night.——It need not be supposed that the body of the sun was then visible. The state of the atmosphere might have admitted a portion of his light and yet not have disclosed his face. In our times we have seen cloudy, dark days, with no sun visible, yet with a manifest distinction between day and night.

7. The true sense of the record as to the origin (1) of vegetable life (vs. 11, 12), and (2) of animal life (vs. 20, 21, 24, 25.)——The important words are, "Let the earth bring forth grass" (v. 11); "and the earth brought forth grass" (v. 12). "Let the waters bring forth abundantly the moving creature," etc. (v. 20); "and God created every living creature that moveth which the waters brought forth abundantly" (v. 21). "Let the earth bring forth the living creature" (v. 24); "and God made the beast of the earth," etc. (v. 25).——Here note that the *historical statements give the true sense of the imperatives*, and show plainly that the earth and the waters are not creative but only sustaining powers, and that they bring forth and sustain only under the fiat of the Almighty—only *when* and *as* God said, Do it. For the whole tenor of these chapters (Gen. 1 and 2) presents to us God himself as sole and supreme Creator.

In the closest connection with the earth's bringing forth the living creature, we are told that *God made* the beast of the field. Though the waters brought forth abundantly, yet it was still God himself who created "every living creature that moveth." The agency of the earth in producing grass is presented in a popular way—the precise, fundamental thought being, that God made the earth his instrument in bringing forth all things that grow; and in like manner in sustaining animal life.

If we will, we are at liberty to push our queries and ask not only *who* gave life, vegetable and animal, but *how?* In just *what way* did he impart that something— be it quality or power or substance—which we call *life?* and deeper still—What *is* life? Is it some subtle form of matter, or only some indefinable force given to matter; and if this be it, To what special form of matter is it given? If it be matter, did God sow the tiny germs thereof in the waters and on the land and leave them to be developed under auspicious circumstances? Or did he breathe forth from his own infinite life these life-forces into material things to make plants or animals?——And yet again; What was the status of that lump of dead matter (small or great) at the point when God put into it the life-force and it became living matter, vegetable or animal? Was the first form of the living animal the egg, or its microscopic cell; or was it the fully developed animal, prepared for all life's functions, and ready to furnish other life-bearing cells for reproduction? On these points what says the record? Not much at the utmost. It does seem to assume that Adam began existence, not an infant in the normally helpless condition of human birth, but with fully developed powers. Beyond this we look in vain to the record for light. We only know that the life-force— that subtle entity which always eludes the most vigilant search—which distances all the strides of scientific scrutiny—which mocks at chemical analysis and never comes to our call;—this life-force we simply know is *from God himself* and *from God alone*. The original gift of it is his prerogative and the secret thereof is for evermore with him.

8. In the passage—"Let us make man in our image, after our likeness" (v. 26) there are two special points to be considered:—(a.) In *what sense* is man made

in the image of God? (b.) The explanation of the plural pronouns, "*us*" and "*our*"—"Let *us* make man in *our* image."

(a.) Inasmuch as God is a spirit and never to be thought of as having a corporeal nature—material, tangible to our bodily senses, we are at once shut off from all reference to man's physical, corporeal nature and shut up to his spiritual nature to find in it the points of this resemblance. Consequently man is made in God's image as being gifted like his Maker with intelligence and with capacities for moral action—beyond comparison the noblest possible elements of being. He has the sense of moral obligation and the voluntary powers requisite to fulfill such obligation. He can find his supreme joy in voluntarily seeking the good of others, even of all other sentient beings, and in laboring even to the extent of self-sacrifice to promote their welfare. This is the pre-eminent perfection of God—the very point ultimately in which man is made in his image, and capable of becoming more and more Godlike, forever approximating toward his holiness and blessedness.——His intellectual powers are only the servants of these highest and noblest activities of his being.——(b.) The use of the plural pronouns—"Let *us* make, in *our* image"—has been accounted for variously. Some would make this plural intensive, corresponding to the emphatic plural in Hebrew nouns. But there seems to be no real analogy in the two cases.——Some make it the plural of dignity ("pluralis excellentiae"), as an oriental monarch puts forth his edict, saying "we," not I. But the great simplicity of this whole narrative goes against this explanation. Moreover, this usage, so far as it appears in literature, sacred or profane, is later by many ages than Moses. Besides, there is no apparent reason why God should assume more dignity in saying—"Let us make man," than in saying, Let us make light, or the sun in the heavens. Indeed, the form of the divine behest—"Let there be light," seems to our ideas the more sublime and the more expressive of God's supreme dignity.—— I see no explanation of this plural that is at all satisfactory save that which assumes a reference to the persons of the Trinity. As one reason for such reference it may be suggested as certainly not improbable—that

MAN MADE IN GOD'S IMAGE. 35

the idea of man, God's chief work in creation, was coupled with his future history (all present to the divine mind)—as fallen, yet also as redeemed, and specially as redeemed *by means of the incarnation of the Son of God in human flesh.* Supposing this incarnation present to the divine thought, the significance of this plural would be—Let us proceed to make in our own image this wonderful being whose nature the eternal Son shall one day assume—this man who is to bear relations to us so extraordinary, so wonderful before the angels, so signal before all created minds, so glorious in its results to the whole moral universe! Have not *we*—Father, Son and Holy Ghost—a most surpassing interest in the creation of this being, man!

9. *The relation of Gen. 2: 4-25 to Gen. 1.*

Here are two points of some importance to be considered.

(1.) Are the two passages by the same author?

(2.) Do they both speak of the creation of the same first man, *i. e.* the same Adam, or is the Adam of Gen. 2 another and different first man, brought into being long subsequent to him of Gen. 1: 26-28?

(1.) That the two passages are from different authors has been maintained on the following grounds.——
(a.) That v. 4—"These are the generations * of the heavens and the earth"—appears like the heading of a new and distinct portion of history.——But nothing forbids that it should be the heading of a new section or chapter of the same continuous history by the same author, resuming his subject with only a very comprehensive allusion to the great facts of creation which he had given in chap. 1, as fully as his plan required. This done he may proceed to a more full account of the creation of man and the events of his early history.
——(b.) That the account here differs somewhat from that in Gen. 1, *e. g.* as to the creation of man, and yet more especially, the creation of woman.——But these differences are not discrepances and are fully accounted for by the scope and design of this portion, viz. to give the history of the first man and woman in much more

* The word, "generations," obtains the secondary sense of family history and then the sense of history in general, from the fact that the earliest written historical records were so largely made up of genealogies—the records of human generations.

detail.——(c.) But especially this diversity of authors has been argued from the different names of God which appear in these two passages. In chap. 1 and 2: 1–3, the name is simply and exclusively God (Elohim). In chap. 2: 4–25 and in chap. 3, the name is "the Lord God" (Jehovah Elohim).——This difference is indeed a palpable fact, and has been the theme of an indefinite amount of critical speculation based for the most part on the utterly groundless assumption that the same author can not be supposed to have used both these names for God. Those critics (mostly German) who have flooded their literature with disquisitions on this subject assume in the outset that none but a "Jehovist" ever used the name Jehovah, and none but an "Elohist," the name Elohim, it being in their view impossible or at least absurd that the same author should use sometimes one of these names and sometimes the other—which assumption seems to me supremely arbitrary, irrational, and uncritical. Authors now use at their option the various names for God, either for the mere sake of variety, or because in some connections one seems more euphonious or more significant than another. Why may not an equal license of choice be accorded to Hebrew writers? It is unquestionable that the same Hebrew author *does* use both of these names for God.——They made far more account than we of the various senses of the several names for the Deity. The names Jehovah and Elohim, were not precisely identical in their suggested ideas, although both are legitimately used of the one true God. Elohim suggests that he is the Exalted, Eternal One, the Infinite Creator of all. This name is therefore specially appropriate in chap. 1. "Jehovah" conceives of him as the Immutable and ever faithful One, coming into covenant relation with his people as the Maker and the Fulfiller of promise. (See remarks on this as God's memorial name in my Notes on Hos. 12: 5). Hence as the narrative in Gen. 2 and 3 brings God before the mind in these special relations to the first human pair and to the race, this name is here specially appropriate. But lest some might suppose that this Jehovah is thought of as another God than the Elohim of chap. 1—the writer uses both names—the Elohim who is also Jehovah to his rational creature man and especially to all his obedient trustful people.

(2.) That Gen. 2: 7 relates to the creation of the same first man as Gen. 1: 26–28, and not of another man ages later, seems to me to admit of no rational doubt. The inducements to make out two distinct creations, *i. e.* of two different first men, come from the supposed proof of the existence of man on the earth ages before the Adam of antediluvian history. I propose to treat below this question of *the antiquity of man.* Let it suffice here to say that we must not mutilate the record or disregard the laws of philology for the sake of making the sacred narrative conform to theories which are yet rather assumptions than scientifically proven facts.—— As to the correspondences and variations in the two narratives of the creation of man, the first makes prominent his being created in the image of God: the second assumes this in the fact that God gave him law in Eden; in the knowledge of the lower animals which his naming them assumes; in the superior dignity which the Lord's bringing them before him for names implies; and in the fact that among them all no help-meet for him could be found. His nature ranked far above theirs.——The earlier narrative says briefly that God "created them male and female." The later one expands this fact much more fully and makes it the foundation for the law of marriage. The later record treats with the utmost brevity the main part of the six days' work and must have been written with the previous record before the mind, to be a supplementary and continuative history, designed to bring out prominently the creation of woman and the scenes of the garden, its moral trial and ultimately its results.——The supposition of a different Adam from that of the former record could never have occurred to the Hebrew mind, and therefore can not be accepted as the sense of the passage.

10. *Invariability of "kind"* in the vegetable and animal kingdoms.

The record in Genesis sets forth that God created grass, herb, and then fruit tree; "each after his kind;" also reptiles, fish, fowl and land-animals, each "after his kind;" and finally man "in the image of God." Over against this the modern theory which bears the name of Darwin holds that all the animals of our globe "have descended from at most only four or five progenitors, and plants from an equal or lesser number;"* and moreover, that man has in this respect no pre-eminence above the beasts, but has descended in the same line with them from some one of the four or five progenitors of the great animal kingdom. More still he says in the same connection—" Analogy would lead me one step further, viz. to the belief that *all animals and plants* have descended from some one prototype."—— These four or five progenitors of the whole animal kingdom correspond substantially with what Webster calls the five sub-kingdoms, viz. Vertebrates, Articulates, Mollusks, Radiates, and Protozoans. The technical classification under these sub-kingdoms into Classes, Orders, Families, Genera, and Species becomes of little or no account in any discussion of Darwin's system, for his theory of "descent with modifications" is reckless of all these lines of demarkation, traveling over and through them all without finding the least obstruction. ——Let it be distinctly understood therefore that though Mr. Darwin makes frequent use of the word "species," and entitles one of his volumes—" *The Origin of Species*," yet his theory takes a far wider range than the question whether "species are variable." In his view not only are species variable, intermixing at will and passing from one into another, but genera also and families and orders and classes—not to say also each of the great sub-kingdoms of the animal world;† even the distinction between animals and vegetables fades away under his analogical argument. Hence the issue between Darwin and Moses is relieved of whatever uncertainty hangs

* Darwin's Origin of Species, p. 420.

† " The Quadrumana and all the higher mammals are probably derived from an ancient marsupial animal, and this, through a long line of diversified forms, either from some reptile-like or some amphibian-like creature, and this again from some fish-like animal. In the dim obscurity of the past we can see that the early progenitor of all the vertebratæ must have been an aquatic animal, provided with branchiæ [gills] with the two sexes united in the same individual, and with the most important organs of the body (such as the brain and the heart) imperfectly developed. This animal seems to have been more like the larvæ of our existing marine Ascidians than any other known form." Darwin's Descent of Man, vol. 2, 372.

over the dividing line between species and varieties, and may fitly be limited to these two points; the invariability of "*kind*" in the sense of Moses in Genesis; and the distinct origination of man.

Under Mr. Darwin's system "community of descent" and not "some unknown plan of creation" is "the hidden bond" which unites together all living existences of our globe. "Looking to some unknown plan of creation" (in his own words) has prevented the truly scientific classification and history of the forms of life in our world. The Bible has stood in the way of the growth of science.——Under his system the changes by natural descent from any given parent to its offspring, taken individually, have been exceedingly small. Hence the theory requires an indefinitely long time from the point of the original creation of the four or five primordial forms to the present status of living things, vegetable and animal, in our world.——The above remarks will suffice for a very general introduction to Mr. Darwin's system.

Wishing to bring this discussion within the narrowest possible limits and yet do justice to Darwin, to Genesis, and to the truth, I propose to state briefly his main arguments; then comprehensively my rejoinder to them severally in their order, and then subjoin some general considerations bearing upon his entire theory.

1. Darwin holds that by natural law the offspring vary, though slightly, from the parent, and hence, that, given an indefinitely long time, he has any desired amount of variation.

2. When animals multiply beyond the means of subsistence, there ensues a struggle for life in which the strongest and most favored in circumstances are the victors and survive. This law which he calls "Natural Selection" (or "the survival of the fittest") works a gradual improvement in the race. A twin argument with this comes from "sexual selection," the amount of which is that in the case of some at least of the animal races, there arises a struggle among the males for the possession of the females, in which struggle the most attractive in beauty or in song, or the champions in fight, being the victors, perpetuate the race and thus improve it. This law of the animal races ("sexual selection") works precisely in the same line with the law

called "natural selection." It may serve therefore to provide a little more of the same thing, but no new or different product whatever. Hence it does not seem to call for a distinct refutation.

3. Homologous anatomical structure is found to obtain very extensively among widely diverse races, *e. g.* in the arm of man, the fore-leg of the monkey and indeed of all quadrupeds, in the wing of the bird and the fin of the fish. This indicates a common parentage.

4. Some animals which, fully grown, differ from each other widely, are scarcely distinguishable in the embryo. Hence he infers their common origin.

5. The fact of rudimentary organs is assumed to be *historic*, proving that some ancient progenitor used them, and that they have gradually passed out of use. This is held to prove that great changes of structure come of genealogical descent.

BRIEF REPLIES.

1. To Darwin's first law, viz. that the offspring always vary though slightly from the parent, and therefore, given indefinite time, he has any desired amount of variation, I reply that this law of variation becomes practically worthless for his theory, because these variations from parent to offspring run in all conceivable directions and not in the one definite direction required for his purpose, *i. e.* toward a higher grade of perfection, or [which his argument requires] toward a new form of animal life. For example, there is always some change in the human countenance from parent to child. Yet who does not know that those changes run in every possible direction and not in one uniform line of progress or advance, as from monkey toward man and from man toward angel? For another example we may take the shape of the skull and of the brain—evermore differing slightly from parent to offspring yet not by any means on one given line. The skulls of Egyptian mummies entombed three thousand years ago do not differ appreciably from those of the Copts (their lineal descendants) of to-day, *i. e.* are no more pithecoid—ape-like. On Darwin's theory three thousand years backward ought surely to approximate toward the ape; otherwise these variations are fruitless. This law of successive genealogical changes amounts to nothing for his argu-

ment unless the changes consent to *come into line* so that their results shall actually *accumulate* with the lapse of ages. The fatal lack in the argument is—no husbandry of these infinitesimal changes—not the least perceivable accumulation.

A second branch of my reply suggests that Mr. Darwin *misinterprets this law of nature*, viz. perpetual variation from parent to offspring. It is doubtless a law, but Darwin has quite missed its divinely ordained purpose—which is to indicate the relationship between parent and child on the one hand, and yet maintain individual identity on the other. The resemblances answer the former purpose; the differences, the latter. Beings constituted to bear personal responsibilities so momentous as those of man must be so organized that every one can identify his own individuality, lest one man be hung for some other man's crime.

2. His second argument comes from the law of "natural selection"—"the survival of the fittest"—with which it is convenient to couple the precisely similar law of "sexual selection"—the ascendency of the smartest over their inferiors, to perpetuate the race. Here a specific case will suffice both to illustrate and to refute. The principle of "natural selection" has a fair chance for itself in the spawn of the shad. It is no doubt true that none but the smartest out of the many thousand spawned at once survive so as to become parents in their turn. Yet who believes that these smartest shad are becoming sturgeon or sharks or whales by this law of progress? Are they actually found to be any thing but shad after never so many hundred generations? It may seem superfluous to push the still more pertinent question—Are these smartest and most ambitious shad really found to be working up out of their watery element, *i. e.* working up into ducks or geese, or into blackbirds and crows? For just this is Mr. Darwin's theory—the line of ascent running up from fish to fowl; from fowl to mammal and so on up to man. The questions here suggested are therefore only the fair and scientific test and touchstone of his argument. A law which has not made its results even perceptible since the birth of the first shad known to human history must be regarded as scientifically worthless.

My second remark here is that Darwin errs not in finding these to be laws of nature—"natural selection," "sexual selection"—but in interpreting them, *i. e.* in detecting their divinely ordained design and their actual working and product. I suggest that these laws, apparently made for the improvement of races, may be requisite to enable them to hold their own against the ever present tendency to degeneracy. Life is a perpetual struggle against death. The life-principle finds an antagonist force in chemical law which is evermore hurrying organized matter back to its inorganic state. Still further, be it considered, races excessively prolific would rapidly lose vitality but for these laws of natural and sexual selection. We may therefore rationally assume that these laws are simply forms of the general principle of *self-preservation*, and not a purposed provision for lifting a lower race up to the plane of a higher.

3. As to homologous anatomical structure, *e. g.* of the arm, fore-leg, wing, fin, paddle—there are abundant reasons for its existence aside from the assumption of Darwin that it proves a common ancestry for man, monkey, calf, bull-dog, eagle, toad and whale. The ball and socket joint at man's shoulder is the perfect thing for use. Equally so is the same kind of joint for the fore-leg of a horse, the wing of an eagle or the fin of a fish. God made the anatomy of man's arm perfect. What forbids that he should make an equally perfect machinery for the motions and various uses of other animals? The reason of this uniformly perfect machinery is found in the wisdom and benevolence of the Great Maker, and proves nothing in favor of a common descent from some one parent, *i. e.* it proves nothing *unless* you may assume that God could not have made two kinds of animals with homologous anatomical structures—two kinds, each with machinery perfect for its purposes.

4. As to the similar appearance of the embryo in very dissimilar races, there may be differences in the embryo which no microscope and no human test have yet discovered. The force of this argument seems to me to come rather from ignorance than from knowledge.

5. As to rudimentary organs, their history is very obscure and their design also. I suggest that Mr. Darwin begin with the history and the reason for the ru-

CREATION: DARWIN'S THEORY. 43

dimentary organs which appear on the bosom of the male in the species man. When he shall have mastered this problem—the history and the reason—we can afford to consider his argument therefrom in proof that man has a common ancestry with whatsoever other animal he may find having this male organ, not rudimentary but in full activity. Probably he will prove that man must have come down by descent from that class of animals which economically combine the two sexes in one and the same individual!

Some objections of a more general bearing upon Darwin's scheme.

1. His system requires indefinite, almost infinite, ages of time back of the Silurian strata, *i. e.* back of the oldest known remains of life, vegetable or animal, on our globe.* That is, he requires for the development of his system an almost infinite extension of time back beyond the earliest traces or proofs of life, vegetable or animal, on our globe. And this, he would have men believe, is the perfection of modern Science!—a science which pushes its sphere *in time* back indefinitely beyond all known facts upon the bare evidence of theories and assumed analogies!——But even this gives not the full force of the objection made by true Science to his system. It is not merely that he builds upon assumed facts where no known facts are—which is building upon nothing—but where no facts *can be*, which is building not merely upon negatives but upon impossibilities. There is no room for his assumed facts where he locates them. If Geology proves any thing it proves that vegetable and animal life commenced on our planet as soon as the planet was ready and *not sooner*, and that we have the remains of the earliest living organisms in the oldest fossil-bearing rocks. His scheme is therefore conditioned upon impossibilities and must be false.

2. His system requires a close succession of animal races, differing from parent to offspring by only the

---

* "If my theory be true, it is indisputable that before the lowest Silurian stratum was deposited, long periods must have elapsed, as long as, or probably far longer than, the whole interval from the Silurian age to the present day; and that, during these vast yet quite unknown periods of time, the world swarmed with living creatures." Darwin's Origin of Species, p. 269.

least possible amount, with no leaps, no gaps whatever. Thus from monkey up to man the system calls for at least a few scores not to say hundreds of intermediate links. Where are they? His suffering theory cries out for their support: there is no answer. The earth's surface responds not to the call; even "the depths say—They are not in me!" From the original monad up to man all the way through at least the long line of the vertebrates—reptile, fish, bird, mammal—that is to say, through the serpent tribe; the fish kingdom; the swallow, blackbird and eagle, and especially through the quadruped family—the horse and camel and particularly the monkey household—through all this remarkable line of ancestry, Darwin's system demands a very gradual upward march by the shortest possible stages of progress, so that the intermediate links must be barely less than infinite. It certainly ought to be very easy to trace a genealogical line so well represented. It is estimated that thirty thousand fossil species have been recognized. How many of these can be formed into this genealogical line from the aboriginal vertebrate—supposed to be aquatic and Ascidian—up to man? Has Mr. Darwin set himself to marshal this proof-line of witnesses to his system? No. Not only has he not *done* this very appropriate thing, but he has *said* little, quite too little on this most vital point, in the way of showing what could be done. He reiterates that the geological records are very imperfect. Doubtless they quite fail to come up to meet the demands of his system. It is the fatal weakness of his theory that just where it should find facts in animal history for its support, they are not there! He himself admits that if you believe in a tolerably full showing of animal history in the geological records of our globe, you must disbelieve his system.* He needs quite another geological record for his proofs.

---

* These are his words—"Why then is not every geological formation and every stratum full of such intermediate links? Geology assuredly does not reveal any such finely graduated organic chain; and this perhaps is the most obvious and gravest objection which can be urged against my theory. The explanation lies as I believe in the extreme imperfection of the geological records."——And again—"He who rejects these views on the nature [*i. e.* the defects] of the geological record will rightly reject my whole theory.

3. His argument is essentially *materialistic*. In his reasonings and assumptions, all there is of mind in man or any animal is *of the* brain and the nervous organism. All animals have wants and are moved by a sense of want to supply them. This begets self-originated activity, and this activity involves thought—yet only as a function of the material brain. Most of the animals are social by nature: hence another member in this family of wants and enjoyments, begetting another class of impulses and activities. But whether it be man or monkey, dog or kitten, these activities and these plans and thoughts underlying them, come of the nervous organism, of which the brain is the center. On his theory and in his words (Origin of Species, pp. 93, 94) "the moral sense is fundamentally identical with the social instinct." Hence it becomes the burden of his argument that the brain in man and in monkey is homologous—almost perfectly the same in shape, in quality, and in its bony incasement. He seems to be quite unaware that there may be something in the human brain that a twelve-inch rule will not measure, nor the nicest made scales weigh, nor the sharpest chemical tests discern. It seems never to have occurred to him that even if the brain of man and of monkey weighed in the same notch, fitted into the same cast, responded alike to the same chemical tests (which, however, is a good way from being the case), yet there might be material qualities in the human brain too subtle and ethereal to be appreciable under any known physical test; and much more still might be a spirit inhabiting the human brain and working through it which the monkey has not. "That the breath of the Almighty hath given to man understanding" is a fact higher than the range of Darwin's philosophy. The *prima facie* probability thence arising that God would fit up a special material organism for the one only mind made in his own image seems to have entirely escaped Mr. Darwin's notice. The record by Moses on

---

For he may ask in vain: Where are the numberless transitional links which must formerly have connected the closely allied or representative species found in the several stages of the great formations? He may ask, Where are the remains of those numerous organisms which must have existed long before the first bed of the Silurian system was deposited?" Origin of Species, pp. 246, 299.

this point—that God created man by a special act, entirely independent of all other forms of life, vegetable or animal, commends itself to the good sense of most men as more than probable, as indeed supremely rational and unquestionably true.

4. It is but a natural result of his materialistic system that he should have no adequate conception of the pre-eminent glory of *man's intellectual and moral nature*. With great ingenuity he labors to make it appear that Tray feels shame and guilt and even the moral sense of oughtness—all the same in kind with those of man. He does not say in definite words that the best developed dog is capable of knowing his divine Creator and of rendering to Him the obedience, love, and homage of an adoring heart—is capable of becoming consciously a trustful child of God and a temple of the Holy Ghost. He does not quite say this; indeed he does not seem to appreciate these exalted functions of a soul made in God's image, or to think them worthy of particular notice. It is a capital fault in his reasoning that he ignores almost entirely these highest, noblest activities of man's nature. Thus ignoring these most vital points which lift man so high above all the lower animals, how can it be expected that his reasoning upon the material relations of man and beast should be otherwise than lame and fallacious?

5. Scientifically it is a sufficient condemnation of this system that it is compelled to fritter away the fundamental law of species which God fixed, not upon its surface but deep in its nature, viz. that hybrids shall be infertile—incapable of propagation. The crossing and consequent interblending of distinct species, genera, families, and orders, if by their nature possible, would long ages ago have thrown the animal world into inextricable confusion, effacing every line of distinction. Such a result must have been simply fatal to all scientific classification. If Mr. Darwin's theories had been taken as the divine plan, the world would have had more grades and orders of animal life than there have been days since the first monad came into being.

6. The scheme is in many points revolting to the common sense and sober convictions of men. Some of its assumptions lie close upon the border of the ridiculous. Think of the stride upward from vegetable life

CREATION: DARWIN'S THEORY. 47

to animal—the plant pulling its roots out from the soil and beginning to use them for legs! And of the very analogous aspirations and endeavors of the fish to live out of water—to push out his fins into wings; convert his superabundant fat into muscle; expand his lungs and soar off in mid-heaven—the very eagle himself! The effort to tone down these absurdities within the limits of sober sense by simply taking it little by little, spreading the change over a few thousands or millions of years and subdividing the work among a vast number of generations may help to confuse some minds and blunt the edge of its absurdity; but soberly considered, the absurdity is still there. Hence we may note the fact that most writers seem to find themselves quite unable to discuss this theory to any extent without sliding, perhaps unconsciously, from sober argument into ridicule and irony.

I am well aware that, to abate if not nullify the force of this apparent absurdity, it will be said that along the actual line between plant life and animal life, the vegetable and animal kingdoms are actually brought closely side by side; that plant life shades off by almost imperceptible stages till it comes so near to the lowest forms of animal life that the dividing line is scarcely if at all perceptible. This fact no scientist disputes. The real question turns upon its purposed object or ultimate reason. Is it, as Mr. Darwin's theory assumes, to bridge over this dividing line and facilitate the march of "genealogical descent with variations" across what else would be a bad if not an impassable gulf?

This being the claim set up by Mr. Darwin, I answer—

(a.) The proper test of this theory is simple: Is there any "*march*" here at all—*i. e.* any *progressive movement* from one form of vegetable life to another, from lower forms to higher, or as this case seems to demand, from higher forms to lower, for along this dividing line we have the lowest known forms of both vegetable life and animal? Is this army of the lowest vegetable species and of animal life-forms, down in this dark microscopic valley, really *on the march*, or is it absolutely moveless and fixed? Are the flora on the vegetable side of the line really doffing their plant-life uniform and regalia, and emerging on the other side of the line into fauna to swell the hosts of animal-life forms? This it would seem must be the test for the proof or disproof of Darwin's theory.

(b.) But again, I would reply in this as in other points; Mr. Darwin misses not so much the facts of nature as the ultimate reason of those facts. What is the ultimate reason for the remarkable fact that the plant kingdom crowds itself so closely upon the confines of the animal? Not, I answer, to facilitate the transit of generations from the one province to the other. Of such transit there is not the first shade of evidence. But the reason is that the Great Author of nature out of his infinite resources has *filled both kingdoms perfectly full of life-forms* so that no territory between their respective domains lies unoccupied. It is simply a fecundity of life-forms or species, analogous to the fecundity of living representatives under most of these species—all alike traceable to the infinite resources of the Creator's wisdom and power.

7. Finally, this theory is reckless of the authority of revelation. It makes no effort to reconcile its doctrines with the testimony of the Scriptures. Especially on the great points of the creation of man—as to his body, independent of all other animals; as to his spirit, made in the very image of God; and as to woman, formed from man—this system stands in absolute antagonism with God's word.——It should not surprise us, therefore, that the common sense of mankind (with rare exceptions) revolts from its absurdities. It should not surprise us that Science—the true Science which builds, not on unsupported assumptions but on ascertained and incontestable facts—should disown these theories and speculations. True Science, here as elsewhere, now and forever, is at one with Revelation; and these pillars of the great temple of Truth are in not the least danger of being shaken.

CHAPTER II.

THE ANTIQUITY OF MAN.

UNDER this head several questions arise:
1. *Is the human family older than the Adam of Scripture history?*
2. *How far back really is the date of Adam?* i. e. How many years intervened from Adam to the flood and how many to the Christian era?

Subsidiary questions are—
(a.) Were there one or more races of primeval men pre-Adamic but now extinct?
(b.) Have there been various "*head-centers*" of the existing human family; or only one and that Adam? Or (the same question in another form) are all the living varieties of race lineally descended from Adam and all from Noah?

The special interest of these questions will hinge upon their relation to the Scriptures—*i. e.* their supposed or real bearing upon the truth of the Scripture history—the friends of the Bible desiring to know whether any well sustained facts exist to affect its credit, or to modify its currently received interpretation: and on the other hand, men whose sympathies are not with the Bible, being inquisitive to see if by any means its authority can be impugned or impaired.——It is obvious that this sort of special interest, for or against the Bible, is liable to affect the candor and fairness of the investigation on either side. The friends of the Bible, however, have really not the least occasion to fear for its stability. It is indeed possible that our interpretation of its chronology may require modification—but always and only toward truth. Also we may have erred in supposing the Bible to have taught what it never intended to teach. But the real word of God can have nothing to fear from the advance of human science—that is to say, from the real knowledge of actual facts.——With the utmost composure, therefore, we welcome all candid investigation, subjecting every new theory to appropriate scrutiny, sifting the evidence on which it rests with no prejudice for or against the conclusions to which it may compel us.

1. *The high antiquity* claimed for man is fitly the first question in order. Here the evidence comes and of necessity must come

(1.) From *traces of man* upon the crust of the earth, *i. e.* in the rock-strata, the drift-deposits, or in caves and lake-dwellings, or in monuments of human labor and skill:

And (2.) from the traditions of the most ancient nations and the high antiquity of their existence, civilization, and monuments.

Under the first head the traces are either:

(A.) *Remains of the human skeleton;* or
(B.) *Remains of man's work and of his tools.*
(A.) As to the *remains of the human skeleton.*

By universal admission these remains are not found in the rocks that bear in abundance the fossil vegetables of the third great epoch of creation; nor in those yet higher strata that contain the oldest forms of animal life whose home is in the waters; nor is man found with the reptiles, say of the fifth day of creation; nor indeed until we come to deposits of the most recent date, of a kind at least similar to those which are known to be forming within the historic age of man.

From these admitted facts I make this special point, viz. that if man had lived on the earth contemporary with the oldest animal species, we ought to find not merely one skeleton or half a skeleton buried along-side of myriads of fossil sea-shells and fishes, but a fair show of specimens, so many at least as to leave no question as to his being a joint occupant with them of the earth as it then was. One or two, or even a dozen skeletons, gathered from every explored portion of the earth's surface, are too few for the base of a theory like this because such scattered cases, in number so meager, are always subject, more or less, to abatement from the following possibilities:

(a.) The human family in all ages have buried their dead, and often, during the earlier ages, in rock-hewn sepulchers or in natural caves;

(b.) In all ages of the world men have been liable to fall into rock-fissures and ravines and to die there; and to leave their skeletons to become fossil there, particularly in calcareous and similar rocks where decomposition or solution in water and new deposits are in progress;

(c.) Men have been wont to frequent caves for shelter, for safety in war or from persecution, and consequently might leave their bones there; or

(d.) Their bones may have been dragged into caverns by flesh-eating animals or borne into strange positions by underground currents of water; or again,

(e.) Since the historic Adam, drift deposits have in some circumstances been forming under water, in which waters men have been liable to be drowned and their skeletons to become imbedded in those deposits. Changes of elevation may bring such deposits to view.

Such possibilities must practically nullify confidence in the proof of man's high antiquity from his bones so long as the specimens are so exceedingly few and even these few found only quite near the surface.

This argument will be appreciated by those who duly consider, on the one hand, that if man were on the earth in those pre-Adamic ages, it is in the highest degree improbable that his population ranged at a dozen for the area of all France, and a few hundreds only to a continent—for what should forbid him as well as the lower animals to "be fruitful and multiply and replenish the earth"? Besides, a population so sparse and consequently weak could have made no stand against armies of hyenas, leopards, bears and lions.——On the other hand, the occurrence of human bones, in numbers so very few and so remote from each other, will be much more rationally accounted for by the possibilities above indicated.

Yet let it be understood:—The way is open for any extent of further investigation. We have no occasion to fear the result of the search. Let the rocks be torn up and examined; let mountains be tunneled and canals be dug; let railroad grading go where it will; if the human skeleton should be found where none of these or similar possibilities admit its date since Adam, we will certainly give the case all due consideration and weight.

(B.) Next is the argument *from man's work and from his tools.*

Here a larger field opens. My limits scarcely allow me to do more than indicate briefly the present state of the question.——Thus far explorations have been mostly restricted to Northern and Western Europe, say north of the Alps and of ancient Greece, in the regions anciently known as Gaul, Germany, Scandinavia and Britain. The supposed remains of man's tools and work are found chiefly in caves and lake-dwellings, or under drift, and only to a small extent in monuments above the present surface. The lake-dwellings specially referred to are in Switzerland, where during the very dry winter of 1853–4 several remarkable villages were found built on piles below the present average watermark, which were once without doubt the abodes of men, with quite abundant traces indicating their modes of life, civilization, implements, and the contemporary animal races.*

The various stages of civilization developed in these ancient remains have been usually classified under three heads:

1. The *Stone age*, in which man's cutting implements, working tools and weapons of war, were of stone. This age is sometimes subdivided, the older part being called "Palaeolithic" [old stone], and the more recent, "Neolithic" [new stone].

2. The *Bronze age*, its implements being chiefly of copper or brass.

3. The *Iron age*, where iron first appears.

Now the great question—the only one that comes within our range of inquiry—is the *date* of these traces of ancient men. When did the men of the Stone age and of the Bronze and the Iron age live?

In the outset, it can not be assumed reasonably that this stone-age civilization, apparent in Northern and Western Europe, was *necessarily universal at that time over all the earth*. It may have been coeval with the very high civilization of Egypt and even of Babylonia, Phenicia, Etruria. We must consider that large portions of the world in those early times were unknown to each other, even as interior Africa has been unknown to the civilized world almost to this very hour. It is therefore entirely an open question—Was this stone-age civili-

* See Thompson's "Man in Genesis and in Geology," pp. 88–90, and Lyell on the Antiquity of Man, pp. 17–29.

zation pre-Adamic? Was it anterior to Noah; or shall its place in the ages be found contemporaneous with the early civilized nations of known history?

It is important here to premise yet further that the earth's surface has at no very remote period experienced considerable elevations and depressions and changes of temperature. Especially there are proofs of an extraordinary period of glaciers and icebergs, by means of which huge bowlders have been transported from their ancient beds and scattered afar, and vast masses of debris, rocks ground down and pulverized, mixed with sand, gravel, and small stones, have been heaped up along the line of the glaciers and spread over their track. It is not easy to conceive the full measure of *utility* resulting from this great ice-flood and glacier movement, in grinding the surface of the rocky strata and mixing this finely pulverized matter with decomposed vegetable elements to prepare soil for our earth's surface.

The opinion is becoming general that man was not placed upon the earth until *after* this glacial and ice-bound age. He could not have lived here then: certainly not in portions reached by glacial action and ice floods; the earth was not ready for him till afterwards. No decisive traces of his presence at an earlier period have been found. Such traces appear shortly after.

The problem of the *time* of man's first appearance upon the earth is for the most part one *of estimates;* and these estimates in the department of geology are comprised, at least chiefly, under these five heads:

(1.) The time required for the *alluvial deposits* underneath which his remains or implements have been found.

(2.) The time required for the *growth of the peat* under which we find man or his works.

(3.) The time required for the succession of forest growths since his first appearance.

(4.) The age of the animal races, extinct or living, whose remains are found associated with his.

(5.) We have next and last another source of testimony which is mainly free from the uncertainties of estimate, viz. the question of commercial relations between the barbarous stone-age, bronze-age, or iron-age tribes, and the civilized nations of the early historic ages.

The estimates on these several points demand distinct consideration.

(1.) The estimate of the time required for the alluvial deposits along the banks of rivers, has been extremely various. Lyell, having visited the delta of the Mississippi river in person, estimated its time-period of accumulation at one hundred thousand years.* But a careful examination made by gentlemen of the Coast Survey and other United States officers, reduces this time-period to four thousand and four hundred years.† Again, Mr. Lyell estimates that 220,000 years are necessary to account for changes now going on upon the coast of Sweden. Later geologists reduce the time to one-tenth of that estimate. A piece of pottery was discovered deeply buried under the deposits at the mouth of the Nile. It was confidently asserted that the deposits could not have been made during the historic period, until it was proved that the article in question was of Roman manufacture.‡ Such diversities suffice to show at least that somebody has blundered. Some of these high estimates are gratuitously extravagant. All estimates from the drift deposits, bearing on the antiquity of man, ought in reason to be made with careful reference to these two modifying considerations:

(a.) That drift deposits may have been, and with the

---

* Lyell's Antiquity of Man, pp. 43 and 204.

† See Report upon the Physics and Hydraulics of the Mississippi River by Capt. A. A. Humphreys and Lieut. H. L. Abbott; 1861, pp. 435.

The following extract will impress the reader as at once definite and reliable.——"If it be assumed that the rate of progress has been uniform to the present day—and there are some considerations connected with the manner in which the river pushes the bar into the gulf each year which tend to establish the correctness of that opinion—the number of years which have elapsed since the river began to advance into the gulf can be computed. The present rate of progress of the mouth may be obtained by a careful comparison of the progress of all the mouths of the river as shown by the maps of Capt. Talbot, United States Engineer, 1838, and of the United States Coast Survey in 1851—the only maps that admit of such comparison. They give two hundred and sixty-two feet for the mean yearly advance of all the passes. This mean advance of all the passes represents correctly the advance of the river. . . . . . Adopting this rate of progress (two hundred and sixty-two feet per annum) four thousand four hundred years have elapsed since the river began to advance into the gulf." Bib. Sacra., April, 1873, p. 331.

‡ Hodge's Systematic Theology, vol. 2, p. 33.

utmost probability were, much more rapid in the earlier ages than at present. At the close of the glacial and ice period vast masses of loose matter were ready to be swept rapidly as drift by river freshets. Any farmer may have an illustration of this if he will plow his side-hill field, running his furrows up and down the hill. He will find that the first powerful shower will bring down far more drift than the fortieth. It would be very short-sighted in him to take the drift of the tenth year after the said plowing for his rate of annual deposition and estimate the whole period from this data. But on this mistaken principle some geologists have made their time estimates for the drift simply monstrous.

(b.) Human remains and tools may in many ways get far below the surface of the drift. They may have been buried under it after its deposition. While the drift lay under water, (soft and pliable therefore,) flints, arrow-heads, knives, or human bones, may have sunk in the mire.——These and similar considerations may demand large abatement from the time-estimates built upon the amount of drift found above the remains of man.

We may apply these modifying considerations to the case given by Lyell (Antiquity of Man, pp. 27, 28) of the drift deposits near the Lake of Geneva. Here are five inches in thickness deposited since the Roman period (known by its enclosed memorials) which we safely put at 1800 years. Next below is a stratum of six inches depth, marked by bronze implements, which he estimates to reach back from the present time, 3000 to 4000 years. Similarly, the next stratum (seven inches) indicated as the Stone age, he counts at 5000 to 7000 years old. But if the depositions were much more rapid in the early than in the later ages of our world, these estimates for the ages of bronze and of stone must be materially shortened, and may reasonably be brought within the historic period of man.

(2.) The time required for the formation of *peat beds* has been usually estimated upon its observed growth and accumulation at the present day. Yet in the case of peat-growth as in the case of drift-deposits, it is at least possible and would seem highly probable that its growth and deposition were much more rapid during the earlier ages of our race than at present. The virgin soil was richer; the climatic influences may have been more propitious. It should be considered also here (as in the case of drift) that the remains of man and his implements, instead of resting invariably upon the surface of the peat, may by various means have gone down much below the surface. The time of man's presence, therefore, as measured by the time estimated to be necessary for the deposit of the peat found above him, may be quite overestimated.

The peat beds of Denmark are put by Lyell (Antiquity of Man, p. 17) at a minimum of 4000 years. In the valley of the Somme (France) they are found 30 feet deep; and in its upper strata there are Romish and Celtic memorials, showing that its depositions continued a considerable time after the historic age of Rome.

(3.) The time required for the succession of forest growths since the appearance of man.

Geologists find in Denmark, earliest, a growth of Scotch fir; next, of oak; last, coming down to the present, of the beech. The age of civilization known as the Stone age synchronizes nearly with the fir; the Bronze age with the oak; the historic period with iron implements answers to the beech.* Now the problem is—How much time is required for one species of forest growths to run its course and become supplanted by another? ——Obviously this problem must depend not on time alone, but on climatic changes. Moreover, one kind of trees may require less time than another to exhaust the soil of the elements specially congenial to its health, vigor and stability. I do not see that any reliable measure of time can be found for estimating the life-period of different species of forest growths.

(4.) Attempts have been made to estimate the antiquity of man from the animal races with which his remains have been found associated. The animals brought into this estimate have been chiefly the mammals, quadrupeds, most nearly related, by anatomical structure, to man. Great account has been made of the fact that the remains of man (his bones or his tools) have been found in connection with the remains of land animals now extinct. The uncertain element in all such calculations is the date at which the said animal

* See Lyell's Antiquity of Man, pp. 9-11.

species became extinct. This is perhaps fully as doubtful as the age at which man began to live on the earth. So far as is known, some species have disappeared within the present century; *e. g.* the Great Auk, or Northern Penguin (alca impennis), last seen alive in 1844. Several species, once quite prominent for their hugeness or other qualities, are supposed to have disappeared within the historic period of man; *e. g.* the mammoth, the mastodon, the woolly rhinoceros, the cave-bear, etc. But precisely *when* they severally became extinct, no existing data suffice to show. Of course it avails little to prove that man was coeval with a few animal races now extinct.

(5.) Far more important in my view is the light thrown upon the antiquity of the Bronze and Iron ages of civilization in Northern and Western Europe by the traces of commercial relations between those respective peoples and the civilized nations of the known historic ages. In this case, the elements of uncertainty common to the preceding estimates are mostly if not wholly eliminated. When among the relics of the Bronze age, say in Switzerland or in Denmark, we find art-specimens, valuable for use or beauty, which manifestly came from Phenicia, Etruria, or Egypt, bearing unmistakably the stamp of their civilization, and specifically, of their art, we need no further proof that the old Bronze age lay *in time* along-side of the reign of Etrurian or Egyptian art and civilization. On this subject the British Quarterly (Oct., 1872) on "The present Phase of Pre-historic Archeology" discusses the question whether the Bronze civilization in Central and Northern Europe was introduced by an invading people from the East, or by peaceful commerce with the peoples contiguous to the Mediterranean, viz. the Phenicians of Palestine, the Etrurians of Italy, and the Egyptians. The argument is strongly in favor of the latter alternative. "The beautiful bronze swords, spear-heads, axes, knives, razors, etc., which lie scattered over Northern and Central Europe are remarkable for the singular beauty of their form and ornamentation"—all bearing so much unity of design as to prove a common origin from the same source. "The double spirals, and dotted circles and spirals and zigzag ornaments which are so common on the bronze articles of France, Germany.

Britain, Ireland, and Scandinavia *are identical with the designs which are found in Etruscan tombs.* Some of the bronze swords and spear-heads are also identical; and the peculiar spuds and bronze axes, used by the Etruscans, are similar to those which are found in Northern Europe." (pp. 247, 248).——The limits of my plan forbid a full presentation of this argument. Suffice it to say briefly that very great progress has been made within the last fifty years toward disentombing the pre-historical ages of Central and Northern Europe, and bringing out their relation to the early historic civilization of Egypt, Phenicia, and Etruria. The results thus far seem to identify the oldest race of man as known by his remains (*i. e.* they of the earlier Stone age) with the Esquimaux of Lapland; the men of the later Stone age, with the Iberian or Basque people of Spain; after whom were the Celts and the Belgæ who were on the field at the period where Roman history touches Britain and Gaul.——How far back in time those Esquimau tribes lie, it seems yet impossible to determine; but the next wave of population—they of the later Stone age—falls far within the period of scripture chronology—not necessarily older than the Phenicians, Assyrians, and Egyptians. Inasmuch as Phenician art and commerce were in their glory during the reigns of David and Solomon, we may at least provide a considerable interval of time for the Esquimau tribes of the older Stone age before we encounter the deluge of Noah, and much more still, before we come up to Adam. It is a fact of no trifling importance that the oldest race detected by the explorers of the earth's crust can be so clearly identified with the Esquimaux now occupying the highest northern latitudes inhabited by man.

More abundant still are the proofs which bring the Bronze and Iron ages of Northern Europe within what were the historic times of the nations on the borders of the Mediterranean.——The estimates made by some geologists and antiquarians which carry the later Stone, the Bronze, and the Iron peoples back into the mighty Past anywhere from 10,000 to 100,000 years seem to me extremely fanciful and unscientific. Thorough investigation into all the facts bearing on the case coupled with sober estimates of the time which they indicate, will at no distant day bring this problem of the antiquity of man to a satisfactory solution. It does not become us to fear any revelations which come legitimately from well ascertained facts.

Another argument for the high antiquity of man has been drawn *from the traditions of the most ancient nations*—China and India; also *from the great population, the early civilization, and the art-monuments of Egypt.*

On the point of the traditions and chronologies of the ancient nations of the East, the first problem is to ascertain what they are and what they claim. If they run up their figures (as sometimes said) to 20,000 years, the extravagance of the claim vitiates its credibility.* We put it to the account of fancy and fiction, or of national pride, and rule it out from the realm of historic science. But if as estimated by Bailly (Kitto; Chronology, p. 434) the years from the Christian era back to the creation are put in Chinese chronology at 6157; in the Babylonian, at 6158; and in the Indian (by Gentil) at 6174, we give these chronologies our respectful attention. The fact that the extreme difference in these three is but seventeen years is certainly striking, and indicates either a common origin of authority or an approximation toward the truth; perhaps both. We shall soon have occasion to compare these figures with the latest and most approved results of Biblical chronology.

As to the age of Egyptian art, civilization, and political power, the time allowed for its development in harmony with Usher's chronology (the one usually indicated in editions of the English Bible) must be admitted to be short—almost incredibly short. Here I submit that the primary question should be—the correctness of Usher. Let the Bible system of chronology be rigidly scanned—not for the purpose of making it tally with Egyptian claims, or with any other system of chronology not sacred; but for the purpose of arriving at the truth as ascertainable from the Bible itself.

* See "Antiquity and Unity of the Human Race," by Rev. Ebenezer Burgess, pp. 25–30.

CHAPTER III.

HEBREW CHRONOLOGY.

From the Birth of Christ to the Creation.

By general consent the birth of Christ is made the central point of all sacred chronology, the Christian ages being reckoned forward from that point (A. D.) and the Jewish or earlier ages being reckoned backward (B. C.). We treat of the latter only.——Going backward from the Christian era, there is general agreement and no reasonable ground for diversity till we reach the period of the *Judges of Israel*. The cardinal points are:

	B. C.
The decree of Cyrus for the restoration of the Jews.	536
The duration of the captivity, from the fourth year of Jehoiakim, 70 years......................	606
(But counted from the fall of the city under Zedekiah, 52 years only.)	
From the revolt, first year of Rehoboam to the fall of the city, 388 years........................	976
To the founding of the temple, beginning of Solomon's fourth year, 37 years.................	1013

This last epoch has chronological importance—the foundation of the temple laid—A. D. 1013.

The first disputed, diversely estimated, point is the *period of the Judges;* yet the proof texts and authorities cover the period from the Exodus to the temple. Usher makes the period of the Judges 339 years; Jahn and many others, 450. Usher relies on 1 K. 6: 1: "In the 480th year after the children of Israel were come out of the land of Egypt, in the fourth year of Solomon's reign over Israel..... he began to build the house of the Lord."

His computation runs thus:

	YEARS.
Hebrews in the wilderness......................	40
Hebrews under Joshua...........................	17

(60)

PERIOD OF THE JUDGES.

	YEARS.
Samuel and Saul together*	40
David (2 Sam. 5: 4, 5)	41
Solomon up to the founding of the temple	3
Judges—to fill out 480	339
	480

The long period for the Judges rests primarily on Acts 13: 20, which states that "after having divided to them the land of Canaan by lot, God gave them judges 450 years until Samuel the prophet." Placing 450 in the above computation in place of 339—an excess of 111 years—we find the date of the Exodus B. C. 1604 instead of Usher's figures A. D. 1491.

In support of this long period for the Judges may be urged—

(1.) The authority of Paul as above (Acts 13: 20) which makes this period 450 years.

(2.) Josephus makes the interval from the Exodus to the founding of the temple 592 years, and not 480. The Jews of China also make it 592—facts which favor the supposition that the Hebrew text of 1 K. 6: 1, is in error. It can not be supposed that either Josephus or the Chinese Jews adjusted their figures to harmonize with Paul.

(3.) The internal dates in the Book of Judges demand the long period and can not be harmonized with the short one.——Thus Judges 11: 26 shows that the Hebrews had then dwelt in Heshbon, Aroer and along the coast of Arnon 300 years. These years lie between the entrance into Canaan and the beginning of Jephthah's judgeship. We have then this computation:

	YEARS.
300 years, minus 17 years for the term of Joshua, is	283
Add for Jephthah (Judg. 12: 6)	6
For Ibzan 7 years; for Elon 10; for Abdon 8 (according to Judg. 12: 8, 11, 14)	25
Servitude to the Philistines (Judg. 13: 1)	40
Sampson (Judg. 15: 20 and 16: 31) not less than	20
Eli (1 Sam. 4: 18)	40

* Josephus states explicitly that Samuel and Saul combined fill out 40 years.

                                                                YEARS.
A period without dates (narrated Judg. 17–21) estimated at 40
                                                              ─────
Makes a total of 454

It is entirely impossible to bring these internal dates in the history within the short period of 339 years for the Judges. We must therefore accept the long period—450 years—and place the Exodus in 1013+591= B. C. 1604.

The next period of conflicting authorities is the *Sojourn in Egypt.* The issue lies between the long period, 430 years, and the short one, 215 years.——The first proof text is Ex. 12: 40: "Now the sojourning of the children of Israel who dwelt in Egypt was 430 years." Next is Gen. 15: 13: "Thy seed shall be a stranger in a land not theirs and shall serve them; and they shall afflict them 400 years":—which is quoted substantially by Stephen, Ac. 7: 6.——On the other hand stands Gal. 3: 17, which makes the giving of the law on Sinai 430 years *after* the covenant made with Abraham. The interval from that covenant to Jacob's standing before Pharaoh is readily computed thus: From the covenant with Abram, he being then 75 years old (Gen. 12: 4) to the birth of Isaac, Abraham 100 years old (Gen. 21: 5) is 25 years.——From birth of Isaac to birth of Jacob (Gen. 25: 26) 60.——Jacob standing before Pharaoh (Gen. 47: 9) at 130, the sum of which numbers is 215. According to Paul, this would leave for the sojourn in Egypt but 215 years.

A distinct class of proofs came from an estimate of the generations between the fathers who went down into Egypt and the sons who entered Canaan. Of this, presently.

Reverting now to the obviously conflicting proof texts above cited, we may note that Ex. 12: 40 is read variously—the Septuagint (Vatican text) adding after "dwelt in Egypt," the words—"and in the land of Canaan;" while the Alexandrian text of the Septuagint adds also—"they and their fathers." Both these additions appear also in the Samaritan text and in the Targum Jonathan; while the Masoretic Hebrew is supported by the more reliable Targum of Onkelos;

also by the Syriac and the Vulgate. These additions as in the Septuagint are clumsily made. The dwelling in Canaan, referring to Abraham and Isaac, should come in *before* the dwelling in Egypt if at all, and not *after*. The diversity between the two texts of the Septuagint is suspicious. The authority of the old Hebrew text stands unshaken.

The passage Gen 15: 13 is strong to the same purport, since it was "in a land *not his own*" (*i. e.* not Canaan), and was a state of tyrannous oppression which was to continue 400 years—points which forbid us to include in this 400 years the life-history of Abraham, Isaac and Jacob.——As to Paul (Gal. 3: 17) his readers had before them only the Septuagint; he would therefore naturally follow its authority, and the more readily because the difference between that and the Hebrew in the length of the interval was a point of no importance to his argument.

The evidence from the lapse of generations during the sojourn in Egypt is of great, not to say decisive, importance to our question. Here, however, opinions as to its bearing differ totally. One of the test passages is Ex. 6: 16-20, which makes the whole age of Levi 137 years; of Kohath, his son, 133; of Amram—apparently his son and the father of Moses, 137. The age of Moses when he stood before Pharaoh (Ex. 7: 7) was 80. Kohath was born in Canaan; his father was older by several years than Benjamin; presumably, therefore, his children were older; yet Benjamin had ten sons when he went down into Egypt (Gen. 46: 21). If we suppose that Kohath was 25 when he went into Egypt, then he lived there 108 years. Amram lived there 137, and Moses at the Exodus had lived 80. With these given generations and ages, this computation is stretched to its utmost extent since it supposes Kohath's death at 133 and Amram's birth to have occurred in the same year; also Amram's death at 137 and the birth of Moses to be in the same year; yet the sum is only 325, which is less by 105 years than the long period. With these data the short period (215) might be readily provided for.

But several circumstances combine to show that there must be several omitted links between the Amram here spoken of, and Kohath. For in this genealogical list (Ex. 6: 16–20) we have but two names between Levi, the tribe-father, and Moses, viz. Kohath and Amram. But between Joseph, a younger tribe-father, and Zelophehad, a contemporary of Moses, there are four intervening names (Num. 26: 28–33); between Judah and Bezaleel there are six (1 Chron. 2: 3–5, 18–20); between Joseph (through Ephraim) and Joshua, there are nine (1 Chron. 7: 22–27).——Again, we have in Num. 3: 27, 28, a census of the four Kohath families. The males, from one month and upward, are 8600. If we set off one-fourth of these to Amram (*i. e.* 2150) and remember that the Amram who was father to Moses had but one other son, Aaron, (known to this genealogy) with four sons, and that Moses had but two, we shall see it utterly impossible that the male offspring of Moses and of Aaron could number 2150. Therefore Amram, the immediate son of Kohath, must have been several generations back of the Amram who was father of Moses.—— The genealogy of Jochebed, the mother of Moses, might also be explained, but space forbids.——The vast increase of Hebrew population, from the 70 souls who went down into Egypt to the 600,000 men of age for war who went out (Ex. 12: 37), suggests a longer time than 215 years. The evidence on the whole preponderates decisively against the shorter and in favor of the longer period, 430 years.

The third doubtful period in Hebrew chronology lies between Abraham and his father Terah, the question being the age of Terah at Abraham's birth. Some authorities make it 70 years; others, 130. The proof texts are—(a.) Gen. 11: 26; "Terah lived 70 years and begat Abram, Nahor, and Haran."——(b.) Gen. 11: 32; "The days of Terah were 205 years; and Terah died in Haran."——(c.) Acts 7: 4; "Abram came out of the land of the Chaldeans and dwelt in Haran; and from thence, *after his father was dead*, he removed into this land wherein ye now dwell."——(d.) Gen. 12: 4; "Abram was 75 years old when he departed out of Haran."——The difficulty is that if Abram was born when his father was 70 and lived with him till his death at the age of 205, he should have been 135 and not merely 75 when his father died and he went into Canaan.——To surmount this difficulty some construe the text (a.) to mean that Terah lived 70 years before the birth of his first son; that Abram was not his first-born but is named first on account of his greater prominence in history and in character; and that Abram was not born till his father was 130.——Others assume that Stephen made the slight mistake of supposing that Terah was dead when Abram left Haran for Canaan, misled by the circumstance that the historian, in order to dispose of his case, narrated Terah's death *before* he spoke of Abram's emigration to Canaan, although (as they assume) it in fact occurred 60 years afterwards.——Others assume an error in the number of years assigned as the full age of Terah, making it 145 instead of 205—the Samaritan text giving these figures.

The assumption that Stephen was mistaken is to be rejected; partly because it was vital to the purposes of his speech that his historic points should be accurately made—at least in harmony with current Jewish opinion—to say nothing of the further fact that he is before us as one "filled with the Holy Ghost" and specially inspired; partly because the history represents Terah as sympathizing fully in the spirit of the removal from Ur to Canaan, and apparently prevented from going only by the infirmities of age.——The choice seems, therefore, to lie between the first named explanation and the last. The first—making the passage (Gen. 11: 26) mean only that Terah lived 70 years before the birth of his eldest, but became the father of three sons—leaving us at liberty to fix Abraham's birth at his 130th year—is a possible construction, but is rendered somewhat improbable by Abram's question (Gen. 17: 17) "Shall a son be born to him that is 100 years old"? How could he have thought this strange if in fact he himself had been born when his father was 130?—— There may be an error in the number of years of Terah's life; the Samaritan text may be right in making it 145. This is below the average age of his fathers; but in those as in all other days, men were subject to die before they reached the maximum age of their generation. It would seem that he set out from Ur with the reasonable expectation of going to Canaan. Hence a probability that he died unexpectedly, and at an earlier age than his fathers. I can express no positive opinion upon this case.

Two other doubtful periods remain to be considered, viz. *The interval from the creation to the flood: and the interval from the flood to the call of Abram.* The question upon these two intervals is substantially the same, so that they may properly be presented together. It hinges in both cases upon the authority of the texts—viz. for the former interval, Gen. 5: 3–32; and for the latter, Gen. 11: 10–26.——In form these tables are not chronological but genealogical. They do not reckon from any given era, as if (*e. g.*) to show the interval from the creation to the flood, but give the age of each member of the genealogical line when his son of the same line was born. It is therefore by adding together these measured portions of each man's life, viz. the years he lived before the next member in the line was born, that we obtain the entire interval.——The tables give three facts as to each man's life; (a.) how old he was when his son in this line was born; (b.) how long he lived afterwards; and (c.) the sum total of his years. If the chain is perfect, with neither missing nor supernumerary links, and if the numbers of the first class are all correct, the result must be reliable. But plainly the result will be changed at once by changing the first set of numbers and the second to correspond,—without changing the third at all.

In the present case from Adam to Noah inclusive are ten generations. The sum of the first class of numbers as it stands in our Hebrew text is 1656, to the year of the flood. The only question of difficulty is upon the *authority of the text*. The Septuagint makes the same interval 2262—an excess above the Hebrew of 606 years.
——In like manner from the birth of Arphaxad to the call of Abram (ten generations inclusive) the Hebrew text makes a total of 365 years; the Septuagint 1015, or by another text of the Sept. 1115, making an excess of 650 or 750 years. The sum of excess in the two periods is 1256 or 1356.——The following tables will serve to show how these diverse footings are produced. The numbers given by Josephus have some interest: I therefore place them in the table for the period before the flood. The numbers given in

the Samaritan text are frequently brought into this comparison. They differ considerably from either of the other authorities, but seem to me of no particular value, and are therefore omitted.

A.

NAMES	HEBREW TEXT.			SEPTUAGINT.			JOSEPHUS.		
	Age at Son's birth.	Rest of life.	Total.	Age at Son's birth.	Rest of life.	Total.	Age at Son's birth.	Rest of life.	Total.
1. Adam............	130	800	930	230	700	930	230	700	930
2. Seth.............	105	807	912	205	707	912	205	707	912
3. Enos.............	90	815	905	190	715	905	190	715	905
4. Cainan	70	840	910	170	740	910	170	740	910
5. Mahalaleel......	65	830	895	165	730	895	165	730	895
6. Jared.............	162	800	962	162	800	962	162	800	962
7. Enoch	65	300	365	165	200	365	165	200	365
8. Methusaleh.....	187	782	969	*187	782	969	187	782	969
9. Lamech..........	182	595	777	188	565	753	182	595	777
10. Noah	500	450	950	500	450	*950	500	450	950
To the flood.....	100	......	......	100	......	......	100	......	......
Total	1656			2262			2256		

* The Vatican text of the Seventy makes this number 167.

Comparing the Hebrew figures with those of the Septuagint, it seems plain that one set or the other has been altered *by design*. It should be borne in mind that the Septuagint is a translation from Hebrew into Greek, made about 285 B. C., which is not far from 1500 years prior to the date of our oldest Hebrew manuscripts. Also that Josephus wrote in the latter part of the first century after Christ, giving Jewish history quite faithfully *as then understood.*——In the first table Josephus sustains the Septuagint with only the one slight exception of making Lamech 182 instead of 188 at the birth of Noah—his total being thereby six years less.

The reader will note carefully how these main differences between the Hebrew and the Septuagint stand. In the first five names and in the seventh, the years in the first column—*i. e.* the age of the father at the birth of his son, are less by 100 in the Hebrew than in the Septuagint, or (what amounts to the same thing) greater by 100 in the Septuagint than in the Hebrew. To correspond, the years in the second column are greater by 100 in the Hebrew than in the Septuagint, so that the totals as they appear in the third column come out the same in both texts.——These are the only important variations. The other is a slight one—the Septuagint adding six years to the age of Lamech at Noah's birth, or the Hebrew taking six years off from the number as in the Septuagint. In this case Josephus is with the Hebrew text.——It may be noted also that in the cases of Jared and Methuselah, the figures agree.——Now the question is—*Which text is pure, and which has been corrupted?*

A better view perhaps of the whole question will be obtained if at this point we study the corresponding table for the period from the birth of Arphaxad (two years after the flood) to the call of Abram, made up from the Hebrew text, from the Septuagint and from the Samaritan text of Gen. 11: 10–26:

B.

NAMES	HEBREW TEXT.			SEPTUAGINT.			SAMARITAN.		
	Age at Son's birth.	Rest of life.	Total.	Age at Son's birth.	Rest of life.	Total.	Age at Son's birth.	Rest of life.	Total.
1. Shem............	100	500	600	100	500	600	100	500	600
2. Arphaxad........	35	403	438	135	400	535	135	303	438
3. Salah............	30	403	433	130	330	460	130	303	433
4. Eber.............	34	430	464	134	270	404	134	270	404
5. Peleg............	30	209	239	130	209	339	130	109	239
6. Reu	32	207	239	132	207	339	132	107	237
7. Serug............	30	200	230	130	200	330	130	100	230
8. Nahor	29	119	148	179 [or 79]	125	304	79	69	148
9. Terah............	130 [or 70]	135	205	130 [or 70]	135	205	70	75	145
10. Abram, his call..	75	......	......	75	......	......	75	......	......
Total	365	......	......	1015	......	......	1015	......	......

Here it will be noticed that the important differences are of the same sort as in the corresponding table before the flood. In a series of six names (Arphaxad to Serug inclusive) the Hebrew has 100 years less in each life than the Septuagint *before* the dividing point. In the first (the important) column, the Samaritan agrees with the Septuagint. The years in the second and in the third columns are quite irregular. In the case of Nahor the Septuagint exceeds the Hebrew either 50, as in the Alexandrian text of the Septuagint, or 150 as in the Vatican text.

On the question—Which of these texts, the Hebrew or the Greek, has been corrupted? it may be said in favor of the integrity of the Hebrew:

(a.) That it is the original.——(b.) That in general it has been preserved by the Jews with extreme care and guarded against corruption with the greatest vigilance.

In favor of the integrity of the Septuagint on the points now in question may be urged—

(a.) As to the period from Adam to Noah, the general concurrence of Josephus—an independent and reliable witness as to the state of all the Jewish authorities of his time. In regard to the period after the flood, the corresponding concurrence of the Samaritan text in all vital points.

(b.) The fact that there is no known reason for intentional corruption; while over against this it has been supposed (with how much probability it is difficult to say) that the Jews during their controversies with the Christians on the great question of the Messiah (A. D. 150–400) found it for their interest to shorten the period from the creation to the Christian era in order to prove that the Messiah had not yet come. This presupposes it admitted on both sides that he was to come within some given number of years after the creation—perhaps 4500 or 5000. We have already seen reason to suppose that the Hebrew text of 1 Kings 6: 1 is in error—perhaps corrupted. It is manifestly less than the truth by the difference between 480 and 591.

(c.) The accuracy of the Septuagint chronology on these contested points does not appear to have been called in question until at least 400 years after the translation was made—never before A. D. 150, about the date when the controversy arose respecting the Christian Messiah.

(d.) It was in use and fully accredited before the Christian era.

(e.) It was used and its authority fully admitted by the fathers of the Christian church.——This fact and the next preceding render it at least probable that the Hebrew text *at that time* was in harmony with the Septuagint.

(f.) The Chaldean and Egyptian annals seem to demand more time back to the flood or to the creation than the present Hebrew text admits, and therefore lend their influence (to be taken for what it is worth) in favor of the Septuagint rather than the Hebrew because of its longer periods.

(g.) In table A it will be readily seen, comparing the figures of the first column in the Hebrew with the corresponding figures in the Septuagint, that the latter are very uniform while in the Hebrew there is a wide diversity between the highest and the lowest, four standing considerably below 100 and two above 180. The probability seems to be somewhat against so wide diversity.——In table B the Hebrew figures in the first column are sufficiently near each other. Out of seven in succession the extremes are 29 and 35. We have an equal uniformity in the first column of the Septuagint and of the Samaritan, six of these figures being the same as in the Hebrew with only the addition of 100. The Hebrew figures seem low relatively to the total years; and on the other hand the Septuagint figures seem too high. Especially is this objection formidable when we remember Abram's surprise that God should promise him a son when 100 years old (Gen. 17: 17). "Shall a child be born to him that is 100 years old?"—as if it were a thing unknown in then recent history. But if all Abram's ancestors back to the flood begat their respective sons in this line at ages ranging from 135 to 130 (or all but Terah) it is somewhat difficult to account for his surprise. The best we could say would be that the average human life was fast lessening. I regard this as the most serious objection of internal character against the integrity of the Septuagint text.——
On the whole the chronological questions at issue between the Hebrew text and the Septuagint, turning

USHER'S SYSTEM TOO SHORT. 71

upon the authority of their respective texts, are very much complicated and not a little doubtful. I have laid before the reader what I regard as the main arguments, and rest the case here, hopeful that greater light may yet arise, leaning, however, toward accepting the authority of the Septuagint.

Reviewing the points made in this examination of Hebrew chronology, it will be seen that we extend the time beyond Usher's system, (a.) In the period of the Judges at least 111 years; (b.) In the sojourn in Egypt 215 years; and (omitting the interval between Terah and Abram as uncertain), (c.) In the interval from the flood to the call of Abram (if the Septuagint be followed) at least 650 years, and perhaps 750; and (d.) In the period from the creation to the flood, 606 years—a total of 1582 or 1682 years.——Or, to put the case in another form, we put the Exodus in the year (B. C.) 1603; Jacob's going into Egypt, B. C. 2033; the call of Abram, B. C. 2248; and by the Septuagint the flood, 3265 or 3365; and finally, by the Septuagint, the creation, B. C. 5527 or 5627.

This approximates toward harmony with the reported results of the Indian chronology which locates the creation B. C. 6174; also the Baylonian, B. C. 6158, and the Chinese, B. C. 6157—the excess of the latter above the longest sacred chronology being only 530 years. The approach toward harmony in these three not sacred chronologies—the Indian, the Baylonian and the Chinese—the extreme difference being only 17 years—is certainly a remarkable fact.

CHAPTER IV.

THE ANTIQUITY OF MAN RESUMED.

As to the antiquity of Egyptian art, civilization and political power, there are two main questions:

1. *How much time, after Noah, is required?*
2. *How much can be allowed in harmony with the most reliable authorities of Hebrew chronology?*

1. Under the head of *time required*, it is in place to note the circumstances which favored the very rapid growth of Egyptian civilization and also of the numerical and political power of Egypt.

(a.) Mizraim, the father of Egypt, who gave his name to the kingdom, was a grandson of Noah and the father of seven sons (Gen. 10: 1, 6, 13, 14). Consequently he started *early and strong*.

(b.) The fertility of the Nile valley was prodigious; it was capable, therefore, of sustaining an immense population, and so would attract other people besides the lineal descendants of Mizraim. Every thing was propitious for the early and rapid peopling of their country.

(c.) Fixed residence, coupled with cheap bread and abundance of it, put the Egyptian on vantage-ground above any other ancient nation for the early culture of art and for rapid growth in all that made Egypt great.

(d.) It is a capital mistake to assume that the arts and sciences *were originated* in Egypt after the flood, and that therefore a very long time must be allowed for their growth and development up from utter barbarism. For there was surely no insignificant amount of art and science among the builders of Noah's ark. The yet earlier history of the race names "the father of all such as handle the harp and organ," and also "an instructor of every artificer in brass and iron" (Gen. 4: 21, 22).

(e.) It is a significant fact that the Chaldean tradition of the deluge as preserved by Berosus sets forth the special care taken by Noah to preserve and transmit to

AGE OF EGYPTIAN CIVILIZATION.

the new-born nations after the flood the arts and sciences which had been developed before that catastrophe. They say he was admonished to put in writing an account of these arts and sciences and deposit it in a place of safety until the flood should be past. This tradition reveals the fact of a current belief that there was such knowledge to be preserved, and that means were used to preserve it.

2. Under the head of *time required* it remains to give a synopsis of the latest and most reliable results of Egyptologists in regard to the Egyptian date of *Menes*, their first king, and of the building of the three great pyramids—these being the most important epochs of the earliest Egyptian antiquity.

The standard historic authority (not, however, above suspicion) is Manetho, an Egyptian priest of Heliopolis, of the age of Ptolemy Philadelphus (reigned B. C. 284–246), who is supposed to have made up from the ancient records of his nation a list of thirty or thirty-one dynasties of Egyptian kings, beginning with Menes and ending with the conquests of Alexander the Great, giving the years of each king's reign. Unfortunately it comes down in a somewhat fragmentary condition, as copied by Julius Africanus (died A. D. 232), who was himself in part copied by Eusebius (of the fourth century) and by Syncellus (flourished A. D. 780).

Until recently it has been the current opinion of the best authorities (still held by many) that these dynasties were at some points *contemporary* and not *successive*—some of them reigning in Upper Egypt, others in Middle or Lower Egypt, *at the same time*. This would raise the problems—How many and which were contemporary? How much is the entire period actually shortened by this contemporaneousness?——Moreover it has been supposed also that on the same throne there has been at some points a joint occupancy of two or more kings—father and son perhaps, or of some rival claimants; so that the entire duration of a given dynasty may be less than the sum of the reigns of its enumerated kings.*——

---

* It is a telling fact that according to Julius Africanus, Manetho's numbers for the entire reigns of all the kings foot up 5404 years, while the aggregate duration of all the dynasties (within the same chronological termini) is 3555 years—*i. e.* the sum of all the dynasties is less by 1849 years than the sum of all the kings' reigns

74 ANTIQUITY OF MAN.

The problem of whole duration being complicated by these elements of uncertainty, it has been the great aim of recent investigation to gather in all possible aid from the monuments and bring their testimony to bear upon the tables of Manetho. The results are variously estimated and the problem can not be regarded as yet fully settled.

I place together the opinions of some of the best authorities:

I. *For the date of Menes, reputed the first king.*

B. C.
Bunsen's latest revised recension of Egyptian Chronology locates him*........................3059
J. P. Thompson at least as far back as............3000
R. S. Poole (Smith's Bible Dictionary, p. 682)......2717
Sir Gardner Wilkinson (see "Aids to Faith," p. 294).2690
Wm. Palmer (Smith's Bible Dictionary, p. 687)....2224
The "Old Chronicle" (very valuable authority)...2220
Eratosthenes and Appollodorus, original authorities, in no respect inferior to Manetho........2793

Other estimates from less reliable authorities carry him back yet further.

For convenience of comparison we place here our corrected Bible Chronology for the call of Abraham—viz. B. C. 2248; and for the flood, by the longest Septuagint text, B. C. 3425, and by the shortest, B. C. 3325. These dates afford ample time for Mizraim, grandson of Noah, to make a home and found a community in Egypt, in which Menes might presently reach the dignity of being the first king.

II. *The date of the Pyramids.*

B. C.
Bunsen in his latest recension, about.............2600
Prof. C. Piazzi Smith, by astronomical calculations.2170
George Rawlinson (in "Aids to Faith," p. 297)....2400

These dates may be compared with the call of Abra-

which make up those dynasties. See Burgess on the Antiquity of Man, pp. 70, 73.

*Bunsen is cited not as the best authority, but as one of the most strenuous for an exceedingly, not to say excessively, long duration.

UNITY OF THE RACE. 75

ham—B. C. 2248.———J. P. Thompson (Genesis and Geology, p. 86) says—"The three great pyramids by the common consent of Egyptologers are assigned to the fourth dynasty of kings of the old empire, as given by Manetho."

It will be seen that these dates for Menes, the first king, and for the oldest pyramids are amply provided for within the extension of sacred chronology as above indicated.———Other points in Egyptian antiquities will be treated of in their place.

On the general subject of the *antiquity of man*, it only remains to touch briefly the subsidiary questions stated above, p. 49.

(a.) *Were there one or more races of primeval men, pre-Adamic, but now extinct?*

So far as reliable facts have yet come to light there is no sufficient evidence of the affirmative. Our investigations into the antiquity of man do not seem to demand a longer time than the extended sacred chronology above presented affords. It is perhaps too soon to say that no evidence will yet appear of a pre-Adamic race not in existence now. But it will be soon enough to recognize the fact when the evidence shall have been adduced. Till then, it is more scientific to believe only so far as we have knowledge based on evidence.

(b.) *Have there been various head-centers of existing human species, or only one, and that Adam?*———Or (the same question in different form) Are all the living varieties of race lineally descended from Adam? and all from Noah?———These questions contemplate the well known diversities of race in the existing human family.

The classification of *race* is made somewhat variously by different authors; but the more common one makes *five* classes: The Caucasian, or white; The Mongolian, or yellow; The Ethiopian negro race, or black; The American, or red; and the Malayan, or brown. (See Webster.)

Let it be premised in the outset that this distinction of race is one of *variety* and not of *species*. It sits upon the surface and does not penetrate to the inner nature. All these races have the same anatomical structure; the same physical organs; and what is far more, the same intellectual and moral nature. Every-where they exhibit the common effects of the fall of

Adam; the same depravity of moral nature; the same common need of redemption by Christ.——These are cardinal traits and tests. What is the color of the skin compared with the stamp of God's image upon the very nature itself?

That these races intermingle and cross indefinitely is sufficient proof that they are only *varieties*, and by no means distinct *species*.——Yet this of itself does not prove that all men have descended from one first man—Adam. For the Lord had power to create five or ten Adams, each the head-center of as many distinct races, yet all, of the one species, *man*. So far therefore as respects the creative power of God or the constitution of man, this is an open question: *What then are the facts?*

1. The Scriptures imply with the strongest form of implication that the Adam of Genesis is the father—the one only father—of the whole human race. The narrative of the creation; of the fall; and of the first promise of redemption—all imply this. Paul implies it in those passages in which he compares the ruin of the race through the one man Adam with the salvation provided for the race through the greater second *Man*, Jesus Christ. The strong passages are Rom. 5: 12–19 and 1 Cor. 15: 21, 22.

2. The diversities of race may be accounted for as produced by either or both of two causes; (a.) Climatic influences; (b.) Sporadic, abnormal peculiarities, appearing suddenly, and perpetuating themselves by inheritance.

3. The geographical distribution of the race from one head-center, Adam, is certainly possible. There is some reason to suppose that the relative position of the seas, oceans, and continents at their points of nearest approach may have been different in the earlier ages from the present.

4. The proofs of a common language from which all known human languages have been derived conspire to sustain the common origin of all the human family.

This list of proofs might be extended and the argument from these points greatly expanded.

On the subordinate question whether Noah was the common ancestor of all the races living since his day, the answer turns mainly on the point of the universality of the deluge; or rather, on this precise point—Did the deluge destroy all the living men except those saved with Noah in the ark?

This question will be considered in its place.

CHAPTER V.

THE SABBATH.

It has been already suggested that the division of the creative work into six days rather than into five or ten or any other number, contemplated the weekly Sabbath and was designed to connect this Sabbath for man with God's rest from this creative work so that the Sabbath should be at once a memorial of the creation and should bear in itself the force of God's example in his relative periods of labor and of rest. God created this beautiful earth for man's abode, and man to dwell upon it; therefore let man remember his Great Creator and Father, thoughtfully contemplating his works, admiring and adoring, worshiping and serving the Glorious Author of both his being and his blessings. God wrought six days and rested one; so let man throughout all the ages of earthly time. Such is the relation of the Sabbath to God and to man.——Note therefore

1. *God ordained and enjoined it.* It is precisely a divine institution—not man-made but heaven-born; an outgrowth of God's wisdom and love for his offspring man—for that one of all his creatures whom only God "made in his own image." "God blessed the seventh day and sanctified it; because that in it he had rested from all his work which God created and made" (Gen. 2: 3). "Blessed and sanctified"—not *as to himself* but *as to man;* i.e. not to make the day a blessing to himself but a blessing to man; not to make the day holy *to himself* but holy *as to man.* It was a day for man to keep holy and a day laden with blessings for man on condition of his sacredly observing it in its true spirit and intent.——In accord with this view are our Savior's words (Mk. 2: 27), "The Sabbath was made for man"—to become a blessing for man, one of the great and sure channels of mercy from the Great Father to his obedient children. Thus the Sabbath was instituted for man when the race existed in Adam and Eve alone—one of the institutions revealed from God and

enjoined in Eden—good for man before his fall, and surely not less needful to the race fallen than to the race sinless. Let it be distinctly considered that this Sabbath was instituted with no limitations of time or race or nation—not for Eden alone; not for the race before their fall only—to become defunct when man began to sin; not for the Jews alone to be only a Jewish national observance and to become obsolete when the ceremonials of Judaism "waxed old and vanished away." It was indeed prescribed anew to the Hebrew nation and enforced with new sanctions, especially by his obligations to his covenant-keeping God for national deliverance from Egyptian bondage; but this weighs not a feather against the doctrine that the Sabbath was made *for man*. While the Sabbath obligation, thus heightened by new mercies, might be said to become more sacred and obligatory upon the Jewish nation, this fact could by no means make the day less sacred to the Gentiles of every land and of all time.

2. As sustaining scripturally this argument for the divine appointment of the Sabbath for the race of mankind, let it be noted that the seven-day division of time is unquestionably traceable to this primeval institution. It did not originate in the revolution of the earth on its axis which makes the common day, nor in its revolution in its orbit round the sun which makes the year, nor in the changes of the moon which mark off lunar months. It is an abnormal—we might say unnatural division of time—one which comes not of nature but from a source above nature—from God directly and from God alone.

Historically we find this seventh-day period in existence during the flood. Noah observed it and sent out the raven and the dove after seven-day intervals of time.——It becomes most distinctly apparent in the recorded history of the manna (Ex. 16: 22–30). By the natural law of the manna, each next day's supply was distilled each night upon the adjacent grounds, ready for the labor of gathering it in the early morning. This would normally make labor a necessity for their subsistence *every day*, leaving them no Sabbath. Therefore God arrested the normal law at the Sabbath point and provided a double supply on the morning next preceding, giving none on the morning of the Sabbath.

Moreover by another special provision, this double supply was kept two days from putrefaction—in this case only, so that it sufficed perfectly for their wants till the Sabbath was past. Some of the people, oblivious of the Sabbath, "went out on the seventh day to gather, and found none. And the Lord said unto Moses, How long refuse ye to keep my commandments and my laws? See, for that the Lord hath given you the Sabbath, therefore he giveth you on the sixth day the bread of two days; abide ye every man in his place; let no man go out of his place on the seventh day" (Ex. 16: 27–30). Most decisively therefore does this narrative assume that the Sabbath was not then a new institution but an old one. This scene and these words, be it remembered, were before (not after) the giving of the ten commandments from Sinai.

To the same purport is the form of the fourth commandment; "*Remember* the Sabbath day to keep it holy." The Lord does not say—I now introduce a new and special precept. His words, "Remember" etc. do not imply this but imply the very opposite of this. So also do the reasons assigned; viz. God's creative work finished in six days with rest on the seventh. If this were a reason for the Sabbath, it was certainly good for Adam in Eden and for all of Adam's children to the end of the world. Corresponding to this we may note that in this fourth command God does not say—I appoint each seventh day for a sign between me and thee and a memorial of your national deliverance from Egyptian bondage (as many have maintained—to make out that the Sabbath was nothing but a Jewish institution) but this is not the form in which the Sabbath stands in the immortal decalogue. These points—a "sign" between the Lord and Israel and a memorial of deliverance from Egypt, came in fitly afterwards as a supplement—an appendix to this fourth command *in its special relations* to the children of Israel. See Ex. 31: 12–17 and Ezek. 20: 12, 20, with my Notes on the passage in Ezekiel. But these special and superadded relations of the Sabbath to the Hebrews can not possibly in reason diminish the obligation of the original Sabbath ordained for man as a race in Eden.

4. To complete the argument for a perpetual Sabbath, it is only needful to add that our Lord re-endorsed it

and gave it the whole weight of his sanction for all future time; and in these several ways: (a.) By re-endorsing the entire decalogue—"I am not come to destroy the law but to fulfill" (Mat. 5: 17). The scope of the sermon on the mount—(of which these words are a part) proves that his eye was on the great moral law of ten commandments. Plainly he could not have spoken of the Mosaic ceremonial law, and therefore must have spoken of that special code of precepts of which the Sabbath was the fourth.——(b.) He endorsed the Sabbath as perpetual and universal by solemnly declaring—" The Sabbath was made *for man*" (Mk. 2: 27).——(c.) Also by affirming it to be his own prerogative to enforce the Sabbath and to set forth its spirit and expound its obligations. "Therefore," because the Sabbath was made for man, for all men of all time, "therefore, the Son of man is Lord also of the Sabbath" (Mk. 2: 28). It was in order to relieve the law of the Sabbath (as then currently expounded) from burdensome, excessive and injurious constructions which human nature could not bear and which were alien from its true spirit, that our Lord confronted the traditions of the Scribes and Pharisees and sought to place this great institution upon its true and eternal basis.—— (d.) Finally as showing historically that our Lord had never a thought of terminating the obligation of the Sabbath at his death but designed its obligation to be perpetual, we have this very incidental word—"Pray ye that your flight be not in the winter, neither on the Sabbath day" (Mat. 24: 20). When the Roman armies should bring down the judgments of the Almighty upon the doomed city of the murderers of Jesus, his followers must flee to the mountains across the Jordan; yet let it be their prayer that they might not be compelled to flee either in the severity of winter's cold, nor on the holy Sabbath. Flight for life might be morally admissible even on this sacred day; yet it would be most appropriate to pray that God would spare them this moral trial and not subject them to the necessity of labor on this holy day.——In these various ways our Lord most fully and undeniably re-endorsed the Sabbath as for all time.

CHAPTER VI.

THE EVENTS OF EDEN.

The first human pair have their first earthly want met by their Maker in a *home*—a quiet, beautiful spot (precisely *where* we know not, but near the source of the great Euphrates) in which trees of beauty for the eye and of nutritious fruitage for subsistence supplied some pleasing occupation for the mind and wholesome labor for the hand; where, happy in each other's love and blessed with the freest communion with their Maker, not a thing was lacking to fill their cup of joy. *If* it might only *last*—and for this, nothing more was needful save that their moral nature should be cultured, their faith and love and obedience strengthened up to the point of being thoroughly, fully confirmed: then their lot would have been most blessed. As a requisite means for such culture, God subjected their faith and obedience to one gentle test—to one point of moral trial. To have endured this successfully would have made them morally stronger and have drawn them yet nearer in love and trust to their Great Father; but to fall before it—Ah! this is the experience of human life, but too well known in its fruits of sin and woe!

The history of these scenes is before us in this third chapter of Genesis. Our leading inquiries may fitly take the following order:

I. Is this description *symbolic* or *historic;* i. e. symbolic of all human sinning; or historic as to this first sin, its antecedents and immediate consequents?

II. *The moral trial;*

III. *The temptation;*

IV. *The fall;*

V. *The first promise;*

VI. *The curse,* being the first installment of the great penalty upon transgression.

I. The preliminary question as to the character of this record demands a brief notice. In my view it is not to be taken as a symbolic representation of the uni-

versal fact that the race yield to temptation and fail before it, but as a historical account of the first human sin—including the person of the tempter and his methods; the working of his temptations upon Eve and then upon Adam; and the first group of immediate results.
——Under this construction of the narrative, I find here a real serpent, and a real, not a merely symbolical, Satan—the serpent supplying the external guise, the sense-medium; but Satan, the intelligent mind, the malign purpose. The narrative seems to indicate that Satan chose the serpent for his service because of his well known subtlety. It is of small account to push our conjectures on this point beyond what is written (here and elsewhere); but it is supposable that the serpent was Satan's fittest instrument as being less likely to excite surprise by his uttered words.

That this record speaks of a real serpent and of a personal devil I am constrained to believe, because,

1. This is the obvious sense of the narrative—is the construction which the mass of readers most naturally put upon it, supposing them to be unsophisticated, holding their minds in harmony with the simplicity of the Scripture narrative and so in a mood to take most readily its obvious sense.

2. This construction is implied and thereby endorsed in subsequent scriptures: *e. g.* Isaiah (65: 25) having said—"The wolf and the lamb shall feed together"— peace and love supplanting violence and cruelty—adds, "And dust shall be the serpent's meat"—with manifest reference to this primal curse on Satan's special agent. See also a similar reference in Solomon's Messianic Psalm (72: 9): "His enemies shall lick the dust." Also Micah 7: 17.——These allusions presuppose a real serpent in the scenes of Eden.

That the real personal devil was there, the responsible agent, is surely implied by our Lord (Jno. 8: 44): "Ye are of your father the devil; *he was a murderer from the beginning* and abode not in the truth because there is no truth in him." So also John (1 Jno. 3: 8): "He that committeth sin is of the devil, for the devil sinneth from the beginning," *i. e.* ever since that first great sin in tempting our common mother. "For this purpose was the Son of God manifested that he might destroy the works of the devil"—according to that first promise—"I will put enmity between thee and the woman, between thy seed and her seed: it shall bruise thy head, and thou shalt bruise his heel." Paul incidentally gives his construction of this narrative: "The God of peace shall bruise Satan under your feet shortly" (Rom. 16: 20); and our Lord also in Luke (10: 18, 19): "I beheld Satan fall as lightning from heaven; and I will give you power *to tread on serpents* and scorpions, and over all the power of the enemy." In 2 Cor. 11: 3, Paul gives us a plain, historic version of this narrative—"But I fear lest by any means, *as the* serpent beguiled Eve through his subtlety, so your minds should be corrupted from the simplicity that is in Christ."—— But Satan is perhaps most sharply identified in the descriptive points made by John (Rev. 12: 9 and 20: 2): "And the great dragon was cast out, that old serpent, called the devil and Satan, who deceiveth the whole world." ..... "And he laid hold on the dragon, that old serpent who is the devil and Satan, and bound him a thousand years." Our Lord, as also Paul and John, saw in this narrative a real Satan and also the veritable serpent, made his instrument.

3. That Satan should use such an instrument is manifestly within and not beyond his power. It has in certain points its analogy in the demoniacal possessions recorded by the Evangelists. As to power he is spoken of as the god and prince of this world, "the prince of the power of the air, the spirit that now worketh in the children of disobedience."

The Scriptures attribute to holy angels great power over material agencies; and with scarcely less fullness to Satan and his legions also. In the case of demoniacal possessions, nothing can be more obvious than the manifestations of *Satanic mind*, mind speaking through human lips indeed, yet giving utterance to Satanic thought. "We know thee who Thou art." "What have we to do with thee, Jesus, thou Son of God? Art thou come to torment us before the time"? (Mat. 8: 29 and Mk. 5: 7 and Luke 8: 28. See also Acts 19: 15.)

4. Other points in this narrative are recognized in the Scriptures as historic and not merely symbolic. Paul wrote to Timothy (1 Tim. 2: 13–15): "For Adam was first formed, then Eve, and Adam was not deceived; but the woman being deceived, was in the transgres-

sion. Notwithstanding, she shall be saved in child-bearing," etc.—all referring very definitely to this narrative as fact and not merely drapery illustrating some universal truth.——To the same purport is Paul in Rom. 5: 12, 19: "As by one man sin entered into the world and death by sin." "As by one man's disobedience many were made sinners," etc. So also 1 Cor. 15: 21, 22.

5. The sin of the first pair stands in its appropriate historic place here (not a merely symbolic place), being immediately connected with the curse upon the serpent (and under him upon the devil); upon the woman also, and the man and the ground; also with the expulsion from Eden and man's changed life, from the ease and the delights of Eden to sweating labor upon a stubborn soil, in perpetual conflict with noxious growths.—— These considerations suffice in my view to prove that this narrative must be taken as simple history, and not as symbolic drapery employed to set forth, not these specific events, but only the general truth of human depravity.

II. *The Moral Trial.*

Provision was made for this trial by one simple prohibition, forbidding to them the fruit of one tree in the midst of the garden. Of all else they might eat as they pleased. All they could need for subsistence or enjoyment was freely permitted them; but the fruit of this one tree they might not eat on pain of death. This was the test of their obedience. This was to discipline their faith and their love toward their divine Father. There the tree stood before their eyes in the midst of the garden—every sight of it suggesting their Great Father's word—not to be eaten at all on penalty of death. Will they cheerfully and even joyfully deny themselves so much for the love they bear their Father? So long it shall be well with them. Every time they put down the temptation to eat of it they will become stronger in their spirit of obedience and more happy in God. It was a means of continual culture in holiness, ever leading onward and upward into deeper communion with God and more assured and joyous submission to his will, more strength of purpose in obedience, more delight in whatever self-denial obedience might involve. Surely it is not too much to say that they might make this means of moral culture a priceless blessing to their souls. How could paradise meet the greatest of all their wants—the want of their new-born souls—without this one provision for proving and invigorating their loving obedience to their God?

Need we then raise the question—*What was God's purpose in this prohibition?* The answer is at hand—To accomplish precisely this result; to give the first human pair a test of obedience which should be naturally a means of moral culture and of growth in holiness.—— The horrible thought—that God meant and sought to make them sin—how can we say less of it than that it is born of Satan! For it assumes, as Satan did in the garden, that God sought, not their good, but their hurt; is not benevolent but malevolent! Our souls recoil from this assumption. Doth not the Scriptures say truly (Jas. 1: 13), "Neither tempteth he any man"? Never, for the purpose of drawing him into sin!——Is it replied:—God certainly knew they would eat that forbidden fruit; the answer is, Undoubtedly he did; but this proves nothing as to his purpose and aim in placing them under this moral trial. If it be yet said— He might have made the trial so much less that they would have borne it successfully: the proper answer is, Who knows that? Who is wiser or more loving in such an emergency than God?——Consider also that while God knew they would fall, he also knew that he could redeem the race through his Son, gloriously; and so could make the wrath of both wicked men and devils subserve his praise. We may account this to be his reason for subjecting the first pair to a form of trial (every way good and wise in itself and well designed)— although he foresaw they would fall before it. It was still (as he saw the case through to its remotest end) better than any other form of trial; better than no trial at all, supposing such a thing in their case possible.

Thus may we vindicate God's ways in this transaction. It was kind in him to grant for their free use every other fruit in the garden—all they could need. It was right that he should impose some test of their obedience and love. Indeed it was a natural necessity of their moral nature that this question of obeying God, always and every-where, should come to issue. As surely as they were moral beings, capable of knowing duty and of doing it, born into being with susceptibilities to happiness which sometimes must be virtuously denied at the demand of God and of the greater good, so surely they must meet this trial sooner or later, in one form or another, until they become so strong in their holy purpose, so fixed in the spirit of love and obedience to God that temptation to sin is of course spurned away and duty is done for evermore without a question. Moral trial, therefore, if not in this precise form, yet in some analogous form, is the necessary means of developing moral strength and confirmed holiness; is therefore the natural pathway to the blessedness of heaven. Thus, with no wavering of doubt, we may vindicate God's ways toward man in this first great moral trial brought on our race.

In what sense was this called, "The tree of the knowledge of good and evil"? (Gen. 2: 9, 17 and 3: 5)——It brought the knowledge of evil by fearful experience; the knowledge of good to a certain extent by the freshened sense of contrast with the experience of evil. Sin gives to moral beings *such* knowledge of good and of evil—knowledge it were better far for them they should never have!

Was the fruit of this tree a natural poison? We do not know. God has not told us. It may have been or it may not. God does not base his prohibition on this ground. There are other grounds, all-sufficient, without this. It might perhaps be urged with some plausibility that the analogy of this earthly life favors the affirmative inasmuch as for the most part, God's prohibitions of food and indeed of animal indulgence in general, are based on this principle—Abstain from poison; do thyself no harm. God is not wont to prohibit aught that is good for food or pleasurable to any sense, except because it is pernicious, poisonous.

What was this threatened penalty? *Death, in what sense?*

In the same sense in which it actually falls upon all who reject Christ and fail of his salvation. Upon such the curse of the law falls without abatement or modification. Their doom must surely be taken as the exponent and measure of the meaning of this threatened death. Of course it includes the loss of God's favor;

the incurring of his frown.——That eternal death did not begin instantly was due to arrest of judgment for a new probation under the scheme of redemption; and to nothing else.

Was natural death a part of this penalty?——Plainly natural death became the doom of the race, equally of the redeemed and of the unredeemed, under the scheme of redemption—a scheme which carried with it more or less of earthly life before the death of the body. But this proves nothing as to the breadth of the original threatening—"Thou shalt surely die." What would have been in respect to natural death if no scheme of redemption had intervened and the original threatening had been executed at once, we have no means of knowing. Mortality as at present resting on the race and terminating in natural death is one of the incidents of the new probation under mercy, and gives us no light on the other question, viz. What if no mercy had come in? In general, it is of small account for us to ask, What would have been if something else had happened otherwise than it did? *e. g.* What would have taken place if the first pair had endured all temptation? How long would the trial have continued? Would it have terminated by removing the tree, or by taking off the prohibition, or only by such complete victory over temptation that its presence could have been only a joy and a triumph?——What part would have been borne by "the tree of life"? And after their sin, what if they had put forth their hand to take and eat of this life-tree?——Speculations of this sort never make men wiser.

III. *The Temptation.*

On this point the history is remarkably full and distinct. To those who have given attention to what may be called *the law of temptation*—the way it works and gains its object—little explanation of the narrative is needed.——We may note that Satan took care not to be recognized as an enemy; that he made his first approaches with subtlest caution and skill, bringing up the case of the prohibited fruit as a question—Is it *indeed so* that God hath said, Ye shall not eat of every tree? As if he would say—What do you think about this prohibition? Is it quite pleasant to be put under such restraint?——When Eve recited the words of God's prohibition and added something more—viz. "neither shall ye touch it," it is at least supposable that Satan had already sprung in her mind the feeling that the injunction was indeed very stringent, perhaps unreasonably and unkindly so. It is plain that Satan is emboldened and now ventures to strike out squarely against God. Putting his word unqualifiedly against God's word, "ye shall *not* surely die," he became "the father of lies," "a liar from the beginning," and threw all the weight of his influence into the scale to break down Eve's confidence in God's veracity as well as in his real kindness. Then with Satanic cunning he took advantage of the name given to this forbidden tree to make Eve think that knowledge, great and enviable like that of the gods, would come from eating this fruit. Artfully he charges that God knew this, and sought by the prohibition to debar them from this boon of knowledge so desirable. The gilded bait was swallowed but too soon and too thoughtlessly! Eve had listened; she had more than half believed these lies; she still dallied with the temptation; she looked again at the tree and its fruit; she saw it beautiful and seemingly good for food; and, far beyond this, it appealed to her imagination as giving her that unknown wisdom, like the wisdom of the gods—so she took of it and *ate!*——Then she brought of it to her husband. Her words to him are not on record. We are left to imagine how her example may have wrought upon him, and sympathy also with her doom if Adam thought of that; how the feeling—I must stand or fall, live or die, with this only human friend I have on earth—may have overcome every scruple. So far as appears he yielded without a word of question, much less of reproof. He yielded—and the awful deed was done!

IV. *The Fall and its Immediate Effects.*

The first human pair are in sin; they have risen against God their Maker in rebellion. Instantly "their eyes are opened." They realize how strangely different are the sensations that come *after* sin from those that are before. The false hopes, the fascinations, the bewildering, bewitching charms of temptation's hour give place to the awful sense of folly and of wrong—a

THE CURSE AND THE PROMISE.

sense of passing suddenly into a world of solemn and dread realities pertaining to God, duty, and doom. "They knew that they were naked"; an awful sense of being unfit to be seen; a consciousness of being ugly, loathsome, as if the inner guilt of their souls stood out visibly over their whole bodies—this seems to have been their first sensation, and they set themselves to sewing fig-leaf coverings. As evening drew on they heard the voice of the Lord God walking in the garden. That voice which up to this day had been their sweetest music now fills their very souls with shame and terror.

——It is remarkable that Adam's words and his acts also make so much account of his nakedness, apparently of person. Was it that his convictions of sin and guilt were yet superficial, so that his sense of shame for his sin turned his thought first to his personal nakedness? Had he yet to learn that "God looketh on the heart"? If so the Lord's searching question must have met his case—"Who told thee that thou wast naked"? How camest thou by this sense of shame, this dread of the eye of thy divine Father? "Hast thou eaten of the tree whereof I commanded thee that thou shouldest not eat"?——Adam could not do otherwise than confess his sin, yet with an apology which almost or quite reflected upon God; "The woman whom *thou gavest* to be with me, she gave me, and I did eat." The woman too sought to screen herself somewhat under the apology of a subtle temptation. "The serpent beguiled me and I did eat."

The secondary results of the fall appear in the curse severally pronounced of God upon the serpent, upon the woman, and upon the ground for his sake.——As to the serpent, since he stands before us in this entire transaction as a double character, so the curse upon him comes in a sort of double meaning. The most obvious sense of the passage assigns a measure of this curse to the literal serpent—the animal under the guise of whom Satan beguiled his victim. But the responsibility and guilt being upon the very Satan, this curse falls chiefly on him. He is degraded, doomed to eternal shame; and in his great conflict against God and goodness, to disgrace, defeat and damning ruin. Words of telling significance were these;—"I will put enmity between thee and the woman, and between thy seed and her seed; it shall bruise thy head and thou shalt bruise his heel." The serpent guilefully assumed to be your friend. I tear off his mask and expose him in his true nature; I ordain eternal enmity between serpent and woman, and pre-eminently between the serpent's seed—the children of the devil—and the great, distinguished Personage known as "the seed of the woman." This enmity underlies the mighty conflict of the ages—Christ and Satan each leading on his host to battle and no peace or even truce arresting hostilities till the victory of the King of Kings shall be complete and ineffably glorious. Thus the first relation between serpent and woman—that of assumed but treacherous friendship—develops into everlasting enmity—God, her real friend, becoming in the person of his incarnate Son, born of woman—her champion and the mighty antagonist of Satan and all his offspring. Here and thus mercy breaks in upon this scene of sin and ruin, and God begins the wonderful process of making the wrath of Satan the occasion of his own infinite glory.——The words which put so tersely the result of this great conflict take their shape and borrow their drapery from the guise under which Satan here appears—that of the crawling serpent. He shall wound the heel of his opponent—the natural place for the serpent's bite; but his own head bruised and crushed, shall end the fight.——This first promise of God to our fallen race sweeps the eye over the whole vast field of moral conflict between Christ and Satan, and testifies of glorious victory over Satan as the sublime result. It was inexpressibly kind in the Lord to bring in these gleams of light and hope upon the trembling souls of the first sinning pair before he proceeded to speak of the specific forms of suffering that must righteously come upon them and their offspring as the testimony of God's displeasure against sin. Having said this, he proceeds to the curse upon woman—sorrow in the birth of offspring; and the curse upon man—toil and struggle for subsistence on a soil prolific in noxious growths and demanding labor as a condition of fruitfulness.

Yet let the minor points of this scene sink into the shade in the presence of the sublime glory of the great first promise. In the light of this we see that though Satan plotted the ruin of the race, yet God counterplotted the ruin of Satan and the salvation of the masses of mankind. When it might have seemed that all was lost, it proved that this extremity was God's great opportunity, for his strong arm was made bare for help and real victory. This is the birth-hour of most momentous issues. Sin came in upon Eden and upon earth; and many a bitter sorrow, many a cup of suffering and woe, must needs follow in its train; but *Redemption comes in also;* it enters upon its co-ordinate work to save the soul from sin and from eternal death and to bring in everlasting righteousness. The history of our world in its most vital aspects is foreshadowed here in this first short meeting of their Maker with this sinning pair. The spoken recorded words were few, but their significance was momentous; the sweep of their bearing, the issues of the divine policy here indicated, were destined to fill up the ages of time with stirring and strange conflict, and to send their influence down through the endless ages of man's being and of God's kingdom.

CHAPTER VII.

FROM THE FALL TO THE FLOOD.

1. *Notes on special passages.*

In Gen 4: 1 our English version stands—"I have gotten a man *from* the Lord." Some critics construe these words of Eve to mean—By the help or blessing of the Lord; but the more direct and obvious sense of the original is this: "I have gotten a man, the Lord"—as if she assumed that this, her first-born son, was really the promised divine "seed of the woman" who was to bruise the serpent's head. The current objection to this construction is that it is too far in advance of Eve's theology:—to which however the obvious reply is—Who knows how far advanced Eve's theology may have been? Her imagination may have outrun the actual revelation at that point made. All we can say is that these words are recorded as indicating her thought, and that this is the most natural sense of her words.

In the Lord's expostulation with Cain (4: 6, 7) we read: "If thou doest well, shalt thou not be accepted?" but better—Would there not be an elevation—*i. e.* of countenance, a cheerful *looking up*, instead of that fallen, sullen look spoken of in the previous verse.——"And if thou doest not well, sin lies crouching at the door"—sin being personified and thought of as some animal, perhaps the serpent, ready to allure him on to deeper, more damning crime: "And *its* (not *his*) desire is toward thee"—its Satanic purpose is to ensnare and ruin thee: "but thou shouldst rule over it"— in the sense of mastering its temptations, commanding them down and ruling them out from thine heart.

The speech or rather song of Lamech to his two wives (4: 23, 24) must be assumed to have a close connection with the occupation and skill of Tubal-Cain, "a workman in brass and iron." Consciously strong and boldly overbearing in view of this new invention and production of death-weapons, he proudly sings: "I have slain (or could slay) a man for wounding me—a young man—for any hurt inflicted upon me; and " (there being in this case some real provocation; Cain had none) "if Cain would be avenged sevenfold, truly Lamech seventy and seven." The lenity shown to Cain was bringing forth its fruits; the invention of improved death-weapons was also contributing to fill the earth with bloody violence.——These little facts indicate the state of society which culminated in so filling the earth with violence that God was compelled to wash out its blood-stains and its degenerate race with the flood.

2. *Abel's offering, and the origin of sacrifices.*

Abel kept sheep; Cain tilled the ground. "In process of time" (Heb. "at the end of days")—the stated time for worshiping God with offerings—Cain " brought of the fruit of the ground"—an unbloody offering: Abel "brought of the firstlings of his flock and of their fat." The reference to their "fat" proves that these animals, lambs of the fold, were slain in sacrifice.——The record informs us that God looked with favor upon Abel's offering, but not upon Cain's. It does not concern us to know *how* God signified his approval of Abel's sacrifice, whether by fire from heaven consuming it, or otherwise; but it does concern us to ascertain if we can *why* he approved it.

We have some rays of light on this point from the writer to the Hebrews who says: "*By faith* Abel offered unto God a more excellent sacrifice than Cain, by which he obtained witness that he was righteous, God testifying of his gifts." Now the simplest idea of faith, the one element always present in it, is *bowing to God's authority with implicit confidence in his word*. But in this case bowing to God's authority implies that God had given some word in reference to bloody sacrifices—the offering of a lamb by shedding its blood upon the altar. And if God had given any such word of command, it is certainly to be presumed that he had also given at least this general idea, that the blood of the innocent lamb took, in some sense, the place of the blood of the guilty offerer, so that the sacrifice would imply the confession of guilt, and also faith in a bloody substitute of the Lord's own providing.——Prosecuting our investigations we find this broad fact of history bearing on the case, viz. that Noah, Abraham and Isaac built altars wherever they were sojourning and offered bloody sacrifices thereon. Further, God directed Noah to preserve in the ark clean animals by sevens, but animals not clean only in pairs—two of a species—a fact which can not be reasonably accounted for save with reference to their customary use in sacrifice. We have then before us the well-established fact of the early custom of bloody animal sacrifices.

How came this custom into existence?
It did not originate *with men*—certainly not with *good men*. Apart from divine suggestion, they could not have supposed that the slaughter of an innocent animal would be pleasing to God. The presumption would be utterly against this. They could not have thought out the divine idea of atonement for sin by the death of Christ, God's own incarnate Son: the very supposition is absurd, for it supposes that men were able to sound the infinite depths of God's wisdom and of his love, and to grasp the relations and bearings of his vast moral government with a reach of thought, not human but divine. Yet further; it is not supposable that, having excogitated and discovered the grand idea of atonement, they could have devised the plan of prefiguring this atonement by the bloody sacrifice of the most innocent, harmless and lovely of the animal races.—— And further, if they could have thought out this miracle of God's wisdom and love—both the divine idea of atonement, and the expediency of illustrating it for ages by a foreshadowing system of bloody sacrifices—it would still have been the height of presumption in them to have started this system of sacrifices without God's special and sanctioning appointment.

We are therefore shut up to this alternative: Either the whole system of altars and bloody sacrifices, as practiced by Abel, Noah, Abraham and Isaac, was an unmeaning farce—a thing of no significance, a mere amusement or fancy, meaning nothing and good for nothing; or, God himself originated the system and enjoined it, and these good men were observing it in obedience to special revelation from God.——Here it will be readily seen that the first side of this alternative is perfectly precluded by the fact that God approved their sacrifices. God "had respect to the offering of Abel." He "smelled a sweet savor" in the sacrifices offered by Noah (Gen. 8: 20, 21.) The other alternative therefore, viz. that bloody sacrifices originated in a direct revelation from God—is the only supposition left us. We must adopt it.

It can not be necessary to draw out an argument to prove that in instituting this system of bloody sacrifices God gave his people some notion of its significance. The whole record shows that he was on most familiar terms with them and therefore can not be supposed to have left a point of so much importance utterly blank. It is not too much to say that unless some light were thrown by the Lord himself upon the meaning and purpose of these bloody offerings, the command to make them would require some apology; for apart from their expiatory significance, they are most revolting to even human benevolence—most foreign to all just notions of what is due treatment of innocent lambs, bullocks and doves from our hand. It should also be considered that their moral value depends on their significance. All these bloody sacrifices must have been practically valueless unless their expiatory significance was in some good degree understood. That God ordained them for the sake of their moral value, who can for a moment doubt?——The conclusion, therefore, seems inevitable that God not only enjoined these bloody sacrifices, but gave his people to understand in general their significance to the extent of fulfilling that unconscious prophecy of Abraham (Gen. 22: 8): "My son, God will provide for himself a lamb for a burnt-offering."

These views, if just, are of vast historic value as showing *how much* God taught his people at that earliest day, pertaining to his great thoughts of redemption for a lost race.

3. *The great moral lessons of the antediluvian age.*

(1.) It may be regarded as God's experiment of a very long life-probation for man. Of course this experiment is not to be thought of as made to satisfy himself as to its wisdom, but to satisfy created finite minds in this and in every other world. In a case where issues so momentous were pending on the results, it must be vital to the honor of Jehovah before all created minds that he should fix the average period of human probation in this earthly life at the best possible point. If he had begun with the same average limit which has obtained since the days of Moses (three-score years and ten), he must have anticipated the general impression that this is much too short for the decision of destinies so vast as the welfare of an immortal existence. It was therefore eminently wise that God should begin (as we see that he did) with a much longer, even a tenfold longer average life-period.——This very long life, moreover, carried with it an extraordinary physical vigor, apparently a very great exemption from sickness, frailty, suffering, save as induced by the violent and murderous passions of man toward his fellows. The discipline of suffering seems to have been at its minimum for all human history. The experiment of almost unimpaired physical well-being was afforded the freest scope for its manifestation.

What was the result? The words of Solomon express it well: "Because vengeance against an evil work is not executed speedily, therefore the heart of the sons of men is fully set in them to do evil" (Eccl. 8: 11). The mass of those generations sunk down morally to the lowest point possible, short of a general and promiscuous destruction. "All flesh had corrupted its way." "Every imagination of the thought of man's heart was only evil continually." "The earth was filled with violence." Human life had no sacredness; society, no safeguard; murderous passions, no restraint. The race were fast becoming too corrupt to live. If the Lord had not swept them by a flood, the earth would fain have opened her jaws to swallow them from the face of the sun.

(2.) This social and moral degeneracy becomes a very instructive lesson for all time upon the results of the non-punishment of murder. It was doubtless wise for God to begin as he did with Cain; but it was not wise to continue that policy after such results had been brought out before both this world and the whole intelligent universe. What men socially related must needs do for their mutual protection in order not merely to make society a blessing but to make the existence of men in society a possibility, was precisely the problem to be solved; and to its solution this first period of human life—the antediluvian age—was definitely adapted. It brought out the solution perfectly. No other experiment can ever be necessary. When the race started anew after the flood, the Lord advanced to the true doctrine and enjoined on social man the solemn duty of shielding human life by taking the murderer's blood. "Whoso sheddeth man's blood, by man shall his blood be shed" (Gen. 9: 6). This was one step of manifest *progress* in the revelation of God's will as to the responsibility and duty of men in their social and governmental relations. It was progress in the origination of society—progress built on the great lessons of human history.

(3.) Here are also lessons of faith and of heroic virtue in the godly lives of the small and it would seem constantly diminishing group of pious men living among the multitudes of the ungodly. Here was Enoch, "the seventh from Adam," who preached a righteous God and a coming judgment to a hardened generation, but seems to have met with only resistance, to the extent apparently of relentless persecution. The remark of the apostle (Heb. 11: 5)—"He was not *found* because God had translated him," may perhaps imply that his enemies sought him for purposes of bloody violence, from which the Lord took him away in his chariot of fire by translation to heaven!——Here too was Noah, also "a preacher of righteousness," who "walked with God"—and was warned by him of the impending deluge of waters. He warned his fellow men of their threatened doom, but warned them only in vain. "They ate, they drank; they bought, they sold;" they revelled and scoffed—till the day that Noah entered into the ark—no longer!——But we speak now of the example of Noah's faith in God. He saw no portents in the sky; heard no muttering thunders in the distant heavens; yet he held on year after year till the ark was ready—himself preaching and warning; fearlessly and heroically witnessing by his labors upon the ark to his positive faith in the forewarnings of God. Thus his faith rebuked the godless unbelief of his generation, and testifies to us of the wisdom and blessedness of taking God at his word and of adjusting our life to his command, though in the face of a scoffing world.

(4.) Yet another point in this cluster of great moral lessons is indicated for us by Peter (2 Pet. 2: 4–9);

"For if God spared not the old world, but saved Noah, the eighth person, a preacher of righteousness, bringing in the flood upon the world of the ungodly:—the Lord knoweth how to deliver the godly out of temptation and to preserve the unjust unto the day of judgment to be punished." That awful word, *retribution*, gathers into itself the fearful significance of these stupendous events. They are God's foregoing judgments, brought out in this world to foreshadow the sorer visitations of that coming day when God shall bring every work into judgment with every secret thing, good or evil. God surely does take note of the sins of men, how long soever he may stay his uplifted hand and delay to smite. If wicked men were wise *they would believe God's words of warning*, and take care not to live over again the life of that doomed generation and meet a final judgment more awful even than theirs!

(5.) Let us not fail to notice those wonderful and beautiful ways of God with his children, coming down in such condescending and most familiar communion, talking with them apparently almost as man talks with his dearest friend; and this not in Paradise only before the fall, but after the fall scarcely less; and onward as the narrative indicates in the case of Enoch and of Noah. What more could he have done to reveal a *personal God* to mortals? Surely the God who thus revealed himself in the fresh morning of our race is no dim abstraction, no impersonal Nature or Essence, diffused and diffusible throughout space, the ideal soul of all matter. This effort to dispose of a God with whom it is man's privilege to walk in positive personal communion, but who also takes cognizance of man's iniquity, and to transmute him into an empty, forceless ideality, finds not the least countenance in these earliest manifestations of himself to our race. Note how he dwells with men; how he walks with them and lets them walk with him! What is this but free and loving communion? What less can it imply than just what the narrative of man's creation witnesseth, viz. that God "made man *in his own image*"—capable therefore of real and most intimate communion of spirit with his Maker? This lesson is written all the way through the Bible. It stands out here with beautiful prominence in this first great chapter of God's revelation of himself to man.

CHAPTER VIII.

THE FLOOD.

1. FIRST, let us note its *moral cause*—the reason why God swept off the living from the face of the earth by a deluge of waters.——It was essential to the moral results which God sought that this reason should be given very definitely. So we find it given (Gen. 6: 5–13): "God saw that the wickedness of man was great in the earth, and that every imagination of the thought of his heart was only evil continually." "The earth was corrupt before God; and the earth was filled with violence." These points are reiterated in most distinct and emphatic terms, showing that, outside of the household of Noah, the whole living race had deeply apostatized from God and were boldly and even defiantly irreligious. Eliphaz in Job (22: 15–17) gives the tradition current in his time, thus: "Who said unto God, 'Depart from us,' and, 'What can the Almighty do for them'"— *i. e.* for Noah and his godly associates? Despite the words of Noah who bore to them God's awful forewarnings and preached the righteousness of repentance, they pressed on in their sins unmoved and reckless—"till mercy reached its bound and turned to vengeance there"! It was a whole generation hopelessly corrupt, daring the Almighty to make good his awful words of warning! The result is on record that all sinners of every age, tempted to like hardihood and defiance of God, may study it with profound consideration.

2. The *antecedent occasions* of this deep apostasy from God as given in the narrative, next demand our attention. They are

(1.) *The pious families intermarry with the godless.*——

(2.) *The Spirit of God, persistently resisted, is withdrawn.*

(1.) "The sons of God saw the daughters of men that were fair, and they took them wives of all which they chose." The "sons of God" were his professed children of the godly race of Seth, Enos and Enoch. The "daughters of men" were of the Cainites, cultured probably in music (Gen. 4: 21); attractive in person, fascinating in manners—but alas, all corrupt in heart as toward God!——The Jews have a tradition that these "sons of God" were fallen angels, once first-born sons of God, who by intermarriage with man's fair daughters, intensified this fearful corruption of the race. This tradition we must reject for the following as well as other reasons:

(a.) Nothing is said here about angels. The record gives us no word which legitimately designates angels— least of all, the fallen angels.

(b.) According to the Scriptures, angels "neither marry nor are given in marriage." The tradition is therefore not only *without* Scripture authority but *against* it.

(c.) If this extreme demoralization had been caused by the marriage connection of fallen angels with the daughters of men, those angels should certainly have come in for their share of the visible retribution. God gave Satan his share of the curse for his agency in the first great sin. The same justice would have made the fallen angels visibly prominent under this curse of the flood.——Either of these reasons singly would be sufficient ground for rejecting this tradition; much more must they suffice, combined.

(2.) The withdrawal of the divine Spirit is the second assigned antecedent of this fatal degeneracy. In our English version we read—"And the Lord said, 'My Spirit shall not always strive with man, for that he also is flesh; yet his days shall be one hundred and twenty years.'"——As to the meaning of "My Spirit," we must reject the sense—*animal life*—that which God breathed into man to make him "a living soul" (Gen. 2: 7), as being incongruous with the verb "strive": also the sense—*rational soul*—that which makes man a rational being; and must accept the sense so amply sustained by Scripture usage—the divine Spirit, sent by Christ to transform human hearts.——The word "strive" to translate the Hebrew verb* is not bad. We must reject the construction of some of the old versions, *dwell*, as not in the original, and as too tame: also the turn given it by Gesenius—to be humiliated, put down— as not borne out well by the original; and say that the

* ירון

verb is currently used of judicial transactions—searching out, convincing, convicting; and seems to have a striking analogy in that leading word given us by Christ; "When he is come, he shall *reprove* the world"—enforce conviction upon the world—as to sin and righteousness.

The next clause is more difficult and perhaps more controverted: "For that he also is flesh." Why is the word "also" here? And what is the logic indicated by "*for that*"? Can it mean that God withdraws his Spirit because man is *human*—with a body of "flesh"? Our translators separated the main Hebrew word into three—the preposition meaning *in*, the relative written elliptically, and the particle meaning *also*. The construction of Fuerst is better—"In their wandering, he is flesh," *i. e.* their degeneracy has brought flesh completely into the ascendant: warring against the spirit, the flesh is absolute victor in the fight. Henceforth all further conflict is hopeless. Hence God may righteously say—nay must in honor to himself say—My Spirit shall not plead my cause in man forever. He is utterly gone over to the flesh, and nothing remains but that he must perish. One hundred and twenty years of merciful respite* for patient warning and exhaustive trial must suffice:—then, if no penitence appear, judgment must fall, and that without remedy!—— Thus God places on record the moral causes and antecedents of this fearful visitation, that its moral lessons may go down to distant ages for their admonition to the end of time.

The hour of doom draws nigh. The Lord gave Noah definite notice to enter his ark (7:1) and allowed him seven days time (7:4) to gather in all whom the ark was provided to save. Then "the fountains of the great deep were broken up and the windows of heaven were opened." Of small avail for safety then was the gigantic frame of the giants of those days or the defiant heart of unbelieving scoffers!

It is scarcely needful to speak of the physical means

---

*Or this one hundred and twenty years may be the reduced standard duration of human life, the thought being—So long a probation, almost a thousand years, is too much; my Spirit shall not prolong his effort in vain to this extent; I reduce the average life-period to one hundred and twenty years.

which God employed to produce this flood. The agencies which appear in the volcano and in the earthquake and which God holds imprisoned at no great depth below the earth's surface, are all-sufficient for these results. We may suppose that they lifted the bed of the adjacent seas, upheaving their waters into the atmosphere to descend in torrents of rain, and sinking for the time the inhabited lands—and the work is done. Such alternate upheavals and depressions are, we may say, chronic to the crust of the earth. The ancient records of geology bear this testimony. It was not strange therefore but was merciful that God should allay human fears by his promise to drown the earth no more. His bow in the cloud, seen when the sun shone forth after the shower, became by God's special appointment the sign and pledge of this covenant.——I see no good reason to suppose that the rainbow never existed before. It must have existed by the laws of nature, unless those laws were greatly changed at the flood—a change which should not be assumed without sufficient reason. No such reasons are apparent. It is better therefore to construe the promise—The well known bow in the cloud I give and ordain to be my sign and pledge that the earth shall be deluged with water no more.——Beautiful symbol, kindly and lovingly ordained; and as we look upon it, delighted with both its beauty and its significance, let it heighten our joy that God says of himself, "I will look upon it and remember my covenant."

Was this flood universal?

1. Was it universal *geographically*, overspreading the entire globe?

2. Was it universal as to all *living men*, leaving absolutely none alive on the face of all the earth, except those in the ark?

1. That the deluge was of limited extent geographically, and not universal, may be fairly assumed on the following grounds:

(1.) The moral reasons for a deluge do not seem to require it to be universal, since obviously that corrupt generation whose sins demanded such a judgment did not overspread all the continents and lands of the globe, but appear to have been confined within a quite limited area in Western Asia.

(2.) While on the one hand we may not limit the miraculous power of the Almighty; on the other hand, it is not legitimate to assume an expenditure of miraculous power indefinitely beyond what the occasion demands.——This objection is designed to apply, not specially to the supply of water requisite to flood the whole earth at once, for there is water enough in the oceans and seas to submerge the continents, provided only that the ocean beds be temporarily uplifted and the continents relatively depressed: but it does apply with great force to the preservation of the living animals and plants of the whole world. The narrative assumes that the deluge will destroy the land animals and the fowls of the air unless they are protected in the ark. It also gives us the dimensions of the ark, and leaves us to estimate proximately how many could be saved alive in it. The narrative, therefore, does not authorize us to resort to miracle for the preservation of these animal races.——Now it is entirely certain that only an exceedingly small part of all the land animals, insects and birds of the whole world were saved in the ark. Men versed in natural science estimate the living species of vertebrate animals at 21,000; of articulates, 300,000—numbers by far too great to be provided for in Noah's ark.——Yet again: To a great extent the "fauna" (as they are called)—the animal species of the several continents—differ widely from each other. South America has its families, many of them unknown to other continents; Australia has its special group, and Africa its own. It is simply incredible that all or even the mass of these animals came to Noah and were preserved in the ark. If they had been destroyed by the flood, there should be traces of their sudden annihilation in the drift of that flood, and geological research might trace the introduction of new races by special creation to repeople those continents. No such line of proofs for a universal deluge is found. The absence of such traces of destruction and of new creation makes it far more than probable that the flood was limited in extent and not universal.

Still further it is urged against a universal deluge— and for aught that appears conclusively—that volcanic cones exist—of Etna in Sicily and of Auvergne in Southern France—which, being composed of loose scoriæ and ashes, must have been washed away by any deluge that should reach them. The cones of Etna are estimated to be 12,000 years old.

(3.) The apparently universal language of the narrative may be readily explained as other similar language must be in the Scriptures, without assuming a range of meaning beyond the writer's personal knowledge. The writer of this narrative (Gen. chaps. 6–9) speaks *as an eye-witness*, especially of the great rain; of the ark borne up upon the waters; of the surging back and forth of the billows, and of their covering "the high hills under the whole heaven," *i. e.* as far as the eye could reach. The same style of universal language appears frequently in the Scriptures, yet subject to limitations from the known nature of the case; *e. g.* Deut. 2: 25: "This day will I begin to put the fear of thee" [Israel] "upon the nations *that are under the whole heaven;*" Acts 2: 5—"There were dwelling at Jerusalem, Jews, devout men, out *of every nation under heaven.*" Mat. 3: 5: "Then went out to him Jerusalem, and *all Judea*, and *all* the region round about Jordan."——It is in point to notice also that the word "*the earth*," so frequently used in this narrative, very often has the sense—*the land*. It should manifestly have a meaning as broad when used of the extent of the judgment as when used of the extent of the sin, and not necessarily any more broad. Of the sin it is said repeatedly—"The *earth* was corrupt before God;" "the *earth* was filled with violence." Obviously this same "*earth*," to the same geographical extent and not apparently any thing more, was destroyed by the flood. It may be noticed also that the word "ground" [Heb. adamah] is used (Gen. 7: 23) as a synonym for "earth"—"every living substance which was upon the face of the *ground*"—but this carries with it no sense of universality as to this globe.

There is every reason to suppose that at this time both the righteous descendants of Seth and the wicked descendants of Cain were living in the great basin of the Euphrates and the Tigris—with great probability not reaching out beyond the area bounded by the Indian Ocean, the Persian Gulf, the Caspian, Black, Mediterranean and Red Seas. This, therefore, we may assume to have been the area submerged by this deluge, and we have no occasion to look for its traces beyond these limits.

2. Whether the deluge destroyed all living men from the face of the whole geographical earth except those in the ark, it is perhaps impossible to decide with absolute certainty. If any were not reached, they must have been such as had wandered early, far from their native home, suppose into China or Africa, where neither the corruption which became the moral cause of the deluge nor the deluge itself reached them. The question is one of probabilities only, for we have no certain knowledge on the subject and can not have. The probabilities are in my view quite against the supposition.

Traditions of a Great Deluge.

All the great nations of history have traditions more or less definite of a vast deluge in the days of their fathers. As should be expected, these traditions compared with the Bible record are variously modified, corrupt we might say, mixed with fable, magnified as great stories are wont to be in passing from lip to lip through many generations. In general those are most pure which are found nearest the locality of Eden and which were earliest committed to writing. Some authors classify them into the *West Asiatic*, including the Babylonian, that of the Sibylline books, the Phrygian, the Armenian, and the Syrian, some of which are remarkably close to the truth. The *East Asiatic*, including the Persian, the Chinese, and the Indian; the *Grecian*, found in Plato, Pindar, Apollodorus, Plutarch, Lucian and Ovid; and those of *peoples and tribes outside of the old world*—the Celts of Northern Europe, the Mexicans, the Peruvians, the Indians of America and the tribes upon the Pacific Islands. Lange remarks that the ethical idea of the flood as a judgment upon men for their sins is every-where apparent. The Chaldean traditions, brought down in the writings of Berosus (wrote B. C. 260), are singularly minute and quite in harmony with the scriptural account in its main outlines, some of which are as follows:

Giving the name of Xisuthrus to the last of the primitive kings, it sets forth that he was warned of the flood in a dream; was commanded to write down all the sciences and inventions of mankind and preserve them; to build a ship and save therein himself and his near friends, and take in also animals with suitable food. After the flood had somewhat subsided, he let fly a bird which came back; a second which returned with slime on its foot; a third which never returned. Then seeing land visible, he opened his vessel and came forth with his wife and children; built an altar and offered sacrifice to the gods. They found the country to be Armenia. Portions of the ark were long in existence, sought for as amulets and charms.

The Chinese story may be taken as a sample of those more remote from the locality of Noah. As given by the Jesuit, M. Martinius, the Chinese date this great flood B. C. 4000; say that Fah-he, the reputed author of Chinese civilization, escaped the flood, and together with his wife, three sons and three daughters, repeopled the renovated world.

Dr. Gutzlaff communicated a paper to the Royal Asiatic Society (as in their Journal xvi: 79) in which he stated that he saw in one of the Buddhist temples in beautiful stucco the scene where Kwanyin, the Goddess of Mercy, looks down from heaven upon the lonely Noah in his ark amidst the raging waves of the deluge, with the dolphins swimming around as his last means of safety and the dove with an olive-branch in his beak flying toward the vessel. Nothing could exceed the beauty of the execution.*

Those which are found among the ancient people of the Western Continent—the Cherokees, Mexicans and Peruvians—have special interest as proving that, remote as these tribes were from the locality of Noah, they must have had a common origin and must have received this common tradition of the flood from the valley of the Euphrates.

* See Smith's Bible Dictionary, "Noah," for numerous traditions of the flood.

CHAPTER IX.

FROM THE FLOOD TO THE CALL OF ABRAHAM.

1. The law against murder and its death-penalty.

When the waters of the great deluge had subsided and Noah and his family found themselves once more upon the face of the solid earth—an unpeopled solitude—that which we read in Gen. 9, was beautifully in place:—"*And God blessed Noah and his sons.*" So long imprisoned in the ark; so long in the presence of this fearful visitation of a righteous God upon a hopelessly corrupt generation, how naturally must their view of human life take on a somber hue, and how refreshing to be assured that the Great God was still their loving Father! "God blessed them and said, 'Be fruitful and multiply and replenish the earth,'"—for God would have it filled again with living men. Moreover, though few and feeble, they need not fear the violence of the animal creation, for "the fear of you and the dread of you shall be upon every beast of the earth; ... into your hand are they delivered." Then by special provision, apparently never made before, God sanctioned the use of animal flesh for human food. Yet lest this sanction should make them dangerously familiar with the shedding of blood, and tend to lesson the sacredness of human life, God solemnly forbade the use of blood for food, and then proceeded to ordain that human blood shed by ferocious animals should be avenged with their life. Then follows special legislation against murder by guilty human hands: "Whoso sheddeth man's blood, by man shall his blood be shed, for in the image of God made he man."——That this is precept and not merely prophecy is so apparent that argument in proof might seem almost an insult to the common understanding of mankind. Yet the passage has been wrested in this way from its obvious significance. It should be construed in harmony with the scope of the context. Note therefore, that its close connection with the use of animals for the food of man and with the "requiring" of human blood shed by the violence of beasts compel us to find here precept and not prediction. Still more does the historic place of this precept, standing upon the ruins of the old world and in the presence of the yet unwasted bones of thousands whose wickedness had culminated in such recklessness of human life that "the earth was filled with violence." In the presence of such gigantic iniquity, grown up under the experiment of pardoning and not punishing the crime of murder and giving unrestrained license to bloody passion, it was pertinent to lay a new and more effectual foundation for maintaining the peace of society and the sacredness of human life. The solemn lessons of the past required, not a prediction of retributive vengeance under the social law of self-preservation, but a divine precept demanding it and enforcing it with its logical reason—that "God made man in his own image." You may take the life of the lower animals for no higher cause than human sustenance—food for man's wants;—but let no man put forth his hand against the blood of man, for he bears the very "image of God."——To make this new law the more solemnly impressive, man must himself be the executioner of this divine behest—"*By man shall his blood be shed.*" Society itself must commit to some of its members this solemn function and they must take the murderer's life. Nothing less can shield the life of man from bloody violence; nothing less will duly honor God's image in man.

2. *The prophecy of Noah.*

In Gen. 9: 25-27 we have the first of those patriarchal utterances of prophetic sort, in various strain—blessing and *not* blessing—of which several examples occur subsequently, as in the case of Jacob (Gen. 49: 1-27); Moses (Deut. 33: 1-29). The form is thoroughly that of Hebrew poetry—the brief parallelism of sentiment and language being the prominent feature.——The circumstances which called out these prophetic words are given briefly in the narrative. Noah having come forth from the ark soon commenced the culture of the vine and experimented (unfortunately) in the free use of its wine. While he lay overcome and personally exposed in his tent, his younger son Ham, lost to all sense of filial duty, reported the sad spectacle. Shem and Japheth, with filial pity and with the most delicate modesty, covered his shame. When Noah awoke to consciousness and came to know what his younger son had done unto him, he said, "Cursed be Canaan; a servant of servants shall he be to his brethren. Blessed be Jehovah, God of Shem, and let Canaan be servant to them. Let God enlarge Japheth, and let him dwell in the tents of Shem; and let Canaan be servant to them."——It had been previously said (v. 18), that "Ham was the father of Canaan." What part, if any, Canaan bore in this transaction, that the curse apparently due to Ham should fall so specially on him, the narrative does not say. The offense of Ham lay in the line of his relation as a son. Perhaps it was for this reason that his punishment lay in the humiliation of *his* son. Be this as it may, the words were prophetic of the future relations of the posterity of Canaan to the posterity of both Shem and Japheth. The devoted nations of Canaan were terribly exterminated by the Hebrew people, sons of Shem; the remnant (*e. g.* the Gibeonites) were made hewers of wood and drawers of water; and in the age of Solomon, were subjected to the most severe labors. See Josh. 9: 20-27, and 2 Chron. 2: 17, 18 and 1 Chron. 22: 2.

When Noah's prophetic eye fell on Shem, the blessings that rose to his view were too rich and grand for description. He could only give utterance to his grateful emotions and thanksgivings in the words—"Blessed be Jehovah, God of Shem"! Blessed be Jehovah, the God of the covenant with his professed people, the God of all blessings, of ever-enduring love and faithfulness! What will he not do for his chosen people, brought into relations to himself so near and so dear!——In this line the sweep of his prophetic eye took in the Hebrew race—Abraham and the patriarchs; Moses and the pious kings and holy prophets; and above all, the Great Messiah—to be born of David's line and to be the incarnation of God's mercy to a lost world. No wonder his soul was moved to devoutest adoration—Blessed be Jehovah who reveals himself as the God of Shem!

Of Japheth he predicts enlargement in the sense of a numerous offspring—"God shall enlarge," *i. e. multiply* "Japheth," with a play on the significance of his name which signifies *the enlarged one*. God will verify his name and enlarge the enlarged son; in Hebrew phrase, will *Japhetize* Japheth.——In the last clause of this verse, the original leaves us in doubt whether the subject of the verb is God or Japheth. Grammatically it might be either—God shall dwell, or Japheth shall dwell, in the tents of Shem. In favor of making Japheth the subject are these considerations:—(a.) The verse preceding gives the prophetic destiny of Shem; this, of Japheth.——(b.) The expression is not altogether apposite when applied to God, for although God dwelt in the Hebrew temple and dwells by his Spirit in the bodies of his people, yet he is not elsewhere said to dwell *in the tents* of his people. The phrase leads the mind to such dwelling as may be said of men but is not said of God.——Applied to Japheth it had a most apposite and beautiful fulfillment when the Gentile races of Japheth came in as proselytes to the Hebrew communion, but far more when in the Christian age, the Jews were broken off from the old stock that the Gentiles might be grafted in, and they were; and may be almost said to have taken possession of the deserted tents of Shem as their own through all the Christian centuries to this hour. All Protestant Christendom is this day of Japheth's line, fully at home in the tents of Shem.

A very extraordinary case of the wresting of Scripture to make it justify crime—so great a crime as the enslaving of men—is the attempt to force from this prophecy concerning Canaan a vindication of the enslaving of Africans by Americans. The wresting appears in these two broad facts:—(a.) That the Africans were not Canaanites, and therefore the prophecy said nothing about the negro race. Admitting for argument's sake that it justified the enslaving of Canaanites, it did not in the least justify the enslaving of African negroes.——(b.) If the passage had named the African negro instead of the Canaanite, even then a prediction *of what shall be* might fall very far short of being a command as to what man *ought to do*. Prophetic predictions of war form not the least justification of war—fall utterly short of a divine command enjoining man's duty. Predictions of the Savior's death could never justify his murderers.

3. *The genealogy of the great historic nations.*

In Gen. 10 the Bible for once departs from its usual

method and gives a chapter of *universal history*—the only one. Elsewhere it traces the history of the one nation which had "the oracles of God," and in later ages, of the Christian church, touching the nations of the outside world only as they come into relations to the seed of Abraham or to the kingdom of Christ. But here we see the sons of Noah branching out to people the countries of the great Eastern Continent and to found the old historic nations of the earth.——Japheth whom Prophecy was to "*enlarge*" (Gen. 9: 27) furnished the tribes from which grew the great nations of Northern and Eastern Asia and for the whole of Europe. At first they occupied the maritime regions bordering on the Caspian, Black and Mediterranean Seas, spoken of here as "the isles of the Gentiles"—conforming to the Hebrew usage which called all maritime countries "isles."——Next we have the sons of Ham, among whom were Nimrod, the builder of Babel; Mizraim with his seven sons who himself gave name to Egypt; Canaan whose posterity long held Palestine, and several names which appear either in the cities or the tribes of the valley of the Euphrates and of Arabia.——Shem seems to have shared with Ham the possession of the great fertile basin of the Euphrates and the Tigris—the cradle of the race—together with portions of Arabia and in general of South-western Asia.

It is a matter of some interest to know that this remarkable record of the birth of the great nations of antiquity is perfectly sustained by the universal history of all subsequent ages. Whether Chaldean or Phenician, Egyptian or Arabian, Greek or Roman, Mongol or Tartar, Indo-Germanic, Celtic, Belgic or Briton—all find the germ of their nationality in this wonderful chapter, and all concur to swell and substantiate the proof that the human race sprang from Noah and that we have no occasion to look for pre-Adamic men or for tribes that escaped the flood and have no pedigree among the sons of Noah. While it was never the purpose of divine revelation to give to any great extent the universal history of the race, it is proper to note that what it does give bears the divine stamp of truth. All historic science does it homage. All the light that comes up from the comparative study of the languages of the race helps us still to follow the track of the emigrating tribes as they diverged from the ancient home of Noah's family. The Science of Ethnography begins with this chapter of inspiration, Gen. 10.

4. *Babel and the confusion of tongues.*

Gen. 11: 1–9 records a very remarkable event, of far reaching consequences toward the geographical diffusion of the race. Up to this point there was but one language—as the record has it—"*one lip and one set of words*," "lip" being (perhaps) used for the mode of speaking, including pronunciation and possibly inflection; while words are the *matter* of language, the roots or ground-forms. The fact that the latter have been far less variable than the former, appearing to some extent in all subsequent ages throughout all the diversities of human tongues, favors this distinction.

Migrating from the Armenian hill country where the ark rested, Noah's posterity reached the fertile plain of Shinar, halted there, and set themselves to the building of a magnificent and lofty tower. There being no stone at hand, they prepared brick, not sun-dried after the common Oriental method, but thoroughly burned for greater durability. As both consequence and proof of this durability, the supposed ruins of this great tower, known as "Birs Nimrood" [tower of Nimrod] are still extant within the area of ancient Babylon, silently witnessing alike to the labors of those fathers of the nations before their dispersion, and to the truthfulness of this sacred record.

This tower was not built for safety in case of another flood (as some have supposed) for, with such an object, a high mountain and not a plain would have been chosen for the site; it could at best have saved but few; and more than all, the record gives a very different view of the motive. This motive was *consolidation*—the aggregation of the masses into one vast nationality or kingdom—a thought due to the ambition of some controlling minds aspiring to power, distinction, fame. Foreseeing the tendency to dispersion they sought to forestall it, to find their own glory in having a multitude under their sway and in building monuments that could not perish. For wise reasons God blasted this scheme. Precisely what divine influence was interposed to confound the language of these men, I doubt if it is possible for us to know certainly. It is supposable that the many became restive under the domination of the few and the severe labor of this enterprise, so that diverse counsels and dissolving social bonds had some influence in blocking the progress of the work. Misunderstandings sprung up and found expression in diversities of tongue. What could be more natural when harmony gave place to discord? So this huge tower-building was arrested and men scattered abroad as they would.——The new tongues which took their rise here had ample opportunity to diverge more and more widely in subsequent ages. The immense variety in language which the history of the world discloses has been a growth—the product of subtle causes, of segregation and non-intercourse in part, and in part also no doubt of diverse mental traits and various influences of culture.

What the original language was, common to the race up to this point, has been much debated by learned men without arriving at uniform and satisfactory results. Whether it was, as some suppose, the veritable Hebrew tongue; or as others think, the Aramaic, *i. e.* the Chaldee; or whether it is utterly lost—these are the alternatives; but for the choice between them we can have no very positive data. Those descendants of Noah who best preserved the religious faith of the fathers would stand most aloof from the scenes of Babel, and be naturally least affected by its many-tongued controversies and its resulting confusion of speech. That they escaped these influences altogether is perhaps too much to assume.——That the Aramaic (Chaldee) tongue, closely allied to the Hebrew, held its place for ages in the valley of the Euphrates, strongly favors its claim to be, if not the very tongue of Noah, at least of the same family.——These points suggest probabilities but fall short of certainty.

CHAPTER X.

ABRAHAM.

ABRAHAM is one of the great men in the world's religious history. Why he is so can not be well understood and appreciated without at least a brief view of the state of the world religiously considered at the date of his call, and the demand thence resulting for the new religious instrumentalities of which Abraham was in a sort "the head-center."

In the age before the flood religion had never really flourished. We read of a time when "men began to call on the name of the Lord," and something approximating toward system and concentration appears to have been introduced. But the record is silent as to any marked result except so far as it may appear in the piety of individual men, *e. g.* Enoch and Noah. Apparently the religious element failed even to hold its own against the on-rushing tides of worldliness. Even the sons of godly fathers formed unhallowed marriage connections, and consequently were borne rapidly down the broad current of degeneracy and moral corruption till only one family remained to represent the piety of all that generation. There was a fatal lack of moral forces.——The flood was a vigorous moral lesson in itself; and besides this, the race started afresh from the seed of this one pious family. Ten generations bring us to Abraham in Ur of the Chaldees, near the old cradle of the race. The history of religion during this period from Noah to Abraham is exceedingly meager. Gathering up the few fragmentary notices which emerge from the general darkness in the age of Abraham, we find that his father's family in ancient Ur "served other gods" (Josh. 24: 2); that Abraham, journeying toward the south country of Palestine, sojourned awhile in Gerar and was there drawn into grave temptation by the apparent godlessness of the people, since he apologizes on this wise for representing Sarah to be his sister and not his wife: "Because I

thought, Surely the fear of God is not in this place; and they will slay me for my wife's sake" (Gen. 20: 10, 11). The same temptation befell him previously in Egypt (Gen. 12: 10–20)—probably indicating the same inward thought based on the same apparent public morality. Then we have the horrible wickedness of Sodom and Gomorrah where not ten righteous men could be found. And sad to say, we see a very low tone of religious and moral life in the family even of Lot, who as the nephew and special associate of Abraham should represent the better elements of society.——
Akin to these special facts is the general one that the personal history of Abraham through a full century of somewhat extensive travels and various experience brings him into contact with God-fearing men in only the single case of Melchizedek. Apart from this one brief but wonderful interview (Gen. 14: 18–20) the recorded history of Abraham gives the impression of a godly man working his way for the most part *alone*, amid godless people on every hand—alone save as the Lord testifies of him—"I know him that he will command his children and his household after him and they shall keep the way of the Lord to do justice and judgment" (Gen. 18: 19).——The case of Melchizedek, "a priest of the Most High God" and also "king of Salem"—a man so venerable in piety, in personal presence apparently, in power and in years, that even Abraham received his blessing and "gave him tithes of all"—this is the one sole bright spot on the otherwise dark religious life of the world as known through the history of Abraham. We marvel that Abraham, so far as appears, never met Melchizedek before and never saw him again. It seems strange that two such men, so kindred in character and spirit, each almost alone breasting the strong currents of prevailing wickedness, should not have formed at least an infant Christian Association to stand by each other and bring their joint light to a common focus in the midst of the world's deep and far spreading moral darkness. But God had a certain great plan to bring out with Abraham and his own way of doing it. It is plain there was need of this new plan. The cause of piety and truth was in peril and called for some "new departure"—some yet untried method and power. The world

was waiting for some Abraham—*i. e.* for just the system of which the great and godly Abraham was the prominent figure and the historic representative.

The patent points in this new system, put in briefest words, were—*Abraham the head* of a great family; the *founder* of a great nation; the *representative* of the family covenant and its first and illustrious exemplar; the *progenitor* of the Great, long-promised Messiah; and coupled with his lineal posterity, the *repositories* of God's truth and promises—*his offspring*, the people with whom God dwelt and was publicly worshiped for ages in the presence of the idolatrous nations of the earth; over whom God became their visible earthly Sovereign, their recognized King and God.——Thus the Lord laid the foundation for progressive manifestations of himself and for a growing development of religious truth and of its legitimate forces from age to age till the Messiah should appear.

Plainly we may recognize among the divine purposes in this new system,

1. In general—to conserve, concentrate, augment and perpetuate the religious and moral forces of revealed truth.

2. In particular:

(1.) To utilize all the best elements of the family relation, turning to fullest account parental care and affection and the facilities furnished by nature to parents for the training and culture of their offspring. The germinal idea of this great family covenant lies in the promise, so often reiterated—"I will be a God to thee and to thy seed after thee" (Gen. 17: 7, 10, 19). A marvellous wealth of significance lies in these brief words; for what can be more rich and all-embracing than this—"I will be a God to thee"—thy God; all that a God can become to man made in his image; his loving Friend, his "Shield and exceeding great reward"; his hope and joy and trust; and to crown all, his glorious salvation! Surely this cup of blessings is rich and full enough to meet the largest wants of any individual human heart. But when man becomes a father—when woman becomes a mother—a new love is born in the soul and new wants are thence begotten, for the parental heart instinctively cries out as the heart of Abraham did—"O that Ishmael might live before thee"! Even so—responds the great parental heart of God—I know the heart of a parent; therefore I said "I will be a God to thee *and to thy seed after thee*;" not to thee alone but to thee, and also, not less, to thy beloved offspring besides.

The *one comprehensive condition* for the fulfillment of this great promise is briefly indicated in the case of Abraham, of whom God said—"I know him that he will command his children and his household after him, and they shall keep the way of the Lord to do justice and judgment; that the Lord may bring upon Abraham that which he hath spoken of him" (Gen. 18: 19). The Lord knew that Abraham would fulfill the conditions so conscientiously and well that he could fulfill his promise. The conditions are thus incidentally brought out—viz. parental fidelity and authority; the early culture and training of his household; consecration, the prayer and the faith which are legitimately begotten of this covenant and naturally correlated to it;— these are obviously the fitting conditions upon which the fulfillment of this covenant on God's part must depend.——But, O, the wealth of blessings garnered up within its bosom for those who walk in the steps of Abraham with like precious faith and like godly nurture! How wonderfully does piety become self-perpetuating in the family line from generation to generation of those who take this covenant to their inmost heart and find God in it ever faithful and ever true and evermore "mighty to save" as he hath said!

Here, strange to say, some good men would thrust in a peremptory limitation, asserting that this family covenant is Abrahamic and Jewish only; good for them, but not good for the Christian age; good in the national but not in the family sense and application thereof.—— But what is the logic of such a limitation? Was the love of parent for offspring lost out of the human heart at the coming of Christ? Or did the Lord forget at that point how deeply he had implanted this love in human bosoms? Or did he think that piety, under the improved auspices of the gospel age, could thrive without the help of this family covenant? Or did he reason thus—

that the gospel age having the advantage of the Jewish in so many points, could afford to forego this family promise, and yet not on the whole fall below the Abrahamic dispensation?——Or in another point of view, looking at the evidence rather historically than logically, it is claimed, as I understand the argument, that Christ did not renew the promise—" A God to thee and to thy seed after thee"; and therefore it did not pass over into the gospel age.——To which I reply; The real question is—not, Did Christ *renew?* but, Did he *annul?* Did he say—I have come to make void the law, not to fulfill? Did he say—That family covenant which the patriarchs loved so dearly, in the faith of which they trained their sons and daughters into the love and service of their fathers' God, has well done its work and can stand no longer? Did he labor to reconcile the parental heart of his Jewish disciples—loving their dear little ones so tenderly—to this sudden withdrawal of divine promise—to this sore bereavement of hope and slaughter of faith? Was this what he meant when he said; "Suffer the little children to come unto me and forbid them not; for of such is the kingdom of heaven"? Or was this the meaning of Peter when in the first Pentecostal sermon he proclaimed—"The promise (of the Holy Ghost) is to you *and to your children*" (Ac. 2: 39)? Or could this have been the purpose of Paul when he testified; "If ye be Christ's, then are ye Abraham's seed and heirs according to the promise" (Gal. 3: 29)?——The proof that the gospel age ruled out the great family covenant is by no means apparent.——It should be considered that the covenant is one thing; circumcision another. The covenant does not of necessity die because circumcision is discontinued. The covenant existed before circumcision and could be operative without it; indeed could live without any visible sign or seal, if so the Lord pleased.——Nor does the perpetuity of this covenant turn on the proof that baptism takes in all respects the place of circumcision. Whether it does fill the same place or does not, the covenant standeth sure. There is value in an external rite or seal—else God had never enjoined it. But it falls exceedingly far short of being the thing of .chief value.

Into the argument respecting the change from the old seal to a new one, it is not in place here to enter.

This class of moral sentiments and social affections looks *forward* in the line of human generations from parent to offspring. Another class of no small value looks *back* reverently, not to say proudly, to *honored ancestors*. Here also Abraham's name became a positive power upon his posterity—not indeed of the very highest efficiency—not altogether proof against being corrupted to the pampering of national pride and even of personal self-righteousness, for bad men might learn to say, "We have Abraham for our father." Yet still it can not be questioned that for long ages the name and history of Abraham bore the precious savor of his faith and of his staunch fidelity as the servant of the living God. It was the prestige of a name both great and good, and served to perpetuate his piety among millions of his offspring. In this direction all those qualities in Abraham which made him truly great as well as eminently good become elements in this new scheme for augmenting the spiritual and moral forces of God's kingdom among men.——It can not be amiss, therefore, to linger here a moment and study this wonderful man. Verily the Lord found the right man for his purposes in Abram, then living in "Ur of the Chaldees." He called him to leave kindred (save the few who joined him in this migration); to leave also all there was to him in country—the land of his fathers' sepulchers; and travel several hundred miles to a strange unknown land. Abram heard and recognized God's voice; he bowed to his authority and went. This first recorded illustration of his faith in God and obedience made its impression upon future ages—as we may see in the words of Joshua (24: 2, 3); of Nehemiah (9: 7, 8); of Stephen (Acts 7: 2–5); and of the writer to the Hebrews (11: 8–10)—which last may be taken as a specimen of all. "By faith Abraham, when he was called to go out into a place which he should after receive for an inheritance, obeyed; and he went out, not knowing whither he went."

Not a little might be said of many of the lesser yet really noble qualities of Abraham's character—how magnanimous he appears in his bearing toward Lot (Gen. 13: 5–9); how dignified before the sons of Heth (Gen. 23: 3–16); how hospitable in entertaining three strangers who came up as he sat in his tent door in the heat of the day (Gen. 18: 1–16) when he "entertained angels unawares" (Heb. 13: 2); how humble, reverent yet earnest in his intercession for Sodom (Gen. 18: 23–33); how fearless, daring and wonderfully efficient in the rescue of Lot from the plundering hordes of the East (Gen. 14: 13–24); how unselfish in refusing to participate in the recovered booty:—but all these qualities fade like stars before the sun when seen in the presence of his wonderful faith and unflinching obedience to the commands of the Lord his God.

The most signal manifestations of his faith and obedience cluster about three several points in his history; viz. his call to go forth from his ancestral home and country; his waiting twenty-five years for the birth of his one son of promise; and the command to offer this only son in sacrifice.

That first call revealed the man. It was but to hear God's voice; and forthwith he "conferred not with flesh and blood." He seems not to have paused a moment to question the Lord about the conditions, or to consider the hardships; and he never "looked back."

Next that promise of a son, standing so long unfulfilled; year by year the human probabilities fading, dying out, till at length they are utterly dead, and nothing remained save the naked promise! This was indeed training Abraham's faith *to wait*. Inasmuch as God's chosen plan of introducing the Messiah involved long ages of waiting and trusting and living on simple promise, this was by no means a profitless or uncalled for illustration of the nature, the value, and the power of *faith* as in man toward God.

High above either of these cases, in point of the fierceness of the trial and the wonderful spirit of calm and steadfast faith and endurance, stands the case of God's command and his consent to sacrifice his son Isaac (Gen. 22). The record puts this case in the foreground as to *trial*: "God did tempt Abraham"—not in the sinful sense—tempting to make him sin; but in a sense appropriate to God—subject him to a terribly searching trial. First, God called him by name, "Abraham"! Then said—" Take now thy son, thine only son "—that son of promise in whom all thy hopes and all thy heart's affections have been so long concentrated—that son "whom thou lovest"—take him and go, far away three days' journey to a mountain which I will point out, and there "*offer him up for a burnt-offering*"!

Was Abraham shocked? Did he stagger under this stunning blow? Did he pause to debate the matter with God? Did he beg that the awful agony might be at least delayed till he could collect himself and prepare for a trial so unexpected, so sudden, so terrible to bear? The record gives no hint of any thing of the sort. Abraham had heard God's voice many times before and could not have had the first doubt as to its identity. If the least doubt had crossed his mind he surely would have said—"Lord, this seems so unlike Thee: Is it not Satan, thine enemy? I can not move one step until I know of a certainty that this is thine own voice."——But there was no relief in this direction. Yet we almost instinctively ask—Did not Abraham expostulate? Did he not say—O my Lord, this Isaac is the son of thine own promise, my only hope for that great and long promised posterity; and what wilt thou do for *thy truth?* Besides, the deed is so shocking, so revolting to a father's heart! Moreover, hast thou not said—"Whoso sheddeth man's blood, by man shall his blood be shed"? And what an example this will be before all the tribes of the earth! How it will encourage them on to murder their children in sacrifice to their gods!

We can readily make up what may seem to us very strong arguments against obedience to such a command; but it does not appear that Abraham whispered in his heart the first one of them. The only hint we have of his deep thoughts in the case comes through the writer to the Hebrew Christians—"Accounting that God was able to raise him up even from the dead." Plainly the Lord meant to show that his command when made known unquestionably is to be obeyed without debate—with no misgivings, no faltering, no fear. So Abraham moved firmly on, saying not a word to Sarah, keeping his counsel even from his two chosen servants and from his son; holding the strange secret in his solitary—shall we say, *sad* bosom?——No; for there is not the first note of sadness throughout this wonderful transaction. Look at those three days of ongoing journey. Ah, was not this a long time to think over the strange deed! And those intervening nights —

was there any sleep to his eyes while this terrible suspense lay still between the command and its execution?——So far as appears Abraham moved on with unshaken fortitude and undisturbed calmness. Certain it is that he never lost his self-possession, for he continued to plan carefully and even sharply against disturbing influences. He could not trust his servants to stand by; so he halted them at a distance back from the scene. He kept the awful secret from his son Isaac until he had him bound and laid on the altar and the uplifted blade was ready to fall!

This was the obedience of faith! The wonderful illustration stands out before all the ages with God's seal of approbation broadly stamped upon it.——When the trial had fully reached its culminating point and no room remained for doubt that Abraham would obey God at every cost, fearless of consequences, or rather committing all consequences to his God, then God's angel interposed! A ram was provided for the sacrifice and the son of promise went back to a more happy home with a more happy father, doubly blessed in the renewed approbation of his covenant-keeping God. No wonder that God proceeded then to make that covenant stronger and broader and richer than ever before! No wonder Abraham stamped into the very name of this ever memorable locality one of the grand moral lessons of the scene—"Jehovah Jireh"—*In the mount of the Lord, himself will provide!* When you come to the mount of last and utmost emergency, the Lord will have salvation ready! His angel will appear; the ram of sacrifice will be there; and Isaac may go in peace!

According to the common law of Christian experience, God's methods with Abraham were *progressive;* his manifestations of himself moved on by successive stages; much this year but more the next; so much indeed at the first that it must have seemed to the good man very great, but more and greater were yet to come. The successive epochs at which God appeared to Abraham to talk with him of the great covenant are very distinctly marked in the history—of such sort as many a Christian might record in his own personal life-history.

GOD'S REVELATIONS PROGRESSIVE.

1. In the outset of Abraham's history is that eventful *call* which brought him out from "Ur of the Chaldees," the narrative of which stands Gen. 12: 1–3. In the promise made to him then the leading points were—"I will make thy name great"; "I will make of thee a great nation"; "thou shalt be a blessing and in thee shall all the families of the earth be blessed"; I will stand by thee to bless all who bless thee and to curse whosoever may curse thee.——This must have raised in Abram's mind large expectations and assured him that Jehovah was indeed his own God.

2. Immediately after Abram's arrival in Canaan (Gen. 12: 7) the Lord appeared to him specially to identify that as *the* land which he had promised (Gen. 12: 1) to show him and to give to his posterity. There, as in each new home, Abram built an altar and in devout worship called on the name of the Lord who had thus appeared to him.

3. Next, after his magnanimous bearing toward Lot (13: 7–9, 14–18) in which he seemed ready to waive all claim to any territory Lot might choose to occupy. The Lord bade him lift up his eyes toward every point of the compass, all round about and reiterated his grant of the whole—"All the land which thou seest to thee will I give it and to thy seed forever." Also, that his seed should be as the dust of the earth. His generous magnanimity toward Lot in nowise damaged his standing with God or his rights in the goodly land of promise.

4. A yet richer scene of divine manifestation followed Abram's rescue of Lot from the plundering horde of the great Eastern kings (Gen. 15). The first words were significant and precious: "Fear not, Abram; I am thy shield and thine exceeding great reward." Abram knew enough of human nature and of the resentful, lawless spirit of those warlike kings to see that he was exposed to their vengeance and that they might return any day with more military force than his household could muster. It was therefore at once timely and kind in the Lord to meet him at this point with this comforting assurance: "Fear not; I am thy shield"; I stand between thee and those vengeful foes: my strong arm shall be a wall of fire round about thee. Moreover Abram had nobly refused to appropriate to his per-

sonal use even a thread or a shoe-latchet of the booty brought back from his routed enemies—whereupon the Lord said, "I will be thine exceeding great reward."——Truly when a man's ways please the Lord, he not only keeps his enemies at peace with him but makes all things go well.——On this re-appearance the Lord promised him a son more distinctly than ever before, and posterity as the stars in number. Here it is said definitely—"Abraham believed God and God counted it to him for righteousness." His faith pleased God, and because of it, God accepted him and he stood as one who is "*all right* before God."——Remarkably the Lord at this time identified himself to Abraham as the same God who had appeared to him in his fatherland and called him forth into Canaan and said, This is the very land I then promised to give thee; to which Abraham replied (v. 8), "Whereby shall I know that I shall inherit it"? At once the Lord proceeded to ratify his covenant in the usual Oriental manner. A heifer, a she-goat and a ram—one from each species commonly used in sacrifice—are brought forward; each is cut into two parts; the parts are laid asunder; a turtle-dove and a young pigeon, also used for sacrifice in certain contingencies, were added but not cut in two. Then when night came on, a deep sleep fell upon Abraham and the Lord gave him in vision certain prophetic views of his posterity; and ratified the covenant by passing (in the symbol of fire and smoke) between the severed parts of the sacrificial animals. Of this method of ratifying covenants we have historical traces in Jer. 34: 18–20. We have also early and decisive indications of the same mode in the fact that at least in the Hebrew, Greek and Latin tongues the word for ratifying a covenant means primarily to *cut*. The phrase is, *to cut a covenant.* The prominent thing in the transaction was the cutting of the animal in twain that the contracting parties might pass solemnly between the parts of it. It seems to be assumed that the contracting parties virtually imprecated upon themselves a like doom if they proved faithless to their covenant.

5. At the next eventful appearance Abraham had been waiting in faith for the son of promise a quarter of a century and was perhaps tempted to think the ful-

fillment fast becoming impossible. Pertinently therefore the first words of the Lord were—*"I am the Almighty God!* Walk before me and be thou perfect"; fear nothing; my covenant stands fast. I will multiply thee exceedingly! Abraham fell on his face and God talked with him, reiterating his promise of posterity, giving unwonted prominence to the family feature of his covenant—" a God to thee and to thy seed after thee"— and instituting the rite of circumcision.

6. The sixth and last recorded appearance followed the triumph of Abraham's faith in the sacrifice of his only son. In this the Lord re-affirmed the great elements of his promise—posterity as the stars of heaven; triumphant over their enemies; a blessing to all the nations of the earth.——Thus at successive and somewhat remote intervals and mostly on special occasions the Lord manifested himself to his servant to confirm his faith, to enlarge the range of promise and to signify his pleasure in the obedient trustful life of his friend.

Such is the religious history of Abraham as related to his covenant God. Corresponding to this is the history of his posterity, the Hebrew nation. To them as to their patriarchal father God manifested himself through long ages, at successive points, *e. g.* in their Egypt life; in his uplifted arm over Pharaoh to bring them forth in the memorable Exodus; at the Red Sea; at Sinai; all through their wilderness life; at the Jordan crossing; in the conquest of Canaan, and onward, onward, till the coming at length of that greater Seed of Abraham in whom most signally were all the nations of the earth to be blessed. But to the details of this latter history we must give more definite attention in their place and order.

One other special feature in the great covenant with Abraham should be noticed.

In many respects this covenant made Abraham and his posterity a peculiar people, discriminating broadly between them and every other nation, and accumulating the blessings of God upon them in no stinted measure. It might be apprehended that such exclusiveness would beget bigotry, national pride and self-righteousness; but, with wisest forethought, the Lord put into this covenant one counteracting element of great power, viz. that *he ordained them to be a blessing to all the nations of the earth.* "In thee and in thy seed shall all the nations of the earth be blessed." It was never the thought of God that the Hebrew people should live to themselves and for themselves—should garner their own store-house full of heavenly blessings and leave all other peoples to shift for themselves as best they might. No; God's plan contemplated the culture in their souls of the broadest benevolence, and this, pressed into service by a sense of largest responsibility to meet the revealed purposes of God as to their work. Into this great system which made them his peculiar people, he put, openly and clearly, the germinal idea of a salvation to be provided for the wide world—this covenant people to be the almoners of all these blessings to the otherwise benighted and perishing nations. Properly understood and duly regarded, this germinal idea would have developed in their hearts and lives the true missionary spirit, would have given at once both breadth and depth to their piety, would have made them feel that God had great thoughts of mercy for the whole race of man, and had honored them as his ministers in giving this salvation to every creature. At the very least here was opened a thoroughly rich field for prayer, the broadest scope for real sympathy with the benevolence of the Great Father of all the nations and a powerful antidote against the narrow exclusiveness which might otherwise have shrunk and shriveled their piety and narrowed their aspirations to themselves and their land. How often in the heart of the good men of later times—the men like Moses, Samuel, David, Isaiah,—must the kindling thought have been sprung by this great germinal promise—*When shall these things be?* When shall the full fruitage of these great promises be realized? What have we to do to hasten the coming of that sublime consummation?

It remains to speak more definitely of the promises made to Abraham *as including the great Messiah.*

In this as in most other Messianic prophecies, the argument is threefold;

(1) The language obviously *admits* the Messiah, *i. e.* may be construed without violence to apply to him, or at least to *include* him:

(2) Its meaning is so broad that it *must* include him; the blessings are too great to be supposed possible without him—apart from him: and

(3) The inspired writers of the New Testament found the Messiah in this prophecy.

The substance of the prophecy is in the words—" In thy seed shall all the nations of the earth be blessed" (Gen. 22: 18 and 26: 4). Beyond question this *may* include the Messiah as the author of these really universal blessings—blessings for all the nations of the earth. Nay more; the blessings are too great, too broad, too far reaching to admit any supposable interpretation short of the Messiah and the gospel age. Historically no fulfillment less broad than the Christian can possibly be made out. In Christ and in him only can this prediction be fulfilled.

And to crown all, our Lord himself testifies; "Your father Abraham rejoiced to see my day; and *he saw it and was glad*" (Jno. 8: 56). It may be noticed that the word used by our Lord was not *me*, my person; but "my *day*"—the gospel age; the great events of it; the wonderful results of my coming—which is no doubt the exact truth. It was rather what was to be achieved by Christ in the way of blessings upon all the nations than what lay in Christ's *person* definitely that Abraham prophetically saw.

Paul adds his testimony that these words refer to Christ; (a.) Affirming (Gal. 3: 8)—"The Scripture, foreseeing that God would justify the nations ["heathen"] through faith, preached before the gospel to Abraham, saying, 'In thee shall all nations be blessed.'" "Preached before" is simply predicted, revealed by prophecy, with the accessory idea that the thing revealed was the gospel, the news of salvation.——(b.) To show that in his view the burden and fullness of this prophecy are Christ and nothing less or other than Christ, he says in this connection (v. 16); "Now to Abraham and to his seed were the promises made. He saith not—And to *seeds* as of many, but as of one—And to thy *seed*, which is Christ."

Waiving any special effort to justify Paul's argument from the singular number of the word "seed," his testimony is certainly valid to the point for which I have adduced it, viz. that Paul saw Christ in this prophecy. How much soever the principles of exegesis may reluctate, they certainly will not deny that he interprets the prophecy concerning Christ. Their complaint would be that he ties it down to Christ too exclusively.

It must be held therefore that the promises made to Abraham really include a prophecy of Christ. We could not infer from the record in Genesis how well Abraham understood the reference to the Messiah. But the allusions to this point in the New Testament give us light, our Savior most distinctly declaring—Abraham rejoiced that he might see my day; *he saw it*—with great joy. The writer of the Epistle to the Hebrews, speaking of Abraham and the patriarchs as not having received the promised blessings but as seeing them from afar and embracing them, has in mind specially their faith in the promised heavenly city (Heb. 11: 10, 13, 14, 16), yet not to the exclusion of him who prepares those mansions for his people (Jno. 14: 2, 3). His testimony is in point to show that Abraham looked beyond the earthly side of those blessings to the heavenly; rested not in the earthly Canaan, not in the multitude of his lineal sons and daughters; but reached out beyond these to the city that hath eternal foundations and to the blessings of the Great Messiah, good for all the nations of the earth. The nearer and lesser blessings had a power of suggestion, lifting his thought to the more remote and greater. A man who talked with God so intimately can not be supposed to have missed these grand ideas of the gospel age and of the heavenly state which we are sometimes wont to regard as the special, not to say exclusive, revelations of the New Testament.

Sodom and Gomorrah.

Involved in this history of Abraham, there occurs this ever memorable case of sudden and most fearful judgment upon the ungodly in this world—the overthrow of the cities of the plain. Sodom and Gomorrah only are mentioned by name in Gen. 13: 10 and 19: 24, 28); in several cases for brevity, Sodom only; but Moses (Deut. 20: 23) and Hosea (11: 8) speak of Admah and Zeboim as also overthrown. These were contiguous and (in Gen. 14: 2) confederate cities. The narrative sets forth their appalling and absolutely universal wickedness. Other references suggest the causes or occasions (Ezek. 16: 49, 50), and intimate that the better life and the reproving testimony of Lot were powerless (2 Pet. 2: 7, 8).

The narrative also makes prominent the immediate agency of God in this destruction. "The Lord rained upon Sodom and upon Gomorrah fire and brimstone from the Lord out of heaven" (Gen. 19: 24). "When Abraham looked toward Sodom and all the land of the plain, lo, the smoke of the country went up as the smoke of a great furnace" (v. 28).

The case became for all future time a standard illustration of God's most sudden, fearful and utter destruction of the wicked. (See Deut. 29: 23 and Isa. 13: 19 and Jer. 20: 16 and 50: 40 and Amos. 4: 11 and 2 Pet. 2: 6 and Jude 7.) It classes itself naturally with the deluge of Noah's time and with the fall of Pharaoh's host in the Red Sea, and the swallowing up of Korah and his company in the wilderness—all combining to show that God never lacks the means or the power to begin his threatened retribution upon the wicked here in time whenever he deems it wise for the moral ends of warning.

The question of secondary agencies is of altogether secondary importance. It may well suffice us that *God's hand was there.* It matters but little whether he made use of the agencies of the natural world—lightning and the combustible materials of that locality, or otherwise. That these natural agencies were employed is perhaps probable.——The locality of those cities is undoubtedly identified, viz. at the southern extremity of the Dead Sea, now and for many ages submerged though in quite shallow water. The adjacent soil affords bitumen and other inflammable substances in abundance, indicating with great probability that a prodigious discharge of electricity ignited the whole region, fire from the Lord out of heaven gleaming and crashing; the atmosphere all ablaze with flames and the very ground on which the city stood burning with terrible fury. It might seem that the deep moral pollutions of its people had doomed that vast plain to be first purified by fire and then sunk from human view for all the coming ages by its subsidence beneath the waters of the Dead Sea.——In view of this appalling scene, how terribly significant become the words of Jude—"Set forth for an example, suffering the vengeance of eternal fire"! How easily and yet how fearfully can the Almighty execute the judgments written against guilty sinners who scorn his words of warning and dare his vengeance!

"The Angel of the Lord."

Cases occur in Old Testament history in which the Lord appears in visible form and is called interchangeably "the Lord" and "the Angel of the Lord." See the personal history of Hagar (Gen. 16: 7, 13); of Abraham (Gen. 18: 2, 16, 33 and 22: 11, 15–18); of Jacob (Gen. 31: 11–13, 16); of Moses (Exod. 3: 2, 4, 6, 7, etc., and 23: 20–23); of Gideon (Judg. 6: 11, 12, 14, 20–23) and of Manoah (Judg. 13: 18, 22). The term "angel" means in general a messenger; but is manifestly applied and therefore is applicable to the visible manifestations of God himself, supposably of the second person of the Godhead, *i. e.* God as made manifest to mortals. The cases above referred to are entirely decisive as to the usage of the phrase, "The Angel of the Lord" in some cases (not relatively many) to denote the very Presence of the Lord himself coming down to reveal himself to his people. In Gen. 18: first three men appear before Abraham; he entertains them. Two of them go on toward Sodom; one remains talking with Abraham. It is said "Abraham stood yet before the Lord"; then drew near and offered that remarkable prayer of intercession for Sodom; after which "the Lord went his way and Abraham returned to his place."——In Gen. 22, when Abraham had stretched forth his hand to slay his son, "the angel of the Lord called to him out of heaven." Shortly after (vs. 15-18) "the angel of the Lord called unto Abraham out of heaven the second time and said, By myself have I sworn, saith the Lord, etc. . . . . . Because thou hast obeyed my voice." This can be no other than the very God.——The passages above referred to from the history of Moses are striking. In Exod. 23: 20–23 we read: "Behold I send an angel before thee to keep thee in the way and to bring thee into the place which I have prepared. *Beware of him*" (*i. e.* not to offend him) "and obey his voice; provoke him not; for he will not pardon your transgressions, for *my name is in him*"—name, as usual in the sense of the very qualities of character of which the name is a significant indication.

CHAPTER XI.

THE PATRIARCHS.

Isaac.

The story of Isaac is brief; his life uneventful, perhaps we might say monotonous. The record shows that the Lord appeared to him on two distinct occasions; at Gerar (Gen. 26: 2–5), renewing the covenant previously made with Abraham, with a very full restatement of all its salient points; also at Beersheba (26: 23–25) where we are told "he builded an altar and called on the name of the Lord," in the steps of his godly father.——We see a point of his character in the fact stated incidentally, that Esau's marriage into Hittite families "was a grief of mind to Isaac and to Rebekah." Esau lacked sympathy with the spirit of the pious patriarchs and utterly failed to appreciate the inheritance of blessings which had lain so near the heart of his grandfather Abraham and of his father Isaac—facts which the historian touches briefly—"Thus Esau despised his birthright." The writer to the Hebrews puts the case forcibly: "Who for one morsel of meat sold his birthright" (12: 16).——We have no means of knowing how persistently and wisely Rebekah had labored to win and hold him by her maternal opportunities and power. In later years she seems to have withdrawn her heart from him to give it (with apparently extreme partiality) to Jacob.——Of her duplicity in the matter of the paternal blessing, it can scarcely be necessary to say that the fact of its being recorded by no means proves that the Lord justified it. Indeed the absence of any explicit condemnation can not be taken as equivalent to a justification. Jacob's exile from his father's house and home for twenty long years—so manifestly the result of this duplicity—must have been to her mind painfully suggestive. It seems plainly to have been one of God's ways in providence to rebuke and chasten her for this wrong, and perhaps we may add, to save Jacob's soul by removing him from a maternal influence which was so defective—not to say faulty and pernicious.

As to Isaac, one point only is named of him by the writer to the Hebrews in his catalogue of illustrious examples of faith: "By faith Isaac blessed Jacob and Esau concerning things to come" (11 : 20). These benedictions (recorded Gen. 27 : 28, 29, 33, 37, 39, 40) must be regarded as far more than a venerable father's good wishes—indeed as nothing less than prophetic benedictions—words uttered under the divine impulses of the Holy Ghost. Their broad outlook embraced the great outlines of the future history of the two nations that were before him in the person of his two sons.

Jacob.

In Jacob's history there is no lack of stirring incident and critical exigency; in his character, no lack of positive elements and vigorous force. *Bethel* where he seems to have found God first; *Mahanaim* where the double hosts of God met him and the murderous rage of Esau threatened every precious life in all his household, and he found help only as he wrestled with the angel of the covenant till he prevailed; the scenes of his sojourning in *Canaan* where Joseph first comes to view, envied and hated of his brethren, and his father mourned for him many days as dead; and finally *Goshen* where the aged patriarch found his lost Joseph yet alive and lord of all Egypt; stood before Pharaoh; saw his sons and sons' sons—a growing host; gave them his blessing and was gathered to his fathers:—surely these salient points of his history indicate no lack of adventure, and in the religious point of view, abundant scenes of moral trial—exigencies that tasked his virtue and endurance, his faith and patience, and in the end brought forth his chastened soul purified by the discipline of suffering and strong in the faith of Abraham's God.

To understand well the scenes of Bethel, we must think of a young man, emerging from boyhood—his fond mother's chief beloved—not to say, her pet boy—never yet thrown upon his own resources; an heir to wealth; a child of ease—perhaps of maternal indulgence;—but now suddenly brought into peril of life from his twin brother's indignant rage and violence. It would be so horrible to the mother to see her Jacob slain by his own brother's hand and to "lose them both in one day"! (Gen. 27: 45). Safety seemed to be only in flight, so she must needs send him secretly to the distant land of her birth—the old maternal family home. Therefore, with many a pang of heart, and (let us hope) with many a prayer, she commended him to the God of the covenant and sent him away.

One day of thoughtful travel had passed slowly over Jacob, his mind traversing by many rapid transitions from the home he had left behind to the new scenes that met his eye; from the brother before whose fury he was fleeing, to the unknown experiences of life among friends he had never seen. At last the sun had gone down; the eye had nothing more to see; weariness called for rest and sleep. With a stone for his pillow, with his tunic wrapt about him, and the broad heavens above for his canopy, he slept and dreamed—dreamed of a ladder with its foot on the earth beside him and its top in the heavens; and wonderful to see! the angels of God descending and ascending upon it! A new sense of communication between earth and heaven came upon him, assuming a strange reality when he saw the Lord standing above it and heard him say, "I am the Lord God of Abraham thy father and the God of Isaac." Before this Jacob had heard of that wonderful covenant of God so often ratified with his venerable grandfather and his father. The transfer of blessing from Isaac to himself as the lineal heir of both birthright and blessing was a thing of quite recent experience. How fully he had comprehended its glorious significance before does not appear; but now that he is cast out alone upon the wide, unknown world—now that he so much needs the Great God for his friend—it comes over him with solemn, precious interest. The words spoken were full of comfort. They reminded him of the great family promise to Abraham, renewed to his father Isaac: "A God to thee and *to thy seed after thee*," and he felt that the promise put its finger upon his own aching, solitary heart. He had a fresh assurance that his life would not come to nought and be a failure, for the Lord said: "The land whereon thou liest, to thee will I give it and to thy seed; and thy seed shall be as the dust of the earth, and thou shalt spread abroad to the West and to the East; to the North and to the South; and in thee and in thy seed shall all the families of the earth be blessed." And lest these blessings might seem too remote to meet his sense of present peril and need, the Lord kindly added—"And behold I am with thee and will keep thee in all places whither thou goest, and will bring thee again to this land; for I will not leave thee until I have done that which I have spoken to thee of." How deeply these scenes and words impressed the soul of the youthful Jacob is apparent in the few words which fell from his lips when he came to the full consciousness of wakeful life. "Surely the Lord is in this place, and I knew it not"! I had not thought to meet God *here* and to meet him *so!* I thought I was utterly alone; but lo! *God is here!*——We must suppose that Jacob had never been so near to God before. Such a meeting with the Majesty of heaven was new to his experience, and a sense of solemn awe—of reverence amounting to fear, came upon him:—as the record is, "he was afraid and said, How dreadful is this place! This is none other than the house of God, and this is the gate of heaven." The ladder stretching upward, its foot resting beside him and its top in the heavens, the open door far in the sky through which the angels seemed to come and go; the voice of the Lord himself and withal uttering such words—ah indeed, the whole effect was as if God and heaven had truly dropped down upon him, and this was God's dwelling-place and heaven's door was there!

The scene was entirely too precious to be suffered to pass into oblivion; so Jacob's thought turned to some memorial of the scene and to a moral adjustment of his future life to this heavenly call. First, he took the stone which had served him for a pillow and set it up for a *pillar* and poured oil upon the top of it—a sacred unction.——To the place he gave the significant name "Bethel"—house of God—by which it was ever after known. Then, by a solemn vow, he gave himself to the Lord who had thus called and comforted him with promise. We read, "Jacob vowed a vow, saying, 'If God will be with me and will keep me in this way that I go, and will give me bread to eat and raiment to put on so that

I come again to my father's house in peace, then shall the Lord be my God, and this stone which I have set for a pillar shall be God's house; and of all that thou shalt give me, I will surely give the tenth unto thee.'"
——If we press the word "*if*" at the head of this sentence so as to make it thoroughly conditional, and withal suggesting some shades of doubt whether God would prove faithful, we shall wrong Jacob, imputing to him what manifestly he could not have meant. His words must be taken thus:—*Inasmuch as* God has so kindly promised to be with me in all my otherwise doubtful way, and to bring me back despite of all peril to my father's house again, I accept him as in very deed my God; and out of all my accumulated wealth, I will surely give one tenth to him.——The spirit is that of one drawn by God's promised mercy—not of one who stands in grave doubt whether God will come up to the full height of his promise. These are the words of one who has *no* doubt on that point and who refers to that promise only to say that because of it, under the joyful assurance of it, he gives himself to God in full, prompt, and perpetual consecration. A reverent soul brought so near to God, impressed with a sense that heaven and God are verily here, does not tempt and provoke God by expressing the fear that he will not prove faithful to his promises!——Late into the morning Jacob lingered in this hallowed spot as one loth to close such an interview with God and break the charm of such sacred associations. And when at length he must go on his journey, it was with far other heart than in his solitary journey of the day before.

Of the scenes of his sojourn at Haran there is no occasion to speak particularly. Perhaps the deception in which his mother and himself were the responsible parties came up fresh and clear to him when he found that Laban had taken similar liberties with him, giving him Leah when Rachel was in the bond. A man never gets so sharp and keen a sense of the wrong of these little deceptions as when he becomes the victim and the sting goes deep into his own bosom. This is sometimes the Lord's way to testify his disapprobation of this wrong and to impress his own view of it upon those who may have sinfully indulged in it.

Mahanaim.

The second great exigency of Jacob's life has its record in Gen. 32. Twenty years have passed away in Haran; he has wives, children, and ample substance of cattle, sheep, camels. Indeed all his children except Benjamin are now about him. Not feeling at home longer with Laban; remembering the Lord's promise to give Canaan to him and to his children; mindful moreover of the scenes of Bethel, and we may hope, somewhat fearful lest the household gods which were dangerously near the heart of Laban, might be a snare to his wives and children, he fully makes up his mind to return to Canaan.

At some point on this return journey, (as the narrative states rather abruptly), the angels of God met him. Jacob saw them and said, "This is God's host"—a convoy—a kind of military guard, the demand for which presently appeared. He gave name to the place from the fact—"Mahanaim"—the double camps or hosts. They seem to have been an intimation to him that danger was near, and that God's hosts were near also for his rescue.

On his way back to Canaan, and consequently approaching the residence of Esau in the land of Seir, Jacob is fully aware that his coming must be known to Esau, and therefore he sends messengers to him for the purpose of conciliating his good will. These messengers soon returned to Jacob, saying; "We came to thy brother Esau, and also he cometh to meet thee and four hundred men with him." In an instant Jacob comprehends the situation and sees his danger. Those four hundred men are led on by Esau with no peaceful purpose. The lapse of twenty years has not sufficed to quench the fire of his wrath and to revive fraternal affection. Still unforgiving he comes on "breathing out threatening and slaughter," exhibiting identically the same character which he impressed on his posterity and which manifested itself in the vindictiveness of the Edomites at the fall of Jerusalem before the Chaldean power. Amos (1: 11, 12) and Obadiah (vs. 10–16) represent this vindictiveness against the posterity of his brother Jacob as the ground and reason of God's overwhelming judgments on their nation and land. "Because he did pursue his brother with the sword and did cast off all pity, and his anger did tear perpetually, and he nursed his wrath for ever."——Such was the bearing of his nation toward the sons of Jacob in the day of Jerusalem's fall; and with this same spirit he is coming, at the point of his history now before us, to cut off Jacob's powerless family.——With admirable self-possession and wisdom, Jacob laid his plans promptly—first, to divide his train into two parts, placing one at some distance in advance of the other, so that if the front column were attacked, the rear might stand some chance of escape: and secondly, to send forward a valuable present to Esau;—"two hundred goats; two hundred ewes and twenty rams; thirty milch camels with their colts; forty kine; ten bulls; twenty she-asses and ten foals" (Gen. 32: 13-15)—enough at least to arrest Esau's attention and perhaps to soothe his spirit toward his brother. These he sent forward with fitting words of conciliation:—but by far the most vital measure of relief yet remained—*prayer to the Great God of the covenant.* Vs. 9–12 record the words of this prayer, apparently as offered to God in the first moments after the messengers returned and apprised him of his danger. The prudential arrangements above named followed, occupying the morning hours of the day. When night came on Jacob was left alone save that the Lord came down in form as a man—the angel of the covenant—and a scene of struggling, wrestling prayer ensued which ceased not till the dawn of the morning. As the narrative has it; "Jacob was left alone, and there wrestled a man with him until the break of day. And when he saw that he prevailed not against him, he touched the hollow of his thigh; and the hollow of Jacob's thigh was out of joint as he wrestled with him. And he [the angel-man] said, Let me go, for the day breaketh. And he [Jacob] replied—I will not let thee go except thou bless me. And he said unto him, What is thy name? And he said, Jacob. And he said—Thy name shall no more be called Jacob, but Israel; for as a Prince hast thou power with God and hast prevailed. And Jacob asked him and said, Tell me, I pray thee, thy name; and he said—Wherefore is it that thou dost ask after my name? And he blessed him there. And Jacob called the name of the place Peniel, for I have seen God face to face and my life is preserved."

What we may call the costume, the purely external *forms* of this scene, are striking, peculiar, but thoroughly significant. In view of the circumstances, there can not be the least doubt that, mentally, spiritually,—*this is a scene of prayer*—nothing else, less or more. The prayer is a struggle of soul on the part of the suppliant. He is in trouble; he is shut up to God alone for help; and he feels that *he can not be denied*. The scene of the wrestling must imply that God debates this matter with the suppliant Jacob, apparently resisting, contending,—certainly delaying, and prolonging the conflict hour after hour of the live-long night till break of day. Seeing that he prevailed not to silence Jacob's supplication, *i. e.* to break his hold as a wrestler, he touched the hollow of Jacob's thigh, crippling the wrestler seriously, yet leaving his arms with strength unimpaired to hold fast his antagonist. Then as if to test Jacob's faith and endurance to the utmost, he said— "Let me go, for the day breaketh;" to which Jacob replied—"I will not let thee go except thou bless me." Jacob as a wrestler with one thigh out of joint had become powerless to cast his opponent; but with his arms in their full strength he could *hold on*—and he did. The culminating point in the struggle is reached in these remarkable words; "I will not let thee go except thou bless me." I can not be denied. I have thy promise: it touches this very case—protection and succor till I return to my country; and I can not let go my hold. I must have help now, or perish!——The change of name is richly significant. Jacob, *i. e.* supplanter, suggested the deception by which he obtained from his blind father the blessing; but with it came the rage of his brother and this present peril to himself and to his great family. "Israel" means *a prince with God*—one who has prevailed in the struggle of prayer and obtained the blessing he sought. The change of name thus indicates the change in Jacob's relations to God and to Esau which followed his victory in this prayer-struggle.

But what is the significance of this example? What was really the animus of this conflict? what the reason for it; what the point in debate, and what the great moral lessons which it teaches?

Our data for the answer to these questions must come from one or both of two sources:

(a.) *The circumstances of the present case;*

(b.) *The principles of God's spiritual administration* of grace to his people in connection with prayer.

(a) As to the circumstances of the present case:—The covenant of God with Jacob is very definite. Jacob understands and manifestly pleads it, as we see in this chapter. These are his words as recorded: "O God of my father Abraham and God of my father Isaac"—the Lord [the *Jehovah*, signifying the faithful God of his people] "who saidst to me, Return unto thy country and to thy kindred and I will deal well with thee: I am not worthy of the least of all thy mercies and of all thy truth which thou hast showed unto thy servant; for with my staff I passed over this Jordan, and now I am become two bands. Deliver me, I pray thee, from the hand of my brother, from the hand of Esau, for I fear him, lest he will come and smite me and the mother with the children. And thou saidst, I will surely do thee good and make thy seed as the sand of the sea which can not be numbered for multitude."——It should be noted that the promise in this covenant precisely meets Jacob's present emergency—"Return and I will deal well with thee: thou saidst, I will surely do thee good and make thy seed as the sand of the sea." These points fully covered his present danger. Jacob doubtless had in mind the very explicit terms of this covenant as announced to him at Bethel: "I am with thee and will keep thee in all places whither thou goest and *will bring thee again to this land;* for I will not leave thee until I have done that which I have spoken to thee of." There is therefore no room for mistake on this point. The Lord's promise to Jacob is explicit, and in its terms guarantees perfect protection in his present peril. Why, then, it will be asked, was this night-long struggle?

We may find some light toward the answer if we remember that every promise of God to man must in the nature of the case *imply certain conditions;* and the promise in this covenant equally with all other promises. "If I regard iniquity in my heart, the Lord will not hear me." "Ye ask and receive not because ye ask amiss."——As bearing on this very covenant let us recall the ground of the Lord's confidence that he should

be able to fulfill his words to Abraham: "I know him that he will command his children and his household after him, and they shall keep the way of the Lord to do justice and judgment, *that the Lord may bring upon Abraham that which he hath spoken of him.*"——Now it will be in point to consider that these scenes of danger from Esau's rage inevitably brought up between the Lord and Jacob the question whether the deception practiced upon Isaac to transfer to Jacob the blessing which legitimately fell to Esau could be passed over by the Lord without rebuke. Was it proper that the Lord should endorse it with no rebuke whatever? If he were ever to bear his protest against it, the present was the time.
——Yet further, the fact had but recently come to Jacob's knowledge that his favorite Rachel had stolen her father's gods and taken them with her as she left the family home. Had Jacob been faithful to the God of his fathers in teaching and impressing the worship of the one true God and in protesting solemnly against idol-worship? And had he been firm and outspoken against such theft and deception as that of his beloved Rachel? Must not things of this sort be inquired into and definitely settled before the Lord could interpose with such manifest deliverance as would virtually endorse Jacob as right before God?——It ought not to escape our notice that while the narrative in the preceding chapter (31) recites the misconduct of Rachel and shows that Jacob then for the first time became aware of the extent of her idolatry, theft, and deception, so a subsequent narrative (35: 1-4) apprises us in a very significant way that both the Lord and Jacob remembered this wonderful night of struggle, and that some of the matters then in issue were set right. "God said to Jacob—Arise, go up to Bethel [that place of so many hallowed associations] and dwell there and make there an altar unto God who appeared to thee when thou fleddest from the face of Esau thy brother. Then Jacob said to his household and to all that were with him, *Put away the strange gods that are among you,* and be clean, and change your garments, and let us arise and go up to Bethel, and I will make there an altar unto God *who answered me in the day of my distress,* and was with me in the way which I went." Yes, "he who answered me in that day of my distress," before whom this whole matter was

reviewed and debated through that long, fearful night—who called me to account in that dread emergency and pointed out my sins and put my soul to most humble confession of past short-comings and to most solemn vows of future service;—let us amend our ways and our doings before the eye of this holy God who mercifully spared us in that fearful hour. These circumstances throw light upon this remarkable scene of prayer.

(b.) We may also call to mind *the principles of God's spiritual administration over his people in respect to answering their prayer.*

Here it is safe to say that God never delays to answer prayer without some good reason. He could not delay from mere caprice.——On the other hand he may delay the blessing sought, for the purpose of holding it before the suppliant's mind till he shall better appreciate its worth, and his own dependence on God alone for it, and that he may accept it more gratefully and prize it more adequately when it comes. The reasons for delay may often lie in this direction; but in the present case of Jacob we must look elsewhere, since in his fearful emergency this particular reason is scarcely supposable. His case was so urgent and involved interests so dear and so near to his very soul that his mind could scarce need to be sharpened to more intense desire or impressed with a deeper sense of dependence.

Again, God often holds the suppliant in suspense for the sake of throwing him upon self-examination. It may be simply indispensable both for the good of the suppliant and for the honor of God that he should be put to the deepest self-searching, to compel reflection and consideration for the purpose of convicting him of some sin that must needs be seen, confessed, repented of and put utterly away. We must not overlook the great fact that when God grants signal blessings in answer to any man's prayer, it will be taken as a tacit indorsement on God's part of this man's spiritual state. It will be considered as God's testimony that he is *not* "regarding iniquity in his heart"—that there are no iniquities palpable to the world and present to the man's own consciousness—indulged and not condemned and forsaken. On this principle it often happens that God must needs compel the praying soul to the most thorough heart-searching and to the most absolute and complete renunciation of known sin, before he can honorably and safely bestow signal blessings.

If now we place this obvious principle of God's spiritual administration alongside of the well-known facts of Jacob's history, we shall readily see reasons, apparently all-sufficient, for this long delay and this remarkable struggle of prayer before the blessing was given. The Lord was searching his servant and impressing some great principles of practical duty upon his mind under circumstances well adapted to insure very thorough reformation.

When Jacob at length prevailed and the Lord blessed him there, the crisis was past, and the danger really over. It was only for the Lord to put forth his finger and touch the heart of Esau:—then the revenge and murderous rage of the Esau that was, gave place to fraternal kindness and sympathy. We read, "Esau ran to meet Jacob and embraced him and fell on his neck and kissed him; and they wept" (Gen. 33: 4). The result therefore was far more and better than a mere escape with life from Esau's murderous purpose. It was the reconciliation of long alienated brothers. At least it secured one precious scene of fraternal sympathy and love.——We read little of Esau's subsequent life. The brothers met at the death-bed and grave of their father (Gen. 35: 29); perhaps their paths never came in contact again.

The scenes of Mahanaim have afforded to the godly of all future ages some new light on the great subject of prayer. This was the first strong decisive case on record of prevalence in prayer. Abraham interceded long for Sodom; but with no further result than to show that God was very condescending to hear such prayer, yet that the thing asked could not be granted.——Here is a case of positive victory—a real prevailing with God, reached, however, only after a most remarkable struggle. It is a great advance in the revealed science of prayer to have a case so illustrative as this of the great laws of prevailing prayer.

Jacob and Joseph.

The group of historic incidents in which Jacob and

Joseph were prominent actors is eventful and striking; in some points without a parallel in human history. If it were fiction, a mere drama, wrought out by some gifted imagination, it could not fail to command the admiration of men as a most finished plot, a wonderful outline of strange varieties of human character. Truth is sometimes "stranger than fiction": and the careful reader of this narrative will testify, far more instructive and impressive.

The points of chief value will be readily embraced under the following heads:

I. The striking developments of personal character in the case of Jacob, Joseph, and his brethren.

II. The hand of God in this history, manifested in two respects: (a.) In the suffering and moral trial of the righteous: (b.) In his overruling control of the wicked to bring forth abounding good from their wickedness.

III. The divine plan and purpose in locating the birth of the great Hebrew nation in such contact with Egypt.

IV. Egyptian history and life, studied in connection with this sacred narrative as affording confirmation of its truthfulness.

I. The reader of Gen. 34 and 35 and 37 and 38 will see that the ten older brethren of Joseph were "hard boys." The sacred historian must have been quite willing to give this impression, else he would not have recorded Reuben's incest with his father's concubine (35: 22), nor Judah's criminal connection with a supposed harlot who proved to be his own daughter-in-law (Gen. 38), nor the pitiless cruelty of Simeon and Levi when stirred up to revenge the dishonor done to their sister Dinah (Gen. 34). Especially do the worst elements of depraved character appear in their treatment of their younger brother Joseph. The narrative (Gen. 37) is brief; gives facts without comments; but *what facts!* Joseph was young and very simple-hearted. Up to the point where the history introduces him, he had been trained in a religious home—which seems scarcely to have been the case with the ten older sons. Their shepherd life took them into distant parts of the country, and seems practically to have removed them much of the time from home and its domestic in-

DEVELOPMENTS OF CHARACTER. 145

fluences. Unfortunately the domestic influences of that polygamous home were by no means so wholesome as a religious home ought to furnish. Envy and jealousy were stimulated into fearful strength.

Joseph was sent to help the sons of Bilhah and Zilpah. Painfully impressed by their misdeeds, he reported them to his father. The special love of this aged father for Joseph, manifested in the "coat of many colors" (really a long tunic reaching to the wrists and ankles) occasioned more rankling jealousy. Finally, Joseph's remarkable dreams which his simplicity related without apparently a thought of giving offense, brought their animosity to its climax. Soon Joseph is thrown into their power. They see him coming and conspire to take his life. "Come,' (say they) "let us slay him and cast him into some pit, and we will say, "Some evil beast hath devoured him; and we shall see what will become of his dreams." We are not told which of them suggested this murderous purpose. Reuben, the eldest brother, was the first to protest. His plan was that they should cast him alive into some pit; and then in their absence he could take him out and return him safely to his father. They consented; stripped him of his new coat, and cast him into a pit without water. [These pits were dug in that poorly watered country for the sake of getting water for their cattle.] Then they sat down to eat bread, perhaps complimenting themselves that they had not murdered him, but had shown their power and for the present had put him out of their way. Manifestly their consciences were dead to that sense of guilt which a few years later forced them to say, "We are verily guilty concerning our brother in that we saw the anguish of his soul when he besought us and we would not hear" (Gen. 42: 21). Just then a caravan of Ishmaelites and Midianites came in sight, moving toward Egypt, and Judah came to the rescue with the proposition to take up Joseph and sell him, to be taken as a slave to Egypt. With some manly feeling he says—"What profit is it if we slay our brother and conceal his blood? Come, let us sell him to the Ishmaelites, and let not our hand be upon him, for he is our brother and our flesh; and his brethren were content."——Reuben's better qualities come up to view again when he returned to the pit, hoping to rescue his brother—but found no Joseph there! "He rent his clothes"; he came to his brethren exclaiming, "The child is not;—and I—whither shall I go?"

In the next scene these brethren were if possible more heartless still. It commonly happens that one crime demands another and yet another to conceal the first. So in this case, the next thing is to deceive their father even though it torture him with the agony of supposing his favorite son devoured by some evil beast. They kill a kid; stain Joseph's coat with its blood; and then send it to their father, saying, "This have we found; see whether it be thy son's coat or not." There was no mistaking the coat, and Jacob's grief is heart-breaking. Remarkably it is said that "all his sons and all his daughters rose up to comfort him, but he refused to be comforted"; and he said, "I will go down into the grave to my son mourning. Thus his father wept for him."——How easily those sons might have said: "Father, we have sinned against God and against thee; but Joseph is not slain by lions; we sold him into Egypt! You may live to see him again." But not even Reuben or Judah had conscience, and truthfulness, and filial affection enough to reveal the guilty secret. Miserable comforters were they all to their father's broken heart!

Leaving Jacob to long years of bitterest grief, we follow the fortunes of Joseph. From this point the thread of the story takes him into Egypt a slave. Sold to Potiphar, an officer under Pharaoh, it soon became apparent that the Lord was with him and made everything prosper under his hand. He rises rapidly in the confidence of his master; is put in charge of all his house—but here springs up a new trial. Joseph is beautiful in person and amiable in manners. Potiphar's wife, lewd and shameless, tempts him with solicitations to adultery. Joseph's bearing in this case was worthy to be put on permanent record to pass down through all future generations to the end of time, a perfect model of both virtue and wisdom—the virtue that resists seductive temptation with unwavering firmness; and the wisdom that comprehends and applies the perfect methods of resisting temptation.

Joseph did not dally with his tempter; did not suffer the temptation to gather new force, but met it instantly with the strongest considerations possible—"How can I do this great wickedness and *sin against God?*" God, said he to himself, is my best friend; I am his servant. He has stood by me through all my trials and given me this great prosperity; his pure eye is on me; I can not do this great wickedness against him!——The sense of a present God settled the question forever. There was indeed another line of considerations—his obligations to the husband of this lewd woman. Potiphar had trusted him most entirely; shall he abuse this trust? Never.——Thus Joseph's course was at once decided. But this vile woman persisted in her solicitations, till at length, maddened by her failure, she plotted his death. She laid hold of his garment; he escaped leaving it in her hands. With this for her proof she accuses Joseph of the crime of which she alone was guilty. Joseph is thrown into prison—because of his virtue and not because of any crime. Of course the Lord was with him still, and again Joseph rises in the favor and confidence of those in power; is put in charge of all matters in the prison, and thus the Lord turned this great trial to account to bring Joseph before Pharaoh. Long was the trial; the story of his relations to the chief butler and the chief baker is in point chiefly as showing how ungratefully the butler could forget his imprisoned friend and prolong his imprisonment. But the hour of deliverance came at last. Pharaoh's two dreams impressed and disturbed his mind so much that he summoned all his wise men to his help—but in vain. At this opportune moment the chief butler remembers Joseph. He should have spoken of him to the king two years before; but engrossed with his own prosperity, he forgot his prison benefactor till this time. Joseph comes to the help of the king. His first answer is beautifully modest and fragrant with piety. "I have heard of thee, said the king, that thou canst understand a dream to interpret it." Joseph replies: "It is not in me; God shall give Pharaoh an answer of peace" (Gen. 41:16). The dreams are interpreted to signify seven years of overflowing plenty, followed by seven of extreme famine throughout all the land. Joseph suggests to the king to store up the excess of the plentiful years against the deficiencies of the famine years. The king sees the wisdom of this suggestion and at once appoints Joseph to this responsibility; in fact, sets him over all Egypt, save only in the honors of the throne.

At this point the historic thread brings Jacob and his sons in Canaan to view again. We are not told whether they had the seven years of exuberant plenty there, but the years of famine were there in terrible power. They were soon breadless. The father hears that there is corn in Egypt; so he sends ten of his sons—all that are with him save Benjamin—to get corn. It was to be brought on the backs of their asses, and therefore it was wise to send them all together.

The scenes that follow are told with masterly simplicity. Joseph knows them; they do not recognize him: What policy shall he pursue? Why, we may perhaps ask, why does he not make himself known to them at once? Why does he treat them so roughly; accuse them of being spies; throw them all into prison for three days; propose to keep them all confined save one and send him back after Benjamin; but finally compromises the matter by taking Simeon as a hostage, binding him before their eyes, and then consenting that the rest may go home and bring Benjamin down as the condition of Simeon's release? Why does he put their money into the mouth of each man's sack of corn? Why this long delay, and these searching, harassing preliminaries?

It was not that Joseph was hard-hearted and rather enjoyed using his power and taking some revenge— nothing of this sort. It is indeed said in the first stage of this interview—"Joseph remembered the dreams which he dreamed of them" (Gen. 42: 9), and thereupon said, "Ye are spies; to see the nakedness of the land are ye come." But this only shows that his policy was settled upon the spur of the moment. He saw what he needed to accomplish and laid his plans accordingly. The whole narrative shows that, so far from being void of fraternal feeling and hard-hearted, in fact it tasked his firmness of character to the utmost to suppress his emotions sufficiently to carry out his purpose. His main purpose was to bring them to thorough repentance.

For this end he must needs throw their thought back upon their great sin and bring the heavy pressure of present calamity upon them with all its suggestive power to show them that God was taking them in hand for that wickedness. He also wished to see how they felt toward their father and toward Benjamin. Their feeling toward both the father and his youngest son would be an index of their penitence for their great sin toward himself.

Joseph was a man of consummate wisdom. Few men have ever lived who understood human nature better than he, or could plan better for a given effect. Consequently we shall not miss greatly if we infer his design from the actual effect. When we see what he accomplished, we are reasonably safe in saying—This is what he aimed to do.

Observe now that the first scene had not fully transpired ere he heard them saying one to another, "We are verily guilty concerning our brother in that we saw the anguish of his soul when he besought us and we would not hear; therefore is this distress come upon us." And Reuben answered them (*i. e.* interposed at that point) saying, Spake I not unto you, saying, Do not sin against the child; and ye would not hear? Therefore, behold also, his blood is required."——Joseph saw that his scheme was taking effect; their consciences were at work. How his own heart must have throbbed! Accordingly we read—"He turned himself about from them and wept." But the work is not yet complete; so he brushed away the tears and "returned to them and took from them Simeon and bound him before their eyes." Why he chose Simeon is not indicated. Perhaps—not to say probably—he was the leading spirit in the cruel scenes thirteen years before. We remember that Simeon and Levi led off in that bloody affray with the men of Shechem. However this may be, he was the eldest after Reuben; and Reuben, though a coarse, rough nature, was on the side of mercy toward the abused Joseph. Simeon, therefore, is chosen for the hostage, to be kept in close confinement while the rest are dismissed to go home. Simeon will have abundant time to think over the guilty deeds of that dreadful past! Let us hope that it brought him to genuine repentance.

The narrative details the return of the nine brethren to their father's house; how they told their story there; how Jacob rebuked them for disclosing their youngest brother; how he struggled desperately against his manifest destiny; how he said—Benjamin shall never go down into Egypt; how Reuben interposed in his rough way, saying to his father: "Slay my two sons if I bring not Benjamin back to thee"—as if he could not see that murdering two of his grandchildren would be infinitely far from helping the matter or affording the least relief. With better good sense and a more just appreciation of his father's feelings, Judah pled with his father:--We shall all die of starvation unless we go down to Egypt for corn: we must take Benjamin with us—else we get no corn. "Send the lad with me; I will be surety for him. Of my hand shalt thou require him: if I bring him not unto thee and set him before thee, then let me bear the blame forever" (Gen. 43: 8-10).
——The heart of their father Israel comes to view here—yielding to the inevitable necessity; wisely getting up a liberal present of the best fruits of their land; double money, to return what came home with them in their sack's mouth, and to buy again. Saddest of all he gave up his dear Benjamin, and then with many a prayer he sent them to Egypt a second time: "And God Almighty give you mercy before the man that he may send away your other brother and Benjamin: If I be bereaved of my children, I am bereaved."——But he did not see the deep thoughts of God in these trying scenes, and perhaps he had not yet fully learned how wise and safe it is to trust Almighty God to bring out his own results in his own way! He will learn more by and by.

Events thicken; the final consummation hastens on. They are in Egypt again and stand before Joseph. His quick eye sees his beloved brother Benjamin among them. At once he gives orders to the ruler of his house to prepare a dinner for all these men and to bring them all into his house. A deeper fear seizes upon them: what, say they, can this mean? What new charges, what prosecutions, what fresh dangers, are coming now? They meet the Steward at the door and tell him their story about the returned money. The recognition of God in his reply seems strange for an Egyptian—unless we suppose that Joseph had given him the words. He said, "Peace be to you; fear not; your God and the God of your fathers hath given you treasure in your sacks. I had your money" (Gen. 43: 23). "And he brought Simeon out to them"—which might well have given some relief to their burdened hearts.——The dinner hour approaches; they are to eat with the lord of the land. They get their presents ready; and when Joseph appeared "they bowed themselves to him to the earth." The historian is careful to mention this for its bearing as the fulfillment of that long past dream of the boy Joseph. With the true politeness of profound sincerity Joseph inquires about his father: "Is your father well—the old man of whom ye spake? Is he yet alive?" "And they answered: Thy servant our father is in good health; he is yet alive; and [again] they bowed down their heads and made obeisance."——Now his eye falls on Benjamin, his own mother's son, and he asks—"Is this your younger brother of whom ye spake unto me? God be gracious unto thee my son."——Ah, but Joseph's heart is too full; "he made haste, for his bowels did yearn upon his brother; and he sought where to weep, and he entered into his chamber and wept there." But the time has not come yet to reveal himself; the searching ordeal through which he must needs make his brethren pass has not fully done its work; so Joseph washes off the tears; refrains himself from shedding more, and orders the food set on. The brethren of Joseph had probably a rather pleasant time—only it seemed strange to them that they were seated by age from the eldest to the youngest and Benjamin had a five-fold mess! How comes it that the lord of Egypt knows so much about us? They can not see.

They are getting ready now for home; their sacks are filled with corn again, and again the money is put back into each sack's mouth, and worst of all, Joseph's silver cup is slipped into the mouth of Benjamin's sack. Ere they are fairly out of the city Joseph posts his steward after them, abruptly charging them with having ungratefully stolen his lord's silver cup. Consciously innocent and deeply indignant, they are rash enough to say—Let the man in whose sack it is found die, and take all the rest of us for slaves! How were they amazed and overwhelmed when the cup was found in Benjamin's sack! They rent their clothes in bitterness of heart, and all return to the city. Judah comes to the front here; it is "Judah and his brethren" who come to Joseph's house, and Judah who makes the plea in behalf of Benjamin. The historian is careful to say again that when they met Joseph "they fell before him on the ground." He also remarks that Joseph was yet in his house, having remained there ever since the caravan left in the early morning, too full of thought on this subject to turn to any other business.——Now he expects to learn how they feel toward Benjamin and toward their aged father. He must be sure they are all right on these points before he lifts the vail and shows them himself.——They are brought back as criminals before him. With a sternness that is not at all in his heart but in his assumed manner only, he says—What deed is this that ye have done? Were ye not aware that I have the power of positive and certain divination?——Judah is in deep perplexity—but he speaks frankly: "What shall we say unto my lord? or how shall we clear ourselves? God hath found out the iniquity of thy servants"—which words can not, it would seem, refer to any iniquity in the matter of the silver cup, but must have referred to the long past crime of the brethren toward Joseph. He can not say less than that they will all become the slaves of Joseph, all including even Benjamin.——No, replies Joseph; I want only the guilty man, Benjamin; all the rest of you may go in peace to your father!——Now the crisis so long dreaded has come. A terrible responsibility falls upon Judah. With wonderful simplicity, with most touching filial affection toward his father, and with masterly skill he rises to the moral sublimity of the occasion. He comes near to Joseph and begins his great plea. Every reader must study it. We shall need to go far to find more touching eloquence, a more masterly setting forth of the facts of the case including the whole story from the beginning to the end. The case of the aged father and of his two younger sons left him by his best beloved wife—put in the aged patriarch's own words—ran thus: "Ye know that my wife bear me two sons, and the one went out from me, and I said—Surely he is torn in pieces, and I have not seen him since; and if ye take this also from me, and mischief befall him, ye shall bring down my gray hairs with sorrow to the grave. Now therefore when I come to thy servant my father and the lad be not with us; (seeing that his life is bound up in the lad's life)—when he shall see that the lad is not with us he will die; and thy servants will bring down the gray hairs of our father with sorrow to the grave. I said to him, If I bring not Benjamin back, I will bear the blame forever. Now therefore I pray thee, let me abide instead of Benjamin, the bond-servant of my lord, and let him go back to his father. For how shall I go to my father and the lad be not with me? Lest peradventure I see the evil that shall come on my father."——This was more than Joseph could bear. He could refrain himself no longer; the tears would come; the swelling emotions must have vent. Joseph cried: "Have every man away from me save these men of Canaan." The proof of their love to their aged father and to Benjamin is unmistakable; Joseph is satisfied. They are penitent for their long past crime against him, and he can therefore at length break the secret and show himself their long lost brother! How do their ears tingle as they hear him say—"I am Joseph: Doth my father yet live?"——The first shock is almost stunning: they can not answer him, for they are troubled at his presence. More kind words and the kindest possible manner are now in place. "Joseph said to his brethren, Come near to me, I pray you; and they came near." Again he says—"I am Joseph, *your brother*, whom ye sold into Egypt." Then with a turn which evinces the exquisite tenderness of his heart, he begs them "not to be grieved nor angry with themselves;" but to think rather of the design of God in permitting and providentially shaping this wonderful series of events. "God did send me before you to preserve life. There are five more years of famine yet to come; God sent me before you to preserve you a posterity in the earth and to save your lives by a great deliverance. So now it was not you that sent me hither, but God." The best thing he could say under just those circumstances to soothe their mind, to assure them of his full forgiveness and to give them consolation in place of the agitation, fear, and remorse that so nearly overwhelmed their spirits.

Arrangements for the future are soon made. Joseph

assures them that the best of Egypt's land shall be given them, and insists that they hasten home and bring their aged father and their little ones—every thing they have—down to Egypt, because five more years of famine are to follow. Egyptian wagons—unknown to Jacob's household—are sent, and the brethren are hastened off. Were they not a happy band? The great agony of fear is past; the surgings of anxiety and solicitude have ceased; the pungent convictions of that dread crime long ago against their younger brother have done their work, and wrought out "the peaceable fruits of righteousness." This is a wonderful crisis in their life history. Let us hope that most if not all of them found God through these fiery trials and these penitent tears!

They are home again. The first thing is to break this strange secret to their father. They make just two points: "Joseph yet alive;" "Joseph Governor over all the land of Egypt." It was too much—was too good to be believed. The English version has it, "Jacob's heart fainted." Better—"Jacob's heart *remained cold*, for he believed them not." It stirred no joyous and warm emotions, for he could not believe it. But when they told him all the words of Joseph, and especially when he saw the wagons which Joseph had sent to carry him, then his spirit rose; his heart waxed warm; he said: "*It is enough;* Joseph my son *is* yet alive; I will go and see him before I die."

Beersheba, the old home of his father Isaac, lay on his route. He stopped there and offered sacrifice to the God of his father Isaac. The night following the Lord met him in vision, saying, "I am thy God and the God of thy father; fear not to go down into Egypt, for I will there make of thee a great nation: I will go down with thee into Egypt and will bring thee up again; and Joseph shall put his hand upon thine eyes"—*i. e.* to close them in death.——How tenderly appreciative of the circumstances and of Jacob's need was this vision of Beersheba! Such are God's blessed ways with his children. He can not send them into scenes of special danger or of critical interest, without some special manifestations of his presence.

II. We are to notice *the hand of God* in this history in its twofold bearings:

1. As active in the sufferings and moral trial of the virtuous;

2. As manifested in his overruling control of the wicked to bring forth from their wickedness abounding good.

1. As active in the sufferings and moral trial of the virtuous.——The most cursory reader of this story will see in it a striking case of the sufferings of innocence. Joseph, envied and hated for no fault of his; coming near to being murdered by his own brothers, and really sold into slavery—a slavery prospectively life-long and in a distant, unknown land; torn away from every thing dear in *home*, at the age of seventeen:—this surely was innocence subjected to the sternest suffering.

How do such things happen under the government of God? When they do happen, *what do they prove?*

a. Negatively: They prove that all the suffering in this world *can not be retribution for sin*. There may be great suffering which can not in any true sense be the punishment of great crime. The greatest sufferers are not necessarily and always the greatest sinners. Suffering is not graduated to crime.——This lesson Job's three friends were slow to learn. Even Job himself seems not to have learned it thoroughly, but was groping toward it, under the lessons of his own conscious experience. It may not be amiss to suggest here that Job and his friends reasoned *without the light* which this history of Joseph would have given them if they had ever heard or read it. They either lived *before Joseph*, or too remote from these scenes to hear or in any way learn the lessons they teach.

b. Positively this case illustrates some of the ends which God aims to secure by permitting the sufferings of the good; *e. g.* to discipline them to patience under suffering, and to trust in God in the midst of darkness and in spite of it. Joseph's slavery and prison-life in Egypt would have been simply miserable without this patience and this trust in the Lord his God. Suppose he had given himself up to fretting and chafing and dashing his head against the strong walls of his prison and to wrenching off the fetters with which they "hurt his feet" (Ps. 105: 18);—What could have come of such adjustment of one's self to dark providences? Certainly not the sweet and blessed discipline which he did in fact get from his afflictions; certainly not the favor and the blessing of his God. Every thing in the future as before his eye was dark enough; but he knew there was a God of loving kindness above—a God who made no mistakes, yet whose purposes were often too deep for afflicted man to fathom, and therefore a God whom his children should learn to trust as certainly doing *all things* well.

Again; the case serves to reveal God's pity and his love in that he *goes with* his children into their slave-life and into their prison-life with such smiles of favor, such tokens of his presence, as may well make them joyful in the most terrible affliction. As Paul and Silas prayed and sang praises within the cold, desolate walls of a prison while yet smarting under the Roman scourge, and with perhaps some prospect of sufferings more severe when another day should dawn; so Joseph found the Lord with him when he reached Egypt a slave; with him when cast into prison because he virtuously repelled a foul temptation to crime. God was there, proving to his servant Joseph that no surroundings are so dark that God's manifested presence will not make them light—that no sufferings and no bereavements are so severe that God can not throw his smile upon the sufferer and fill his soul with overflowing joy!

Yet again; this lesson teaches that God uses means apparently rough and stern to prepare his servants for higher responsibilities and more signal blessings. We can not say what Joseph would have been if he had remained in the bosom of his doting father's home through all those years from seventeen to thirty, instead of being in God's school of suffering and trial; but it is safe to say that he made rapid strides forward in this school of God—in his knowledge of human nature; in his quick and manifest sympathy with every one in trouble; in his skill to gain the confidence of those about and above him; in his capacity for business; and not least in his living piety and his humble walk with God. His surroundings threw him roughly upon his own resources, and at the same time sweetly upon God's resources; and in consequence he rose, as few men have even been fit to rise, from slave-life and from prison-life, to be the actuary of a great kingdom—the almoner of bread and of life to the nations of the then civilized world; and also to become one of the most exalted and spotless characters of all history. Are not the ways of God truly wonderful?

The ways of God toward Jacob must not be overlooked. We need not debate the question how far his sufferings were those of innocence, and how far he was criminally responsible for the lack of moral culture and the power of fearful depravity in his sons. Be this as it may, it was hard for him to lose Joseph—the one son who was a comfort to his heart among so many who were quite otherwise. Even after thirteen years his heart seems still to be sore with that great sorrow, so that when his ten sons say that Benjamin must go with them to Egypt, he exclaims, "All these things are against me"! And when at length he is compelled to consent, his words indicate that he bows to an inexorable fate rather than yields in sweet trust to a divine hand believed to be wise and kind, though utterly and inexplicably mysterious;—"If I am bereaved of my children, I am bereaved."

Jacob lived to see the clouds of darkness lifted and rolled away. He lived to learn that all those things were *not against him* by any means, but were in fact shaped of God to save his great household alive through a seven years' famine; and (what is far more than even this)—were designed of God for the salvation of those sons of his whose wickedness had brought these sorrows upon him, and whom God had faithfully taken in hand to bring them to repentance. Had he not learned ere this that it was always safe to trust in his father's God? Had not the Lord said to him, "I will surely do thee good"? As to being "bereaved of his children," was not the covenant very definite: "A nation and a company of nations shall be of thee, and kings shall come out of thy loins"? (Gen. 35: 11).——This discipline of the aged patriarch was sharp but wholesome. He might have said, "In faithfulness hast thou afflicted me." The clouds of life's stormy day cleared before sunset. It would be pleasant to hear, if we might, the experiences of his closing years when he came to understand God's ways and to reap the blessed fruits of such chastening sorrows.

These methods and ends of God in the discipline and culture of his people *reach onward into eternity.* The faithful here are the rulers there (Mat. 25: 21). Those who take God's discipline kindly here and turn it to best account according to his thought and will, have their reward above. It is not needful that we know in their details what the heavenly responsibilities are, and what the dignities and the honors of those who have been faithful over a few things here; but we are safe in the belief that earthly discipline and culture are not lost attainments as to the after life.——As one short day transferred Joseph from the prison-house of the kingdom to the lordship of that kingdom, so one day is long enough for the transfer of many a humble, suffering saint of God from dungeons of darkness and pain to palaces of royalty and bliss. In the story of Joseph these great truths of God's administration with his people were breaking forth upon the minds of men by most interesting stages of progress.

2. From these lessons in God's ways with the righteous, we turn to other lessons pertaining to his *ways with the wicked.* This history of Joseph shows how skillfully and mightily God manages the wicked, making their wickedness work (wholly against *their* purpose) to evolve abounding good.

We have seen how Joseph directed the thought of his brethren to these ways and designs of God. "Be not angry with yourselves that ye sold me hither; for God did send me before you to preserve life." "So now it was not ye that sent me hither, but God" (Gen. 45: 5, 7, 8). And again seventeen years later, after Jacob's death, his brethren being apprehensive lest Joseph might then relapse into revenge, he said to them; "Fear not, for am I in the place of God? But as for you, ye thought evil against me; but God meant it for good, to bring to pass as it is this day, to save much people alive (Gen. 50: 19, 20). We should quite under-estimate Joseph's knowledge of human nature and his sense of moral distinctions if we were to press his

GOD OVERRULES SIN FOR GOOD. 159

words to mean that God's agencies in those crimes superseded theirs; lifted off their responsibilities and left them essentially faultless.——The reason why Joseph's remarks took this turn seems to have been this. He saw that conviction for sin had done its vital work in their souls; that they were apparently penitent and leaning toward the most severe self-condemnation—at a stage where it was both safe and kind to turn their attention to God's hand as evolving good from their sin. In so far as we can have confidence in Joseph's judgment as to their moral state, his words afford proof that his brethren were truly penitent, and at a stage where consolation might properly be suggested as some relief to their mental anguish.

The use which God made of the sin of Joseph's brethren exemplifies his consummate, far-reaching wisdom. He knew all the future. He saw the coming famine; knew how to advance Joseph to the lordship of all Egypt, and to put him there just in time to garner up the surplus of seven years of overflowing abundance, and then dispense these stores of corn for the sustenance of thousands less provident throughout all Egypt and all adjacent countries. The resources of God's providence, guided by such wisdom, are simply boundless. What can he not do when he wills to do it?——The case is equally demonstrative of his *love*. Mark how he bends the great powers of his infinite being to the production of good, to multiply the means of happiness. This view of his character is doubly, yea infinitely precious when studied in its developments in a world, or rather a universe, *with sin in it*. If the Lord were obliged to say—I must content myself with the co-operation of the good, the unfallen, turning their agency to best account for the promotion of happiness; but as to the wicked, they are beyond my reach; I can do nothing with them; the evil they do must be endured as so much dead loss to the universe, never to be of any service toward virtue and happiness—the case would be, so far, one of unrelieved sadness. We may bless the name of our God that his resources of wisdom and power and the outgoings of his love are not thus limited. No indeed; some good results will be extorted from even those horrible crimes of Joseph's brethren. Even the devil's wickedness in which he exults as availing to frustrate God's plans and to shake his throne, he will find at length to his everlasting confusion and shame, has been made, by the over-mastering wisdom, power, and love of God, to subserve the very cause he thought to break down, and to break down every thing he had vainly hoped to build up! For is not God wiser and mightier than the devil? The final result of the conflict will prove it.——But it is in place here to note that this story of Joseph's brethren and of God's over-ruling hand in their case was shedding some rays of light on these previously dark problems, and therefore was indicating progress in the revelations of God and of his ways with sinful men.

Nor let us overlook this one other point—that the case evinces the consummate skill of God in managing the free moral activities of men without the least infringement upon their free agency and moral responsibility. We see this in the way they went into their sin—purely of their own free purpose—after their own envious and proud heart, although God had purposes to answer by means of this very sin. We see it still more, if possible, in the means he used to bring them to repentance; how he put his great hook into their jaws and brought them down to Egypt; took the pride out of them; pressed them with one calamity after another till they came to feel very weak before Almighty God; aroused their long slumbering consciences and kept their thought upon that long past, almost forgotten crime against Joseph—till at length they seem to have become thoroughly penitent. Only by legitimate means and influences, and only by such a use of these as still left their moral activities under their own responsible control—were these grand results reached.——Thus we may take lessons in the masterly skill with which God's agencies interwork with man's, effective to the result he proposes because God is more and mightier than man.

III. Taking a broader range of view, we may next study the purposes of God *in locating the birth of the Hebrew nation in the land of Egypt.*

Since God's purposes never come to nought but are always accomplished perfectly, the ends he has in view being surely secured, it is safe to reason backward from known results to original purposes. It would amount practically to the same thing if we were to ask—What great results were actually secured by locating his people in Egypt when and as he did; by shaping their history as he did, and by bringing them out at length with his high hand and outstretched arm?

1. In answering these questions we may note that Egypt in that age stood at the summit of the world's civilization, a fully organized kingdom, a great and highly cultured people. There is most ample proof that Egypt was then eminent above any other nation in learning, wisdom, science, and art; in jurisprudence, and in the administration of law; in industry and in wealth; in short, in all the main appliances and results of a high civilization. The antiquities of Ancient Egypt are the marvel of our times. Her temples, pyramids, and obelisks; her paintings and works of art, have come down to our age in most wonderful preservation, living witnesses to her ancient greatness. There was no other kingdom on the face of the earth where a man like Moses could have been educated and trained to become the law-giver of the Hebrew nation, or where such a system of civil law as God gave his people by the hand of Moses could have taken its rise and could have been understood, accepted, appreciated, and ultimately wrought into established usage and into the national life. We shall have occasion in its place to inquire how far the civil system given through Moses was borrowed from the Egyptian Code, and consequently how far the scenes of their Egyptian life prepared the way for the new national life instituted in the wilderness.

2. The plan of transferring his people from their nomadic, pastoral life in Canaan, to a settled residence in Egypt provided scope for all those developments which we have been studying in the history of Jacob, Joseph, and his brethren.

3. Yet more and greater developments of God's mighty hand were provided for in the deliverance of his people from their bondage in Egypt; in his judgments on Pharaoh and his land; in the destruction of his hosts in the Red Sea; in the wilderness life of Israel during forty years; and at length in their location in the land of promise. All these points will come under review in their order.

IV. *Some notice should be taken of ancient Egypt as affording confirmation to the historic accuracy and truthfulness of Moses in Genesis.*

1. Moses assumes that Egypt had a king and a fully organized government. The evidence of this from Egyptian history and antiquities is too abundant and accessible to need citation.

2. Also that the people subsisted mainly by agriculture, not pasturage; that their soil was exceedingly fertile and the country one of great wealth. The facts on these points also are beyond question. The Nile has always made Egypt rich in soil and in agricultural productions. Its periodical inundations have sustained the fertility of that valley for thousands of years. Alternations of years of plenty with years of famine have been their common experience in all ages, though probably never so extreme and protracted as in the age of Joseph.

3. The history by Moses records the fact that in the early stages of this great famine the lands passed over largely to the crown, but were leased to the farmers for a certain portion (one-fifth) of the crops (Gen. 47: 20-26).——Testimony from sources other than sacred proves these points. Herodotus was told by the priests of Egypt that the king gave each Egyptian laborer a square piece of land of equal extent and collected from each a yearly rent. Diodorus states that all the land of Egypt belonged either to the king, the priests, or the military caste. Strabo says that the farmers and tradesmen held their lands subject to rent. In the Egyptian sculptures as shown by Wilkinson, only kings, priests, and the military orders are represented as land-owners. [See "Hengstenberg and the Books of Moses," pp. 62-70.]

4. The history by Moses makes an important exception in the case of the priests. Being supported directly from the royal treasury, they were not obliged to alienate their lands during the great famine and consequently continued to hold them (Gen. 47: 22). With this all profane testimony concurs.

5. This fact implies an organized priesthood as a favored and therefore powerful class in Egyptian society. Egyptian history confirms this and shows more-

over that they were not merely priests, performing religious functions, but were the learned and scientific men of the nation; had charge of education; held in their body the art and the "wisdom" of the nation and performed largely the administrative functions of government. "The thirty judges (says Drumann) priests of Heliopolis, Thebes, and Memphis, were maintained by the king, and without doubt, the sons of the priests also, all of whom over twenty years of age were given to the king as servants; or, more correctly, to take the oversight of his affairs." "The ministers of the court were in Egypt the priests, just as the state was a Theocracy, and the king was considered as the representative and incarnation of the Godhead." (Hengstenberg, p. 68).——It was by virtue of this usage that Joseph married into the class of the priesthood, Asenath his wife being a daughter of Potipherah priest of On (Gen. 41:50).——The reader will perhaps recall the striking analogy between the Egyptian system and the Hebrew Theocracy, particularly in the point that the ministers of religion were also ministers of civil law and prominent in its administration. The judges in the civil courts were taken chiefly from the tribe of Levi.

6. Joseph's arraignment of his brethren—"Ye are spies; to see the nakedness of the land are ye come"—suggests an inquiry into the relations of Egypt to foreign powers. The suspicions of Joseph obviously assume a consciousness of great liability to foreign invasion. Such was the fact; and the reasons for it will readily appear. We have only to think of the powerful tribes scattered over vast Arabia, the Hittites and other tribes of Canaan and of the regions North and East—all stalwart men, all poor and subsisting on precarious supplies, yet possessed of fleet animals—horses, dromedaries, camels—with which they were able to move masses of men with great celerity. Let such men see the tempting bait of corn in plenty in Egypt, and the marvel is how Egypt could protect herself against sudden and formidable invasion. The monuments of her early history testify to her long and bloody wars with the Hittites and other tribes of Western Asia, often carrying the war into their country as a wiser policy no doubt than to stand behind her own walls on the defensive. Suffice it to say here that

when those Asiatic countries were famishing for bread and it was well known there was corn enough in Egypt, the suspicion expressed by Joseph that those ten men were spies was not only natural but perhaps even a necessary measure of policy to satisfy the Egyptians. *They* must naturally apprehend danger though *he* might personally know that these men were harmless.

7. Sacred history drops this incidental remark—"For every shepherd is an abomination to the Egyptians" (Gen. 46: 34). To some extent this feeling was a natural outgrowth of their relations to the nomadic tribes of South-western Asia—to which we have recently referred. But there is some reason to suppose among them a certain special antipathy against the sheep, more intense than against any other domestic animal unless swine be an exception. They had so much respect for the cow that they made her and her species objects of worship. Although they attained great skill in the manufacture of linen, cotton, and silk, I meet with no allusion to wool. Woolen cloths are never found upon Egyptian mummies; linen and cotton were used.——Some writers have supposed that shepherds were held in special abhorrence because their country had been conquered and ruled by a dynasty of shepherd kings from the North-east; but the precise date of their invasion and of their rule over Egypt is very much in doubt.

8. Both Joseph and his father were embalmed after death (Gen. 50: 2, 3, 26)—a service performed by the physicians. The antiquities of Egypt furnish most conclusive testimony to their skill in this art—a skill far surpassing that of any other people known to history. Great numbers of those embalmed bodies ("mummies") have been found in Egyptian tombs within the present century, in perfect preservation. On this point the coincidences between sacred and profane history are striking.——The practice was very ancient, some mummies bearing the date of the oldest kings. It was performed by a special class of physicians. In harmony with Moses, Herodotus and Diodorus state that the embalming process occupied forty days; the entire period of mourning seventy. Classic authorities give accounts similar to those in Gen. 50 of great

mourning for the dead. The monuments contain representations to the same effect. Funeral trains, processions, of such sort as Gen. 50 records, are represented abundantly in the oldest tombs at Elithias, also at Sagguarah, at Gizeh, and at Thebes. (Hengstenberg's Egypt and Moses, pp. 70-78).——A coincidence so minute as this is noticed; that mourners forbore to shave their hair or beard; but none might appear befor the king unshorn. Consequently we observe that in the mourning scene of Gen. 50, Joseph does not come before the king in person but "spake unto the house of Pharaoh" requesting them to speak in his behalf to the king (Gen. 50: 4-6).

Quite in contrast with the usual oriental custom, women were exempt from seclusion and moved in society with apparently entire freedom. This appears in the family of Potiphar. The ancient sculptures and paintings found in their tombs give a very full view of the domestic life of the ancient Egyptians, no point of which is more striking than the high social position of woman and the entire absence of the harem system of seclusion. "The wife is called the lady of the house." (See Smith's Bible Dictionary, p. 677). According to the monuments the women in Egypt lived under far less restraint than in the East, or even in Greece. Wilkinson's Egypt is full of testimony to this point (Vol. II, p. 389). Hengstenberg's Moses, p. 24.

Sad to say there is abundant evidence from profane sources of a very lax morality among married women— of which the history of Joseph in Potiphar's house is an illustration. Herodotus gives a fact in point: "The wife of one of the earliest kings was untrue to him. It was a long time before a woman could be found who was faithful to her husband. When at last one was found, the king took her without hesitation for his wife."

Yet other points might be adduced of coincidence between the sacred and the profane records of Egypt as the former appear in Moses. The above may be taken as specimens. Most amply do they testify that the author of Genesis was entirely familiar with Egyptian life and manners. The sharpest and most unfriendly criticism has hitherto detected no point of discrepancy between these respective records—no point in which it

Some special passages occurring in these latter chapters of Genesis should receive attention.

Jacob going down into Sheol to his son Joseph.

In Gen. 37 : 35 Jacob, supposing Joseph to be dead, says—"I will go down into the grave (Sheol) to my son mourning." The reader of the Hebrew text of Genesis has not met with this word before, and may reasonably expect to see its meaning discussed here.

In the outset it should be observed that these words can not possibly mean—My dead body shall go down into the grave proper, the sepulcher—there to lie by the side of Joseph's dead body. He could not have meant this because the place of Joseph's supposed dead body was entirely unknown to him. He had seen his bloody coat and inferred that Joseph was no doubt torn in pieces; *where*, he knew not; and whether devoured by flesh-eating animals he could not know. We must therefore reject this construction of his words.—— Plainly the Joseph he thought of was the undying soul. He expected at his own death to meet Joseph in that state or place which the Hebrews indicated by the word "Sheol."

What is the primary significance of this word? What were the views of the ancient Hebrews in regard to its location and the state of its occupants?

The noun "Sheol" is made from the verb Shaal * having the sense, to ask, to demand; and conceives of the place as evermore demanding, insatiable; that which is never full; never has enough. The current Hebrew conceptions of the word may be seen in Prov. 30: 15, 16, and Isa. 5: 14, and Hab. 2: 5. "There are three things that are never satisfied; yea four say not, It is enough: the grave" [Sheol], etc.——"Therefore hell [Sheol] hath enlarged herself and opened her mouth without measure; and their glory, and their multitude and their pomp, and he that rejoiceth shall descend

* שאל

into it." " Who enlargeth his desire as hell " [Sheol] and is as Death, and can not be satisfied," etc.

As to the location of Sheol it seems clear that they thought of it as an *under-world*, as somehow beneath the surface of the earth. We see this in the case of Korah and his company (Num. 16: 28–34), of whom Moses said:—" If the earth open her mouth and swallow them up with all that appertain to them, and they *go down* alive into Sheol [Eng. " the pit "], then shall ye understand that these men have provoked the Lord " . . . . " As he had made an end of speaking these words, the ground clave asunder that was under them and the earth opened her mouth and swallowed them up," etc.——We find the same view in Deut. 32: 22. "For a fire is kindled in mine anger and shall burn unto the lowest hell [Sheol], and shall consume the earth with her increase and set on fire the foundations of the mountains."

In regard to their conceptions of Sheol as a state of being for the righteous and the wicked dead, it is easy to see that holy men of the oldest time lacked the clear light of the gospel age. Then it had not yet been said—" In my father's house are many mansions "; " I go to prepare a place for you, and I will come again and receive you to myself that where I am, there ye may be also (Jno. 14: 2, 3). They had not heard these words of Jesus—" This day shalt thou be with me in paradise " (Luke 23: 43); nor those of Paul: " Having a desire to depart and to be with Christ which is far better " (Phil. 1: 23).——But the patriarchs did expect to "be gathered to their people"—the good men who had gone on before. This is said of Abraham (Gen. 25: 8); of Ishmael (25: 17); of Isaac (35: 29); and of Jacob (49: 29, 33). David said of his deceased infant child: " I shall go to him, but he shall not return to me." Job said of that little known world—" There the wicked cease from troubling, and there the weary are at rest " (Job 3: 17), and yet he sometimes thought of it as intensely dark, for gospel light had not then fallen upon it :—" Before I go whence I shall not return, even to a land of darkness and the shadow of death; a land of darkness as darkness itself; and of the shadow of death without any order, and where the light is as darkness " (Job 10: 21, 22). Conceptions of this state as well illustrating the full and doom of wicked kings and kingdoms, tinged, it would seem, with the spirit of poetry, may be seen in Isaiah 14, and Ezek. 31: 15–18.

How far these notions as to the locality of Sheol are to be ascribed to direct inspiration, and how far to a merely human speculation, following the leading thought that the body *goes down* and back to dust at death, it seems by no means easy to determine positively. We may be allowed to doubt whether the Lord intended to reveal definitely the *location* of human souls after death. It was a point of the least conceivable importance; and moreover our knowledge of celestial geography may be yet quite too limited to admit of any intelligible revelation on this point.

Jacob's benedictions upon his sons on his death-bed—more or less prophetic—present some points that call for special notice. Remarkably they seem in most if not in all cases to start from the then existing present, and to build their allusions to the future upon it. We see it in the case of Reuben—noted for his outrage of his father's nuptial bed; of Simeon and Levi, whose history suggested their cruelty toward the men of Shechem; of Judah, whose name bore the thought of *praise* and whose record in the case of Joseph put him at once in the front among his brethren; of Joseph, whose relations to his father and indeed to all the family had been surpassingly precious. The special address of Jacob to each of these was closely linked to their past history. The prophetic feature in all these cases seems to have been suggested by these salient points of their history. Reuben as the first-born might have kept his supremacy—if he had been worthy of it—but he was not. Simeon never rose to any distinction, and scarcely held any well-defined territory in Canaan. Levi came into prominence as the ancestor of Aaron and of Moses, and redeemed himself also by the religious zeal and energy of Phineas in a great emergency during the wilderness life (Num. 26: 6–13). The tribe were scattered in Israel, yet not in the bad sense. Judah and Joseph had each a future more resplendent and distinguished than any other of the twelve—their prominence in Jacob's benediction being fully carried out through the history of their nation.

Some special passages and phrases should be briefly explained.

In v. 4, the phrase, "Unstable as water," does not compare water to the solid earth or to more solid rock as treacherous to the foot and unsafe to stand on; but rather as bubbling, effervescing under heat or applied force—as therefore a fit image of ungoverned passion; of wantonness, impatient of restraint. Reuben had no moral stamina, and therefore could not hold his natural place of headship as the first-born—a moral lesson worthy of thoughtful consideration. A young man given to licentious indulgence can have no solid bottom to his character. The sagacious will never trust him.

v. 5. "Simeon and Levi are brethren"—of kindred spirit; "instruments of cruelty are in their habitation"; better, instruments of cruelty their swords are. Most solemnly does the dying patriarch disavow all sympathy with their cruelty!——The phrase—"Mine honor" in the sense of myself—my nobler powers—is specially significant here, for their spirit was dishonorable, treacherous, basely cruel. Jacob had a sense of honor which utterly forbade all sympathy with them in this thing.——In the last clause of v. 6, the English margin gives the sense of the Hebrew: "They houghed oxen." They slew not one man only but man as a species; and cut the hamstrings of their cattle.

The benediction upon Judah (v. 10) stands unrivaled in importance and is not without difficulty. The main question is whether the word "Shiloh" signifies the Messiah, in the special sense of the Peace-giving One; or refers to the city of that name in Canaan. If it refers to the Messiah, the sense, the application and the fulfillment of the passage are facile and truly rich—thus: Judah shall head the tribes and give them kings until the Great Messiah shall come: then all the nations (Gentile and Jew) shall obey him—obedience rather than "gathering" being the best established sense of the word. It occurs elsewhere only in Prov. 30: 17.

No facts of Jewish history are better known than these—that Judah led the march through the wilderness, and that from David to Christ the scepter was in Judah—until the Messiah came, when it dropped from his hand. "We have a law," (said the Jewish Sanhedrim in the age of Christ) "and by our law he ought to die"—*i. e.* for blasphemy. But under their law, capital punishment was by stoning (Lev. 24: 15, 16, and Mat. 26: 65, 66, and Jno. 19: 7). Having lost the power of life and death over criminals, they were compelled to take the case to the Roman authorities. *Their* mode of capital punishment was crucifixion. Thus the "cross" stands through all the ages to prove that the scepter had departed from Judah and that the Messiah had come.——But he came not only to die but to reign, and the nations of the wide earth are to bow to his scepter.——Such is the construction of this passage, provided the term "Shiloh" refers to the Messiah.

That it does refer to him may be argued on two grounds:

(a.) This construction is facile, natural, and supported by analogous prophecies;

(b.) The other which makes Shiloh the name of a town in Canaan, labors under serious, not to say insurmountable difficulties.

(a.) "Shiloh" is derived readily from the verb Shalah,* kindred with Shalam, both words being in frequent use in the sense of being at peace and in rest; expressing good wishes for peace—*i. e.* for all prosperity—the noun from which might naturally mean the author of peace, as we see in Mic. 5: 4. Furthermore, this distinctive feature of the Messiah's character and mission is the theme of Ps. 72 and of many passages in Isaiah, *e. g.* 9: 6, 7, and 11: 1–10, and 60: 18–22. These prophecies naturally follow the lead of this and therefore sustain the construction here given it.

Moreover, it is natural and highly probable that Jacob whose twelve sons were to found the twelve tribes of Israel and who knew that the Messiah was to come in the line of *some one* of his sons, should indicate which. Noah had designated Shem: God had designated Abraham, Isaac, and Jacob; now the choice is naturally made out of these twelve. That the long promised Seed was in Jacob's thought is forcibly and beauti-

*שלה

fully suggested in the midst of these dying benedictions by the words—"I have waited for thy salvation, O Lord" (49:18). In the sustaining hope of a coming Savior he had waited and trusted through many long years; for these words express the precious experiences of a life. As Jesus himself testified of Abraham, "He rejoiced to see my day," hailing it joyously from afar, so Jacob witnesses of himself, "I have waited for thy salvation, O Lord."

(b.) Those who give "Shiloh" here the geographical sense argue that in every other case of its use in scripture, it refers to the town of that name. This name for a town appears first in Josh. 18: 1, 8, 10, and often subsequently in Judges, 1 Sam., etc. But there is no evidence that in Jacob's day it had come into use in geography. This usage, so far as appears, was long subsequent. Nothing forbids, therefore, that Jacob should use it simply for its significance—the Peace-giving One.

Again, the most marked supremacy of Judah began *after* the nation had reached Shiloh. It is therefore bad history and very inept prophecy to represent Judah as holding the scepter *until* the nation came to Shiloh; the fact being that he had not held it in the full sense previously to reaching Shiloh, but did hold it for many centuries after Shiloh had lost its pre-eminence as the religious capital. I see therefore no good ground for setting aside the Messianic interpretation of this passage. The argument in its defense is ably and fully drawn out by Keil in his Commentary, and yet more fully by Hengstenberg in his Christology, vol. 1. pp. 50–63.

The less readable portions of Genesis.

We have passed several portions of Genesis with little or no notice; *e. g.* the genealogical tables, and some of the less important sketches of family and tribal history; *e. g.* that of Abraham's sons by Keturah; of Ishmael, Esau, Laban, etc.

Of these less readable passages, let it be noted:

1. They are such as never could find place in a tale of fiction, gotten up in some later age to interest and amuse the reader. The fact that nobody finds interest

and amusement in reading them now proves conclusively that no writer of fiction could possibly have concocted such chapters from his own fancy and have foisted them into a professedly ancient history. The men who forge books of fiction to pass them off as truthful history are careful not to put in unreadable chapters—void of rational or even imaginative interest to the men of after ages.

2. Consequently these passages are incontrovertible proof of the genuineness and real antiquity of these writings. In their time they had interest—just that interest which attaches to sober truth: none more or other than this.

3. The Scriptures were written with special adaptation to their first readers, and must include therefore those matters which had real value and interest *to them*, whether they would continue to have interest and value many thousand years onward or not. This fact, often overlooked, has many important bearings.

4. By far the greater portion of these historic books has a permanent interest and value to us and will have to their readers through all future ages. We see in these ancient books not only the earliest developments of human nature in the primitive society of the race, but also the earliest manifestations of God to men, and can trace their progressive unfoldings step by step age after age by new methods and with clearer light as we move on toward the great era when God became manifest in human flesh.

5. It may well reconcile us to the annoyance (if such it be) of some unreadable portions that precisely these above all others afford us the strongest evidence of the genuineness and high antiquity of these entire books. They constitute an internal mark of antiquity and genuineness which by the laws of human nature never could be counterfeited. The man who should attempt to counterfeit such proofs that his fiction is true history would not prove himself very sharp save in the skill of spoiling his book and frustrating the only conceivable object of a fiction—for the sake of what?

We lay down Genesis, profoundly impressed that this oldest volume of human history is unsurpassed in simplicity and beauty, and wonderfully rich in its revelations both of man and of his Maker.

CHAPTER XII.

EXODUS.

This second book of the Pentateuch takes its modern name from its principal event, the exodus of the Hebrew people—their marching forth out of their house of bondage from the land of their oppression, to be replanted under God's gracious providence in the goodly land promised to their fathers.——This one main event as recorded in this book includes many subordinate points, *e. g.*

I. The *oppressions* of the Hebrews by the Egyptians.

II. *Moses*, who became in the hand of God their great Deliverer; his history; his early training and his call from the Lord to this great work.

III. *The great mission of Moses to Egypt's king;* his reception; the ten successive plagues—miraculous judgments from the hand of God; the case of the magicians; the hardening of Pharaoh's heart, and the ultimate result.

I. *The Oppression.*

The narrative shows that this oppression consisted in part in the exacting of terribly severe labors, especially in building, including the making of brick, the preparation of mortar, the transportation of these materials, and the erection of buildings. The ancient monuments of Egypt confirm the statements of sacred history, showing that the Egyptians employed national bondmen in the construction of their vast national works; that they placed over them task-masters; that when the workmen fell short of the required tale of brick, their masters put them to more severe labors, and in some cases to labors of other sort. It has been supposed by some that the ancient paintings represented some of these laborers with the well-known physiognomy of the Hebrews.

It should be noted that this bondage differed from the slavery of modern times in this one respect—that the bondmen were held by the king and the nation in their national capacity and not by individuals. The Hebrews were not held as private but as public property. The king and the nation as such bore therefore the responsibility and guilt of this oppression, and God let his judgments smite them for the most part in such a way as to indicate their sin.

A second feature in this oppression was the king's cruel edict to murder the male infants. This was first enjoined upon the Hebrew midwives. Fearing God more than Egypt's king, they evaded obedience; whereupon the king commanded all his people to cast the male infants into the river.——The reason assigned for both these measures was *public policy*, to prevent the rapid increase of Hebrew population which the king assumed might be dangerous to his throne and people in case of a foreign invasion. Such a policy is at once short-sighted and wicked; short-sighted, since kind treatment would have made this rapidly growing people their fast friends and helpers; wicked, because it violates common morality, insulting God, and provoking his wrath by outraging all the obligations which he imposes on men toward their fellows. Egypt's king and court presently found themselves arrayed against Almighty God and saw him take up the challenge in a fearful conflict for mastery. We shall see in the final issue that the Lord improved this occasion to illustrate some of the noblest principles of his government over nations and indeed over individuals as well, showing that he abhors oppression; takes the side of the oppressed; hurls his fiercest thunderbolts against giant oppressors in every age; and every-where holds men to the responsibility of using their power to befriend and not to oppress their human brethren.

This oppression began with "a new king over Egypt who knew not Joseph." It is generally held that these words indicate a new dynasty—one royal line superseded by another, perhaps a foreign power coming in to supplant the former dynasty. The points of historic contact between Egyptian and Hebrew chronology may at some future day be adjusted with reasonable certainty. They are not yet. The subject is undergoing a somewhat thorough investigation with some prospect of ultimate success. At present I am not prepared to express positive opinions.

Two of the disputed periods in Hebrew chronology are necessarily involved;

(a.) The period of the Judges, which as shown above some reduce to 339 years; others extend to 450;

(b.) The period of the sojourn in Egypt, made by some 215 years; by others, 430. Some of the theories which attempt to locate this new king of Egypt in his relation to Hebrew history place the Exodus about B. C. 1600; others B. C. 1491. Some put the commencement of the sojourn in Egypt B. C. 2030; others B. C. 1706; yet others B. C. 1815. I have given my reasons for adopting the longer periods. It is possible that Egyptian authorities may yet throw a strong influence upon the decision of these much disputed points of Hebrew chronology.

The narrative shows that the Hebrews had become numerically strong and were rapidly growing stronger. Joseph had been dead probably a considerable time and all the men of his generation. Being 39 years old when his father came into Egypt and dying at the age of 110, he lived to protect his people 71 years. Moses was 80 years old when he came before Pharaoh, bearing the command of the Almighty—" Let my people go." It is probable that the terrible edict to destroy all the male infants did not long precede the birth of Moses. The interval between the death of Joseph and the birth of Moses will depend on the duration of the entire sojourn in Egypt, since from this entire sojourn we must subtract the years of Joseph's life after the sojourn began and the years of Moses before it closed, *i. e.* $71 + 80 = 151$. This sum must be subtracted either from 215, leaving 64; or from 430, leaving 279. The latter I assume to be the true period. It provides abundantly for the great increase of the Hebrew people, and accounts for the fear felt by Egypt's "new king."

II. Moses.

We shall study the history of Moses without *the key* if we overlook the point made by the writer to the Hebrews (11: 23): " *By faith* Moses when he was born was hid three months because they saw that he was a proper child, and they were not afraid of the king's commandment." Faith in God made them fearless of Egypt's cruel king. It would seem also that they saw in the peculiar beauty of this child a sort of prophecy of his future, something at least which raised expectation and put them upon special ventures to save his life. Three months they secreted him within their home. When this expedient could suffice no longer, they prepared an ark of bulrushes—a little box, water-tight, constructed to float—and moored it with its treasure among the flags on the river's bank. We may suppose that his mother knew the spot where the king's daughter was wont to take her baths, and that her faith and prayer lay back of this venture to throw her darling infant upon the compassion of a stranger woman's heart. It need not be supposed that she foresaw his future adoption into the royal family, his training for forty years in all the wisdom of the Egyptians, and his consequent qualification to become the great Hebrew Law-giver and Deliverer. Suffice it that these results lay in the thought of God. She had faith enough to commit her darling to God's care and to leave all the future unknown results to his adjustment.

The ways of God were mercifully kind toward this Hebrew mother. She stationed his elder sister as a sentinel to watch the issue, and then (let us presume) gave herself to prayer. When this elder sister with palpitating heart saw the daughter of Pharaoh take the beautiful child to her bosom, she felt that her time had come. Modestly advancing, she said, "Shall I go and call to thee a nurse of the Hebrew women that she may nurse the child for thee"? Pharaoh's daughter said, Go. How joyfully did she go and call the child's own mother! God's finger was there. The mother's faith has come up as sweet incense before Him and her heart is made glad, as only a praying mother's can be. There was no occasion to tell us that she consecrated this child to Israel's God for any service he might have for him in his after life. Such a mother, drawn by her sweet faith into such relationship to God, could do nothing less. Moreover, this was no barren consecration—was not a vow once made and soon forgotten. Nothing can be more certain than that she cared diligently for the moral training and culture of this marvelously saved son. Else how could it happen that "when he was come to years, he refused to be called the son of Pharaoh's daughter; choosing rather to suffer affliction with the people of God than to enjoy the pleasures of sin for a season; esteeming reproach for Christ greater riches than all the treasures of Egypt, for he had respect to the recompense of the reward" (Heb. 11: 24–26)? The seeds of this world-conquering faith must have been dropped early into his tender mind. This hired Hebrew nurse, permitted to come into the royal palace by some back-way, was indulged this privilege freely, we know not precisely how long; but let us presume that the same faith and prayer kept this door open, at least for her occasional visits in his future years. How many testimonies of God's love to the fathers of their nation she dropped into his youthful ear; how much she told him of God as "the exceeding great reward" of his believing people; how well she put the contrast between "the treasures of Egypt" and the treasures laid up for God's then persecuted people:—these points are rather left to our inference than definitely stated; but we may be very sure that the faith of Moses took hold of these grand truths of then extant revelation; fixed its hold early; and held fast through all his future life.

We have three co-ordinate narratives of the early years of Moses: that given in Heb. 11: 24–27, very brief, and touching only its specially religious side; while that of Stephen (Acts 7: 20–29) is full, even somewhat more full than the narrative in Ex. 2: 10–15. Particularly Stephen adds that Moses was "learned in all the wisdom of the Egyptians and mighty in words and in deeds"—a man like Joseph of immense efficiency:—also that he was "full forty years old" when it came into his heart to visit his brethren the children of Israel—a statement which shows that he distinctly recognized this relationship of brethren. Seeing a brother Hebrew abused by an Egyptian he interposed, smote the Egyptian dead, and buried him in the sand. Stephen's words suggest that this was not merely one of those quick, spontaneous impulses felt by noble souls in view of outrageous wrong, but was a first step toward a contemplated career of interposed force for the rescue of his people from their oppression. "For he supposed his brethren would have understood how that God by his hand would deliver them; but they understood not" (Acts 7: 25). The whole of the fact seems to be that the Lord was not yet ready and had not fully prepared Moses for this great life-work of his yet, and certainly had not inaugurated him into it.*——Interposing the next day in a quarrel between two of his own Hebrew brethren, he learned that his slaying of the Egyptian was known, and immediately sought safety by flight to the land of Midian. The Lord had more objects than one in turning his steps thither; not only his then present safety, but the spiritual culture of so much solitude and of long-continued, unbroken communion with God and of long tried faith, coupled with the incidental advantage of becoming perfectly familiar with that great wilderness through which he was to lead the hosts of Israel for forty years.

Scarcely had he penetrated this desert land in his flight when he made the acquaintance of a priest of Midian [Jethro], and of his seven shepherdess daughters, one of whom became his wife. Like the somewhat similar experience of Abraham, falling in with the priest of Salem, Melchisedek, the circumstance suggests the inquiry how much of the true knowledge and worship of God existed in those early ages outside the line of Abraham's family. The historical traces of such piety are certainly very few, yet they recur so incidentally that we are justified in the hope that these cases are not exhaustive; stood not altogether alone. When we come to consider the history of Job we shall take occasion to observe that his location is certainly in this great region of Arabia, and that his date must in all probability have somewhat preceded this residence of Moses in the land of Midian. Here Moses may have found the story in a traditional form; may perhaps have seen Job's immediate descendants; may possibly have put the story in its present form as one of the pastimes of a literary shepherd's life; and then, retaining it in his possession during his subsequent years, may have himself solved the problem—How came this book in the archives of the Hebrew nation, on an equal footing as to inspired authority with their historical books?

*Many an American reader will be reminded of John Brown striking for the redemption of the American slave.

The Great Mission of Moses.

Of the second forty-year period in the life of Moses, little is reported save its first scenes and its last. Ex. 3 opens the latter. Moses is keeping the flock of his father-in-law, the priest of Midian. He has "led them to the back side of the desert"—*i. e.* to the west side of it, for in designating the points of compass the Hebrews always turned the face toward the east. The east is in front—*before;* and of course the west is behind. Horeb and Sinai lay on the western margin of the great Arabian desert.——Here "the angel of the Lord appeared to him" (v. 2), called "angel" however only as one who comes or is sent with divine manifestations; for in every subsequent mention he is called "the Lord" and "God" (vs. 4, 6, 7, 11, 13, etc.)*——Remarkably this visible manifestation was made by the symbol of fire in a bush—the bush all aflame yet not consumed. This strange sight attracted the attention of Moses, and he turned aside to look into it more closely, when a voice from the bush called him by name; warned him not to approach in the spirit of mere curiosity, but to take off his shoes because the place on which he stood was holy ground. The mystery before Moses' mind is solved—the Lord is there! His purpose in this appearing is soon told. He has heard the cry of distress from his oppressed people, has come down to deliver them and to bring them forth into Canaan. He has a mission for Moses in this work. "Come," said he, "I will send thee to Pharaoh." Moses knew the power and the pride of Pharaoh, and saw at a glance the difficulties of this enterprise. No wonder he shrank back saying—"Who am I that I should do this"? God replied: "I will certainly be with thee"—a sufficient answer to any amount of conscious weakness and faintness of heart. The Lord added—"This shall be a token to thee that I have sent thee; when thou hast brought the people out of Egypt, ye shall serve [*i. e.* worship] God in this mountain." From that moment this token was God's pledge to Moses of success in bringing the people forth from

---

* See on the Scripture usage of "the angel of the Lord," p. 130.

Egypt; and when it was fulfilled in the scenes of national worship and consecration on Horeb, it became doubly a sign to all the people that the Lord their God was in this great movement.

Moses anticipates that the people will ask for the name of God, and he therefore inquires--What shall I answer them? To which the Lord replies: "*I am that I am*;" and then abbreviating the phrase, adds, "Thus shalt thou say to Israel, *I am* hath sent me to you." What immediately follows should be carefully noted. God said moreover to Moses (still reiterating the same thought though in other and more familiar terms): "Thus shalt thou say to the children of Israel: The Lord—*i. e.* Jehovah, God of your fathers, hath sent me unto you; this is my name forever and this is my memorial through all generations." This v. 15 is without doubt the key to the true sense of the names as previously given—"*I am that I am*," and in briefer form, "*I am*." Their true meaning is in the name *Jehovah*. This name contemplates God as evermore existing, the same unchangeable God, and therefore ever faithful to his promises. This view of God assumes that he reveals himself personally as the God of his trustful people, entering into covenant with them and never failing to remember and fulfill that covenant.

In order to see the full force and pertinence of the passage, it should be considered that by common Hebrew usage, the names of persons were significant. They were words with a meaning. This is true of all the names by which the true God is made known. And when Moses suggests that the people will ask for God's name, it is not implied that they had never heard any name for God and did not know what to call him; but this—They would know what new or special feature of his character was to be manifested then. Their question was equivalent to asking—What does God propose to do now? What new movement does he contemplate? What new development of God may we expect?——To the question so understood, the Lord made a direct answer:—I have come to reveal my eternal faithfulness to my covenant with your fathers. I pledged myself to Abraham, Isaac and Jacob that I would bring their posterity into the goodly land of Canaan: I have come down to fulfill that word and to put into your national history an enduring testimony that my name is truly, "I am that I am"—the immutable and eternal God, whose word of promise faileth not forevermore.

The same course of thought appears again Ex. 6: 1–8—a passage which should be studied in connection with this. "God said to Moses, I am the Jehovah. I appeared unto Abraham, unto Isaac, and unto Jacob by the name of God Almighty; but by my name Jehovah was I not known unto them"—the meaning of which is, not that the name Jehovah was never used by them, or given of God to them; but that its special significance had not been manifested to them as he was then about to make it manifest. His *power* God had revealed—his power to protect them in their perils, his power to fulfill to Abraham the promise of a son; but such a glorious testimony to his faithfulness in fulfilling promise as was then to be given, the patriarchs had never seen. The redemption of Israel from Egyptian bondage was destined to stand through all the ages of their history as the crowning manifestation of God's faithfulness—the standard and unsurpassed testimony to the significance of his most honored name *Jehovah*. By this shall ye know that I am Jehovah your God when I bring you out from under the burdens of the Egyptians and bring you into the land given by solemn oath to your fathers and to their posterity for a heritage (vs. 7, 8).

In entering upon this redemption of his people the Lord understood well the difficulties to be overcome and fully comprehended the situation. If Moses saw them at a glance, so did the Lord also. It was not possible that Moses could have a deeper sense or a juster view than God had of Pharaoh's great pride, of his consciousness of power and stubbornness of purpose. The Lord expected a conflict; was ready for it; and by no means disposed to shun it. "I am sure that the king of Egypt will not let you go; no, not by a mighty hand"—not even under fearful visitations of God's supernatural power. The precise sense of this seems to be that Pharaoh would resist God's will *for a long time* despite the inflictions of his mighty hand and would yield only in the last extremity. In fact he never honestly yielded his will to God's will, but only bent for the moment before the blast, to rally again with more desperate madness after it had swept by. When at length he saw that the people were really gone, his unsubdued will rose again in towering hardihood, to rush more madly than ever before against the uplifted arm of the Almighty and meet his doom in the bottom of the Red Sea!

This chapter closes (vs. 21, 22) with directions to the children of Israel to *ask* the Egyptians for gold, silver, and raiment. The Lord promised to give them such favor with the people that they would readily grant them what they asked. Our English version puts it "*borrow*"—as if the Israelites at least tacitly promised to bring these borrowed things back, or if nothing more, left the Egyptians to expect this. But this English word "borrow" misrepresents the Hebrew and consequently the sense of the passage. The Hebrew verb used here never has the sense of *borrow*, but means simply to *ask*. Indeed borrowing was out of the question because the Israelites were not coming back again. It was never God's thought that they should come back. He had come down to deliver them from their bondage and to bring them into Canaan. There is no reason to suppose that the Egyptians expected them back again. They gave what Israel asked, therefore, not as a loan, but because the Lord brought them into such relations to Israel that they were glad to get them out of the country any way, and perhaps hoped to avert more fearful plagues by these gifts to God's people. The historian in this case says (Ex. 12 : 33)—"The Egyptians were urgent upon the people that they might send them out of the land in haste; for they said—We be all dead men"; which the Psalmist confirms (Ps. 105 : 38)—"Egypt was glad when they departed, for the fear of them fell upon them." Manifestly the Lord counted it simple justice that Egypt should pay her slaves for long years of unrequited toil, and not send them away empty. Therefore he took measures to make the old masters but too glad to do this tardy justice.

A new instrumentality of most vital importance now came to view, designed to bring about the redemption of God's people from Egypt, viz. *supernatural agencies—miracles* in the legitimate sense of the word. Noticeably these miracles were two-fold in character and purpose;

one class designed to identify God to the people and be a witness to his present hand, to confirm their faith in him as their Deliverer: the other designed by terrible inflictions of calamity, to force upon Pharaoh's hardened heart the conviction of Jehovah's power and compel him to let God's people go. These two objects were to be accomplished; the Hebrew people were to be assured that their own God had indeed come; Pharaoh must be made to know who Jehovah is; how fearful the judgments of his uplifted hand are; and how vain it is for mortals, though on thrones of human power, to lift up themselves against the Almighty.

In the list of miraculous signs sent to convince the Hebrew people, we have (Ex. 4: 1–8) the rod of Moses turned to a serpent and then turned back again to a rod; then his hand withdrawn from his bosom leprous, white as snow; then again withdrawn, perfectly restored.

The narrative gives the reader a strong sense of the reluctance of Moses to enter upon this new mission. Over and over again, in varying forms, he pleads his want of adaptation; that he is slow of speech, not eloquent; that he sees no improvement in this regard since the Lord first spake to him; and finally he begs the Lord to send by any body else he pleases, only (he implies) excuse me. Plainly he pushed this plea for excuse not merely to the verge of modest propriety but beyond it, for we read—"The anger of the Lord was kindled against Moses." Yet he did so far regard the plea of Moses as to give him Aaron his elder brother to speak in his behalf. "Thou shalt speak to him and put words into his mouth; he shall be thy spokesman to the people," and to Pharaoh.

The way is now prepared for Moses and his family to return from Midian to Egypt. He took his wife and his two sons and proceeded on his journey. The scenes of the first night at the inn are recorded in these words: "And it came to pass by the way in the inn, that the LORD met him, and sought to kill him. Then Zipporah took a sharp stone, and cut off the foreskin of her son, and cast *it* at his feet, and said, Surely a bloody husband *art* thou to me. So he let him go: then she said, A bloody husband *thou art*, because of the circumcision." This account is very brief, leaving various points unexplained. Probably the facts were substantially these. Of their two sons, one had been circumcised; the other had not—the prescribed rite having been disobeyed or at least neglected out of the deference of Moses to the opposition or reluctance of his wife. But as Moses is now about to assume the highest responsibilities between God and the Hebrew people, it is vital that his example in this respect should be spotless. The Lord therefore called him suddenly to account in this manner, threatening his very life. The cause is instantly understood; the wife of Moses yields and herself performs the rite, though perhaps not in the most submissive and amiable spirit. After this transaction and the developments attending it, we must suppose that Moses (prudently) sent back his wife and the two children to remain with her father until the redeemed Israelites should reach the home of Jethro. We hear no more of her and her children till the narrative in Ex. 18 brings them to view thus: "When Jethro had heard all that the Lord had done for Moses and Israel, he took Zipporah, Moses' wife, *after he had sent her back*, and her two sons and brought them to Moses" etc.——Shortly after this scene at the inn, Aaron, sent of God for this purpose, meets Moses yet in the wilderness and is introduced to his responsibilities in the issues then pending before Pharaoh and the people. Their first introduction to Pharaoh and the reception he gave to their message (Ex. 5) revealed his character and gave pre-intimations of the conflict. They put their case before him:—"Thus saith the Lord God of Israel, Let my people go that they may hold a feast unto me in the wilderness." "And Pharaoh said—Who is the Lord that I should obey his voice to let Israel go? I know not the Lord, neither will I let Israel go." Am not I king over all Egypt? Do you tell me there is some higher king than I and bid me obey his command? I know nothing of your Jehovah: I will never submit to his authority! And as if to show how fearlessly he could resist their summons he at once puts heavier tasks upon the people, in proud defiance, daring the vengeance of their Great Defender! Verily the issues hasten to their crisis!

The suffering people are entirely disheartened and evince a painful lack of faith in the God of their fathers. When Moses rehearsed to them the inspiring words re-

THE PLAGUES ON PHARAOH AND EGYPT.

corded Ex. 6: 1-8, "They hearkened not unto Moses for anguish of spirit and for cruel bondage." Ah, how frail is poor human nature! How weak is the faith of this long-oppressed people! But God's compassions are a great deep and he does not frown severely upon them, broken down though they were in their manhood and in their religious trust.——Moses too seems to falter before this stern reception from Pharaoh and this disheartening attitude of Israel (6: 12); but the loving kindness of the Lord endures, despite of these sad imperfections in his servants. For the glory of his own name and not for the worthiness or virtue of his people, he has entered upon this redeeming work and he will carry it through.

The narrative pauses a moment more (Ex. 6: 16-27) to give us the genealogy of Levi, for the obvious purpose of showing the place of Moses and of Aaron in this record; and then proceeds (Ex. 7 and onward) with the impressive scenes of *the ten plagues on Pharaoh and on Egypt.*

A brief preliminary explanation of some of these plagues will be in place, after which the following points will have special attention:

1. That these ten plagues on Egypt were really supernatural, miraculous.
2. That several of them were very specially adapted to Egypt.
3. The case of the magicians.
4. The divine purpose and policy in shaping the demand made upon Pharaoh to let the people go.
5. The hardening of Pharaoh's heart.
6. The final result as shown in the last of the ten plagues.

The ten plagues in their historical order stand thus:
1. Water turned to blood (Ex. 7: 14-25);
2. Frogs (8: 1-15);
3. Lice (8: 16-19);
4. Flies (8: 20-32);
5. Murrain upon cattle (9: 1-7);
6. Boils (9: 8-12);
7. Hail (9: 18-35);
8. Locusts (10: 4-20);

9. Darkness (10: 21–27);
10. Death of all first-born (11: 4–8, and 12: 12, 29–33).

References to these plagues by name may be seen in Ps. 78: 43–51, and 105: 27–38.

By way of preliminary explanation it should be said—that the turning of water into blood should not be toned down to a mere discoloration of the waters of Egypt—a reddening of such sort as customarily attends the annual rise of the Nile, only carried in the present case somewhat beyond the ordinary degree. For, be it noticed, the record is that the waters were *turned to blood;* that fish could no longer live in it but died (were the fish deceived by the mere appearance, the color?); that the river became offensive to the smell; its waters could not be drank; "there was blood throughout all the land of Egypt." If this language does not mean far more than a mere *discoloration*—something totally different from a visual deception; in short, if it does not mean "*turned to blood,*" then no language can be found to express it.

In the third plague, the Hebrew word for "lice"* were better rendered *gnats*, yet an insect unknown to our country. Herodotus (B. C. 400) speaks of the great trouble which they cause and of the precautions used against them. Hartmann testifies: "All travelers speak of these gnats as an ordinary plague of the country." † "So small as to be scarcely visible to the eye, their sting notwithstanding causes a most painful irritation. They even creep into the eyes and nose, and after harvest rise in great swarms from the inundated rice fields." (Keil.)

In the fourth plague, the word translated "swarms of flies"‡ does not mean a mixed mass or swarm of various insects as our translators assumed, but "a stinging, scorpion-like insect" [Fuerst], "so called from its sucking the blood" [Gesenius]. Sonnini (in Hengstenberg's Moses, p. 117) says—"Men and animals are grievously tormented by them. It is impossible to form an adequate conception of their fury when they

*כנים
†Hengstenberg's Egypt and Moses, pp. 115 and 116
‡ערוב

wish to fix themselves upon any part of the body. If they are driven away they light again the same instant, and their pertinacity wearies the most patient. They especially love to light in the corners of the eyes or on the edge of the eyelids, sensitive parts to which they are attracted by a slight moisture." "They are much more numerous and annoying than the gnats; and when enraged, they fasten themselves upon the human body, especially upon the edge of the eyelids and become a dreadful plague" [Keil].——Obviously the American house-fly gives us no adequate idea of this fourth plague on Egypt.

Of the sixth plague, "boils with blains," it need only be said that they were inflamed ulcers breaking forth into pustules, intensely painful. The word for "boils" is the same which describes the plague brought by Satan upon Job.

The seventh plague, *hail with lightning*, was not unknown in Egypt, yet was by no means common, and was specially rare in Upper Egypt—more frequent in Lower.——The other plagues will be readily understood.

1. It is now in place to show that these plagues were really *supernatural*—miraculous inflictions from the hand of the Almighty.

(1.) Note, they were wrought in response to Pharaoh's challenge to Moses and Aaron to "show a miracle for themselves" (Ex. 7: 9). The Lord accepted this challenge. Of course the achievements wrought can be nothing less than miracles. Given on the side of the Lord honesty and power; then nothing less than miracles can follow.

His purpose in these terrible inflictions God announces to Pharaoh in these words: "By this shalt thou know that I am the Lord" (Ex. 7: 19 and 9: 14). Events in the common course of nature do not suffice for this purpose upon such a heart as Pharaoh's. The case demands real miracles—things done outside and apart from the ordinary laws of nature.

(2.) The plagues came and went at the behest of Moses acting under God; in some cases, at a definite time previously indicated (9: 5, 18, 29, 33 and 10: 4); while some were removed at a time which Pharaoh himself for his more full satisfaction was allowed to fix (8: 9, 10). So I construe the somewhat disputed words (v. 8); "Moses said to Pharaoh—Glory over me: When shall I entreat for thee," etc. Moses would say—I yield to you the honor of fixing the time: say when; and I meet your time.——Some critics translate simply—Explain; declare yourself (Gesenius); or utter plainly, definitely (Fuerst); but the usual sense of the verb, coupled with the preposition ("over") which follows, strongly favors the construction above given.

(3.) Most of these plagues if not all discriminated sharply between the Hebrews in Goshen, and the Egyptians elsewhere in Egypt—*e. g.* flies (8: 22, 23) and murrain (9: 4–7), etc. This discrimination assumes that the plagues followed no general law of nature, but were altogether special, *i. e.* were truly miraculous.

(4.) They surpassed and even totally eclipsed the achievements of the magicians; in fact, routed them utterly from the field and showed before all Egypt that the Almighty God was there!——The case of the magicians will be considered more fully below.

(5.) The conviction was forced upon Pharaoh and the confession extorted from his lips (utterly against his will), that God's hand wrought these achievements; that these calamities came at his command, and could be removed by his power and not otherwise. Hence over and over he begs Moses to pray to his God for their removal. See this in the case of the frogs (8: 8); of the flies (8: 28, 29); of the hail (9: 27–29); and the locusts (10: 16–18). It is not easy to see how stronger testimony to the reality of miracles can ever exist.

(6.) That these plagues were real miracles, direct from the hand of God, it is unquestionably the intent of the whole narrative to set forth and affirm. So much, no candid reader of the account has ever questioned. Some may say, the narrator was himself deceived: none will deny that he saw God's finger there and meant to make all his readers see it. None can deny that according to his account even proud Pharaoh saw and felt the very finger of God in them. In fact the narrative makes this its *main purpose*, viz. to show that these judgments were nothing less than immediate visitations from the hand of the Almighty. Take out this element and there is nothing left.

(7.) Or thus: If there is any truth in history, the children of Israel were for a long period bondmen in Egypt. Ultimately the day of their deliverance broke and they came forth free. *How came this to pass?* Was it by forcible insurrection—the uprising of slaves cutting their way out of bondage into freedom with brave hearts and strong arms of their own? Or was it achieved by diplomacy? Or did Pharaoh relax his grasp and let the people go, under the impulses of humanity, or as a measure of political economy? All suppositions of this sort are not only unhistorical but utterly chimerical. No solution of this great problem—the redemption of Israel from bondage in Egypt—can ever find rational support save the one given in this record, viz. that the Almighty wrenched them from the grasp of Egypt's proud and hardened king by a series of terrible judgments launched upon him and his people in quick and hot succession, until they were only too glad to hasten and drive the people out lest they should all be dead men. They were made to feel that the battle was against Almighty God and that they could not succumb too soon.

The events of this wonderful conflict and victory were stamped into the national life of Israel; they reappear all along the course of future ages, interwoven into the very warp and woof of her national history and into the moral forces which developed the nation's piety. It might as reasonably be maintained that there never was any Hebrew nation as that God did not bring them forth out of Egypt with a high hand, first loosing Pharaoh's grasp by these ten plagues, and last, burying his pursuing hosts and himself in the waters of the Red Sea.

The supernatural character of these plagues will stand out yet more distinctly when we shall place them in contrast with the things done or attempted by the magicians.

2. *Several of these plagues were very specially adapted to Egypt.*

This does not mean that they were at all less miraculous than any other supposable inflictions would have been; but only that they had more or less special fitness to the ends God had in view and were made to touch the sensibilities of Egypt and her king in tender points. Thus, the Nile was Egypt's pride and glory, indeed her very life, and not improbably (as some maintain) was worshiped by the Egyptians as one of their gods. How terrible then to wake in the morning to find it one vast sea of blood!—to have only blood for themselves and their cattle to drink; blood every-where for the eye to rest upon in place of the glory of the Nile! How terribly suggestive of their national sin—of the male infants of the Hebrews murdered there, and of the resources of Israel's God to punish the guilty!

So we must suppose that frogs were often inconveniently plenty in Egyptian waters. This visitation of such masses of them brought an evil by no means foreign to their experience. The miracle lay in their numbers and was none the less a miracle because there had been frogs there before. It must have been excessively annoying and humiliating,—if the frog as a near neighbor is as unamiable in that country as in this.

Essentially the same must be said of the lice [gnats]; of the flies; and of boils. All these were forms of evil not unknown in Egyptian life; but yet in the present case were truly miraculous and fearfully afflictive.

Their cattle were so useful and so highly esteemed that some of them were made objects of idolatrous worship. The golden calf of Hebrew history was an Egyptian idea. There was special pertinence therefore in this fearful slaughter among Egypt's gods!

The hail, with most terrific lightning, was by far the more appalling because rain rarely falls there; hail and lightning yet more rarely.

In the natural course of events, locusts are among the fearful visitations of Oriental countries—not unknown in Egypt. In this case the fearfulness of the plague lay in their numbers, and the miracle was none the less because they had had some experience before of this form of desolation.

3. *The case of the magicians.*

The entire account of them is in these words. After Aaron had cast down his rod before Pharaoh and it became a serpent, "Then Pharaoh called the wise men and the sorcerers, and they also, the magicians of Egypt, did so with their enchantments. For they cast down every man his rod and they became serpents; but Aaron's rod swallowed up their rods" (Ex. 7: 11, 12). Again, after the miracle of turning the water to blood, "The magicians of Egypt did so with their enchantments" (7: 22). After the miracle of the frogs, "the magicians did so with their enchantments and brought up frogs upon the land of Egypt" (8: 7). Next, when all the dust became lice, "the magicians did so with their enchantments to bring forth lice, *but they could not:* so there were lice upon man and upon beast. Then the magicians said to Pharaoh—This is the finger of God" (8: 18, 19). Finally, under the plague of boils, "The magicians could not stand before Moses because of the boils, for the boil was upon the magicians and upon all the Egyptians" (9: 11). We hear of them in this history no more.

The Hebrew word for "sorcerers" involves the practice of magic arts and incantations. The word for "magicians of Egypt" contemplates them originally as *writers*, the learned class, but couples with that the idea of special skill in horoscopy—the interpretation of dreams and the doing, or at least pretending to do, things beyond the skill of the uninitiated. The word for "enchantments" originally suggests secret arts, things covered, veiled from the public gaze.——The passage Deut. 18: 10–14, gives most if not all the nearly synonymous words by which this class of men and their arts were designated, showing also that they were regarded before the Lord with most intense abhorrence as an abomination. By the Mosaic law the practice of these arts was punishable with death (Ex. 22: 12).

In regard to the case of the magicians as presented in this history, the point of chief interest will be this— Did they really perform miracles? Did they in fact turn rods into serpents, and water into blood, and produce some frogs in addition to what were there before? ——I am not sure that we have data sufficient to determine with certainty whether these things ascribed to them were simply tricks of hand, arts of jugglery; or whether there was really some power exerted, more and other than human.——The cases were of a sort in which deception was at least supposable. All the waters it would seem were turned to blood before their effort was made. If so, they had to do with what was already blood and had only to make it appear to be water before they began operations.——So of the frogs. When frogs were every-where in such numbers, it would not be specially difficult to make it appear that they produced yet more. The turning of rods into serpents is not unknown in the tricks of jugglery the world over.

Of two facts we may be very sure. (1) They had no help from God. Their wonders were not wrought by God's power. We may put this denial on two independent grounds:——(a.) The moral purpose of their work utterly forbids the least participation on God's part. God never fights against himself.——(b.) Their power was infinitely less than divine. Compared with God's, it was shown to be simple weakness. "Aaron's rod swallowed up their rods." Before the plague of lice they were compelled to succumb, and (utterly against their will and against their interest) they declare to Pharaoh—"This is the finger of God"! It utterly distances all our skill. We can not approach it. Before the boils, they writhed in agony. They could not even screen themselves from the terrible infliction. Moreover it is made plain throughout the whole transaction that they were powerless to remove even the slightest of these plagues. If they had possessed this power Pharaoh would have put them to this service. It is plain they shrank from even the attempt. The whole scene was a competition between God's power as manifested through his servants, Moses and Aaron, and the power of Egypt's magicians—resulting in most overwhelming proof that the latter had not the first element of God's power in it.——It follows therefore that if the magicians had extra-human help—if they had any power beyond human skill, *they obtained it from Satan.* We may readily suppose they were in league with him, working according to his will. He may have sharpened their wits by his influence, helped their arts by his suggestions, and possibly may have given them superhuman aid in the line of physical power. It is not given to us to know the exact limits of his power to aid his servants. It is not essential that we should know precisely where these limits are. We know enough to impress the injunction—"Be sober, be vigilant, because of your adversary the devil" (1 Pet. 5: 8).

It may always be our consolation that whenever he matches his power or his skill against the Almighty, he will come off, as in the case before us, utterly worsted in the fight, overwhelmed with defeat and shame.

4. Some attention should be given to the divine purpose and policy in shaping the demand made upon Pharaoh to let the people go.——The point of special importance here is one which has been thought to involve the question of strict moral honesty—it being claimed that the divine demand at first ran on this wise: "Let us go three days' journey into the wilderness that we may sacrifice to the Lord our God" (Ex. 3: 18)—leaving Pharaoh to assume that, this being granted, they would return to his service.

The facts on this point are:

(1.) It was never promised or even intimated that they would return. If Pharaoh construed the words of God and of Moses to imply this, he did so on his own responsibility.

(2.) The demand made upon him that he should let the people go was based in part at least on the religious duty of sacrificing to God in the wilderness (Ex. 5: 1, 3)—an entirely appropriate demand—one which Pharaoh ought to have appreciated, and one which would be more likely to have weight with him than any other. For he was himself a worshiper of his own gods; he knew the strength of the religious element in human nature; he was able to recognize the universal rights of conscience by which every man may claim to worship God according to his own convictions of duty. If Pharaoh would not yield to this request he would yield to none. The policy pursued was, therefore, the most hopeful and the least likely to arouse opposition.

(3.) Even the severest honesty did not require that the Lord should put this demand in its most revolting form in the outset. True, he might have said from the beginning: "My people shall never return"; but this would have at once foreclosed all hope of gaining Pharaoh's consent.

(4.) If the question of the return of the people was thus left a very little open—or more correctly, was not peremptorily closed, it served the better to test the heart of Pharaoh. It left the way open to ply him with inducements most likely to be successful; and at the same time if he proved obstinate and self-willed, he might show it by bantering over the conditions, higgling as tradesmen and their customers sometimes do over the price, negotiating like diplomatists for the most favorable terms. But this was the fault of Pharaoh, not of God.

(5.) Most frequently the demand was made in these significant words: "Let my people go that they may serve me" (Ex. 8: 1, 20, and 9: 1, 13). Israel is my son; his service is due to me and I claim it (Ex. 4: 22, 23). You have no right to his services; I demand therefore that you let my son go that he may serve me.——This is at least sufficiently definite, and is by no means open to the slightest imputation of lacking in the point of honesty.

5. *The hardening of Pharaoh's heart.*

In this topic, as in the one next preceding, the point of chief interest is the moral one—that which locates the moral responsibility for the hardening of Pharaoh's heart—that which defines and places truthfully the really responsible agency in the case. Was this hardening the work of God, by his immediate hand? Was it wrought by his power so exclusively and in such modes as to overrule and throw out of account Pharaoh's own responsible agency?

Or was the responsible agency that of Pharaoh only, altogether his and his alone? Did he harden his own heart, in the exercise of his own free will, in carrying out the purpose and desire of his own soul, essentially as other sinners and as all sinners do?

This question is one of immensely vital moment. Let us approach it with both care and candor.

We may reach the true answer by studying,

(1.) The history of the case;
(2.) What is said of God's purpose in this matter;
(3.) What he has taught us of his character, and of his agencies in the existence of sin.

(1.) The history of the transaction will doubtless throw light on the question—How came Pharaoh's heart to be hardened? *How was it done?*

WHO HARDENED PHARAOH'S HEART?

The history of the transaction, developing the steps of the process, bears more vitally upon the question, Who is responsible?—than may at first view be realized. For, let it be carefully considered: God's ways of working by his immediate, direct, exclusive agency will forever be mysterious and inscrutable to us. It is idle for us to ask—*How* does God work a miracle? Of course it must be idle for us to inquire after the natural law of such working because the very idea of a miracle is that of a work *not* wrought according to any known laws of nature. If now the hardening of Pharaoh's heart were wrought by God's miraculous, direct, immediate hand, we shall look in vain for the law of his operations. It would be simply preposterous to inquire after the laws of mind in accordance with which the thing was done—the supposition being that it was done according to *no* known laws of mind whatever.

On the other hand if Pharaoh hardened his own heart, there will be no mystery about it. It so happens that we all know but too well how sinners harden their own hearts. There is rarely the least difficulty in tracing the operations of the human mind and the influences of temptation which produce this result. Therefore, if the history of the hardening of Pharaoh's heart brings out the working of his mind, according to the common modes of human sinning—if we see that his mind worked as the minds of other proud sinners are wont to work under like circumstances, then the whole question is settled at once and forever. If we can actually *see* how Pharaoh hardened his own heart and can identify the whole process as being the very same which occurs in the case of all proud sinners who resist God's power and especially resist the appeals of his love and mercy, what more can we ask? It were worse than idle—it were impious to exonerate Pharaoh from the least portion of the moral responsibility for his hardened heart and to seek to cast it over upon God.

In entering upon the *history of the case*, it is well to note the attitude of Pharaoh's mind toward the God of Israel in the outset. We have it brought out fully (Ex. 5: 1, 2): "Moses and Aaron went in and told Pharaoh: 'Thus saith the Lord God of Israel; let my people go that they may serve me.' And Pharaoh said—*Who* is the Lord that I should obey his voice to let Israel go? I know not the Lord, neither will I let Israel go."——This is plain; he says he does not know this God; he does not recognize his authority or admit his claims. His soul is full of practical unbelief in God—a fact which commonly lies at the bottom of all the hardening of sinners' hearts in every age.—— Pharaoh did not at first contemplate crossing swords and measuring strong arms *with the Almighty God.* If he had taken this view of the case, he might have paused awhile to consider.——So it usually is with sinners. Unbelief in God conduces to launch them upon this terrible conflict. Once committed, they become more hardened; one sin leads on to more sinning till sin becomes incurable—shall we say it? an uncontrollable madness.

We may now fitly proceed to give attention to each particular case.

The first miracle (Ex. 7: 10-13) that of changing Aaron's rod to a serpent, was rather a *test* than a *plague.* Pharaoh met it by calling in his magicians to try their hand—his thought being, My men can do that! They did *seem* to do it, and though Aaron's rod-serpent swallowed up theirs, yet Pharaoh did not love to be convinced and therefore was not. Under this result, which perhaps seemed to him a partial victory, he braced himself against God this time.

Next, in the turning of water into blood we read (Ex. 7: 22): "The magicians did so with their enchantments, and Pharaoh's heart was hardened." This seemed to him a complete success for his side. Naturally, therefore, his heart is hardened to withstand God yet.

Under the plague of frogs—not by any means one of the most severe—Pharaoh seemed to yield; he at least begged the prayers of Moses and Aaron; and promised to let the people go (Ex. 8: 8). To make God's hand the more distinctly visible, Moses said—Set your own time, and I will pray that this plague may cease. Done: "but when Pharaoh saw that there was *respite*, he hardened his heart and hearkened not unto them" (8: 15). Alas, how he abused God's mercy! God lifted the plague—and up springs the old rebellion of his soul against God. Perhaps he flatters himself that this is the last, or he hopes that Moses will pray the rest away as he has this; or, as often happens, the simple sense of respite without any particular reasoning in the case makes him feel strong again to withstand God. Not the least sense of gratitude for the favor—the mercy of removing the plague! O how many of the sinners of our world have done this very thing! Stricken down with sickness, have they not begged for life and besought the prayers of all the good, and promised the Lord that with restoring mercy they would give him their hearts and their lives? But when the respite came their vows were forgotten; their hearts were hardened.

The plague of lice brings out another element of depraved hearts. The magicians try, but make an utter failure, and (what is to Pharaoh more provoking still) they frankly declare to him, "This is the finger of God." They retire from the contest, and leave Pharaoh to fight it out alone. They can help him no longer. He is apparently vexed and maddened, but not at all subdued. Rather, he rouses himself to greater desperation, for the record puts these points in the closest connection: the frank admission, "This is the finger of God"; and the stiffening of Pharaoh's rebellious will—"*And* Pharaoh's heart was hardened and he hearkened not unto them."

The plague of flies brings out yet another element of human nature which not unfrequently comes into play in the hardening of men's hearts against God—viz. the habit of bantering—shall we say dickering, driving a bargain and quibbling over the terms and conditions of God's requirements. The flies are terribly annoying: Pharaoh sees that something must be done; in fact he concludes he must make some concessions: so he calls for Moses and Aaron and says—"Go ye, sacrifice to your God *in the land.*" The last words were emphatic—in *this* land: stay here, and you shall have time to offer your sacrifices. I can not let you go three days journey into the wilderness lest ye never come back.——Moses insists on the original terms; and then Pharaoh concedes yet a little more: "I will let you go that ye may sacrifice to the Lord your God in the wilderness, only ye shall not go very far away. Entreat for me"—*i. e.* entreat the Lord to take away these flies—the same word being used here as in v. 8. Moses entreated: the Lord removed the plague, and according to the record "Pharaoh hardened his heart at this time also, neither would he let the people go." Allowing himself to make terms with God and to banter him upon the conditions, coupled with the respite—the temporary relief found in the removal of the plague—are manifestly the causes and modes in this case of his hardening his own heart.

Next is the plague of murrain—a terrible loss of their cattle. In the antecedent threatening of this plague, Moses said to Pharaoh, "The Lord will *sever* between the cattle of Israel and the cattle of Egypt: there shall nothing die of all that belongs to Israel." So it was; for we read—"Pharaoh sent [*i. e.* to inquire] and lo! not one of the cattle of the Israelites was dead. And the heart of Pharaoh was hardened, and he did not let the people go" (9: 1–7). This discrimination gave a keener edge to the plague; it cut the deeper; but in the result it only maddened him the more. It showed most clearly that God's hand was in these plagues and that he was on the side of Israel; but Pharaoh was committed to the contest and seemed to have but the one ruling purpose—to fight it out to the bitter end.

The plague of boils was a visitation of physical suffering, perhaps somewhat adapted to make a fretful man irritable. The narrative notes the circumstance that the magicians were completely broken down by this plague: "They could not stand before Moses because of the boils, for the boil was upon the magicians and upon all the Egyptians [not upon the Israelites]. As to Pharaoh, all human help fails him; every man among his people seems to quail and give up the contest; yet his proud heart is only the more maddened and the more determined! It is said, "The Lord hardened the heart of Pharaoh and he hearkened not unto them;" but such mad infatuation is wont to appear in depraved human souls without any miraculous infliction of hardness from the hand of God. There is not the least occasion to assume any other influences than those of a proud, maddened human heart, working out its own obstinate will against God.

The hail with attendant thunder and lightning

(next in order) were fearfully appalling. All Egyptian hearts seemed to quiver with terror under this infliction. Pharaoh is brought (shall we say) to his knees: he sends hastily for Moses and Aaron and says to them: "I have sinned this time; the Lord is righteous and I and my people are wicked." Truly this seems hopeful. For the first time he appears penitent. "Entreat the Lord (for it is enough) that there be no more mighty thunderings and hail; and I will let you go and ye shall stay no longer."——This seems to be a final victory over the proud heart and the long time inflexible will of Pharaoh. He confesses sin; he begs again for prayer; he promises to yield to God's entire demand and let the people go. Consequently the plague was removed. "And when Pharaoh saw that the rain and the hail and the thunder were ceased, he sinned yet more and hardened his heart, he and his servants."——Alas for man's perverse and false nature—his proud heart and his lying lips! How readily he relapses back into his old and much-loved sin and becomes more hardened than ever! The judgments of God extort confessions and tears and prayers; but God's mercies let off this pressure and leave the guilty soul to fly back to its old sins again. So it was with Pharaoh. God's mercies, abused, worked out his ruin. But it were simply monstrous to say that this showing of mercy is on God's part a moral wrong and that it throws over upon him the moral responsibility of hardening the sinner's heart. Yet it was precisely in this way—perhaps more really and potently than in any other—that God hardened the heart of Pharaoh.

The plague of locusts brings to view a new group of elements. Egypt had known something about locusts before: so when this scourge was announced, Pharaoh's servants beg him to yield the contest. "How long shall this man" [Moses] "be a snare unto us? Let the men go that they may serve the Lord their God. Knowest thou not yet that Egypt is destroyed"? (10: 7).——Pharaoh yields to their entreaty only so far as to send for Moses and Aaron, and again try his hand upon bantering with them and with God over the conditions. "Go serve the Lord, said he; but *who are they that shall go*"? Moses answers, Every thing must go; we with our young and with our old; with sons and with daughters; with flocks and with herds—all, absolutely *all* must go.——No indeed, replies Pharaoh—with what we must take as his royal oath—with the most fearful threat he could make and the most solemn asseveration—he says, "*Not so;* go *ye that are men* and serve the Lord, for that ye did desire." That was all ye asked at first: it is the utmost I shall give! "And they were driven out of his presence." Pharaoh is thoroughly mad! This allowing himself to banter them as to the terms of the arrangement helped him to a stronger feeling of his own importance. He seemed to himself to be yet more a king on his throne, and why should not he dictate the conditions?——Soon the plague comes, and for the moment it quite changes the face of affairs. "Pharaoh called for Moses and Aaron in haste, and said [again]—" I have sinned against the Lord your God and against you. Now, therefore, forgive, I pray thee, my sin only this once, and entreat the Lord your God that he may take away from me this death only." Apparently he remembers that once before he confessed, and more than once has begged their prayers, and more than once has promised to let the people go. So he labors to give a little more emphasis to his beseechings this time by confessing his sin against Moses, and especially by the limitation—"*for this once*"—once more *do* hear me—this time only. But he has been through this very process once before; most of its points, many times before; and it is much more easy for him to turn back upon every promise and break every most solemn vow than it ever has been before. It is safe to predict that any sinner who has broken so many solemn vows of amendment will never do any thing better than break vows when God's mercy lifts off the plague. So Pharaoh's heart is hardened yet again. The statement is—" But the Lord hardened Pharaoh's heart "—yet the way he did it, here as before (9: 34), was by removing the plague; by hearing his prayer for relief and apparently trusting his sacred promise to let the people go. This was the way and these the agencies by which the Lord hardened Pharaoh's heart.

The plague of darkness is next in order. Again Pharaoh sets himself to negotiate as to the terms. He will consent that not only the men may go, but their wives and their little ones; *but their flocks must be left behind.* He must have some hostages—something left in his hands that will bring his bondmen back. Moses says *No!* we need our flocks for sacrifice; not a hoof is to be left behind! Pharaoh is more mad than ever: he not only drives Moses out from his presence, but adds—"Take heed to thyself; see my face no more; for in the day thou seest my face thou shalt die." In this case it is said—"The Lord hardened Pharaoh's heart"; but these terrible uprisings and outbursts of madness well up from the depths of a depraved sinner's soul. No supernatural miracle of divine hardening is at all needful to create them. Pharaoh is too proud a king to bear such confrontings of his will. Shall he yield to such a man as Moses, or even to the God of Moses? Not he. It stirs up all the elements of his pride and madness to have his propositions of compromise so peremptorily rejected. It is this in special that works in this present case to the hardening of his heart.

There remains but one more plague—that awful night on Egypt when the wailing cry rang out over all the land, "for there was not a house where there was not one dead"! and that the *first-born!* Under this, Pharaoh for the time really broke down; he called for Moses and Aaron by night and said—Go ye and all your people, and take your flocks and herds as ye have said and be gone, and bless me also." This conceded everything, closing off with begging their blessing upon his consciously guilty soul! The Egyptians too were all astir; "they were urgent upon the people to send them out of the land in haste; for they said—"We be all dead men." And the people of Israel do really go.—— But strange as it may seem, when "it was told the king of Egypt that the people had really gone, then the heart of Pharaoh and of his servants was turned against the people and they said—"Why have we done this that we have let Israel go from serving us"?——Forthwith armed chariots are made ready and are off in hot pursuit;—till they find themselves battling the mighty waves of the Red Sea, quailing before the awful eye and under the uplifted arm of the Almighty!——This last instance of hardening the heart seems most like pure and simple infatuation. No doubt Pharaoh and his servants had a fresh sense of what they had lost in letting go such a host of hard working bondmen. No doubt they also felt the mortification of having been worsted in the long-fought struggle over this national question of letting the people go; but after all they had seen and felt of God's power to curse and to plague and to crush them, nothing but the most senseless infatuation can rationally account for this last desperate dash upon Israel with the armed force of the nation. Yet no one will say that such infatuation does not often appear in the history of human sinning. In his own sphere many a poor sinner is just as madly infatuated as Pharaoh and his people were—is altogether as senseless, as void of wisdom, as reckless of the hot thunderbolts of the Almighty! It is an awfully sad fact, a most humiliating confession as to the manner of human sinning; but it is only too true! There is no need of assuming any direct supernatural divine interposition to produce it.

Nothing more seems necessary to complete the argument from the history of the case unless it be to suggest that when we have accounted for the hardening of Pharaoh's heart satisfactorily on the one principle—the well-known proclivities and activities of a proud, stubborn human heart, it is entirely unphilosophical to bring in another principle, viz. the miraculous, immediate, direct action of Almighty Power. When we have proved the former power adequate to produce all the results, we have virtually precluded the latter. There can be no reason whatever for assuming a joint, co-ordinate action of both the natural laws of the human mind and of the supernatural power of God. If the former suffices, the latter is uncalled for. Miracles are never to be assumed where non-miraculous agency is fully adequate.

If it be still argued that the very words declare, " God hardened Pharaoh's heart," the answer is: God is said to do what he foresees will be done by others and done under such arrangements of his providence as make it possible and morally certain that they will do it. Joseph said to his brethren (Gen. 45: 5, 7, 8), "Be not angry with yourselves that ye sold me hither, for God did send me before you to preserve life. So now it was not you that sent me hither but God." Yet it is simply impious to put the sin of selling Joseph into Egypt over upon God. God did it only in the same sense in which he hardened Pharaoh's heart. He had a purpose to subserve by means of the sin of Joseph's brethren; and he did no doubt permit such circumstances to occur in his providence as made that sin possible and as resulted in their sinning and in the remote consequences which God anticipated.

It is of no particular use for us to find fault with the way in which the Scriptures speak of God's hand in the existence of sin. There is no special mystery about it. It certainly does not involve the least moral obliquity on God's part; and it is therefore every way prudent and wise to interpret such language in harmony with the common sense of the case and with the well-known character of God.

2. We proceed to notice what is said of *God's purpose* in the hardening of Pharaoh's heart. It is the more important to speak of this because an extreme view is sometimes taken of the central passage (Ex. 9: 14–16); "And in very deed for this cause have I raised thee up for to show in thee my power," etc. The extreme view referred to is that God made Pharaoh a great king, put him on a high throne, for the avowed purpose of displaying his own great power in his sin and punishment.

By consent of Hebrew lexicographers, the verb translated "*raised up*" means in this case *preserved alive*—have *caused thee to stand* or continue among the living. The previous context moreover seems not to be quite accurately put in our English version. It should rather be thus, beginning with v. 14: "For at this very time I am sending [present tense] all my plagues to thine heart and upon thy servants and upon thy people that thou mayest know that there is none like me in all the earth. For I might now have stretched out my hand and smitten thee and thy people with pestilence [*i. e.* might have smitten you all dead], and thou wouldest have been cut off from the earth. But truly for this very reason have I preserved thee alive to the end that thou mightest show forth [make others see] my power, and for the sake of proclaiming my name in all the earth." To the same purport are the words (Ex. 14: 17, 18) with reference to the final destruction of Pharaoh's host; "And I will get me honor upon Pharaoh and upon all his host, etc. And the Egyptians shall know that I am the Lord when I shall have gotten me honor upon Pharaoh and upon his chariots and his horsemen." The great thought is that God turns to account the sin and madness of Pharaoh for the purpose of making known his power to save his people and to crush their foes. He shapes his ways of providence to this end. He might have swept off Pharaoh and his people with the same pestilence which destroyed so many of their cattle; but he had a wiser purpose. He could make a better use of their sin and of their life; so he spared them till he had wrought all his wonders upon Egypt before all the nations of the earth; and then he let them plunge into the mighty waves of the Red Sea and make their grave there!——Now if wicked men *will sin*, who shall object against God that he makes the best possible use of it? Why may he not reveal his power thereby and exalt his name as one "mighty to save" or to destroy?

3. It only remains to ask—What has God taught us of his character as bearing on the question before us, and of his agencies in the existence of sin?

Here few words ought to suffice. Nothing can be more plain than the revelations of scripture concerning God's character as infinitely pure and holy—as a Being who not only can never sin himself but can never be pleased to have others sin, and above all can never put forth his power to *make them sin*. God can not be tempted with evil, "*neither tempteth he any man*" (Jam. 1: 13). When he declares so solemnly and so tenderly: "O do not that abominable thing which I hate"! shall it still be said—But he puts men to sinning; pushes them on in their sin; inclines their heart to sin and hardens them to more and guiltier sinning? Never!

Shall it be claimed that with one hand God gives his Spirit to impress the truth on human souls unto their salvation; and with the other sends his Spirit to augment the forces of temptation and to harden men's hearts unto their damnation? Shall the same fountain send forth both sweet water and bitter? Shall the same God renew some human hearts unto holiness and harden other human hearts in sin—all by the same direct and similarly purposed agency, each work being

done under the same impulses of infinite love?——
Surely there must be some egregious misconception of
God's character involved in supposing him capable of
acts so fundamentally opposite and incompatible—not
to say, in supposing him capable of tempting men
into more and greater sin!

The fact that He wisely and mightily over-rules sin
to bring good forth from it should never be construed
to imply that he abhors sin any the less because he can
extort some good results from its existence.

CHAPTER XIII.

THE PASSOVER.

The first of the three great annual festivals of Israel,
and the one which above all was commemorative in
character—a memorial service—was the *Passover*. It
was designed to commemorate the deliverance of Israel
from Egyptian bondage—the great birth-hour of the
Hebrew nation. Especially did it commemorate the
scenes of that last eventful night when God caused his
angel of death to *pass over* the houses of Israel as he
went through the land of Egypt, smiting the first-born
in all her households.——The central thing in this institution was the slaying of the paschal lamb—one for
each household—and the sprinkling of its blood upon
the two side-posts, and upon the lintel over the door of
each house. This sprinkled blood, seen by the destroying angel, became his authority for *passing over* and by
that house, sparing its first-born, while he spared not
one first-born of all the families of Egypt.

There were numerous collateral points in the institution, designed to fill it out more completely and
make it most impressively a memorial service for all
the future generations of Israel; *e. g.* the following:

As to *time;* it was on the fourteenth day of the month
Abib, corresponding to our March or April—the night
next following this day being that of the last plague
on Egypt—the night which broke their yoke of bond-

age. Henceforth, this was made the first month in the Hebrew year.

The paschal lambs were *taken by households*. If the family was large, it stood by itself; if too small to consume one lamb, then two or more were united, the aim being to have the flesh of the lamb eaten entire. If any thing remained, it was to be burned in the morning.—It was to be roasted with fire, not eaten raw, and not boiled in water. (Ex. 12: 8, 9.) The arrangement *by families* looked toward the great fact of the original event—that Egypt was *smitten by families*—there being not a house in which there was not one dead. Its influence must have been precious through all the ages of Hebrew history in cementing family ties and sanctifying the family relation.

It was eaten with *unleavened bread*—the rule on this point being most stringent. No leaven might be eaten or even seen in their households during the entire feast of seven days. So prominent was this fact that the feast was called interchangeably, "The Passover," or "The feast of unleavened bread."——The original design of this prohibition seems to have been commemorative—the great haste of their departure precluding the preparation of leavened bread for their journey. The allusions to "leaven" in the New Testament (Matt. 16: 6, 11, 12, and Luke 12 and 1 Cor. 5: 7) indicate that leaven was associated with "pride that puffeth up," and is quite the opposite of that simplicity and purity of heart which God loves.

It was also eaten with bitter herbs, the vegetable condiments of the supper suggesting the bitterness of that bondage in Egypt out of which they came (Ex. 12: 8).——Yet another suggestive memorial usage was to eat with loins girt, shoes on, staff in hand (Ex. 12: 11), and in haste, as men ready to start a journey at a moment's warning.

The feast continued seven days (Ex. 12: 14–20), beginning with the evening of the paschal supper. The first day and the last were specially sacred, all labor being prohibited except that which was necessary in preparing their food (Ex. 12: 16).——The object in allowing so much time was to provide for extended religious ceremonial services and for wholesome social communion, not to say also for cultivating national sympathy and patriotism As all the males from every tribe in the whole land were required to come together on this great feast to the one place which God should appoint, the convocation was vast, and its social and religious influences were naturally both wholesome and great.

In the original institution it was specially enjoined that the history and purpose of this great festival should *be made known to their children.* "And thou shalt *show thy son* in that day, saying, This is done because of that which the Lord did unto me when I came forth out of Egypt" (Ex. 13: 7). "And it shall be when thy son asketh thee in time to come, saying, What is this? that thou shalt say unto him, By strength of hand the Lord brought us out from Egypt, from the house of bondage," etc. (Ex. 13: 14, 15.) How naturally would this wonderful story thrill the young hearts around the paschal board! How swiftly would the hours fly away while fathers rehearsed to sons the great national traditions, or read from the book of the law the narrative, and sung again and again the song of triumph over Pharaoh fallen with which this story closes! Jewish history has it that in ancient times it became the custom, after the paschal table was fully spread and the family had taken their places about it, for the servant suddenly to remove the prepared food away. Then when the hungry children opened their eyes wide and eager lips cried out—What does this mean? the head of the household rehearsed slowly and solemnly the meaning and purpose of the feast, with the history of its original institution; then when the curiosity of the little ones had been both aroused and enlightened, the provisions were replaced and partaken with a freshened sense of the grand significance of the Passover.

Closely associated with this festival and fraught with solemn significance as a memorial institution was the *consecration to God of all first-born males,* both the first-born of man and the first-born of beast (Ex. 13: 11–16). Of the lower animals the first-born males, if without blemish and if suitable for sacrifice, were to be offered in sacrifice to the Lord. If not suitable (*e. g.* the ass), it must be redeemed with a lamb—in which case the lamb became the sacrifice, and the ass might be used at the pleasure of its owner.

In the family, the first-born son was consecrated to God. In carrying out this principle, a substitution was made by which the entire tribe of Levi were put in the place of all the first-born males of Israel and held to be specially consecrated to God. The language (Num. 8: 14–18) is—"Thou shalt separate the Levites from among the children of Israel, and the Levites shall be mine. They are wholly given unto me from among the children of Israel, instead of such as open every womb, even instead of the first-born of all the children of Israel, have I taken them unto me. For all the first-born of Israel are mine both man and beast: on the day that I smote every first-born in the land of Egypt, I sanctified them for myself. And I have taken the Levites *for* [in the place of] all the first-born of the children of Israel."——The law prescribed the rites by which the Levites were set apart (Num. 8: 5–15).

The original institution of the Passover is rehearsed quite fully in Ex. 12 and 13; is referred to again briefly Ex. 23: 15, and 34: 18–20—this last giving emphasis to the consecration of the first-born. A brief notice of it appears Lev. 23: 5–8; the accompanying ritual services and offerings may be seen in Num. 28: 16–25; and a brief resume of the institution as given in Exodus 12 and 13 stands in Deut. 16: 1–8.

The Paschal Lamb with its sprinkled blood became a pertinent and impressive illustration of the central idea of the atonement by the blood of Christ, the elements common to both being—the shedding of blood—the blood of an innocent one—and especially the passing over the sprinkled souls by the destroying angel, while the unsprinkled were smitten by God's angel of death.——It is under the force of these and similar analogies that Paul speaks of Christ as being "our Passover"—[rather our Paschal Lamb], and as "sacrificed for us" (1 Cor. 5: 6–8). Pushing the analogies of the Passover feast one step further, he thinks of the exclusion of all leaven; then of leaven as naturally diffusive, and so as representing the pernicious influence of bad men in the Christian church; and therefore exhorts the Corinthian church to cast out the man guilty of incest lest his influence work like leaven.——These remoter analogies were forcible to persons familiar with the feast and its usages; yet we can not say they were properly involved in the typical significance of the Passover. The easy and natural manner in which Paul speaks of Christ as our Paschal Lamb shows that so far the resemblance was a well recognized fact, wrought into the current views of inspired men, not to say, of the church of that age. Without the shedding of blood there is no remission; with it and by means of it remission comes to the guilty, accepting it with penitence and with faith.

The long route to Canaan.

Scarcely had the Hebrew hosts set forth for Goshen before the question of the *route to Canaan* must be determined. That Canaan was their destination was settled long before. The first call of Abram designated the land of Canaan as the home of his posterity. Every renewal of that original promise specified the country which was given them. Now, for the course of their journey, the route along the south-eastern shore of the Mediterranean through the land of the Philistines was short and direct; but it must have brought them into contact inevitably with those powerful tribes from whom their descendants suffered so much during all the centuries intervening between Joshua and David. Just emerging from a bondage which spanned several generations and which had emasculated them of all national courage and spirit—but slightly trained moreover yet into the moral heroism which comes of living faith in God—they were in no condition to encounter such enemies. The record puts these points briefly: "God led them not through the way of the land of the Philistines although that was near, for God said—Lest peradventure the people repent when they see war and they return to Egypt; but God led the people about through the way of the wilderness of the Red Sea"* (Ex. 13: 17, 18). The long circuitous route is therefore chosen.——Wheeling suddenly to the

---

* That this fear was by no means groundless appears in the panic which smote their hearts when they saw Pharaoh's host pursuing (Ex. 14: 10–12), and also in the unbelieving fear manifested on hearing the report of ten of the spies returned from their forty days traversing of Canaan (Num. 13: 28, 31–33, and 14: 1–4).

right they put their faces squarely toward the Red Sea, beyond which lay the vast Arabian desert. Ultimately they entered Canaan on its Eastern and not its Western side—the quarter most remote from the Philistines.——In this wilderness route there were great purposes to be accomplished in the moral training and culture of the nation and in the manifestations of the God of their fathers before their eyes. That way lay the passage of the Red Sea which God provided as the burial-place for the proud hosts of Pharaoh: that way lay Sinai—those grand mountain cliffs which God was to shake with his thunders and invest with the smoke and the flame of his glorious presence that the law might be written in letters of fire upon the souls of the whole people: that way lay the long, breadless, waterless route of almost forty years wandering and sojourning in which the Lord fed the people with angels' food—bread from the lower heavens—the manna of the desert, and with water once and again from smitten rocks, flowing in dry places as a river—that they might learn the power and the love of their God:— that way lay also their long tuition and training into their religious system—a wonderful arrangement of sacrifices and ordinances for which the life-time of a generation was scarcely too long. All these great results and yet others were contemplated and provided for in this choice of the wilderness route as their way to the land of Canaan.

The March and the Pursuit.

The night of the fourteenth day of the first month was one to be long and gratefully remembered. Little sleep was there in the homes of Israel or in the dwellings of Egypt on that eventful night. The feast of the Paschal Lamb beginning with the early evening; the dread visitation upon Egypt of the angel of death at midnight; the hasty preparation for their journey throughout all the families of the children of Israel; the gathering and mustering of their hosts for the march of the next day:—such was the work of that memorable night. The stages of their march are definitely chronicled; one day from Rameses to Succoth (Ex. 12: 37); another day from Succoth to Etham, "in the edge of the wilderness" (Ex. 13: 20); another from Etham to Pi-hahiroth between Migdol and the Sea over against Baal-zephon (Ex. 14: 2). The same stages appear in the official record (Num. 33: 3–8) in which it is added that "Israel went out with a high hand in the sight of all the Egyptians, for the Egyptians buried all their first-born whom the Lord had smitten among them; upon the gods also, the Lord executed judgment"*—so that the shock of such and so much death and their funeral services for the dead diverted their attention from Israel and detained them from the pursuit for a season, giving the slow moving hosts of Israel time to reach the Red Sea before Pharaoh's swift chariots could overtake them.

The guiding Pillar of cloud and fire.

At this stage commenced that striking but most precious manifestation of God's guiding presence, of which the first record is—" And the Lord went before them in a pillar of a cloud to lead them the way; and by night in a pillar of fire to give them light; to go by day and night. He took not away the pillar of the cloud by day, nor the pillar of fire by night, from before the people (Ex. 13: 21, 22). If the order of the narration corresponds in time to the order of the events, this manifestation of the pillar commenced on the second day of their march as they moved from Succoth to Etham "in the edge of the wilderness." All through those otherwise dreary days of their marching and halting for forty years in the wilderness, this pillar was before them, appearing as a pillar of cloud by day but of fire by night—the symbol of Jehovah's presence in all their way, leading their path as they journeyed; marking their place of rest where they were to halt and pitch their tents.——Subsequent allusions to this pillar of cloud or of fire are somewhat numerous, *e. g.* Ex. 29: 43—showing that *in* this pillar God met his people and sanctified the tabernacle with his glory: Ex. 40: 34–38,

---

*Connecting the fact given in profane history that Egypt worshiped the ox and the cow as gods, with the fact of sacred history—that all the first-born of their cattle fell in this fearful plague, we shall understand how signally God "executed judgment on *Egypt's gods.*"

setting forth that when the tabernacle was in readiness, the cloud covered it and the glory of the Lord filled the most holy place, making that henceforth his special locality. Yet the pillar of cloud was lifted above the tabernacle as the signal for striking tents and moving forward. Its service as the signal for marching or resting is detailed minutely and beautifully in Num. 9: 15–23; and the prayer of Moses on these special occasions in Num. 10: 35, 36. When the ark set forward—"Rise up, Lord, and let thine enemies be scattered and let them that hate thee flee before thee"; and when it rested—"Return, O Lord, unto the many thousands of Israel."——Other allusions may be seen, Deut. 1: 23 and Neh. 9: 12, 19 and Ps. 78: 14, and 99: 7, and 105: 39 and Isa. 4: 5.

Remarkably when the Egyptian chariots and horsemen drew near toward evening of the third days' march, "the Angel of God, [embosomed in this pillar] which had been in front of their host, removed and went behind them"—putting himself thus between the men of Israel and the armed hosts of Egypt—"And it was a cloud and darkness to Egypt's hosts but gave light by night to Israel, so that the one came not near the other all night." Thus the angel of God in the cloud became, not their guide only, but their protector, their guardian angel. If there were godly men in Israel who like Moses could appreciate the salvation and the glory of Jehovah's presence, their hearts must have been a thousand times gladdened, and inspired with ixexpressible hope and consolation as they lifted up their eyes in their otherwise deepest darkness to see the pillar of fire ever near, the witness that God was near in all their wanderings. But especially *there* with the Red Sea before them and the chariots of Pharaoh behind—how safe they might have felt! for who is not safe under the wing of God's pillar of fire?

When Pharaoh's chariots and horsemen came in sight, rapidly gaining upon the slow-marching footmen of Israel's host, the latter were sore afraid and cried unto the Lord (Ex. 14: 10). This crying to the Lord would have been all right if only they had believed and trusted; for then they would have honored their great Protector, and they would *not* have chided Moses for leading them out of Egypt, nor would they have thought so readily of turning back to their cruel bondage.——With touching forbearance and grace the reply of Moses (from God) breathes scarce a whisper of rebuke: "Fear ye not; stand still and see the salvation of the Lord which he will show to you to day; for the Egyptians whom ye have seen to day, ye shall see no more again forever. The Lord shall fight for you, and ye shall hold your peace." The Lord did not propose to bring the people into direct battle with the trained hosts of Egypt at this early stage of their new life of freedom. They were in no manner prepared for the conflict of arms. This time the Lord alone would go into battle against Egypt. Israel might stand still and look on!

Moses, it seems, cried unto God; but whether because there was some implied unbelief in it, or because there was no time and no further need of prayer, the Lord answered—"Why criest thou unto me? *Speak unto the people that they go forward"!* The time for action and for placid trust in God had fully come.——But that deep Red Sea lies across thy path; lift up thy rod and stretch out thy hand over the sea and *divide it;* let Israel march through it dry-shod. The uplifted rod of Moses was the signal for the uplifted hand of God by which he forced the waters from their channel by a strong east wind all that night and made the bed of the sea dry for his people to pass over. The miracle in this case was exerted upon the wind rather than upon the water. God caused the east wind to blow strongly just when its effect was needed for the end in view. He turned the wind and hurried the waters back upon the Egyptians just when the opportune moment came for burying them beneath its mountain waves. If his wisdom had chosen to do so, his Almighty hand could just as easily have annihilated so much of the Red Sea waters as lay in the way of his people till they had passed its dry bed, and then have reproduced them for the destruction of Egypt. But in his mighty works God does not seek display but rather results, and these ordinarily by using only the least amount of supernatural agency which will suffice. It is of little account to attempt to fix the law of miracles, yet we may not infrequently observe the same method as is apparent here.

The historian alludes to yet another element of divine agency. In the morning watch as the host of Pharaoh were pressing on through the very midst of the bed of the sea, "the Lord looked unto the host of the Egyptians through the pillar of fire and of cloud, and troubled [rather confounded, smote with panic] their marching hosts; and took off their chariot wheels that they drave them heavily; so that the Egyptians said—Let us flee from the face of Israel, for Jehovah fighteth for them against the Egyptians."——It may not be possible, certainly is not specially important, to draw the line here between the natural and the supernatural. We may suppose that the pillar of cloud which had been darkness to them blazed forth fearfully in their faces, appalling the stoutest hearts with fear; that both horses and drivers were confounded; that wheel crashed into wheel and made advance impossible; that turning back for flight, their disorder and confusion became a rout, and that in this hour of crisis the returning waters surge and dash upon them and bury them en masse beneath the mountain waves! So perished the slave-holders and oppressors of God's ancient people! Thus signally did Jehovah exalt his name and win glory to himself as the Avenger of the oppressed and the faithful God of his Israel. The case falls into the same class with the flood and the fires on Sodom, to show before the ages how readily the Lord can find fit instruments of retributive justice for the swift punishment of the wicked even in this world whenever examples are needed to set forth his dipleasure against sin, and the certainty of his retributions upon the wicked. Under a system which normally puts over this retribution till after death, it might obviously be wise in the early ages of time to give some exceptional cases to stand as illustrations squarely before the eyes of living men, witnessing to the terrors of that retribution which can not linger long under the government of a just and holy God.

The night of doom to Pharaoh was the night of redemption to Israel. With the morning light they "saw the Egyptians dead upon the sea-shore"—men in their armor of battle; horses in the proud trappings of Egypt; broken chariots, all powerless now—are dashed up by the waves of the turbid sea and lie strewn upon the eastern shore—memorials at once of the danger that was and of the victory and triumph that are, and that are to be, the joy of God's redeemed people. Most fitly the deep emotions of the people seek expression in song. The oldest song known to history and one of the grandest, is here before us. "I will sing unto the Lord, for he hath triumphed gloriously:"—Ah, indeed, it was the Lord who wrought the victory; who went down alone into that eventful battle and who came back the mighty conqueror! "The horse and his rider hath he thrown into the sea." Over and over this central idea appears: "Pharaoh's chariots and his host hath he cast into the sea; his chosen chariots also are drowned in the Red Sea." "Thou didst blow with thy wind; the sea covered them; they sank as lead in the mighty waters." Let the Great God of Israel be praised for all this! Appropriately this is the burden of the song: "The Lord is my strength and my song, and he is become my salvation." "Who is like unto thee, O Lord, among the gods? Who is like to Thee, glorious in holiness, fearful in praises, doing wonders"?

Let us hope that the hearts of the saved people were deeply moved in the spirit of this sublime song; that they saw God as never before, and gave him the homage of their hearts, grateful, trustful, and adoring!

It may be noticed that Moses leads the thought of the people forward to the remote results of this redemption: "The nations shall hear and be afraid; sorrow shall take hold on the inhabitants of Palestine; all the inhabitants of Canaan shall melt away; fear and dread shall fall upon them . . . . till thy people pass over and thou hast planted them in their promised inheritance."

The moral results of this scene, we may hope, were really wholesome and effective upon the multitude. It amazes us to find that so soon afterward there were some among them who murmured for water, rebelled against Moses, made and worshiped a calf of gold: but the young, less depraved by their Egyptian life and perhaps more impressible by such manifestations of God, seem to have drank in the solemn lessons of these grand events.

The locality of the Red Sea crossing has been not a little controverted—until the researches of modern times. Since Dr. Robinson's personal examination of that region, including the site of Goshen, the route of their three days' travel till they reached the sea, the width of the sea at the various points between which the selection must be made, there has been a general if not universal concurrence in the conclusions to which he came. The location a little below Suez where the sea was supposably not far from one mile in width; where a strong easterly wind would drive out the waters from the channel—seems to fulfill all the historical conditions of the problem. See his Researches in Egypt and Palestine, Vol. I. pp. 74-86.

CHAPTER XIV.

THE HISTORIC CONNECTIONS OF MOSES WITH PHARAOH AND EGYPT.

THE thread of our history having now reached a point where we leave Egypt and have seen the last of that one particular Pharaoh, it is in place to take a final review of the questions—Who was this Pharaoh? Can he be identified in the annals of Egyptian antiquities? Have any points of chronological contact between the records of Egypt and the records of Moses been fixed reliably so that the one system can be laid alongside of the other and positive correspondence be made out?

Comparing the Hebrew records with Egyptian monuments and history, the following points of coincidence may be regarded as established.

1. That (as already observed) the kingdom of Egypt was thoroughly organized, was powerful, and had, apparently, the ripeness of age, in the times of Joseph and of Moses. In all these respects it was far in advance of the adjacent populations of Northern Africa and of South-western Asia.

2. That the state of the arts, the attainments of the learned in science, the usages of the people, the reign of law and of social order, indicated a state of civiliza-

tion much in advance of any thing else known in that age.

3. That all the minute references in sacred history to the common life of the people, to their occupations, to their skill in the arts, to the productions of the country, to their political relations with outside powers, are abundantly verified in the numerous monuments and authorities which testify what the Egypt of that age really was. The reference to many of these points in the history of the ten plagues admits of most ample verification from the ancient Egyptian authorities.

4. Particularly we find in Egyptian history the means of explaining how a new king might arise who "knew not Joseph (change of dynasty being a chronic infirmity); and how the monarch of an empire so magnificant, wielding a sway so despotic, might be tempted to defy Jehovah and proudly scorn to obey his command to "let the people go."

5. Yet again as to the sort of labor exacted unmercifully of the Hebrew people the evidence from Egyptian antiquities is fully corroborative. "They built for Pharaoh treasure cities, Pithom and Rameses," and were put to the severest toil in making brick; in the erection of buildings, including the transportation of the heaviest materials; and to "all manner of service in the field" (Ex. 1: 11, 14).——These treasure cities are identified with a high degree of certainty; and proximately some of the very kings by whom this service was exacted. Mons. Chabas* thinks he has found the Hebrews under name in official Egyptian records. He argues well that it must be in vain to look in the public monuments [e. g. in their temples] for any thing disastrous to the king or to his people—those monuments being consecrated to the triumphs and glories of the kingdom—official bulletins for this very purpose. This consideration rules out the ten plagues; the escape of the Hebrews; the overthrow of the Egyptians in the Red Sea. Events so disreputable and disastrous to Egypt need not be looked for on her sacred monuments. ——But the records on papyrus, consisting of both official and private correspondence, military reports, surveys of public works, financial accounts, etc., may furnish their name. The Hebrews were an important

* See Bibliotheca Sacra, Oct., 1863, p. 881.

colony, held forcibly upon the soil of Egypt, employed largely upon her public works. Consequently some notice of them may be reasonably looked for in the class of documents pertaining to the business of the realm.——Mons. Chabas maintains very sensibly that we should look for this people under the name "*Hebrews;*" not "children of Israel"—this being rather a religious than an ethnic designation; not "Israelites"— this name not having then come into use; not Jews, this name being first used many centuries later.

Three documents have been recently discovered which speak of a foreign race under the hieroglyphic name "Aperiu.". On principles of comparative philology, Mons. Chabas makes this word the equivalent of *Hebrew*. ——In the first document the scribe Kanisar reports to his superior: "I have obeyed the command which my master gave me to provide subsistence for the soldiers and also for the Aperiu who carry stone for the great Bekhen of King Rameses. I have given them rations every month according to the excellent instructions of my master."*——The second is similar: "I have furnished rations to the soldiers and also to the Aperiu who carry stone for the sun of [the temple of] the sun, Rameses Meriamen, to the south of Memphis."

Furthermore, Egyptian records show that they put their prisoners of war to such labors; for their kings record on the temples the number of captives they have taken to labor upon the temples of their gods.

Two of these documents on papyri belong to the reign of Rameses II, whom Mons. Chabas assumes to be the king whose daughter adopted Moses and whose son and successor, Mei-en-ptah, experienced the ten plagues and fell in the Red Sea. (Bib. Sacra, Oct., 1865, p. 685.)

6. It is a well-established fact of history that at one period—not yet located definitely—Lower Egypt was subdued and held by a Shepherd race, called by Josephus, "Hyksos," supposed to have come from adjacent provinces of Arabia or from Phenicia or both, and to have held the country from 350 to 500 years—a Vandal race, savagely desolating the noble monuments of Egyptian art and civilization, and known by the native Egyptians

---

* The term "Bekhen" is used for any kind of building—a temple, palace, or even a common house. Descriptions of what they built correspond to the sacred record, "treasure-cities."

as "the Scourge." This Shepherd race was ultimately driven out by the kings of Upper Egypt (a Theban dynasty)—probably before the age of Moses; perhaps before Jacob went down into Egypt. It may be considered certain that Josephus and others err in confounding them with the Hebrew people.——Geo. Rawlinson [in Aids to Faith, p. 293] says—"The period of the Shepherd Kings is estimated variously as continuing 500, 600, 900, and even 2,000 years; that historic monuments were generally destroyed during their dominion; that no reliable historic records exist older than the beginning of the eighteenth dynasty which expelled the Shepherd Kings; and that previously to their times, 'Association' in Royalty was practiced, two or even three kings sitting on the same throne at the same time, dividing its labors and its honors between themselves."

As to the date of this Shepherd rule, the diversity in opinion among the best informed students of Egyptian antiquity is by no means comforting or assuring. Dr. Lepsius and others have placed their invasion of Egypt directly after the twelfth dynasty (B. C. 2101), and their expulsion about B. C. 1591. In his chronology, Jacob went down into Egypt B. C. 1414; Moses led the people out B. C. 1314—neither date having the least regard to the scripture chronology.——Mons. Mariette dates it in the eighteenth century B. C., *i. e.* between B. C. 1700 and B. C. 1800. With this we might compare the sojourn of the Israelites in Egypt from B. C. 2033 to B. C. 1603; or on the chronology of Usher, from B. C. 1706 to B. C. 1491.——Brugsch dates their incursion B. C. 2115, and supposes them to have been Arabs from Arabia Petraea.——Bunsen's latest recension places their invasion B. C. 1983; their expulsion, B. C. 1548; and the Exodus of the Hebrews B. C. 1320—the last date being certainly wide of the truth.——The evidence is conclusive that their expulsion preceded the resplendent eighteenth dynasty whose kings ruled over all Egypt, and among whom was the Pharaoh who "would not let the people go." Dr. Thompson argues at considerable length that the entire occupation of Lower Egypt by the Hyksos must have *preceded* the residence of the Hebrews there; but feels the difficulties of the problem. He says—"As yet the *terminus a quo* remains in obscurity" [the point at which their occupation begins];

"while the *terminus ad quem* is beginning to take a fixed place in history." The date of their expulsion is mostly relieved of doubt. The war which resulted in their expulsion was begun by Seneken-Ra, about the commencement of the 18th dynasty of Thebes [Upper Egypt], and was prosecuted by Ahmes I, otherwise called Nebpeh-Ra, in whose fifth year they were finally expelled. The reign of Ahmes I is proximately assigned to the 17th century B. C., *i. e.* from B. C. 1600 to B. C. 1700.——A curious inscription has recently been discovered by Mons. Dumischen, referring to a brilliant triumph over the Lybians, achieved by a certain king Menephtah—this war being dated nearly 400 years after the expulsion of the Hyksos. The scribe appended the remark—"One could not have seen the like in the time of the kings of Lower Egypt when the country of Egypt was held by the "*Scourge*," and the kings of Upper Egypt could not drive them out."——This authority seems to prove that the Hyksos held only Lower Egypt; that Upper Egypt was under another dynasty, for a time unable to expel the Shepherd race, but ultimately successful, and subsequently attaining much greater military power; also that the Hyksos people were accounted a savage and barbarous race.

In conclusion I am constrained to say that the study of Egyptian antiquities, though richly remunerative and satisfactory in regard to almost every thing else, is still very dubious and perplexing in the point of *definite chronology.* The views of the ablest scholars are widely conflicting; the original authorities still wait for some master mind to put them into system, or what is perhaps nearer the truth, for the discovery of competent data from which a system can be constructed which shall harmonize all the authorities in the case. We want to know the Pharaoh to whom the Lord sent Moses, whose reign synchronizes with the Exodus. We find a series of powerful monarchs in the eighteenth dynasty and also in the nineteenth; but which of them answers to this particular Pharaoh, it seems yet impossible to determine with satisfactory certainty. Rameses II, all agree, was a powerful king; built immense public works; reigned at least sixty, perhaps sixty-six years;—but some authorities place him in the eighteenth and some in the nineteenth dynasty, and the extreme difference in the assigned dates for his reign is three hundred years.

The difficulties that invest Egyptian dates and dynasties seem at present to be aggravated rather than relieved by the progress of modern discoveries. Thus we find in the Bib. Sacra, Oct. 1867, (pp. 773 and 774) four parallel lists of the first three Egyptian dynasties, viz: (1.) That of Manetho; (2.) The Turin Papyrus; (3.) The Tablet of Sethos; (4.) The Tablet of Sakharah or Memphis. Compared with Manetho, the last three are of quite recent discovery. They are somewhat defective; yet it is not specially difficult to discover a striking similarity and in many cases an obvious identity in the names given. But the names in Manetho's list almost utterly lack even similarity; much more do they refuse to come into identity. The authority of the last three must, it seems to me, be decidedly greater than that of Manetho.——The same difficulty appears when we compare Manetho's names in the later dynasties (*e. g.* 18th–20th) with names constantly coming to light in recently discovered Egyptian monuments. I know not how this fact affects other minds. It can not but lessen my confidence in the lists of Manetho. It certainly goes far to lessen their practical value.——It is somewhat disheartening that these chronological difficulties clear up so slowly. It still remains to be hoped that light will yet break in and that conclusions will be reached in which all important authorities will be shown to concur.*

It would be a very great acquisition historically if we might know what Egypt was doing while the Hebrews were wandering in the wilderness forty years. Various circumstances conspire to favor the opinion that during this period her king made a vast military crusade upon Palestine and the regions farther north, occupying several years and greatly crippling the powerful tribes [kingdoms so called] then in possession of the land of Canaan. Both Josephus and Herodotus give accounts of a great military expedition of this sort—leaving, however, the main chronological prob-

---

* See Burgess on "The Antiquity of Man," pp. 68–84, on the unreliability of Manetho's lists and on the relative value of other authorities in Egyptian chronologies.

lem *When?* to be determined.——As to the great power of the kings of Canaan, the Lord said to Moses, "I will send a hornet before you to drive them out," *i. e.* to break down their power and facilitate the subjection of the country before the arms of Joshua. The original word translated "hornet" does not suggest the insect now commonly known by that name; but is equivalent to *scourge*, yet not precisely defining of what sort. It is supposable that Egypt and her next king after the Exodus, were more maddened than subdued by the escape of Israel and by the humbling disaster at the Red Sea; that this great expedition was inspired by the expectation of finding the Hebrew people in Canaan and of punishing them there; that God's providence shielded them with perfect protection in the great Arabian desert where no Egyptian host could follow them or even subsist; and then with that marvelous wisdom which so often turns the wrath of man to his own praise, used their prowess in arms to break down the military strength of Canaan and prepare that land for easy conquest before the arms of Joshua. It seems obvious that in point of military strength a great change had come over the tribes of Canaan between the visit of the spies and the conquest by Israel. Did the Lord use the chariots and horsemen of Egypt to produce this result? To have done so would be quite in keeping with that great law of his operations in this sinning world under which he so often turns the wrath of wicked men to account most signally and even gloriously to promote the ends of his own kingdom.

The Manna.

The divine plan of leading Israel to Canaan by the way of the great desert involved the question of *subsistence*—bread and water for such a host through so long a journey. It was perfectly obvious that the ordinary resources of this desert were entirely inadequate, so that the alternative was simply, miracle, or starvation. In the choice of miracle God had in view not only physical subsistence but moral culture—the perpetual impression upon the millions of Israel that their covenant-keeping God was feeding them every day with bread immediately from his own hand.

THE MANNA.

This bread took the name "manna" from the question asked by the people when they found it upon the ground in the morning—*What* is this? Their Hebrew words were—Man-hu; what this? All the ancient versions and most ancient authorities concur in deriving the name "manna" from this original question as put in Ex. 16: 15. [Our English version has the only correct rendering in the margin.]

The manna fell by night as the dew falls, and it would seem, fell with and in the dew so that when the dew evaporated under the morning sun, there remained this very fine deposit—"a small round thing, as small as the hoar frost upon the ground." "It was like coriander seed, white, and the taste of it was like wafers made with honey" (Ex. 16: 13–15, 31). A subsequent description (Num. 11: 7–9) adds—"The manna was as coriander seed and the color thereof as the color of bdellium. And the people went about and gathered it, and ground it in mills, or beat it in a mortar, and baked it in pans, and made cakes of it; and the taste of it was as the taste of fresh oil. And when the dew fell upon the camp in the night, the manna fell upon it."——The gathering, the preparation of it for cooking, and the cooking itself, cost labor, yet obviously none too much for the health and morals of the million. The physiological facts to be noticed are that it was sufficiently palatable for all practical purposes and had the necessary elements for the real bread—the staff of life—for a whole nation during forty years of wilderness life, with its alternations of marchings and encampments; of labor and of rest.

The points which evinced the miraculous hand of God were—that it came from no known or possible source of supply in the kingdom of nature; that it fell in the full amount needed for the thousands of Israel; fell on each of six mornings but not at all on the seventh, the Sabbath; that the average amount on five of these mornings was a supply for one day, while on the morning next preceding the Sabbath, a double quantity fell, being a supply for two days; that the gathering for the first five days of the week could be kept only one day, but the double supply of the sixth day remained sweet and pure for two days; and moreover, a quantity laid up by God's command in the sacred ark remained unchanged for many generations. Thus wonderfully did the Almighty impress his hand upon every feature of this bread from heaven!*

The allusions to manna in the Scriptures take note of the fact that "God *suffered them to hunger*" before he sent them this supply (Deut. 8: 3, 16). The record (Ex. 16: 1) states that it was already the fifteenth day of the second month since they came out of Egypt when the whole congregation murmured for bread and seemed to themselves about to perish of hunger in the wilderness. One month and a half must have quite exhausted the hasty and scanty supplies which they brought from Egypt. The marvel is how they could have subsisted upon this so long, even though coupled with all the supplies possible in that desert. That "God suffered them to hunger" is however only in harmony with his usual method of dealing with his people—subjecting them to a certain pressure of want for purposes of moral trial—the object being to test their faith in himself; to draw out their soul in prayer for help and in trust under darkness and in straits; and to make the blessing when given doubly precious. What Christian has ever lived long under any circumstances of this earthly life without some discipline under this great law of the Christian life—"He suffered thee to hunger" and then "fed thee with angels' food"?

Moses (Deut. 8: 16) makes a special point of the fact that this bread was such as neither they nor their fathers had ever known before. The Psalmist (Ps. 78: 24, 25) takes the lofty poetic view of this great gift of God: "He commanded the clouds from above and opened the doors of heaven and rained down manna upon them to eat and gave them of the corn of heaven. Man did eat angels' food: he sent them meat to the full."——Josh. 5: 12 shows that the manna ceased as abruptly as it began, precisely when it was needed no longer. The people having arrived in Canaan and supplies being within reach from the old corn of the land, the manna ceased and fell no more.

An article of commerce known under the name of

* The passages which treat of it are Ex. 16: 14–36 and Num. 11: 7–9 and Deut. 8: 3, 16 and Josh. 5: 12, Ps. 78: 24, 25 and Wisdom 16: 20, 21.

"manna," produced in the Arabian desert and in other Oriental regions, has scarcely any points in common with the manna of Scripture save the name. It exudes from shrubs; does not fall from the lower heavens in and with the dew; it is obtained at the utmost only about four months of the year; is most abundant in wet seasons—fails in the dry; is somewhat useful as a condiment and a medicine, but can never take the place of bread; and never has been known in such quantities as would supply bread for the hosts of Israel.

How long the pot of manna was preserved in the ark of the covenant can not be known definitely. We have the fact that the Lord directed its preservation there (Ex. 16: 32-34); and the further fact that when the ark was placed in the new temple of Solomon there was nothing in it save the two tables of stone (1 Kings 8: 9). It was doubtless kept long enough to subserve all the valuable purposes of a memorial to the generations of Israel. It has been embalmed in the Christian consciousness of the Christian age by its symbolical use in the teachings of our Lord in which it represents his flesh which he gave for the life of the world—the far more real bread of life from heaven (John 6: 31-35, 47-58).

Water Supplied by Miracle.

The subsistence of the Israelites during forty years in the desert of Arabia involved not only a supply of bread but of *water* also. On two distinct occasions—the first at Rephidim, close to Horeb, during the last half of the second month from Egypt; and the second at Kadesh, in the northern border of the great desert, and during the first month of the fortieth year from Egypt,* water was supplied them by miracle.

So great a multitude of people, including their animals, must have required a large supply of water.

---

* The precise date of the scenes at Kadesh (Num. 20) may be inferred from the death of Aaron which followed shortly after (Num. 20: 23-29), and is definitely dated (Num. 33: 38), viz. on the first day of the fifth month in the fortieth year from Egypt. The "first month" therefore, spoken of Num. 20: 1 must have been that of the fortieth year.

Nothing therefore is more probable than that the supply should often be short, and sometimes utterly fail. At Rephidim the people most unreasonably chode with Moses as if he alone was responsible for bringing them out of Egypt and for the lack of water, and as if their sufferings were so great as altogether to eclipse all the blessings of that great deliverance. Moses had no help but in the Lord his God. In answer to prayer the Lord provided for a miracle, to be well attested by the presence of a body of the elders of the people. "Take them with thee," saith the Lord, "and take also thy rod wherewith thou smitest the river" (the Nile) "and go. I will stand before thee there upon the rock in Horeb and thou shalt smite the rock, and there shall come water out of it that the people may drink."—— The names given were significant—"Massah" of their *tempting* the Lord by their unbelief; Meribah, of their *chiding* and *strife* as to Moses.

The scenes at Kadesh (Num. 20) were almost forty years subsequent, and consequently involved another generation. The spirit of their complaint was quite the same however—chiding Moses most unreasonably, petulantly wishing they had died before the Lord as so many of their brethren who had fallen under God's judgments in the wilderness since the unbelieving report of the spies and the consequent wrath of God upon the people. Sadly we must note here that this unreasonable and even cruel reflection upon Moses stirred his indignation, excited him unduly, and found expression in ill-advised words from his lips. The Lord had told him to take Aaron his brother, to gather the people together before the rock, and then *speak* to the rock before their eyes and it should give forth water. When the eventful moment came, Moses, instead of saying— Ye have sinned against the Lord your God, yet in his mercy he will give you rivers of water from this rock upon the word of command from his servant—said as in the record—"Hear now, ye rebels, must *we* fetch you water out of this rock"? In circumstances where man should be nothing and God all in all—man only a consciously unworthy instrument, and God the Supreme and ever to be honored Power, it was one of the sad infirmities of the best of men to put himself so prominently forward and thrust the Great God so ungratefully into the back-ground. Then, moved by the same excited passion, instead of speaking to the rock, he smote it with his rod, not once only but twice. Yet the Lord did not rebuke him with failure, but despite of his bad spirit, gave forth water abundantly. The rebuke upon both Moses and Aaron came shortly after in the form of an absolute prohibition upon their entering the land of promise. They had *so* dishonored the Lord in this case at Kadesh that he must needs express his disapprobation by denying to both of them the long-desired consummation of entering the goodly land.——If the Lord's rebuke of Moses seem severe, let it be considered that his sin was very great because he had been admitted into so near communion with God— such communion as had never been granted to any other man. If the guilt of sin be as the light sinned against, we are not likely to overestimate the guilt of his. The Lord speaks of it as rebellion (Num. 27: 14). And manifestly his sin was so public as well as so flagrant that it became vital to the honor of God's name and government to rebuke it unmistakably.

The exclusion from Canaan fell sorely upon the heart of Moses. He prayed earnestly that God would reverse this decree, but in vain. The Lord shut off all hope, saying, "Let it suffice thee; speak no more unto me of this matter" (Deut. 3: 23-27). Sorrowful are the words of Moses: "I must die in this land; I must not go over Jordan" (Deut. 4: 21).

The question arises naturally: Were these two cases—at Rephidim and at Kadesh—the only supplies by miracle during those forty years? One of them occurred during the first year of the forty; the other, during the last: was the whole intervening period barren of all miraculous supply? Or were these two cases put on record rather as specimens than as exhaustive history?——Yet another question comes up: How long did the supply in each of these two cases continue? Rephidim was adjacent to Sinai, and the hosts of Israel remained before and near that mountain many days. Did the supply from the Rephidim rock hold good during this entire period? Did it follow them along their journey in the wilderness still further?

To these questions the first answer is—that the history is silent as to the duration of the supply in either case. Moses might have told us definitely, but he has not.——Beyond this it only remains to take note of the allusions to this supply, made elsewhere in the Scriptures, and to suggest the probabilities of the case.—— The writer of Ps. 78 sings: "He clave the rock in the wilderness and gave them drink as out of the great depths. He brought streams also out of the rock and caused waters to run down like rivers" (vs. 15, 16). In Ps. 114: 8. we read—"Who turned the rock into a standing water; the flint, into a fountain of water." These words imply a great abundance for the time and seem to assume an ample supply so long as the hosts of Israel remained in those places. They do not necessarily imply that the waters followed them as a river in their journey onward from Rephidim or from Kadesh. ——The allusions in Isa. 43: 19, 20, and 48: 21 are decisive as to the temporary supply but indefinite as to its duration.——The words of Paul (1 Cor. 10: 4) should be noted. "Our fathers all drank the same spiritual drink (for they drank of that spiritual Rock that *followed* them and that Rock was Christ").——In this passage, drinking of the Rock can be nothing else than drinking *of the waters* that issued from the rock. The only question of importance exegetically is—whether the words "followed them" refer to the waters or to the presence of Christ as in the pillar of cloud and of fire. The former seems the more obvious and natural reference, and, in so far, favors the view that these waters, furnished miraculously, did follow them to some extent on their journey—perhaps in the way of fresh supplies provided for them in a similar manner. It can not be doubted that the hosts of Israel *had water* through all their journeyings; they could not have subsisted long without it. The natural supply must have been vastly greater in that age than in this if it sufficed for this great host at all other points of their journey save at Rephidim and at Kadesh. The fact of a constant supply of bread by miracle favors the assumption of water miraculously provided whenever the supply from natural sources failed to meet their necessities. This is perhaps the utmost we can say in the way of probabilities.

The Battle With Amalek.

While Israel was on the march near Rephidim, the Amalekites fell savagely upon their rear in a dastardly, unprovoked assault, described by Moses (Deut. 25: 17, 18): "Remember what Amalek did to thee by the way when ye were come forth out of Egypt; how he met thee by the way and smote the hindmost of thee, even all that were feeble behind thee when thou was faint and weary; and he feared not God." The day following, Moses summoned Joshua to choose men for war and go out against Amalek, proposing for himself to take his stand upon a hill adjacent with the rod of God in his hand. His uplifted hand and rod became the symbol or rather the visible manifestation of prayer. While held up aloft, Israel prevailed; let down, Amalek prevailed. To achieve victory despite of the weariness of Moses, a stone was placed for him to sit upon; then Aaron and Hur on either side held up his hands until the going down of the sun. Thus victory was achieved; Amalek was defeated, and what is specially to be noted, a signal illustration was afforded of the power of prayer and a sublime testimony placed on record before all Israel that in God they were mighty against their foes and could have nothing to fear. So important were these great moral lessons that the Lord directed Moses to "write this for a memorial in *the* book" [not merely *a* book]—the well-known public record in which the wonderful works of God for Israel were to be permanently preserved.——Another reason for the record was that Amalek was doomed for this outrage, and the future kings and warriors of Israel received from time to time their divine commission to execute this sentence of extermination. (See Deut. 25: 19, and 1 Sam. 15, etc., etc.)

There are some differences of opinion as to the history and geographical location of these Amalekites. The name "Amalek" appears (Gen. 36: 12) as the grandson of Esau; whence some have found the origin, genealogically, of this people there; but they appear much earlier (Gen. 14: 7).——As to their *home* geographically, their nomadic habits require a somewhat wide range of territory within which they may be found. The passages 1 Sam. 15: 7, and 27: 8, locate them in the district lying between the Philistines and Egypt, along the eastern shore of the Mediterranean in Arabia Petrea. We find them repeatedly associated with the Midianites, Moabites, and Ammonites in raids upon the children of Israel during the time of the Judges and onward to the reign of David (Judg. 3: 12, 13, and 6: 3, and 1 Sam. 30: 1). They come to view in the visions of Balaam (Num. 24: 20), spoken of there as "the first of the nations"—a phrase which can scarcely refer to their high antiquity (though this construction is barely possible); but more probably it refers to the fact that they were the first to make war upon Israel after the latter assumed her distinctly national character. So understood, the description of Amalek looked historically back to the facts before us Ex. 17. Balaam foresaw their early destruction—their case being in this respect solemnly admonitory to the king of Moab.

Let us not pass this historic fragment without a passing allusion to its admirable fitness as the opening scene in Israel's relation to hostile foreign powers. She had and was destined to have national enemies. It was clearly in the policy of the Lord her God that she should fight these enemies with arms in deadly combat. Hence it was vital that she should be taught in the outset where her strength for victory actually lay. This onslaught of Amalek upon her rear and the ensuing battle, terminating in victory through prayer without ceasing—the uplifted arms of their Moses sustained till the sun set upon the victorious arms of Joshua—became their standard lesson—the first and the permanent example to show them the fountain of their strength—the ground of assured victory while they lived in obedience to God and trusted his arm alone.——It scarcely need be said that all the spiritual conflicts of God's people with sin and Satan fall under the same general law—victory through prayer sustained and unfaltering—victory in the strength of Israel's God alone.

Jethro.

In Ex. 18, Moses narrates a visit from his father-in-law who brought to him his wife and children, left in his care ever since the scenes of which we read Ex. 4: 18–26. Jethro is before us here as both a good and a wise man—*good* in that his heart is shown to be with God and with God's people, "rejoicing for all the goodness which the Lord had done to Israel whom he had delivered out of the hand of the Egyptians" (18: 9); and *wise* in that he saw at a glance that the burdens then borne by Moses in the administration of justice among the people would soon break him down; and in his admirable suggestions of a better method which from that day became established among the Hebrew people. For both reasons such a visit deserved a permanent record. It refreshes us to think of that good man who had known Moses forty years as his worthy son-in-law, yet moving only in the humble sphere of a shepherd's wilderness life; but now meeting him God's recognized Leader of the thousands of Israel and hearing from his lips the wonders God had wrought on Egypt and on Pharaoh; the deliverance from national bondage; the passage of the Red Sea and the entrance upon a wilderness march underneath the cloudy pillar; subsisting on the "corn of heaven" and on rivers of water from the rock of Rephidim; and withal having just then achieved their first victory over the first foreign power that dared assail them:—all this recital from the lips of such a son must have moved the aged father's heart with unwonted emotions. We are not surprised that he should exclaim: "Blessed be the Lord" [your nation's own Jehovah] "who hath delivered you out of the hand of the Egyptians and out of the hand of Pharaoh. Now I know that the Lord is greater than all gods, for in the thing wherein they dealt proudly, he was above them" (18: 10, 11).——Then, being a priest, ["priest of Midian" Ex. 2: 16 and 18: 1], he proceeded to offer sacrifices in the manner which had come down traditionally from the earliest fathers. "He took a burnt offering and sacrifices for God; and Aaron came and all the elders of Israel to eat bread with Moses' father-in-law before God" (v. 12). The term "burnt offering" is usually applied to a sacrifice which is burnt entire upon the altar. The phrase "sacrifice for God," refers here to a peace-offering upon portions of which the worshipers partook in the manner of a religious feast—an act at once religious toward God and social toward man.

The next day Moses resumed his accustomed routine of labor, sitting for the administration of justice to the people from morning till evening. The spirit which we see in Moses where he appears first in active life (Ex. 2: 11-13) would naturally put him to this service. His prestige as the recognized Leader of Israel under God would turn the eyes of all the people to him as their Judge. Hence naturally this overwhelming burden, from which relief came through the wise suggestion of Jethro. This was that a gradation of subordinate courts be instituted so that cases of lesser magnitude and difficulty might be administered by others, and only the more difficult be brought before Moses. The guiding principle in the classification was at first both tribal and numerical—following their division into tribes and their numbers. After their location in Canaan the numerical element gave place to the geographical. Judges had their province and their responsibility limited, not by thousands and hundreds directly but by cities and localities. With this modification the system passed into established usage among the Hebrews.——In a parallel passage (Deut. 1: 9-18) Moses recites the same transaction, omitting all allusion to his father-in-law, and giving prominence to the qualities requisite in judges, and to the principles of justice and righteousness by which they were to be governed.——At the close of this brief interview Jethro returned to his home and people. His son Hobab, brother-in-law of Moses, appears in the history somewhat later (Num. 10: 29-32), and seems to have consented to act as guide to Moses and Israel in their march from Sinai to Kadesh, and not improbably until they reached the Jordan. The home of the family had been on the East and South of Horeb. In the period of the Judges and onward they are in the Northern border of the great Arabian desert. (See Judg. 1: 16 and 4: 11 and 1 Sam. 15: 6).

THE SCENES AT SINAI.

The National Covenant and the Giving of the Law.

Events of most vital bearing upon the national life of the Hebrew people are now before us. No longer one family as in Abraham and Isaac and Jacob; no longer a mere tribe, clustering several families under one or more patriarchs, but a group of many tribes, enlarging fast toward the proportions of a great nation;—and what is more, a people no longer under the emasculating incubus of bondage, but emancipated, and free to rise and assume the duties of self-government with all its possibilities of growth and improvement, personal and national—this great people, were at this point summoned of God to enter into solemn national covenant with himself. In its spirit and significance this covenant differed in no essential point from that which God made with Abraham more than six hundred years before. In that earlier covenant Abraham spake for himself, and so far as it was naturally possible, for his posterity as well; and God on his part promised to be a God not to him only but to his seed after him; yet when this seed of Abraham became a great people, there was special fitness in summoning them to renew this covenant *for themselves.* Precisely this was done before Sinai.

The Lord reminded them most appropriately of what he had so recently done for them. "Ye have seen what I did unto the Egyptians, and how I bare you on eagle's wings and brought you unto myself." It was as if he had lifted them up from earth toward heaven and borne them forth and out from their national bondage—as the eagle might take up her young and bear them aloft beyond the reach of whatsoever hostile power were tied down upon the earth's surface. God had done this for the definite purpose of *bringing them to himself.* "Now, therefore, (he proceeds) if ye will obey my voice indeed and keep my covenant, then ye shall be a peculiar treasure to me above all people, for all the earth is mine; and ye shall be to me a kingdom of priests and a holy nation" (Ex. 19: 4–6). In this divine proposal the central word, translated here "peculiar treasure," appears in Ps. 135: 4 translated in the same way; but in Deut. 7: 6 with a different translation—"A *special people* unto himself, above all people that are upon the face of the earth." The sense is—a special property— a people by the choice of God and by their own voluntary consecration, made peculiarly his own. Moses in Deuteronomy (as above) labors to impress upon the people the thought and purpose of God in this covenant relation: The Lord did not set his love upon you nor choose you because ye were more in number than any [other] people; for ye were the fewest of all people; but because the Lord loved you and because he would keep the oath which he had sworn unto your fathers, hath the Lord brought you out with a mighty hand and hath redeemed you out of the house of bondmen from the hand of Pharaoh king of Egypt." Of kindred significance are the other phrases used to express their new proposed relation to God—"A kingdom of priests and a holy nation." This strong language—"a kingdom of priests"—gives us the thought of a *whole people*—every man in all the nation, personally consecrated to God, as if the nation were made up of priests and of such only. God would have them understand that the holiness he required of them was not the professional service of a chosen few, but the free-will offering of every man's own heart and life. The whole people—every individual man—was summoned to come into this national covenant. Would they come?

Moses called for the elders—who acted as the representatives of the whole people and "laid before their faces all these words from the Lord." At once all the people answered together and said—"All that the Lord hath spoken we will do."——Let us hope that a fair proportion, including at least many of the representative men of the nation, were thoroughly sincere in this profession. It would be grateful to our feelings to believe that they all both understood and meant what they said. But, alas! subsequent developments forbid this belief. It was however the formal consent of the nation. As a whole people they gave their voice to this definite proposal from the Lord their God—that he would be their God and that they would be his people.

The next thing in order, is the *giving of the law*. A people who propose to be the Lord's and to obey his voice, should be made acquainted with his will in the form of *law*. They must be informed what he would have them *do*. Rules of heart and life, precepts defining the reverent homage and worship due to God, and the acts required or forbidden as toward their fellow-men should be made unmistakably plain. Prepara-

THE GIVING OF THE LAW.

tions are accordingly made for the formal and solemn promulgation of this great moral law. It is noticeable that in these preparations nothing seems to be omitted that might conduce to a deep and solemn impression. The people are specially enjoined to sanctify themselves, and two full days are set apart for this purpose. They were commanded to "wash their clothes"—significant of the personal purity of heart which God required.——Then the surroundings were of the most imposing and impressive character. The whole people were gathered in an open plain which lay at the foot of Sinai. The most stringent precautions forbade all curious, irreverent approach. Not a man or beast might touch the mountain on pain of death. Definite bounds were set for the people over which no one might pass. There before them full in view stood the awful mount—rugged, grand, cleft with fissures, broken with deep ravines, towering in sublime height and all enwrapped in thick clouds out of which lightnings flashed—the whole mountain rocking under the footsteps of the Almighty and reverberating with his awful thunder, and the voice of trumpet exceeding loud so that all the people in the camp trembled. The written description of this scene gives us a sense of its ineffable grandeur and sublimity. "Mount Sinai was altogether on a smoke because the Lord descended upon it in fire; and the smoke thereof ascended as the smoke of a furnace, and the whole mount quaked greatly. When the voice of the trumpet sounded long and waxed louder and louder, Moses spake and the God answered him by a voice."——Essentially the same descriptive points are repeated after the record of the law as promulged from Sinai (Ex. 20: 18-21). "All the people saw the thunderings and the lightnings and the noise of the trumpet and the mountain smoking; and when the people saw it, they removed and stood afar off, and said to Moses: Speak thou with us and we will hear; but let not God speak with us lest we die." See also the renewed mention of this scene in Deut. 4: 10-12.*

---

* Bearing in mind that the Israelites had lived in the valley of the Nile, all unused to mountain scenery, we may readily understand how these scenes around the base of Sinai must have impressed them. It is quite in place here to bring before our mind

The Moral Law as given from Sinai.

Passing from the natural surroundings and scenes of Sinai to the law itself, let it be observed carefully that this law of ten commandments (Ex. 20: 1–17 and Deut. 5: 6–21) is to be somewhat broadly distinguished from the other "statutes and judgments," whether civil or

the physical features of this wonderful pile of rocks and cliffs. A modern writer supplies the following sketch:

"The entire Sinaitic group presents the most impressive indications of the terrible convulsions by which its labyrinth of mountain heights has been rent and torn since its first upheaval. From the summit of Mt. Serbal, as from a watchtower in high heaven, one looks down upon a perfect sea of mountain ridges, often precipitous, always intensely steep, and culminating in a sharp edge at the height of two, three, or four thousand feet from their base. The entire line of these mountains is seen to have been rent transversely by clefts from the base to the summit, filled with injections of basaltic rocks, striping the mountain on every side with black bands. The whole assemblage is a perfect ganglion of ridges thrown up in wild confusion with its strata dislocated, disjointed, dipping in all directions and at every angle from horizontal to perpendicular. The mountains of Sinai form no system, no regular ranges, like the Alps, the Appenines, the Pyrenees, or the mountains of America." (Bib. Sac. April 1867, p. 253).

——Dr. E. Robinson gives his impressions from personal inspection—thus: "Here the interior and loftier peaks of the great circle of Sinai began to open upon us—black, rugged, desolate summits; and as we advanced, the dark and frowning front of Sinai itself (the present Horeb of the monks) began to appear.——The scenery reminded me strongly of the mountains around the Mer de Glace in Switzerland. I had never seen a spot more wild and desolate.—— As we advanced the valley still opened wider and wider, shut in on each side by lofty granite ridges with rugged, shattered peaks a thousand feet high, while the face of Horeb rose directly before us. Both my companion and myself involuntarily exclaimed: "Here is room enough for a large encampment"! Reaching the top of the ascent, a fine broad plain lay before us, sloping down gently toward the S. S. E., inclosed by rugged and venerable mountains of dark granite, stern, naked, splintered peaks and ridges, of indescribable grandeur; and terminated at the distance of more than a mile by the bold and awful front of Horeb, rising perpendicularly in frowning majesty from twelve to fifteen hundred feet high. It was a scene of solemn grandeur, and the associations which at the moment rushed upon our minds, were almost overwhelming." [Robinson's Researches Vol. I. p. 130, 131.]——This plain stretching out from the foot of this precipitous mount, is supposed to have been the identical place where the people were gathered to see the mountain all aflame—to hear the sound of trumpet long and loud, and to listen to the voice of God proclaiming the words of his law.

THE LAW OF TEN COMMANDMENTS. 237

religious, which the Lord gave to Israel by the hand of Moses;—this distinction being apparent in the following points and for the reasons which they suggest:

1. It was proclaimed by God himself in a most public and solemn manner in the hearing not of Moses alone, but of the elders of the people at least, if not of the people en masse, assembled before and around the glorious mount.

2. It was given under circumstances of most appalling majesty and sublimity—the mountain being enveloped with clouds and thick darkness, yet at some moments all ablaze with the lightning's flash and rocking beneath Jehovah's feet.

3. It was written by the finger of God on two tables of stone (Deut 5: 22).

4. It differed from any and all other laws given to Israel in that it was comprehensive and general rather than specific and particular.

5. It was complete, being one finished whole to which nothing was to be added—from which nothing was ever taken away. ("And he added no more" Deut 5: 22. See also Mat. 5: 18). The other statutes, as we shall see, were subjected to future modification.

6. The law of the ten commandments was honored by Jesus Christ as embodying the substance of the law of God enjoined upon man. With a master's hand he grasped and brought out its two great principles, underlying all the precepts: Love supreme to God: love equal and unselfish toward fellow-men. "Thou shalt love the Lord with all thy heart, and thy neighbor as thyself." (Mat. 22: 36-40, and 19: 18, 19 and Mk. 12: 28-34).

7. It can scarcely be doubted that Jesus had his eye specially if not exclusively on this law (Mat. 5: 18) as one *never to be repealed*—from which not one jot or tittle should ever pass away.

To this great moral law of ten commandments we now give special attention and note—That its introduction (Ex. 20: 2), "I am the Lord thy God which have brought thee out of the land of Egypt—out of the house of bondage"—is special—not general and universal; is adapted to the circumstances of Israel, and gives a special reason why *they* should honor this law as coming from the God of their national covenant, the Redeemer and Savior of their nation. On the one hand this special reason why Israel should render supreme homage to Jehovah as their Deliverer from Egyptian bondage neither applies specifically to all mankind, nor does it imply that this law is not binding on other people than Israel. It was pertinent that as given originally to them it should be preceded and introduced by this special consideration, so pertinent to their case. Yet it should be thoughtfully considered—God might have said most truly to every child of his great human family—I am He who gave thee thy being and every good; and therefore I claim thy supreme love and homage.——I see no reason to question that this clause was put on the two tables of stone—its special introduction as given to the children of Israel.

I. In the first precept, the words "before me" are construed variously. The most usual and obvious translation of the Hebrew words is—*before my face*. In some connections the preposition might mean *upon* or *above*. "My face" is thought by some to be merely equivalent to *myself*. Keil translates—"literally *beyond me*, or in addition to me, equivalent to except me, or by the side of me." He rejects the construction, "before me" (in my presence) as incorrect, and also condemns *against me*—in opposition to me. Fuerst has it "above *i. e.* except me." Murphy says—"before me" is literally "upon my face." It supposes those other gods to be set up *before* the true God as antagonists in the eye of God and as casting a shade over his eternal being and incommunicable glory in the eye of worshipers."—— The two constructions—*beyond* me and *above* me—are open to the objection that they seem tacitly to admit other gods provided they are inferior and that God is supreme. I prefer as the more obvious and natural construction—*before my face*. Thus the precept forbids homage to any other god in the presence of the supreme and omniscient Jehovah; and by consequence, forbids divine honor to any other being or thing whatsoever. "Thou shalt have no other gods *before my face*" seems to imply that the least acknowledgment of other gods is in its very nature an insult to Jehovah, as if it thrust those gods into his very face—held them up before his eye as more worthy of homage than he. Moreover, as no possible worship of other gods can escape his eye, or be otherwise than thrust up before his face, the prohibition necessarily shuts off all such worship. You may never worship other gods than the One Supreme Being, for it is simply impossible that any such worship can elude his eye, and you must not put it before his face.

II. The second command prohibits the making and worshiping of images designed to represent idol gods— imaginary powers, supposed to have more or less control over human welfare. It equally prohibits images designed to represent the true God. All such sensuous conceptions of God are necessarily debasing. They rest on false views of God; tend to fearful and fatal degeneracy; and must therefore be forbidden under most stringent penalties. The whole history of our race witnesses to the infinite mischief wrought by such sensuous conceptions of God, as well as by the notion of subordinate powers, lower than the one supreme yet more than human. This has been one of Satan's devices to rule God out of his universe and transfer to other objects the worship due to God alone.

This prohibition as it stands here is not enforced by specific penalties, but in a way far more impressive it bears us back to the very heart of God, revealing his holy *jealousy* of any rival to his throne who would wrest and steal away from him the supreme love and homage of his creatures, and give it to supposed gods that are no Gods at all. "For I am a jealous God, visiting the iniquity of the fathers upon the children unto the third and fourth generation of them that hate me."——By the very law of the family relation, the great sins of the father send their curse down upon his children. He makes them heirs to an inheritance of shame and sorrow. He entails calamity upon his offspring. Godless and idolatrous himself, he makes his family also godless and idolatrous. The influence of his sin will naturally and almost inevitably blight the morals and the souls of his children after him, and of his children's children. Let this fact throw its shield like a wall of fire around him and his family, so that, if not for his own sake, at least for the sake of his unborn offspring, he will most sacredly obey this command and abstain from the least infringement of it in spirit or in letter.

"Visiting iniquity" and "showing mercy" are set over against each other—the penal visitations of judgment for this sin warning men against it; and the great promises of mercy to the obedient alluring them to its most diligent observance. Judgment is God's strange work, while mercy is his delight. Therefore we have here the forceful antithesis—the visiting of the iniquities of fathers upon children to the third and fourth generation, but the showing of mercy unto thousands of generations of them that love and obey. To a Hebrew mind this last clause of the second command would naturally suggest God's mercies to Abraham, the well-known friend of God, upon whose posterity God was shedding forth his blessings to thousands of generations. So richly does the loving God reward his dutiful and trustful children! So much more grateful to his heart it is to bless even to the thousandth generation than to visit iniquity even so far as to the third and fourth!

It should be carefully noted that the visiting of the iniquities of fathers upon sons falls only *upon those who hate him*. If sons in any future generation turn from their sinning to the love of God, his merciful loving-kindness to them is sure. The curse visits only those who persist in the sin of their fathers despite of all the warning judgments that should admonish them to fear God. (See Ezek. 18).——This injunction against image-making and worship would naturally suggest to the men of Israel the idolatrous Egyptians. Their early fathers received from Noah the knowledge of the one only true God. But they did not love this knowledge, nor the God whom it revealed; therefore, not liking to retain these views of the pure and holy God, they chose to think of him as being like some of his works and began to worship such imaginary gods; or they put in his place some lower beings or powers as objects of worship. Hence the terrible judgments which the children of Israel had seen falling upon Egypt and her idols.

"Upon those that love me" is delightfully suggestive of the great truth that the essence of all acceptable worship is love. God looks complacently on his human children when they delight in his glory, love his character, rejoice in his blessedness, and make it the best joy of their souls to please him by doing all his will. Such love legitimately flows out in reverent worship and adoring homage. Over against this the worship of idols in place of God is congenial only to the souls that hate God. This command assumes that those who wor-

THE LAW OF TEN COMMANDMENTS. 241

ship other gods really hate the one Supreme Jehovah. Therefore it is that his jealousy burns against them. They withhold from him the love and the homage of their hearts.

III. In the third command the exegetical question is whether it refers primarily and properly to perjury, or to profanity, *i. e.* whether the Hebrew word for "*in vain*" * is precisely falsehood, or emptiness, a nothing, a thing of no worth. The current of critical opinion (Gesenius, Fuerst, etc.) goes for the former, falsehood; and makes the precept in its strict sense condemn perjury. Thou shalt not take up the name of Jehovah to a falsehood—shalt not use it to affirm the more solemnly what is false. Yet as what is false has no foundation in fact, and in point of truth is nothing—is only an emptiness—it comes to pass that this Hebrew word takes not infrequently this secondary sense—what is *empty, vain*. Hence some able critics [*e. g.* Keil] construe this precept to prohibit "all employment of the name of God for vain and unworthy objects so as to include not only false swearing, but trivial swearing in the ordinary intercourse of life and every use of the name of God in the service of untruth and lying—for imprecations, witchcraft, or conjuring."——The construction of Keil, being the more broad and comprehensive, and withal being clearly within the established usage of the original word, is to be preferred. The doctrine of inspiration is—"Thy commandment is exceeding broad" (Ps. 119: 96).——The *name* of God is associated closely with the idea and thought of God. Hence all irreverent use of this name naturally begets irreverence of spirit toward God, and must be fearfully pernicious. Using God's sacred name to affirm the more solemnly a falsehood is more than mere irreverence, and must incur his highest displeasure.

The fourth command—the law of the Sabbath—has been already treated somewhat fully in connection with the original institution of the Sabbath in Eden. I must dissent entirely from those critics who deny the existence of any Sabbath law prior to Sinai. To "bless the seventh day and sanctify it" (as said in Gen. 2: 3) has no meaning if it do not mean that God required the day to be one of rest from labor—a day of holy

* שׁוא

time, devoted to other than ordinary uses.——Fully in harmony with this construction of these words is the allusion to the Sabbath in the history of the manna (Ex. 16: 22–30), and also the *form* of the precept here (Ex. 20: 8), which is not precisely—Thou shalt do all thy work during six days, but none on the seventh;—but it is this: "*Remember* the Sabbath-day to keep it holy." The implied injunction of the words spoken in Eden was—make it a holy day. God blessed the seventh day and made it holy: now, therefore, *remember* that original injunction. To remember a previous day made holy, must surely imply a precept setting it apart as holy time.

As given here the law of the Sabbath is expanded into its legitimate details. The prohibition of labor is applied to children, to servants, to cattle and to strangers. Then the reason for the command, essentially as given in Eden, is reiterated; "For in six days the Lord made heaven, earth, sea, and all creatures; but rested on the seventh day; therefore he blessed and hallowed this Sabbath-day." Noticeably, the statement following "therefore," uses the same Hebrew verbs—"bless," and "sanctify" [or "hallow"] which are used Gen. 2: 3.——It seems plainly implied that God places before men his own example of creative work during six day-periods and of rest from this work on the seventh as a reason or motive for their observance of the Sabbath—one day of rest after six of toil. A secondary consideration is doubtless that by this arrangement the Sabbath would be perpetually suggestive of man's relation to God as his Infinite Creator and Father. The linking of the Sabbath to God's creative work and rest would naturally make that work a fact ever present to human thought—blending its influence with the sacredness and with all the employments of this holy day. Man desists from labor. Why? Because God did. After what labor? That of making the heavens and the earth and man. Therefore let man remember God as his Creator and render him the homage of obedience and the homage of adoration, gratitude and praise. Thus the historic origin of the precept became suggestive of the thoughts, the words, and the divine worship appropriate to this holy day.

It is scarcely in place here to discuss the Christian

change from the seventh to the first day of the week, further than to remark that a similar suggestive influence came in as the purpose and object—*the choice of the day suggesting the resurrection of Christ.* The original reference to God as Creator need not be practically lost: but we may practically gain a second group of suggestive and most vital truths—those which cluster round the resurrection of our Lord.

V. The fifth command consecrates its strength to the family relation. Addressed to children it requires them to honor their father and their mother, and makes obedience the condition of long life and prosperity in the land of their promised inheritance. As read in Ex. 20: 12 the command specifies only long life, but as repeated in Deut. 5: 16, "that it may go well with thee"—is added. General prosperity is however involved and implied in length of days.——Obviously this honor carries with it obedience as well as due respect. Such honor is vital to the happiness and the value of the family relation. Without it no foundation can ever be laid for a useful and worthy after-life. It should not be overlooked that the earliest training of the infant mind Godward should begin with cultivating the honor and obedience due to father and mother. Through all the earliest developments of the infant and youthful mind, the parent is to the child in the place of God. The same qualities of character, the same obedience, respect, and deference, which God requires toward himself are to be first implanted and developed in the mind toward the human parent. Failing of their due development in this antecedent relation, they are almost certain never to be developed toward God: a fatal defect in character is fastened upon the child; a cast of mind is determined which but too surely ends in hopeless ruin.——It is noticeable that this very association of ideas, uniting the homage due to parentage and years with the honor due to God appears in the Mosaic law (Lev. 19: 32); "Thou shalt rise up before the hoary head and honor the face of the old man; and *fear thy God:* I am the Lord."

VI. The next four precepts are a series beginning with the most vital, designed to protect the rights of person and life; of chastity; of property; and of reputation. The precepts forbid murder, adultery, theft, false witness, or defamation. The prohibition of murder must be construed broadly enough to forbid personal injuries on the one hand; and on the other all those passions—hate, malice prepense—which naturally lead on toward violence and murder.——The prohibition of adultery in like manner forbids not only all illicit sexual connection, but even unchaste desire (Matt. 5: 27, 28). So the prohibition of theft devolves the duty of caring for our neighbor's property so far as the law of loving our neighbor as ourself would require. It is not enough that we do not take his property and appropriate it to our own use. We must protect his right to his property as he should ours. In like manner the law forbidding the bearing of false witness against our neighbor involves the duty of protecting and cherishing his reputation. We may never forget that our neighbor's good name is a treasure to him which we not only must not steal away, but must so far as in us lies guard and defend as if his good were worth as much as our own. The one comprehensive principle which embraces all these points of law toward our neighbor and determines their true interpretation is given in the law of Moses as well as in the law of Christ—"Thou shalt love thy neighbor as thyself" (Lev. 19: 34 and Matt. 22: 39 and 19: 19). As to this passage from Moses it should be noted that *in terms* it speaks not precisely of one's neighbor but of the *stranger*—one toward whom you are wont to think your obligations less than toward any other human being; for he is not a brother born of the same father—not a relative of the same tribe—not a citizen of the same commonwealth or nationality; but an alien, a foreigner, a stranger toward whom you recognize no other relation than that of a fellow-being of human kind. Of such an one the law holds—"The stranger that dwelleth with you shall be unto you as one born among you, and *thou shalt love him as thyself;* for ye were strangers in the land of Egypt: I am the Lord your God"—and I enjoin upon you this all-embracing love for the lowest of human kind.

It should be carefully noted that although this group of four commands (6-9) in each case specifies the extreme form of the sin, the law by no means limits its prohibition to this extreme form. Killing is the extreme of personal violence; adultery (strictly the crime of the married) is the most aggravated form of unchastity; theft is more than simply being reckless of your neighbor's property; and false witness naturally contemplates a case in court—public, formal, and of most grave and momentous consequences;—yet in each and every one of these prohibitions it behooves us to remember that God looks at the heart; that the spirit is more than the letter; that the law which specifies the extreme form of a special sin forbids with its full force all the lower grades and all the less flagrant and revolting forms of the same sin. We wrong ourselves most fearfully when we labor to ease our conscience by limiting the prohibitions of God's law to the extreme forms of sin which may be named in the statute. It is always our highest wisdom to deal very honestly with our own conscience as before God in the construction and application of his law.

The tenth and last commandment is peculiar, as compared with all others of the second table, in this point—that it specifies no external act whatever but lays its prohibition directly *upon the heart.* "Thou shalt not covet"—shalt not allow thyself to *desire* in such a way as might tempt thee to try to obtain—thy neighbor's house, wife, servants, cattle, or any thing that he has. This law aims to forestall temptation. It strikes at the root of such sins as theft and adultery by forbidding any such desire as might move you toward the sin. It may be regarded as shielding both of the two parties; the one who might commit the sin, and the one against whom the sin might be committed. It throws its shield over him who might otherwise be tempted, and it also becomes in so far a safeguard around him who holds treasures which lustful eyes might covet.

Let us not omit to notice that it was this precept which opened the spiritual eye of Paul and gave him a new view of the breadth and true significance of God's law. "I had not known sin, (said he) but by the law; for I had not known lust except the law had said, Thou shalt not covet" (Rom. 7: 7). His Pharisaic training (we may suppose) had been scrupulous over the tenth part of the mint and anise and cummin—had taken even ostentatious care of the external matters of the law; but, alas! had *left the heart out.* Here at the close of the law of Sinai—last among the precepts that treat of duty to our neighbor—stands one which puts its finger squarely upon the *heart*. It says—"Thou shalt not *covet*." It not only suggests that God looks within the soul of man for sin, but it demands that every man shall look there too and put his own restraining hand directly upon those rising desires which, indulged, would push him into overt sin. Moreover, this one precept may be supposed to have suggested to the mind of Paul that the whole law of God must be construed on this heart-principle—that every precept it contains goes beyond the letter to the spirit—pushes its demand deeper than the outward act, even to the inner thought, passion, and purpose of the soul. This view put the law of God in a new light—we might even say—revealed a new law to his soul. It gave him a new field for self-examination; brought up new sins never seen or dreamed of before, and at once demolished hopes of favor before God and of salvation on which he had perilously leaned through all his Pharisaic life.——"Thy commandment" (said one of the Psalmists) "is exceeding broad" (Ps. 119: 96). We are not to think of all the Old Testament saints as Pharisees. Let us rather hope that many of them read in the law of Sinai the law of love, and adjusted to it, not the outward life only but the very heart as well.

Progress in the Revelation of God to Man.

The first twenty chapters of Exodus cover a period eminently rich in point of *progress* in revealing God to the race.——More fully than ever before God manifested those special elements of his character which are unfolded in the new name Jehovah—I am that I Am (Ex. 3: 14). He had given promises before; then he came forth to *fulfill* them. He had talked with the patriarchs about faith, and had sought to inspire it in their souls. In these great deeds for his people he gave them demonstrations of his eternal faithfulness—a basis on which their faith might rest, and also the faith of every child of his through all the future ages. God came exceedingly near to his afflicted people in Egypt, and never missed any opportunity of suggesting and impressing the idea that these tender testimonies of his love were in proof of his *fidelity to promise*—were the very acts which his covenant with Abraham involved and called for—called for of their covenant God not in vain.

Again, we see here the *possibility of very great intimacy of communion between God and man.* As bearing on this point the reader will review the scene between Moses and the Lord at the burning bush; in his mission to Pharaoh; in the special directions given him in regard to the sending of each several plague, and usually as to its removal as well. Did ever earthly Potentate stand on more intimate terms with his prime minister? Or military chieftain with his subordinate officer? If Moses was at any point reluctant, under a conscious sense of capacities unequal to the work and of difficulties he could not surmount, did he not bring the matter before the Lord with at least as much freedom as the case could justify?——Especially when we think of Moses coming so near to Jehovah in his majesty wielding the terrific agencies of flood and storm and fire, of darkness and lightning and the voice of trumpet exceeding loud—Mt. Sinai rocking beneath his feet, and Moses alone drawing near the Awful Presence and talking with God face to face there—what shall we say of the possibilities of communion between man and his Maker? Whatever speculations we may have as to the means and methods by which the thought of God was borne to the mind of Moses and the thought of Moses to the mind of God, the great fact of *communion* of mind with mind—thought meeting thought—of command from the superior party, received and obeyed by the inferior—is on the outer face of the whole history and admits of no question. God can speak to man so that man shall know the voice to be his and comprehend perfectly its significance. Relations of obedience, confidence, and love on the part of man toward his Maker are established, and God meets them with appropriate manifestations of his favor.

This great fact is one of telling significance in the whole province of Christian experience. Its significance can not terminate with the present life but must pass on to be unfolded far more gloriously in the revelations of the eternal world. "It doth not yet appear" [in all points] "what we shall be"—but it does appear that God has made us capable of exceedingly intimate relations to himself—as we shall know more perfectly when we shall see as we are seen and know as also we are known.

Yet again; This portion of historic revelation *abounds with testimonies to the power of prayer* and to its place in the relations of God to man and of man to God. We see these revelations in the history of the plagues on Egypt. So palpably manifest was the power of Moses with God in prayer that even proud Pharaoh saw and recognized it. Over and over again the king besought the prayers of the man of God—apparently with unlimited confidence that God would grant whatever he should ask. Though he never had seen such power in prayer before, the force of the facts was too great to be resisted. For once he became so far a believer in the communion of man with God, and also in the power of God to work wonders which man's power alone could never reach.

The war scenes with Amalek and the prayer which turned the victory to Israel's side will be readily recalled. As already suggested, this specimen case, brought out so perfectly in the first national conflict of arms, was well adapted to send down to future ages the great secret of success against their national enemies. How happy for Israel if it had never been forgotten! How well for the Christian world if the lessons of that scene were faithfully transferred and applied in all spiritual conflicts against foes within and foes without which pertain to this ever militant state!

It is scarcely necessary to speak in fuller detail of the revelations of God to man *through miracle.* Every page of this history teems with miracles. Take the miracles away, and truly there would be nothing left. The revelations of God's will to Moses; the judgments on Egypt; the redemption of his people from bondage there; the scenes at the Red Sea; the bread and the water for his needy people; the pillar of cloud and of fire; the glories of Sinai and the giving of his law in voice of majesty:—what are all these but miracles—the Great God overstepping the ordinary course of nature to impress himself, the power of his arm, the mandates of his will—upon human minds? No other such chapter on miracles appears in the Old Testament. Nowhere else do they cluster so grandly; not elsewhere do they so much supersede the common laws of nature and give character to the entire course of the divine administration. Most abundantly do they testify that the arm of the Lord is equal to any result which his wisdom may devise. If he has purposes to accomplish he can not lack the means or the power necessary. The age of miracles can be brought round again if so he wills it. But more to our purpose is the inference to the adequacy of his resources in general, whether with or without miracle.——Yet let us not miss the more vital truth that this cluster of miracles aimed to witness to God's present hand working with Moses, endorsing his mission and accrediting his words from the most High. God was then specially active in "making history" (shall we say?)—*making history to put into his Bible.* The Bible was growing; the great crisis which developed into the birth of the Hebrew nation was then transpiring; God's plans for training a people who should be holy to himself—the repository of his truth—the church of the living God—were then rapidly unfolding; and no vital step in this process could spare the agency of miracle.

Yet again; In this portion of sacred history much new light has been thrown upon *God's management of great sinners.* Pharaoh was a standard case of this sort. As already suggested, there are many aspects of this management. On one side we see the strong arm, putting his hook into the jaws of Leviathan—curbing his spirit, breaking down his power; burying him and his hosts in the sea. On another side are unfolded the nice relations of even this resistless power to the free moral activities of the great sinner; the wonderful blending of mercies with judgments; the patient waiting—if possibly these manifestations of God's hand may bring the proud king to real submission; and coupled with this, the steady purpose on God's part to turn all Pharaoh's pride and guilt and moral obduracy to best possible account—setting forth his mode of dealing with wicked men in making known his power to save his people and to crush their foes, and his unfailing wisdom in making the wrath of the proudest of mortals evolve his own glory and praise.

The scenes of Sinai were a long and magnificent step

of progress in the revelations of God to men. We may think here not so much of the external surroundings—the bringing into service of all the grandest agencies of nature to impress men with reverence and fear and awe, and so to plant the more deeply in their souls the idea of law as emanating unmistakably from the Infinite One; but we may consider the *great fact itself of a revealed law.* It is surely a point in the progress of God's revelations of himself second to nothing that has gone before—second to nothing in all the ages save the greater mission of his Son for the purposes of redemption. God revealing to man a rule of duty; expressing it in terms at once so simple and so comprehensive; including the duties we owe to God on the one hand and to fellow-beings on the other; putting it on permanent record; accompanying it with demonstrations of majesty and glory, endorsing it so surely and so sublimely; adjusting it so nicely in harmony with the intelligent convictions of rational minds, and so commending it to every man's conscience as intrinsically and eternally right:—truly the promulgation of such a law through such agencies is surpassingly grand and glorious; and, in the line of our present thought, is one of the great epochs in the march of God's revelations of himself to mortals. We pause before it to take in the value of this revealed law; the new relations into which the race are brought thereby toward their Great Father; and the bearings of this law upon the whole plan of God's moral administration toward our fallen race.

CHAPTER XVI.

THE HEBREW THEOCRACY.

NATURALLY following the national covenant (Ex. 19) and the giving of the law from Sinai (Ex. 20) and preliminary to the civil code—"the statutes and judgments"—comes in the *Theocracy*—a term used to designate the system of government established for the Hebrew people.

Here we may consider briefly the following points:

I. *The Supreme Power.*

II. The powers of *Jehovah's vicegerents*—his chief executive officers.

III. The *general assembly* or congregation, and their *elders.*

IV. The scope afforded for self-government-democracy.

V. The fundamental principles of this entire system.

VI. Its union of church and state.

VII. Its principles and usages in respect to *war*, with a notice of the war-commission against the doomed Canaanites.

I. *The Supreme Power.*

God himself was *king*. In every respect the supreme power was his. Precisely this is the sense of the term "*theocracy*"—*a government of God.*

This comprehensive fact appears in the following particulars:

1. God demanded supreme homage as their king (Ex. 19: 6 and Deut. 6: 4–15, and 7: 6–11, and 10: 12–21, and 33: 4, 5 and 1 Sam. 8: 6–8, and 10: 18, 19 and Judg. 8: 23).

2. God enacted the statutes. He was the Supreme *Lawgiver.* We sometimes speak of the "Mosaic code," of the "statutes of Moses," meaning by these phrases only that the statutes came from God to the people by the hand of Moses; never that Moses was himself the

author of these statutes—the true legislator. (See Ex. 21: 1 and Deut. 6: 1).

3. God *nominated the chief executive*. He called Moses (Ex. 3: 10, 12, and 4: 16 and 1 Cor. 10: 2); and Joshua (Num. 27: 18–23 and Deut. 3: 28, and 31: 3 and Josh. 1: and 5: 13–15). The same was true of the Judges, raised up for special emergencies (Judg. 2: 16, 18, and 3: 9, 15, and 4: 6, and 6: 12, etc., etc.) God called the kings:—Saul (1 Sam. 9: 17, and 10: 1); also David (1 Sam. 13: 14, and 16: 1 and 2 Sam. 5: 2 and Ps. 78: 70, 71); and to name no more, Solomon (1 Chron. 28: 5).

4. In all cases not otherwise provided for, the ultimate appeal was to God. In point we have (Num. 16 and 17) a case of resistance to the authority of Moses—incipient rebellion. God interposed with his supreme authority. We have a case in civil law, not reached by the statutes, viz. the entailment of real estate in a family of daughters only. Moses brought it before the Lord for adjudication (Num. 27: 5). A special provision respecting the marriage of daughters holding property in land became necessary: this new law was sought from God (Num. 36: 6).——A criminal case occurred in which the law was not explicit; "it was not declared what should be done" with the criminal (Num. 15: 32–36). The Lord gave them the law for the case.——In the case of Achan (Josh. 7) the Lord interposed, not so much because there was no law for its decision as because the sin was flagrant and the demand for exemplary punishment was very great. ——In cases which would appropriately require the calling of a Supreme Council, the people sought direction from God. (See Judg. 1: 1, and 20: 18, 27, 28 and 1 Sam. 14: 37, and 23: 2, 4, 9–12, and 28: 6, and 30: 8 and 2 Sam. 2: 1). God made provision through the prophets for a direct revelation of his will to the people in special cases not otherwise provided for (Deut. 18: 18).

5. In later times the demand of the people for a human king seemed to be constructive treason. It might be so understood, and therefore the Lord reasserted his prerogative, although he yielded to their demands (1 Sam. 8: 6–9, and 10: 17–25).

6. It scarcely need be said that God bound himself by promise to reward the people with all national prosper-

ity if obedient, and by threatening, to punish them with national calamity for disobedience. These points are expanded fully Lev. 26: and Deut. chapters 27–30. ——That God inflicted these threatened punishments early in their nation's history may be seen Num. 11: 33, and 16: 1–50.

Thus it appears that in every appropriate way and in numerous vital respects God manifested his supreme authority over his people Israel.

II. *The powers of Jehovah's vicegerent.*

Of this we have illustrations in the cases of Moses, Joshua, the Judges, and the kings. These cases show that they were precisely the Lord's prime ministers, commissioned to execute his will. If a law touching the case existed and its application was clear, they simply adjudicated the case and put the law in force. If no statute touching the case was extant, they sought one. If the application of the law baffled their wisdom, they sought counsel from God. Hence the Scriptures speak of these prime ministers as the Lord's "servants," to serve him in this high capacity. (See Num. 12: 7 and Heb. 3: 2, 5 and Josh. 1: 1, 2, and 5: 13–15 and 2 Sam. 7: 8, etc.)

Of the officers holding under the chief executive there is no occasion to speak in great detail. The system of subordinate judges—lower courts—has come to view in the history of Jethro (Ex. 18). In Canaan they held their courts in the gates of large cities, and (for certain criminal cases) in the cities of refuge which were cities of the Levites—from which tribe judges seem largely to have been drawn.

The "elders"—"heads of the house of their fathers"—held important responsibilities—a fact due largely to the influence of the patriarchal system which had come down from the earliest times, the usages of which, therefore, had essentially the force of common law in Israel. It was in great measure due to them that after the death of Joshua the processes of government went on without any chief executive, with no king, and with no Supreme Judge except as the High Priest may have performed that function.

III. *The General Assembly or Congregation, and the Elders.*

We read of great conventions, congregations, assemblies, in which it is not definitely said that *all the people* were there; and also of convocations in which "all the people" were present. In some at least of the cases of the latter sort, the elders seem to have acted distinctly from the masses of the people, being the media of communication (as the case may be) between the Lord or his servant Moses of the one party and the people at large of the other. Thus shortly before the giving of the law from Sinai when God ratified a national covenant with the people, we read—"Moses called for the elders of the people and laid before their faces all these words which the Lord commanded him. And all the people answered together and said—All that the Lord hath spoken we will do" (Ex. 19: 7, 8). Moses spake to the people *through* their elders. It was naturally impossible that any one human voice could be heard by six hundred thousand men.——So in 1 Sam. 8: 4–10 "the *elders* gathered together and said to Samuel, Make us a king;" "and the Lord said unto Samuel, Hearken unto *the voice of the people.*" "And Samuel told all the words of the Lord *unto the people* that asked of him a king."——These elders—chiefs of the people—seem to have been a well-defined class. Note how they are designated (Num. 1: 16); "These are the renowned [Heb. the *called ones*] of the congregation, princes of the tribes of their fathers, heads of thousands in Israel." Also Num. 16: 2: "Two hundred and fifty princes of the assembly, famous in the congregation" [Heb. the *called ones* of the congregation, *i. e.* the men summoned to represent their constituents], "men of renown."—— The question will arise whether these *called men*, the recognized heads and representatives of the people, held specially delegated powers; whether they were appointed for an occasion and were instructed by the people: or whether they held the headship, this representative power, by virtue of the ancient usages of the patriarchal system. The latter is the true view, for the patriarchal system had the prestige of common law; and we find not the least hint of any *election* of these "heads of the house of their fathers" for any special

function—no notice of their receiving special instructions to act as delegated representatives of the people.
——Let it be noted carefully that on all really great occasions when the vital issues of their covenant relation with God were pending, "all the people"—the solid masses—were convened, and of course their elders and high officers with them. We see such a case before Sinai (Ex. 19); another, shortly before the death of Moses, in a solemn ratification of their national covenant: "Ye stand this day *all of you* before the Lord your God; your captains of your tribes, your elders and your officers, with all the men of Israel" (Deut. 29: 10–12), "that thou shouldest enter into covenant with the Lord thy God," etc.——Again; after they had entered Canaan in the scene of rehearsing the blessings and the curses of the law from Mt. Gerizim and Mt. Ebal: "And all Israel and their elders and officers and their judges, stood," etc. (Josh. 8: 33). See also Josh. 23: 2 and 24: 1 and Judg. 20: 1 and 1 Sam. 8. It was supremely appropriate that every man of Israel should give his voice and heart in these great national consecrations of themselves to their nation's God. The Lord sought to call into action every mind—to make a deep moral impression on every heart. Therefore none could be exempted; no man could be excused for absence.

IV. The scope afforded under this system for *self-government—democracy.*

It is readily obvious that under this theocracy, the function of *legislators* was out of the question. The people did not make their own laws: these were *given* them—made by the Lord alone. It only remained for them to say whether they would accept the Lord their God as their Lawgiver and Supreme King. Such assent and consent on their part was appropriate; and precisely this they gave—as we may see in the case of the moral law of Sinai (Ex. 19: 3–8 and Deut. 5: 27, 28); and of all the statutes and judgments of their civil code (Ex. 24: 3). This national recognition of God as Supreme Lawgiver was renewed from time to time with subsequent generations of Israel (Deut. 29: 10–15 and Josh. 24: 15–27 and Neh. 10: 28, 29), etc.

Thus it appears that the laws under which they lived were not arbitrarily imposed upon them without their consent—much less, against their will; but only with their formal and solemn consent. So far forth, their government involved an element of freedom and of self-control. They were not tyrannously coerced into subjection to laws which they repudiated. A system of law, in itself most excellent and entirely unexceptionable, was presented to them for their adoption or rejection. They adopted it—apparently with the warmest approbation.

Essentially the same principle obtained in regard to their highest human executive officer. They did not nominate and choose Moses of their own motion. No caucus, no primary meeting, no formal election brought out his name as the choice of the people. The Lord alone raised up Moses, prepared him for the position he was to hold and brought him before the people. Then they received him as their leader (Ex. 4: 29-31 and 20: 19 and Deut. 5: 27). In the same manner they accepted Joshua (Josh. 1: 16-18). In the case of Saul, their first king, the Lord nominated, and the people ratified his nomination (1 Sam. 10: 24 and 11: 14, 15). The Lord called David also (1 Sam. 16: 1-12), but the people accepted him as king and cordially ratified his divine nomination (2 Sam. 5: 1-3). Through his prophet Nathan the Lord gave the kingdom to David's posterity (2 Sam. 7:) and prophetically indicated Solomon (1 Chron. 22: 8, 9 and 1 Kings 1: 13, 29, 30); but the people still gave their full-hearted consent (1 Kings 1: 39, 40). The same powers were asserted by the people in the case of Rehoboam (1 Kings 12: 1-20).

It should be specially noted that when the government assumed the form of a *human* monarchy—an earthly king reigning under God in this real theocracy, it was a limited, not an absolute monarchy. The Mosaic law anticipated this change and imposed certain constitutional limitations upon the prospective king (Deut. 17: 14-20). He must be one whom the Lord should choose; of native and not foreign birth; must not multiply horses, nor wives, nor treasures of silver and gold; must keep by him a copy of the law given through Moses, must read it and regard it as the constitution under which he reigned. When the demand for a king arose Samuel forewarned the people of the assumptions of power which, by the usages of mankind, they must expect in their king (1 Sam. 8: 10-17), and took the precaution to put in writing "the manner of the kingdom"—the constitutional provisions and safeguards under which he was to reign (1 Sam. 10: 25). No copy of this constitution has come down to us; but it doubtless corresponded essentially with the limitations made by the law of Moses as in Deut. 17: 14-20.

The voice of the people in self-government appears also in the appointment of the judges who were to administer the law in courts of justice. We have seen how the old patriarchal system was enlarged and modified at the suggestion of Jethro (Ex. 18: 13-26). This first narrative seems to rest the appointment of these judges entirely with Moses; but his own more detailed account (Deut. 1: 9-18) shows that the people were heard in the nomination: "Take you wise men and understanding, and known among your tribes, and I will make them rulers over you. And ye answered me and said—The thing which thou hast spoken is good for us to do. So I took the chief men of your tribes, wise men and known, and made them heads over you," etc. Plainly these men had acquired position by merit, and held their place and power (before this special appointment) by the general consent of the people.——The general law in the case runs—"Judges and officers shalt thou make thee in all thy gates, etc., and they shall judge the people with just judgment" (Deut. 16: 18).

Self-government is further developed in the independent action which we may notice occasionally in the several tribes. Especially in the period from Joshua to Saul, the several tribes acted singly, or in union with one or more of their fellow-tribes at their option (Judg. 1: 1-3, 22 and 4: 10 and 7: 23, 24 and 8: 23, and 20: 11-46). Special cases of this independent action appear in 1 Chron. 4: 41-43 and 5: 18-23.——On great occasions, the people convened en masse for deliberation and united action as in Josh. 22: 12, 16 and 2, 3: 2 and Judg. 20 and 21.——Obviously they assumed the right to disapprove the action of their princes as in the case of the Gibeonites (Josh. 9: 18, 19)—"All the congregation murmured against the princes."

V. *The Fundamental Principles of this entire System.*

1. Jehovah being their Supreme King, supreme love and worship must be rendered to him.

2. Idolatry was a state offense, nothing less than high treason, and therefore a capital crime, punishable with death. Any one of their cities, given to idolatry, must be utterly exterminated (Deut. 13: 1–18 and 17: 2–7).

3. The most stringent laws ordained non-intercourse with idolatrous nations and non-conformity to their customs. Inter-marriages with them were strictly prohibited; trade and commerce were at least discouraged if not forbidden. These laws may be seen in Ex. 34: 11–17 and Deut. 7: 1–5, 16, 23–26; and cases of their application in Num. 25 and 31; also in Ezra 9 and 10 and Neh. 13: 23–31.

Sundry customs, some of which might in themselves be of small account, were prohibited, apparently because associated with idolatry in the usages of other nations and in the ideas of the people of Israel (Deut. 14: 1–21 and Lev. 20: 23–26). The distinction between clean and unclean beasts seems to fall under this principle.

4. This Hebrew Theocracy was engrafted upon a previously existing patriarchal government, and therefore it recognized this previous system as substantially the common law of the land, to be in force except so far as modified by special legislation under the new regime given from the Lord through Moses. This principle is illustrated in the powers and functions of the *elders*, known as "heads of the house of their fathers"; "princes"; "heads of the thousands of Israel" (Ex. 6: 25, and Num. 3: 24, 30, 35, and 1: 16, and 10: 4).

5. It was manifestly an accepted principle, underlying the entire system, to give the people as wide a range of free responsible action as a theocratic government would admit. Democracy must of necessity be subordinate to *theocracy;* the self-ruling of the people must find its place *under* the supreme ruling of Jehovah. Consequently the law must come entire from God, not from the people. The chief executive must receive his commission from God, though he might be formally accepted and his appointment in this way ratified by the people. The Lord sought the willing homage of the

people—the obedience of their heart—and therefore encouraged the most cheerful and hearty expression of their will and of their homage in entering into covenant with himself, and from time to time in solemnly renewing it. He would have them feel that they were the people of the Lord by their own real consent and hearty acceptance. So much democracy therefore entered into their scheme of national polity. So much there might be. In the nature of a theocracy, there could not be more.

6. As elsewhere shown, the statutes were within certain limits graduated in moral tone to the moral status of the people, being as high as they would bear—as near theoretical perfection as could be made effective—*i. e.* as could secure a general obedience.

VI. *Its union of Church and State.*

By this modern phrase is currently meant the subordination of the church to the civil or state authorities. Such a union in the Hebrew nation was a natural consequent upon a theocratic government. The civil code coming from God himself, the religious code must come from him by obvious fitness, not to say necessity. In his entire policy with Israel, God sought the most effective moral culture. We find this purpose underlying the entire civil government with its code of civil laws; it must of course underlie their religious institutions. Hence the church and the state were worked not only by the same hand but for the same general purpose.

In practice certain crimes against the religious law were enforced by the state. Idolatry was a state offense, punishable as other state crimes. So of perjury and blasphemy. (Deut. 19: 16–19.)——It was due to the common relations of church and state that to a great extent the religious orders were civil judges. In the absence of a king or other chief executive, the High Priest seems to have held that function. (See Deut. 17: 12 and 2 Chron. 19: 8–11). The subordinate judges were largely taken from the priests and Levites (Deut. 21: 5, and 33: 10).

Since the system provided for an ultimate appeal to God, extreme cases were taken up for the sake of such appeal to the one place which was for the time the seat of God's special manifestations to his people (Deut. 17. 8–13, and 19: 17).

The wisdom of this joint action of the civil law with the religious admits in their case of no question. It may suffice to refer in proof to the omnipresent power of idolatry through all the ages from Moses to the captivity, to show the vital need of the civil arm to sustain the true worship of God and save the nation. On the other hand the state was the stronger for her religious institutions. The great religious festivals, bringing the masses of the male population from every tribe three times a year for a sacred week of communion must have been of priceless value in sustaining the national unity and a national patriotism. Jeroboam was sharp enough to see that the calves at Bethel and Dan must take the place of the festivals at Jerusalem, or his kingdom would melt away from under him, and his people give their civil fealty as well as their religious homage at the old center. Hezekiah would have brought the ten tribes back if he could have drawn their people in a body to the great Passover, as he sought to do.——Hence it is quite safe to say that the state was the stronger for the national religion, and their religion the stronger for the aid of the state.—— Yet let none rush to the inference that such mutual relations of church and state are therefore wise and useful in the Christian age of the world. The providences of God shut off from the primitive church the possibility of such union and shut up Christianity to make her first great conquests under the sturdy opposition of the greatest civil power of the age. Experience has long since disproved the inference above referred to. The cases are too dissimilar to admit of any logical reasoning from that age to this.

In the Hebrew economy we are struck with the fact that both the religious and the civil code were enforced chiefly by considerations and influences, rewards and punishments, coming in from the present world—not from the future. Let it be supposed that religious duties were in our age enforced by such motives chiefly—and we should see at a glance the change that has passed over the world since Moses uttered the concluding chapters of Deuteronomy. Idolatry, then the head sin of the ages, was fitly resisted, not only by the civil arm, but by the most fearful array of civil pains and penalties. The capital sins of Christendom are now of quite other sort; and the motives to repentance come appropriately from the other worlds yet before us and not from this. It may be difficult for us to realize how stern the necessity was that God should in the earlier ages govern the world, and not least his own people, by motives from the visible and not from the invisible world—from earth and time and the present life, and not from the eternal, the future and yet unseen state.

[This subject will receive further attention near the close of this volume].

VII. *The principles and usages of the Hebrew code in respect to war;* with some notice of the *war-edict* for the extirpation of the Canaanites.

By their constitution the war-power was with God. The power and the right to declare war rested in him alone. He forbade them to make war on Edom; he commanded them to exterminate Amalek and the devoted nations of Canaan, and to "vex the Midianites and smite them" (As to Edom, see Deut. 2: 5; as to Amalek, Ex. 17: 8, 14, 16 and Deut. 25: 17–19; as to the Midianites, Num. 25: 17, 18, and 31:).——Their rulers were expected to bring the question before the Lord—Shall I in this case go up to battle, or shall I forbear? (Judg. 1: 1, and 20: 18, 23, 28).——Any one tribe might go out to war alone, or might call in the aid of another or of all:—a fact which shows that the tribes were confederated rather than united and consolidated. On great occasions, of common danger, all the tribes associated together, and, with certain specified exceptions, every man able for war was required to go. The exceptions are given (Deut. 20: 5–8); viz. the man who had built a house, but had not dedicated it; he who had planted a vineyard but had not eaten of its fruits; he who had betrothed a wife, yet had not taken her; and finally, every fearful and faint-hearted man;—*i. e.* all who had special attractions homeward which might tempt them to desert the ranks, and they whose timid hearts made them worthless and might be contagious:—in the words of the statute, "Lest his brother's heart faint as well as his heart." Personal heroism was of prime account—a heroism inspired by faith in Israel's God. The history every-where shows that such armies, fired with religious enthusiasm, strong by faith in the mighty God, were terrible in battle, and for the most part certain of victory. Often as we read these annals of the wars of Israel, we can not resist the conviction that they were means of grace as well as of manhood—an illustration of which may be seen in David before Goliath the Philistine (1 Sam. 17).—— When only a small number of men were needed, they were chosen, picked men, naturally the brave, skilled, and renowned. See Joshua's first battle (Ex. 17:9); his assault upon Ai (Josh. 7:7), and the sifting of Gideon's army (Judg. 7:1-8).

The grant of Canaan to Israel and the commission to extirpate the Canaanites.

These points call for special examination.

It has been objected against the morality of the Old Testament Scriptures that this war-law enjoining the extirpation of the Canaanites was cruel and unjust; hence that it either misrepresents God and therefore disproves the divine authority of the Old Testament; or if it truly represents the God of the Bible, then he does not deserve the homage and the love of his creatures.——These are grave charges and should be candidly examined.

The grant of Canaan and the commission to destroy the Canaanites have been vindicated by Michaelis and others on the following grounds.

1. The right of prior possession and occupation.

2. This right kept good by burial there, and not by any means relinquished when Jacob was driven by stress of famine into Egypt and then detained there by force.

3. This right protected according to their ability by reassertion, perpetually holding forth their purpose to return and their recognition of Canaan as their land of promise.

4. That no argument prejudicial to their right of war against the Canaanites can be drawn from the absence of formal manifesto, setting forth the causes of the war, inasmuch as such a setting forth of grounds

and causes of war is a thing of modern and not of ancient usage.

This course of argument in defense of the war-law in question seems to me defective and quite below the truth in the following points:

1. Its primary position—*prior occupancy*—seems not fully made out.
2. It makes too little account of God's original and perfect title to all the earth, and his consequent right to give his people any portion of it at his pleasure.
3. It fails to give due prominence to the moral grounds assigned by God himself for the extirpation of the Canaanites, viz. their extreme debasement in character; their abominable wickedness; their horrible violations of the common humanities of social life.

As to prior occupation, Michaelis says the original home of the Canaanites was Arabia; that Herodotus testifies that at first they dwelt near the Red Sea; Justin, that they had another country before they came to Palestine; and Abulfeda that they dwelt in Arabia. But in proof that they were in Palestine before Abraham was, Moses affirms (Gen. 12: 6) that when Abram first passed through, "the Canaanite was then in the land;" also that when Abram and Lot, being rich in cattle and "the land unable to bear them," "the Canaanite and the Perizzite were then in the land" (Gen. 13: 7); and further still in his earliest account of the location of primitive families after the flood, he says—"The border of the Canaanites was from Sidon as thou comest to Gerar unto Gaza as thou goest to Sodom and Gomorrah," etc. (Gen. 10: 19). This is the oldest known historic testimony, and unquestionably locates the Canaanites in the original land of Canaan.——Moreover, it is said that Abraham went with his flocks and herds wherever he would as if lord of the country. It may be replied—So apparently did the Canaanites also. If Abraham dug wells, so did they; if he buried his dead there, so did they—with this incidental fact in their favor; viz. that Abraham bought ground of them and paid money for his cemetery at Macpelah. This special argument from prior possession can scarcely be sustained.

But it may be maintained that Abram was there *very early;* and what is more, God's first call to him to leave his native country named Canaan as his promised land; and every successive promise reaffirmed this gift. Abraham's title to Canaan therefore rests on God's right to give a perfect title. If the Lord of heaven and earth, the Great Creator of all lands in all the ends of the earth had not a right to give Canaan to Abraham and his posterity, then *he is not God.* Unquestionably he assumed this right and in the exercise of it pledged Canaan to the posterity of Abraham with perpetual reiteration and most solemn covenant. This fact is the more significant because it is the first step in a series of acts all of which aimed to reveal himself before the world of mankind as the true God and the Lord of the whole earth. With these ends in view he chose this people and made them his own; manifested himself among them and before all the world as their covenant-keeping God; gave them Canaan, and by manifold miracles helped them to gain possession of it. Nor is this argument weakened by the fact that by means of a special series of providences he led them down into Egypt to dwell there 430 years; suffering the Canaanites meanwhile to hold Canaan, not driving them out earlier because "the iniquity of the Amorites was not yet full" (Gen. 15: 16). Here is suggested the real ground on which the edict for extirpating the Canaanites was made to rest. God suffered them to remain there until they had forfeited their title not to Canaan alone, but to life itself and to any further national existence.

This point is too vital to be passed without careful attention. In Lev. 18 we meet with a series of crimes against moral purity—violations of the seventh commandment—culminating in sodomy and bestiality; and classed with these is the burning of children in the worship of Moloch (v. 21). Then God says—"Defile not yourselves in any of these things; for in all these the nations are defiled which I cast out before you, and *the land is defiled;* therefore do I visit the iniquity thereof upon it, and the land itself vomiteth out her inhabitants."——The same sentiments are repeated (vs. 26-30). Unnatural lusts had sunk both men and women not only down to a level with beasts, but even below them. Idolatry had so far quenched the sweet humanities from the parental heart that fathers and mothers could burn their own sons and daughters to Moloch. These horrible, unnatural crimes were not only an outrage against the heart of God the Great Father; but, as he forcibly puts it, they defiled the very land itself. The earth was nauseated with these abominations and spued out such inhabitants. God's fair and much abused world could bear them no longer. Nature herself lifted her voice of protest against such wickedness; or, as the strong figure suggests, her stomach sickened even to nausea over such unnatural lusts and such a torturing death of innocent sons and daughters. What could a holy and righteous God do with such a people but wipe them out of existence and wash the land they had defiled clean of such pollutions?——Lev. 20 reiterates substantially the same list of abominations against which God warns his people;—"Ye shall therefore keep all my statutes and all my judgments and do them, that the land whither I bring you to dwell therein, *spue you not out*. And ye shall not walk in the manner of the nations which I cast out before you; for they committed all these things, and therefore I abhorred them (vs. 22, 23).—— Perfectly definite and explicit is the repetition of the same point in Deut. 12: 30, 31. When the Lord shall have cut off the Canaanites before thee, be not snared into their ways; inquire not after their gods and ways of worship:—"Thou shalt not do so unto the Lord thy God, for every abomination to the Lord which he hateth have they done unto their gods; for even their sons and their daughters have they burnt in the fire to their gods." No fact could be more telling; none more damning. A people so given up to devil-worship as to burn their own offspring at his supposed behest, must be too debased and corrupt to live! The earth itself cries out against them, demanding their utter extirpation!

A more full description of the varieties and forms of the devil-worship and fellowship common among the Canaanites may be seen in Deut. 18: 9-14, to which it must suffice to refer the reader.

I am well aware that some Jewish doctors, wishing to vindicate their fathers from crimes so unnatural have sought to prove that "causing children to pass through the fire" was a rite of purification and not actual murder. The attempt is futile:——(1.) Because some of the expressions are perfectly unequivocal; *e. g.*—"Even their sons have they burnt in the fire to their Gods" (Deut. 12: 31). See also the cases in 2 Kings 17: 31, and 2 Chron. 28: 3, and Jer. 7: 31, and 19: 5.——(2.) The phrase—"To make to pass through the fire unto their gods" is used in the same sense as the phrase—"to burn in the fire."——(3.) That the Phenicians and Carthagenians, closely related to the ancient Canaanites, did offer human sacrifices is a well established fact of history. (See Smith's Bible Dictionary; "Moloch.")

We have seen that the title of Israel to Canaan falls back upon God's prior title—upon his right to deed it to whom he would. On the same principle the question whether it was right and just for them to extirpate the Canaanites falls back upon two prior questions— (a.) Was it right and just for God to extirpate them? ——(b.) Was it wise for Him to command the Israelites to do this work of extirpation, rather than do it himself by miracle, and without human hands? Here are our two great questions.

(a.) As to the first—the right of God to destroy them for their crimes and the justice of doing it—I see not how it can be denied or questioned without denying to God the right to punish sin at all. Has God any right to govern his own universe—any right to resist the influence of sin and rebellion in his kingdom—any right to protect innocent children from being burned to death in homage to the devil? Alas for the universe if this doctrine can be maintained!——Truly we may say—If God has no right to exterminate from the earth any one individual sinner, or a nation of many thousands who are too corrupt to live, then he lacks the essential rights of a God! If he has not the power to do it, he lacks the power necessary to a God. If he has not the firmness—the nerve (shall we say?)—the sense of justice and right that would forbid his evading the duty, then he lacks the essential attributes of a God. If he has so little love for his offspring that he can see their welfare sacrificed in the worship of the devil and in the sweep of unutterable social pollutions, then he is incompetent to govern a world of sinners!

(b.) But the objector will make his chief stand upon the secondary question—Was it wise for God to employ Israel to extirpate the corrupt Canaanites?

The objector will perhaps say—He might have sunk all Canaan under a second flood like that of Noah's time, and no complaint could stand against him. He might have engulfed those cities in fire as he did guilty Sodom, and all the living, cognizant of the moral grounds of the act, would have said, Amen! But that he should set such an example of *war*—the most horrid of all wars—before the nations of all history—before the ages of all time, giving it his holy sanction—nay more, setting his own most holy people to the bloody work—this is unpardonable. That he should put them to such barbarities—subject them to such demoralization of all the finer sensibilities of the human soul, seems too horrid to be thought of!

It is perhaps well to meet this question in its strongest form, with its objectionable points in their most revolting aspect.

I do not feel called upon to say one word to soften down any man's sense of the horrors of war. War *is* horrid—but sin is more horrid—certainly such sin as that of the old Canaanites. In fact war is horrid—not mainly because of the suffering but because of the *sin* that may be in it. And this suggests the true and just reply to be made to the objection now before us, viz. that such a war as that of Israel against the Canaanites, waged in obedience to God; waged for the destruction of such sinners and to cleanse the earth from such unutterable abominations and pollutions, is *not* demoralizing—is not so either necessarily or even naturally; but if done in honest obedience to God and with a due sense of the grounds on which God commanded it, must have been the very opposite of demoralizing; must have educated the nation of Israel to a juster sense of the abominations of idolatry and of the righteous moral government of God over the wicked in the present world. It can not be doubted that these were the ends which God sought to secure in putting this service upon Israel. A lower object to be reached was to vacate the land of Canaan for Israel to occupy; but the far higher object was to wash the land of its moral pollutions; to break down and blot out nations too corrupt to live. The Lord devolved this extirpation upon Israel that they might thereby get a deeper sense of his abhorrence of such sin—not to say also, a juster view of the intrinsic abominations which God commissioned them to punish.

Or we may put the argument thus: Given—the great historic fact, the moral corruption of the nations of Canaan and the moral purpose of God to exterminate those nations for their corruption. The choice of methods lies between *miracles* on the one hand, and the war-force of Israel, backed up by God's providential agencies, on the other:—miracles as in the flood and on Sodom: or the war-commission given to his people Israel.

Now consider.——1. Miracles had already been employed repeatedly before the eyes of mankind, and the Lord might for this reason wisely vary his methods, for the greater and better effect.

2. As already argued, the moral effect upon Israel of being made the executioners of God's righteous justice may be presumed to have been naturally wholesome. But not to push this argument—we may at least maintain,

3. That seen historically—estimated in the light of the facts of the case, this method *was morally impressive, instructive, elevating, wholesome.* Recur to the first war—that against Amalek; and to the scope it gave for illustrations of prayer, and to the sense it inspired of their relations to their covenant God. Turn to the record of the war against Moab and Midian (Num. 25 and 31). Mark its powerful protest against the lewdness involved in those forms of idol-worship, and note how Phineas arose to the sublime grandeur of the emergency and made a record for himself and for his whole tribe indeed in the history of the nation (Num. 25: 11–13 and Mal. 2: 4–7). Study the wars of Joshua and the moral heroism developed there, and ask if any generation of Israel appear on the page of her national history, exhibiting a truer consecration to God or a more conscientious devotion to his will. And what shall we say of Deborah and Barak, and of the heroism that shines and gleams in the record of their achievements, or of the piety that flavors their triumphal song? The same may be said of the wars under David, Jehoshaphat, and Hezekiah, and of the songs of praise and of proud triumph in Israel's God which gave expression to the moral results of those

wars and victories. That man reads the history of the heroic age of Israel very imperfectly who does not see in it ample demonstration that staunch obedience to God in this matter of war against the idolatrous, corrupt Canaanites, fostered piety, developed Christian heroism and toned up the standard of morality. When they compromised, accepted tribute, and tried their own policy of living side by side with such idolaters instead of God's policy of vigorous extermination, then came disaster, religious decline, and most perilous moral corruption.

4. The great conflict of those early ages between God and Satan was fought on the point of idolatry—the real question being whether God or the devil should have the worship of men; whether the supremacy and the moral right to rule the world are with God or with Satan. This being the great conflict of the ages, it should not surprise us that God should let Israel's land of promise be in a sort the battle-ground, and should bring into play the physical force of arms and let his covenant people come into the fight hand to hand against the hosts of his foes. This arrangement gave scope for his own hand in various providential agencies— thunder, hail-storm, the day prolonged miraculously; panics often smiting the hearts of his enemies, and victories that witnessed visibly to Jehovah's present hand. In an age when men were waiting for God to manifest himself visibly and tangibly; when their spiritual perceptions were but dim, and when of necessity the first step in the process of revealing God to men demanded an appeal to the senses, it was certainly no mistake in wisdom for God to suffer this great fight to take on visible form and stand out palpably before human eyes. In the result God made it unmistakably manifest that his soul abhorred such unnatural and horrid crimes as those of the men of Canaan, and also that he had both the power and the will to inflict on them the extremest and most fearful judgments.

CHAPTER XVII.

THE CIVIL INSTITUTES OF MOSES; OR THE HEBREW CODE OF CIVIL LAW.

In scripture phrase, the code is most often called "The statutes and the judgments"—the "commandments and precepts" which the Lord gave by Moses (Deut. 6:1 and Ex. 21:1).

I approach this subject with a feeling of regret that the necessary limits of this volume forbid any attempt to make my presentation of this topic exhaustive. The utmost I can do within the limits prescribed is to give an outline rather than a full development of this code. I shall aim to make this outline full enough to show the *steps and stages of progress* in the science of legislation which are obvious in these "statutes and judgments."

I must first call attention to certain points of a general nature, most of which will need only a brief statement.

1. This code of laws was *given to the Hebrews by God himself, through the hand of Moses.* For the sake of brevity and to distinguish it from other codes we may speak of it as the code of Moses and may speak of Moses as the Hebrew lawgiver; yet let it be said once for all that we recognize no authority—no authorship other than that of God himself.

2. This code was built upon the moral law of Sinai—the ten commandments. It simply expands and applies the general principles expressed or implied in that summary.

3. It was framed with the purpose of reaching the highest moral standard practicable in the circumstances of the people—the highest which it was possible to enforce. This doctrine assumes that any special statute which is so far above the moral status of the people as to be practically inoperative and void may be for this very reason an evil rather than a good inasmuch as it may break down rather than build up the law-abiding

spirit of the people. Consequently the best statute for any given people may be the best that can be in the main enforced—the best which they can be brought up to respect and obey. Hence it may happen that some of the statutes in the best practicable system will be only second best—*i. e.* not theoretically perfect, but only the best practically for the circumstances. We may illustrate this by the law of divorce, as to which Jesus himself remarks that Moses "because of the hardness of your hearts suffered you to put away your wives, but from the beginning it was not so" (Mat. 19: 8). The provisions for an easy divorce were a concession to a sadly low morality among the people—the best under the circumstances—the best that could be made operative with that people, but by no means theoretically perfect.——The reader will take note that we had no occasion to apply this principle to the moral law of the ten commandments, nor indeed to the underlying principles of this code of "statutes and judgments," but only to some of its practical applications of these principles.

4. It is an inference from our last-named point that this code must needs *take the people as they were;* must have regard to existing usages, to the common law under which they had been living, and perhaps must be compelled to tolerate some undesirable usages until better principles could be inculcated and a higher moral tone of public sentiment could be established. Illustrations of this principle appear in the prevalent system of servitude, and in polygamy.

5. Another inference from the point above made is that this code can not be held responsible for what was in existence before its promulgation; *e. g.* personal slavery. It can be held responsible only for doing the best that could be done with such a people—a people so educated, accustomed to such usages and trained in such ideas.

6. That this code, though given by the Lord himself, was not theoretically perfect but only the best practicable, is obvious from the fact that it was from time to time modified. Cases of this appear in the law respecting the six years' emancipation of Hebrew servants (compare Ex. 21: 2-7 with Deut. 15: 12-17); the taking of pledges from the poor for the payment of

debts: (compare Ex. 22: 26 with Deut. 24: 6, 10–15). See also the law of inheritance in a family consisting of daughters only (Num. 36).

7. That this code was framed with the design of a special adaptation to the Hebrew people appears in such facts as these, viz. that though it went into immediate effect and continued in force during their wandering life in the wilderness forty years, yet it anticipated their ultimate residence in Canaan, especially in its land-law and its provision for the entailment of real estate. Also it anticipated the future demand for a king according to the usage of contiguous nations and provided for this modification in the general government.

8. At the point where the administration of justice first appears, the sole responsibility seems to have rested on Moses (Ex. 18). At the suggestion of Jethro (as we have seen) important modifications were introduced. Further modifications were made after the settlement in Canaan. In consequence of the close connection between the church and the state—the religious law and the civil—the same class of men were to a great extent put in charge of both. The tribe of Levi became the ministers of religion and the administrators of civil law as well. Exempted chiefly from agriculture and from military service, they became the learned class—the lawyers of the nation. "The priests' lips should keep knowledge and they should seek the law at his mouth" (Malachi 2: 7).

9. The question how far this divinely revealed code of law is authoritative upon human legislators and should control legislation in this Christian age, should be carefully considered. With no attempt to exhaust this question, I may suggest briefly:—(1.) That the great principles of this code should underlie every code of human law. These principles must be good for all time—for man in his social and civil relations everywhere. For example, its doctrine of equity; its law of love; its regard for the personal rights of life, chastity, property; its doctrine of the essential equality of every man's rights before the law; and its assumption that the poor, being otherwise defenseless, have special need of the protection of law, and should be regarded therefore as the special wards of government and its of-

ficers.——(2.) As the moral law of the ten commandments is obviously the compend and summary of the great principles which underlie this Hebrew code, so should this moral law be the compend and summary of the principles that should underlie every human code of law in whatever age of the world and in whatever stages of civilization.——(3.) As the Hebrew code while accepting the supreme authority of the ten commandments and aiming to embody and apply its principles did yet allow to itself a certain latitude in adjusting its "precepts and statutes" to the condition of the people, so may human legislators. Lessons of wisdom may be drawn from this code in both these lines of its example; viz. its fidelity to the principles and doctrines of the perfect moral law of Sinai; and its careful adaptation of these principles to the actual status of the people so as to reach the highest possible amount of practical efficiency in securing the ends of justice and of virtue.

The brief analysis and treatment of the *civil code* here attempted will follow mainly the same order of subjects which appears in the law of Sinai; thus:

I. Crimes against God:
   1. Idolatry;—2. Perjury;—3. Presumptuous sins;—4. Violations of the Sabbath;—5. Blasphemy;—6. Magic.
II. Crimes against parents and rulers (Fifth commandment).
III. Crimes against the person and life (Sixth commandment).
IV. Crimes against chastity (Seventh commandment).
V. Crimes against property; laws respecting property (Eighth commandment).
VI. Crimes against reputation; violations of truth (Ninth commandment).
VII. Hebrew servitude.
VIII. Judicial procedure.
IX. Punishments.

I. Crimes against God:
   1. *Idolatry.* The laws against idolatry included both the professed worship of the true God by means of images, and the worship of other gods. As the law of Sinai for-

bade both these practices with no special discrimination between them, so did the "statutes and judgments"—the law apparently holding it of small account to attempt any discrimination. In the case of the golden calf (Ex. 32) Aaron having more knowledge of the true God than the body of the people, may have thought only of worshiping the Lord ("To-morrow is a feast to the Lord"); but the people bringing their notions from their Egyptian life, may have had no thought beyond the calf, and so may have worshiped it as their God. Plainly the professed worship of God by means of images was a perpetual temptation to let slip all just conceptions of God and to worship images only, or some other object than God. No discrimination in point of penalty appears in the law. Both forms seem to have been condemned and punished with no attempt to discriminate between them. Individual idolaters, after careful examination and clear proof of guilt, were stoned—the witnesses casting the first stone (Deut. 17: 2-7). No man might allow himself to be seduced into the worship of other gods—no, not by a brother, or a son, or a wife, or by friend dear as his own soul, but must expose the sin of his seducer and spare not his very life (Deut. 13: 6-11). A city given to idolatry, if the case be proven, must be utterly destroyed and made a perpetual desolation (Deut. 13: 12-16). The statutes were absolutely sweeping against any possible form of similitude, image, or representation, made for an object of worship; and also against the worship of the heavenly bodies—a form of idolatry both ancient and widely diffused (Deut. 4: 13-19).——To guard them against temptation in the social line, they were forbidden to eat in idolatrous festivals (Ex. 34: 15). Apparently many special usages were forbidden because of their associations with idol worship (Lev. 19: 27, 28). The prohibition to eat blood or fat may have been in part sanitary, but probably was also anti-idolatrous. The distinction between things clean and unclean helped to make them a peculiar people, and may have been so intended.

2. *Perjury.* The law of Sinai tacitly indicates that the Lord himself would take the perjurer in hand, would never hold him guiltless, and would be responsible for his punishment. The statutes touch only a

single case—"A false witness rising up against any man to testify against him that which is wrong"—ordaining that the case be brought before the judges who are to make diligent inquisition. If found guilty, the evil he thought to bring upon another must be visited upon himself (Deut. 19: 16–21).——In general the sanctity of the sacred oath was shielded by Jehovah himself, searching out and punishing the guilty. Oaths seem to have been far less frequent than in the modern administration of law—less frequent, but more sacred, this binding force being laid on every conscience and left to the awful sanctions of Jehovah.

3. *Presumptuous sins.* The law against such sins sought to impress due reverence for God's authority. A broad distinction was made between sins of ignorance and sins where knowledge of duty was presupposed and the offense involved deliberate contempt of God. The external act was of smallest consequence. The law said, "The soul that doeth *aught* presumptuously"—no matter what it be. Certain cases are specified having these common elements—that the law was plain; the duty palpable; and innocent ignorance not even supposable;—*e. g.* the law of the Sabbath against all [needless] work (Ex. 31: 14, 15 and 35: 2, 3). The case (Num. 15: 32–36) of the man who gathered sticks on the Sabbath, stands in the closest connection with the law against "presumptuous sins," showing that the offense was seen in that light. The most emphatic condemnation of presumptuous sins immediately precedes (vs. 30, 31) in these words: "The soul that doeth aught presumptuously, the same reproacheth the Lord; and that soul shall be cut off from among his people" (*i. e.* by capital punishment). "Because he hath despised the word of the Lord and hath broken his commandment, that soul shall be utterly cut off; his iniquity shall be upon him." He must bear it himself, with no atonement provided for his pardon.—— Other cases specified are—the eating of unleavened bread during the Passover (Ex 12: 15); neglect of the Passover when its observance was practicable (Num. 9: 13); eating certain sacrificial offerings while unclean (Lev. 7: 20, 21); eating fat or blood (Lev. 7: 23–27). The reason for laws of this sort, apparently so strin-

gent and severe, lies in the facts—that God was their king; that he looked on the heart; and that whatever acts manifested contempt of his authority and treason against his throne were in their very nature the highest possible crimes.

4. *Laws against violations of the Sabbath* have been indicated sufficiently under the previous head. The statute was so entirely definite; the line of duty so easily defined and understood, it seemed to be assumed that palpable violations of the Sabbath were presumptuous sins, and they are treated accordingly. The case of the man who gathered sticks was carried up to the Supreme King, apparently because though the law was clear, the external act was in itself trivial. God's answer amounted to this; No offense *can be trivial* if the spirit of it contemns God's authority and reproaches his name.

5. *Blasphemy.* A case of blasphemy is specially described (Lev. 24: 10–16, 23). It was referred to God, the Supreme Ruler. "They put him in ward that the mind of the Lord might be showed them." The Lord replied through Moses: "Bring forth him that hath cursed without the camp; and let all that heard him lay their hand upon his head, and let all the congregation stone him." The law was enacted accordingly: "He that blasphemeth the name of the Lord shall surely be put to death, and all the congregation shall certainly stone him." The majesty of the Great King—the infinitely holy God, must be held sacred. No punishment could be too severe for a crime which struck so fatally against the reverence and homage due to Jehovah.

6. *Magic Arts.* In examining the statutes on this point, we are struck with the number and variety of names which designate these arts. The standard enumeration (Deut. 18: 10, 11) gives at least *eight ;* viz.——
(1.) "He that useth divination"—professing to gain knowledge and power more than human and in some sense divine:——(2.) "An observer of times"—the Hebrew word being related to *cloud*, perhaps in the sense of covering, hiding, as the cloud shuts off the sun's

light; practicing covert arts:——(3.) "An enchanter"—the original suggesting the serpent, and implying either a hissing, in imitation of the serpent; or the practice of charming serpents, yet always connected with the arts of divination:——(4.) "A witch"—the Hebrew word signifying one who mutters incantations, its cognate words having the sense of praying, but in Hebrew only in the bad sense of seeking help from others than God:——(5.) "The charmer"—a word which suggests *binding* as with the spell of enchantment—"spell-bound"; often used of the charming of serpents:——(6.) "A consulter with familiar spirits"; (Heb.) one who prays to the bottle-man—the Hebrew word for bottle being applied to the ventriloquist from whose body came forth unearthly sounds as from a second being imprisoned within him. Ventriloquism was one of the arts practiced by the ancient magicians to excite the wonder and to command the belief of the credulous.——The English phrase—"familiar spirit"—signifies spirits who stand in such a relation to the performer that they *come at his call*, like servants of his *family*, he having the power to evoke them at his will. Of course it is pretended that these spirits are other than human and greater than human spirits can be while yet in the body. The original Hebrew [Ob] comes down to us in the African "Obe-man" who still follows the same profession, by means of similar arts.——(7.) "The wizard" is one who claims superhuman wisdom—the old English accurately translating the Hebrew: the distinctively *wise one*. Of course the word is restricted in usage to this sort of superior wisdom—that which is gained by the arts of magic.——(8.) "The necromancer"—precisely the spiritist of modern times—or rather, of all time—who claims to have communion with the spirits of dead men.*

I have led the reader through this analysis of the original words, to aid him toward some just conception of the associated ideas which cluster round the *magic arts* of the Hebrew age. Their name and their arts are legion. Think of so many classes—professions—of men and women naturally shrewd, sharp, cunning; prac-

---

*The word necromancer comes from the Greek; necros—a dead one; and "mantis" divination—gaining superhuman knowledge from the dead.

ticing upon the superstitions, the fears, the gullibility of the millions; gaining an almost unlimited control over them; working upon their imagination, haunting them with the dread of unknown powers, bringing up to them ghosts from the invisible world, claiming to give auguries of the future, playing in every way that may be for their own selfish interests upon their fears and their hopes to extort their money or to make sport of their fears, or to gratify their own or others' malice. Or go still deeper and see all this machinery subsidized by the devil to impress men with his supremacy, to extort their homage, or at least their fear of himself; and perhaps, most of all, to turn them utterly away from the true God and to displace him from his proper sphere as the supreme hope and joy and trust of mortals.——It will always be an unsettled question—How much help in the line of superhuman knowledge and power does Satan give to his servants who work the infernal machinery of magic arts? But on the point of his interest and sympathy in these arts, there need not be the least question whatever. A system so near akin in spirit and influence to idolatry—which so thoroughly displaces God from the hopes and fears of men, and which seeks so successfully to instal these horrible superstitions in his place;—a system which perverts the powers of the world to come to subserve ungodliness and which practically rules out the Blessed God from the sphere of men's homage, fears, and hopes;—this system has always been worked by wicked and never by good men—has always subserved all iniquity, but piety and morality never;—this has been a master stroke of Satan's policy and one of the most palpable fields of his triumph through all the ages.——Let it not surprise us that God's law given through Moses denounced it unqualifiedly and made it punishable with death.

The nations whom God drove out of Canaan were steeped in its abominations and ripened under its influence for their righteous doom.——I am not aware that even one pagan, idolatrous nation, known to history since the world began, has been free from this abomination—the arts of magic. Egypt, Canaan, Babylon, India, Africa, historic Greece and Rome; the old nations of Northern Europe, the savages of America—all come up to testify that they have been cursed by its presence and power. The latest edition, modified slightly to adjust it somewhat to an age of Christian civilization, is the "spiritism" of our day—of which I need at this point to say but two things:—(1.) That its principles and policy, its spirit and its influence, are essentially the old "*necromancy*" of the ages of all history: and (2.) That it naturally becomes the nucleus around which chrystallizes whatever elements in society are irreligious and unchristian.——This last remark would not deny that some are attracted toward it temporarily by curiosity; but it would maintain that the animus, the soul of the system, is congenial to those who know not God, and who choose not to know him;—who therefore gladly seek a substitute for God, for his Bible, for prayer, and for trust in his providence in these new revelations from the future, unseen world.

Passages in the Old Testament treating of this subject are Ex. 22: 18 and Lev. 19: 26, 31, and 20: 6, 27, and Deut. 18: 10, 11, 14, and 1 Sam. 28: 7-20, and 1 Chron. 10: 13, 14, and 2 Kings 21: 6, and 2 Chron. 33: 6, and Isa. 8: 19, 20.

II. *Crimes against Parents and Rulers;* (Violations of the Fifth Command).

Of crimes against parents, the statutes of Moses specify smiting and cursing (Ex. 21: 15, 17); the penalty in both cases, death. The precept forbidding to curse a parent is repeated impressively (Lev. 20: 9); "For every one that curseth father or mother shall be surely put to death: he hath cursed his father or his mother; his blood shall be upon him." This crime stands in the list of those that are anathematized—in Deut. 27: 16: "Cursed be he that setteth light by his father or his mother; and all the people shall say, Amen."——In Mat. 15: 3-6 and Mk. 7: 9-13, our Lord seems to give this law forbidding a son to curse father or mother, coupled with the fifth command, a construction broad enough to require him to give them an adequate support—of course in their years of infirmity and want.—— That God had a high regard for this filial duty toward parents is manifest in the place of priority accorded to the fifth command and in the special promise made to those who fulfill its obligations.

In Deut. 21: 18–21, the case is supposed of a son incurably stubborn, rebellious, gluttonous, and drunken, upon whom parental chastisement is unavailing. The law very considerately provides that his father and his mother shall lay hold of him and bring him before the elders of his city unto its gates (*i. e.* into open court), and there, as a public example and warning, the men of his city shall stone him with stones that he die:— "So shalt thou put evil away from you and all Israel shall hear and fear."——Parental love and partiality would guaranty this law against abuse. It is pleasant to note that no case of its execution is on record. Perhaps the severity of the law forestalled its violation. ——The spirit of this precept is so fully in harmony with the book of Proverbs that we naturally expect to find it there. (See Prov. 20: 20 and 30: 11, 17.)

A precept forbidding insult and reproach of magistrates stands in Ex. 22: 28: "Thou shalt not revile the gods [Elohim used probably in the sense of *judges*], nor curse the ruler of thy people." The word "gods" here can not refer to false gods, idols (as the English reader might suppose), for the Hebrew word can not bear that sense, nor would it be pertinent. The parallelism with "ruler of thy people" favors the sense above suggested— *judges*—acting under God and in his behalf before the people. Their sacred office under God is assumed to be good reason for treating them with respect and against offering them insult.——No penalty is attached to the violation of this law—perhaps because the penalty ought to depend so much upon the aggravation of the offense. ——Under the kings, it was apparently a capital crime, for when Shimei cursed king David (2 Sam. 19: 21–23) Abishai assumed that he ought to die; and his temporary pardon was manifestly due to David's sad consciousness of deep personal ill-desert and of God's righteous visitations upon him.

III. *Crimes against Person and Life;* (Violations of the Sixth Command).

Under this head the salient and vital points are:

1. That the *real murderer must be put to death*, and no "satisfaction" be ever taken in place of his life.

CRIMES AGAINST PERSON AND LIFE. 281

2. That the law discriminated with the utmost care and wisdom between real murder, and homicide, more or less justifiable. [Special laws touching injuries done to servants will be treated under the head of Hebrew servitude.]

3. A special law provided cities of refuge.

4. Another special law met the case of murder by unknown hands.

5. Inexcusable carelessness causing injury or death was punished.

6. Personal injuries not fatal were specially punished by statute.

1. Real murder was punished capitally. "He that smiteth a man so that he die shall be surely put to death" (Ex. 21: 12 and Lev. 24: 17). The law appears fully in Num. 35: 9-34 and Deut. 19: 4-13, 20, 21, in connection with provisions for the cities of refuge. With firm and solemn tone the law declared "Ye shall take no satisfaction for the life of a murderer who is guilty of death, but he shall be surely put to death. So shall ye not pollute the land wherein ye are; for blood it defileth the land, and the land can not be cleansed of the blood that is shed therein but by the blood of him that shed it. Defile not therefore the land which ye shall inhabit wherein I dwell, for I the Lord dwell among the children of Israel" (Num. 35: 31-34).——This reaffirms and amplifies the doctrine of the law as given to Noah and to the repeopled world; "And surely your blood of your lives [life-blood] will I require; at the hand of every beast will I require it, and *at the hand of every man;* at the hand of every man's brother [such a case as that of Cain and Abel] will I require the life of man. Whoso "[with no exception] sheddeth man's blood, by man shall his blood be shed; *for in the image of God made he man.*" Human life is sacred, and God protects it under the sternest possible penalties—nothing less than the life of the murderer. That God intended this law *for the whole race, for the entire repeopled world* from and after Noah, is too plain to be denied or even doubted. It is not easy to see how another word could be said to make this more plain. The law of Sinai and the code given through Moses are intensely emphatic, indeed, perfectly decisive.

CRIMES AGAINST PERSON AND LIFE.

The law does not prescribe the mode of this capital punishment. In various other crimes punishable with death, the mode is by stoning, done, however, not by any one executioner, but by many; in some cases by "the men of the city." The penalty for murder would often be executed by the blood-avenger—the nearest relative of the murdered man; and it seems to be assumed that he would use any deadly weapon he might choose (Num. 35: 19, 21, 27 and Deut. 19: 6, 11–13).

2. The law discriminated with the utmost care and wisdom between real murder, and homicide, more or less justifiable. Real murder was to be proven as follows:

(1.) By previous hatred and enmity. Of course this could be known by human judges only by its manifestations.

(2.) By violent passion in the act—which I take to be the sense of the words in our translation: "If a man come *presumptuously* upon his neighbor; [in Heb.] if a man *boil up with rage* against his neighbor to slay him with guile," etc. (Ex. 21: 14).

(3.) By evidence of premeditation—"lying in wait" (Ex. 21: 13, and Num. 35: 15–23, and Deut. 19: 4–6).

(4.) By the sort of instrument used (Num. 35: 16–18). "An instrument of iron;" "a stone;" "a hand-weapon of wood," *i. e. wood of the hand*, large enough to fill the hand and deal a death-blow.

On the other hand it would be in favor of homicide if one had killed his neighbor "ignorantly"—"whom he had not hated in time past;" or thrust upon him suddenly without enmity; without lying in wait; or cast upon him a stone seeing him not, nor seeking his harm, etc. (Num. 35: 22, 23 and Deut. 19: 4–6). A case for example is given—the head of a man's ax flying off when he is at work and killing his neighbor.

3. A special law provided for *cities of refuge*. (See Ex. 21: 13 and Num. 35, and Deut. 19 and Josh. 20).——At the era of Moses it was already a time-honored usage that the nearest blood-relative should avenge the blood of his slain friend. The prevalence and strength of this sentiment were due of course, primarily, to the instincts of human nature; but secondarily to the fact that as an institution for the protection of person and life, the family was prior to the state.——The Goel [as

he was called in Hebrew]—the blood-avenger or Redeemer, could not be expected to exercise cool and impartial discrimination over the questions lying between murder in the first degree and homicide. To obviate this evil the Lord introduced an important modification upon the previously current usages of blood-revenge. It was this. Six cities in Palestine—three on each side of the Jordan were selected in such convenient geographical position that from any point of the whole country the man-slayer might make the nearest one within less than one day's run.——All these were cities of the Levites; hence the leading men of the city would be competent to hold a preliminary investigation. The man-slayer fled for his life to the nearest of these cities. The legal authorities there protected him against the Goel—the blood-avenger. The elders of his own city, if the case seemed to demand it, might send and fetch him; try him, and deliver him up to the blood-avenger; or remand him back to his city of refuge. Thus this city shielded him against sudden and indiscriminate vengeance, and secured for him a trial before the congregation or elders of his own city. If his case was proved to be homicide, he must remain within the city of refuge till the death of the high priest, after which the avenger's right to take his life (outside the refuge-city) ceased and he could go at large in safety. This provision affixed a limit to his quasi-imprisonment. Perhaps it was also significant of the pardon for sin provided for in the death of our Great High Priest.——If the man-slayer allowed himself to be caught by the blood-avenger outside his city when he should be within it, the avenger might take his life with impunity.

The law was specific on the point that human life must not be taken on the testimony of one witness only—a plurality of witnesses being required (Num. 35: 30, and Deut. 17: 6, and 19: 15).——It was no crime before the law to kill a thief breaking into a house by night (Ex. 22: 2, 3). After sunrise, it became a crime of blood to take his life—it being assumed that he might be caught and compelled to make restitution, and that the peril to your own life and that of your family is materially lessened. The law carefully guarded the defenseless hours of sleep by night. If a thief in defiance of this law played the burglar by night, he must run his own risk of death in the attempt.

4. A very remarkable statute met the special case of a murder done by unknown hands (Deut. 21: 1-9). The authorities from all contiguous cities took up the case; measured carefully to fix upon the city lying nearest to the bloody spot. Then the elders of that city were to take a heifer never worked in yoke; bring her down into a wild, uncultivated valley—the home of all weird and thrilling associations—and there strike off the heifer's head—the priests coming near and all the elders of that city washing their hands over the headless heifer, solemnly protesting—"Our hands have not shed this blood, neither have our eyes seen it. Be merciful, O Lord, unto thy people Israel, and lay not innocent blood unto thy people Israel's charge." "And the blood shall be forgiven them. So shalt thou put away the guilt of innocent blood from among you when thou shalt do that which is right in the sight of the Lord."
——The entire scene was well adapted to make the impression that murder is no trifle, and that God held the whole people responsible to some extent for the safety of every human life.

5. *Inexcusable carelessness*, followed by fatal results, was punishable by law. A supposed case for a specimen appears in Ex. 21: 28, 29. The goring ox—wont to push with his horns—reported to his owner but not "kept in" by him—killing man or woman—must be put to death and *his owner also*, for his culpable negligence.

6. Personal injuries, not fatal, came under special statute. In the case of a mutual quarrel and fight, personal injuries, less than fatal, were punished by requiring their author to pay for the wounded man's loss of time and for his being "thoroughly healed" [nursing and medical services].——The master who smote his servant unto immediate death, must surely be punished. But if the servant survived a day or two, the presumption would be that the master did not intend to kill. His loss in the services of his servant was considered his punishment.——Other special cases appear Ex. 21: 22 and Deut. 25: 11, 12 which were better read than rehearsed.——The principle of punishment by retaliation—["lex talionis"]—like for like—was applied

in all appropriate cases (Lev. 24: 18–21). "If a man cause a blemish in his neighbor, as he hath done, so shall it be done unto him: Breach for breach; eye for eye," etc. (Ex. 21: 23–25 and Deut. 19: 21).

IV. *Crimes Against Chastity;* (Violations of the Seventh Command).

The necessity for laws on this point at once discriminating, wise, and stringent, will be sufficiently obvious when we consider (1.) The strength of the passion to be controlled—constitutionally common to all ages of the world:——(2.) The sacredness of the marriage relation and the inestimable value of moral purity in all human society—also common to all ages of the world's history:——(3.) (Peculiar to the earlier ages) the necessity of defining the limits of consanguinity within which marriage should be prohibited, and all sexual connection sternly forbidden. Perhaps we need to remind ourselves that the race having sprung from a single pair and the world having been repeopled a second time from one family, those primitive examples may have sent down for many generations a certain looseness which called for special restraint and a carefully defining law:——(4.) The crimes of Sodom, their polluting influence in so good a family as that of Lot; the low morals of Egyptian life; some sad manifestations in the early history of Jacob's family; the horrible contagion of Moab and Midian when the tribes of Israel came socially near them;—these and kindred facts will be readily recalled as in point to show the necessity of vigorous legislation in the Mosaic code to counteract these untoward influences of their antecedent life and of surrounding society.——The thoughtful student of the Mosaic code as expanding and applying the seventh commandment will be painfully impressed with the disadvantages under which it labored by reason of the toleration of polygamy, concubinage, and domestic servitude. In some points the law bore with special severity upon woman as compared with man—a sort of imperfection which was simply an inevitable result of tolerating those ancient evils.——It scarcely need be suggested that the value of this part of the Mosaic code as a definite model for Christian legislation is greatly lessened by this class of facts. Woman's place in society then was by no means that which the genius of Christianity has given her. Unquestionably this code alleviated her condition as compared with what it had been, and brought to her relief as large a boon of blessing as the genius of the age would bear.

In view, partly of the difficulty of treating this subject with minute detail in a way to make its discussion really useful, and partly of its inferior value in some points as an example, for reasons above indicated, I shall excuse myself from any minute and extended presentation of these laws.

In general: The laws accord ample space to the condemnation of the unnatural crimes of sodomy and bestiality (Lev. 18 and 20, and Deut. 23: 17, 18, and 27: 21): also to incest, which for historic reasons needed to be thoroughly and stringently defined (Lev. 18 and 19 and 20): to adultery proper; to the case of a suspected wife (Num. 5: 11–31);—to seduction and rape; to aggravated whoredom in the form of public prostitution; of prostitution to an idol; of impurity in a priest's daughter; in a woman betrothed, etc., etc.—— The study of these laws would impress pure-minded readers with a sense of the great pains taken to lift up and regenerate a sadly low and debased condition of social morals on these points; and also with a sense of special difficulty arising from the fact that society was quite too low to bear the introduction and enforcement of the Christian law of marriage as against concubinage, polygamy, and the debasement inseparable from even modified slavery. We shall rise from the careful study of this department of the Hebrew code with gratitude for the wisdom and goodness which attempted so much, yet with a deeper gratitude that a purer and higher code came to mankind through the law of Christ and the spirit of an enlightened Christian age.

V. *Statutes Protecting Rights of Property;* (Expanding the Eighth Command).

In Ex. 22: 1–15, 25–28, and 23: 4, 5, we have the earliest instalment of statutes on this point. The staple penalty for theft was restitution, yet varying widely in amount to meet the peculiarities of the case. In pastoral life cattle were specially exposed; therefore the law ordained that if the thief had killed the animal or sold it, he must restore—of oxen five for one; of sheep, four. But if the animal was found alive in his hand, the restitution was only double—two for one. The law made the charitable supposition that the thief might yet repent and bring back the stolen property, and purposely favored this result. On the other hand the selling or destruction of the animal would indicate a fixed purpose to have the avails of it, and also to render detection more difficult—both of which purposes the law punished sharply.——It may well be noted that restitution was a telling, stinging penalty, touching the sensibilities of the thief in a very tender point. The indolent or unprincipled man who thought to live upon his neighbor's toil, would find stealing very unprofitable. The law had the more grip in those times because if a man tried to put his property out of his hands to evade the demand for restitution, or were in fact too poor to restore four or five fold, there was always the last resort—the law could take him for a slave ("servant") and make him *work it out.*——This was one of the incidental benefits of a hard system: it could be applied so as to make the penalties for theft very effectually stringent.

The law punished trespass upon another's property and want of care for its due protection—on which points, subsequent statutes reaffirm and expand what we first find in Ex. 22. (See Deut. 22: 1–4.)

While the law was vigorous, not to say severe, against criminal theft, it was yet *exceedingly lenient towards the unfortunate and innocent poor*, e. g.,

(1.) It gave permission to eat another's property for the supply of present want. The specifications are—The grapes of thy neighbor's vineyard; and his standing corn. Thou mayest eat grapes, but not put one in thy vessel; mayest pluck the heads of grain in thy hand, but never move thy sickle against thy neighbor's grain (Deut. 23: 24, 25).

(2.) It regulated thoughtfully and compassionately the whole subject of *pledges, i. e.* securities for the payment of debt. As first announced (Ex. 22: 26, 27), it provided that if the poor man's garment were taken in pledge, it must certainly be restored to him by sundown, because it was his bed-covering for the night; and God would surely hear the poor man's cry if he were compelled to lay himself down to sleep with no covering. ——As subsequently revised or enlarged (Deut. 24: 6, 10-13, 17), the statute peremptorily forbade taking the upper or the nether millstone in pledge, because no oriental family could subsist without these. It also forbade the creditor to go in to the poor man's house to get his pledge lest he fix his covetous eye on something there, but required him to wait patiently outside for the poor man to bring it out—a provision which manifests a specially delicate regard for the feelings of the poor. He was not obliged to expose his deep poverty, nor to disclose all he had to the greedy gaze of his more wealthy neighbor.——The law also forbade the taking of a widow's raiment in pledge.

(3.) The law was entirely explicit and positive in its prohibition of *usury*. By "usury" the Hebrew meant, not merely excessive or illegal interest, but *interest* itself—*all* interest—money paid for the use of money, or any thing valuable paid for the use of any other property borrowed.——The first statute (Ex. 22: 25) was general, yet fully covered the principle: "If thou lend money to any of my people that is poor by thee, thou shalt not be to him as an usurer, neither shalt thou lay upon him usury." The law contemplated the poor only; for the rich are presumed to be above the necessity of borrowing money. The borrowing of money as capital to be used in trade, or in manufacture, or in the purchase of land, had no place at all in the business economy of Israel. The borrowing which the law contemplated was only that of the poor man to meet his imperative necessities. A man who had no accumulations to draw from for a sick day or a casualty, must borrow or go hungry. God speaks of such poor as "my people," and forbids taking interest on what they must needs borrow.

In the later books (Lev. 25: 35-38 and Deut. 23: 19, 20) we have perhaps a later and revised form of the statute. "If thy brother be waxen poor, thou shalt relieve him. Take thou no usury of him or increase;

LAWS RELIEVING THE POOR.

fear thy God, that thy neighbor may live with thee. Thou shalt not give him thy money upon usury, nor lend him thy victuals for increase." In Deut. (as above) the law discriminates between "thy brother" and a stranger. "Thou shalt not lend upon usury to thy brother; unto a stranger thou mayest lend upon usury." The ground for this discrimination against the stranger may be a purpose to discourage his residence in the land; or it may be related to the general fact that foreigners were the men of traffic. (The original words for Canaanite and for merchant were the same.) Tradesmen, doing business on borrowed capital, might afford to pay interest; and on every principle of right and justice, ought to do so. But God did not encourage the Israelites in traffic with other nations. It would have been quite too perilous to their morals, and to their religion.

The reader will scarcely need the suggestion that the Hebrew law against interest applies in our Christian age only to the case of loans made to the poor to meet their necessities. The spirit of the law unquestionably *does* apply in such cases, and does *not* apply to any other.

(4.) *Many special statutes contemplated relief for the poor.* ——The corners and the gleanings of the harvest field; a forgotten sheaf; a few clusters of grapes also and some olives on the olive tree, must be left for the poor and the stranger (Lev. 19: 9, 10, and 23: 32, and Deut. 24: 19-22)—each of these successive statutes adding somewhat in detail to the preceding.——The day wages of the poor laborer must be promptly paid, even on the very same day (Lev. 19: 13 and Deut. 24: 14, 15). But especially the sabbatic year (each seventh) was designed to be a special benefaction to the poor. This law (Deut. 15: 1-11) uses chiefly the word "release" in regard to the debts of the poor. Critics are sharply divided over the question whether this release was an entire *remission of debts,* or only a *stay of collection,* putting it over for this one year. In favor of the latter view, Michaelis and others urge that the reason for stay of collection was that no cultivation of land was permitted during this year, and hence there were no crops of this sort, and therefore only diminished means of paying debts. Also that the law might be so abused as mostly to annihilate all rights of property, inasmuch as the statute (v. 9) would virtually put the property of the more wealthy within the control of the less wealthy. Thou shalt not withhold because the year of release is at hand, etc.

On the other hand, the arguments for construing the law to mean an actual release of debt in the case of "thy poor brother" or neighbor, are strong, and in my view, conclusive; *e. g.*

(a.) This is the legitimate meaning of the original word translated "release." There should never be any deviation from the legitimate sense of the original staple word, without cogent reasons—a principle which is doubly strong *in the words of a law.*

(b.) This construction is fully in harmony with the genius of the entire code in all its statutes for the relief of the poor.

(c.) On this construction the limitations of the statute are precisely in place; *e. g.*—to the case of "thy poor brother." "Thou shalt release *save when there* shall be no poor among you": also—"If there be among you a poor man of one of thy brethren, etc., thou shalt not harden thy heart nor shut thy hand from thy poor brother, but shalt open thy hand wide unto him, and shall surely lend unto him sufficient for his need in that which he wanteth"—[not all your property: you are not required to make over every thing you have]. "Beware that there be not a thought in thy wicked heart, saying—The year of release is at hand" [and I shall never get my money or my grain back again], "and he cry unto the Lord against thee, and it be sin unto thee." This shaping of the statute plainly contemplates a real remission of this sort of debts on each seventh year.

(d.) To the same purport is this—that the law excepts debts against a foreigner: "Of a foreigner thou mayest exact it." Our translators have taken the liberty to add the word "again," but without the least authority from the Hebrew. The word "again" seems to come from the theory that this statute required a stay of collection for one year in the case of the foreigner: but of this there is no proof in the law as it came from the hand of Moses.——In the time of Nehemiah (5: 1–12) there was unquestionably an entire remission of debts to the poor, and not the least hint that this was going beyond the Mosaic law. On the contrary it is implied that "the fear of our God" (v. 9)—equivalent to obedience—would require just this.

This seventh or sabbatic year had other special features besides the remission of the poor man's debts as in Deut. 15: 1–11. These additional features appear in Lev. 25, which provides (vs. 2–7) that this year shall be a Sabbath of rest to the soil—rest from its usual cultivation.——In this chapter we find also a kindred institution—the Jubilee—each fiftieth year—next following each seventh Sabbatic year. Inasmuch as this arrangement would bring two years of land-rest together, the Lord gave a special promise that the fertility of the year immediately preceding should suffice against the necessities of these two years of rest—a fact which testifies that God ruled his people Israel under a system of special providences. If Moses is to be considered as even in a secondary sense the legislator of the people, he must have had unbounded confidence in God's special direction and counsel in these statutes.

The law of the Jubilee gave personal liberty to all bondmen. Of this, more must be said under "Hebrew servitude." It also provided for the return of all real estate—all the lands of Canaan—to their original possessors. Lands could be alienated only till the jubilee. They were sold, if at all, subject to this law. Consequently a sale of land was only a lease for at longest forty-nine years—*i. e.* for the years intervening till the next jubilee. They were subject to redemption at any time—the price to be graduated by the years which the lease had to run. Houses in walled cities were redeemable only within one year from sale; but in unwalled cities, houses followed the law of land, returning with the land to their original owner at the jubilee. The houses of Levites were accounted as land.——These statutes had a twofold purpose; to afford relief to the poor; and to prevent the entire alienation of the lands of Canaan from the tribes, families, and individuals to whom they were originally given.——The question, how far these institutions—the Sabbatic year and the Jubilee—were observed in the future history of Israel is foreign from our present purpose.

VI. *Crimes against reputation;* (the details of the **ninth** commandment).

Here are stringent statutes against *false accusation* and *false witness*. Under this general head fall two distinct cases:—(a) Testimony given to favor the guilty (Ex. 23: 1, 3);——and (b) allegations designed to condemn the innocent (Deut. 19: 16–21).

(a). The former class (as given Ex. 23: 1, 3) forbids not merely originating ("raise"), but *taking up* a false report and seconding it by indorsement. It warns men not to be drawn in to help the wicked in their malicious plots to screen each other, though they be many. The cause of the poor man which you may not favor (v. 3) is certainly supposed to be a bad one. Your sympathy for him as poor must not override justice and truth.

(b). False witness, purposed to condemn the innocent, is met by the statute (Deut. 19: 16–21). The accuser and the accused are to be brought face to face before the Lord and before the priests and the judges who are to "make diligent inquisition," obviously hearing both parties, and if the accuser is proved to be a false witness, "Ye shall do to him as he thought to do to his brother; thine eye shall not pity, but life shall go for life; eye for eye," etc.

Tale-bearing, *i. e.* tattling, retailing scandal maliciously or for a past-time, needed the force of law to abate and suppress it in those times as in most other ages. "Thou shalt not go up and down as a tale-bearer among thy people, neither shalt thou stand against the blood of thy neighbor. I am the Lord" (Lev. 19: 16–18)— "Standing against the blood," must mean—taking ground against the very life, and must not be construed to forbid truthful testimony against the real murderer. But the informer should constantly remember that his neighbor's interests and life are too precious to be lightly tampered with. Thy neighbor may have said or done something wrong. Your duty in the case is not to scatter broadcast all you know and more than you know of his misdeeds; but first of all—"Thou shalt not hate thy brother in thy heart," but "love him as thyself" (v. 18); and next, "Thou shalt in anywise [by all means] rebuke thy neighbor, and not suffer sin upon him."——This last clause has been understood in two ways:—(a) Thou shalt not suffer the sin to lie upon him with no effort on thy part to bring him to repentance: or (b) Thou shalt not bear on thine own conscience the sin of neglecting to admonish him; *i. e.* thou shalt not submit to bear this sin on his account—a sin which comes of knowing his crime and of failing in your duty to save him by means of judicious and fraternal rebuke. The latter construction is best sustained by Hebrew usage of the words. See the same words, Lev. 22: 9 and Num. 18: 32, and the preposition "*upon* him," in Ps. 69: 8—"*For thy sake have I borne,*" etc. The verb in this clause means rather to "*bear*" in your own person, than to "suffer" to exist in another.——The passage, so interpreted, assumes it to be your solemn duty to labor to bring your neighbor to repentance if you are cognizant of his wrong-doing, and implies that you must lie under a load of sin if you fail to do so. But do it *in love* (loving him even as yourself) as well as in all fidelity to his soul, as also to your own. Do this instead of going up and down to scatter this scandal among those who will do nothing to save your erring neighbor, and nothing to relieve your conscience of your responsibility in his behalf.

While this statute bears against giving information about misdeeds of minor sort, there were two crimes of such magnitude that every man was bound to testify in the proper form against them; viz. idolatry and murder. See the case of idolatry in Deut. 13: 6–14: "Neither shalt thou conceal him, but thou shalt surely kill him: thy hand shall be first upon him to put him to death, and afterward, the hand of all the people." (Also v. 14)——The expiation for murder by an unknown hand included this most solemn protestation: "Our hands have not shed this blood, neither have our eyes seen it." Of course, whoever might have seen was most sacredly bound to testify.

CHAPTER XVIII.

THE CIVIL INSTITUTES OF MOSES, CONTINUED.

VII. *Hebrew Servitude.*

Servitude existed before Moses. It was no part of the mission of the Hebrew code to *create* it. Let it be forever admitted that the laws given of God through Moses can not be held responsible for the existence of slavery. They found it existing and proceeded therefore to *modify it;* to soften its more rigid features; to extract its carnivorous teeth; to ordain that the slave *had rights* which the master and the nation were bound to respect—in short, to tone down the severities of the system from unendurable slavery to very tolerable servitude.

By what means was this change wrought? What new elements were introduced to abate the severities of real slavery?

1. *Man-stealing was punished with death.* "He that stealeth a man and selleth him, or if he be found in his hand, he shall surely be put to death" (Ex. 21: 16). The law as recited in Deut. 21: 7 applies to a man stealing one of his brethren of the children of Israel. As stated in Ex. 21: 16 it is universal, with no limitation. Stealing a *man* is the crime. I see no reason to doubt that the law was intended to apply to men of every nationality—to men as made in God's image of whatever nation.

This statute struck at the very root of real slavery. Both stealing and selling contemplate property—assume the fact of a property value. The spirit of the law is—Men shall never be degraded into merchandise. Every body knows that all American slavery began with stealing men from Africa and selling them. Servitude, involving a certain right to service and property in service, there might be, despite of this Hebrew law; but real slavery—property in man as distinct from property in his services, there could not be under this law. Moreover, the severity of this penalty must have thrown its shield of protection over the entire system of servitude. It was a very palpable indication of God's stern displeasure against the whole system of chattelizing human beings.

2. The Hebrew law positively forbade the rendition of fugitives. "Thou shalt not deliver to his master the servant that has escaped from his master unto thee: he shall dwell with thee, even among you in that place which he shall choose in one of thy gates where it liketh him best; thou shalt not oppress him" (Deut. 23: 15, 16).——Observe it was not only impossible to have any law for the reclamation of fugitives—*i. e.* to have "a fugitive slave law" of the recent American pattern; but the law was put on the other side. It declared—"Thou shalt *not* deliver him up to his master"—shalt not give his master information and help the arrest; but shalt let him choose his abode by his own free and manly will. If his hardships are such under his bondage that he prefers to take his risk of finding a better living elsewhere, let him try it. Let no man stand in his way. He would not leave his master if his personal rights and interests were properly cared for. But if his master is too selfish, or too cruel, or too exacting of labor, or too stingy of bread or clothing, who shall judge but the servant himself? Therefore let the servant better his own condition if he can, and let all selfish, savage-hearted masters take warning!——Such laws exorcise the real spirit of slavery with blessed rapidity. It would require but few such ameliorating statutes to tone it down from unendurable slavery to very tolerable servitude.

The spirit of this law is altogether the spirit of the Great Lawgiver when he found the Hebrews sorely oppressed in Egypt; smote off their chains; brought them forth from their house of bondage, and placed them beyond all reclamation. What he required his people now to do in behalf of any oppressed servant was only in spirit what he had done for them.

3. Severe personal injuries gave the slave his freedom. "If a man smite the eye of his servant or the eye of his maid that it perish, he shall let him go free for his eye's sake." So of the tooth (Ex. 21: 26, 27).

The eye and the tooth are but specimen illustrations of the principle. A charge of shot in the leg could not be less under this law than a passport to freedom.—— Moreover, the statutes very specifically enjoined clemency and forbade rigor in the treatment of Hebrew servants (Lev. 25 : 39–43, 46).

4. Of wider sweep in its influence and of inexpressible value was *the system of periodical emancipation*. The term of service for the Hebrew-born was limited to six years. At the end of this term they went out free. Servants of foreign birth (as we shall see) went out at the Jubilee, each fiftieth year.——The effect of this law was at once to lift from the heart the terrible incubus of a life-long bondage—that sense of a hopeless doom which knows no relief till death. Whatever the amount of discomfort or suffering involved in servitude might have been, the Hebrew servant had under this law the prospect of his freedom at no distant day.—— Moreover the accompanying provisions of this law were thoroughly humane. The servant who had sold himself through extreme poverty (Lev. 25: 47–55) might be redeemed at any time by a friend, or if he could command the means by extra labor or skill, he might redeem himself.——When his term expired, his master must not send him away empty, but must furnish him liberally out of his flock and out of his floor (grain), and even out of his *wine-press*—of any thing and every thing wherewith the Lord had blessed the master, he was to impart liberally to his manumitted servant (Deut. 15: 12–15). So the servant would have a fair start in his new self-supporting life. It was a forethoughtful provision, full of the milk of a more than human kindness.

Apparently this periodic emancipation applied to every class of Hebrew servants—to him who had sold himself because he had become too poor to provide for his family; to him who had been taken and sold for debt; and to him who had been sold into servitude for crime. This latter case, however, is doubtful.

Noticeably, this law provides for the family rights of the servant. If he had brought his wife with him into this state, he took her out with himself, and of course his children also. If his master had given him a wife, he retained her because of his property interest in her services, and her children with her for humanity's sake; for children under six years of age need their mother's care. Wives in that age of the world were paid for.

Let it be noticed, the law assumes that possibly the servant may love his wife and his children and even his *master* so well that he chooses not to leave them. Very well; if he will consent to come before the judges and in a solemn judicial manner, testify to this love of his heart, and moreover, will consent to endure the rather uncomfortable operation of having his ear bored through with an awl, then he may remain forever—*i. e.* during life. But the discomforts of this operation were intended to bear somewhat against this unlimited servitude. The law seemed to say to every servant—"It would probably be better for you to be your own master and live in freedom, rather than in even this very comfortable servitude.——Every provision of this statute had a purpose. The servant must be brought before the judges to express in this public manner his choice to remain in servitude; for this method would make it impossible for the master to misrepresent the will of his servant. Moreover, it seems probable that boring the ear was no badge of honor but the opposite, and therefore would bear against the man's choice of perpetual servitude.

The law made special provision for the case of female servants. The original statute (Ex. 21: 7–11) put her case on a different footing from that of her brother. "She shall not go out as the men-servants do." The language—"If a man sell his daughter to be a maid-servant"—may seem at first view to be a case of slave-sale, involving real property in human flesh and bones. A closer examination will show that it comes under the usage of *selling daughters to become wives;* for this purchase "betrothed her to her master," or to "his son," and the law made special provision for her rights as such; viz. that in case her master is not pleased with her, he shall let her be redeemed, "and shall have no power to sell her unto a strange nation." If betrothed to his son, he shall deal with her as with a daughter; if the son take another wife, he shall not abate from his duty as a husband toward her; and if he refuse to do all the law demands, she is free—redeemed by law, "without money."——These statutes of course shape themselves to the existing usages in respect to polygamy, concubinage, and easy divorce, sedulously protecting the rights of a female servant under these most unfavorable usages.

It seems probable that these kind and considerate provisions failed to protect her rights as fully as the spirit of the law intended, and therefore a further modification appears at a later period; for Deut. 15: 17 declares that the six years' emancipation law shall apply to her also as truly as to her brother;—"and unto thy maid-servant thou shalt do likewise."

5. In view of the fact that what we may call "religious privileges" included rest from labor and more or less of religious and social festivity, the law was very specific in stipulating that the man-servant and the maid-servant must share in all these equally with the son and the daughter. We see this in the law of the Sabbath; in the feast upon the second tithes (Deut. 12: 17, 18); and in two of the great festivals, viz. the Pentecost and the Feast of Tabernacles (Deut. 16: 11, 14).——Thus they were put religiously and socially upon the same footing as children in the family. No ban of exclusion, no stigma of caste, could attach to their condition so long as these statutes were duly observed.

6. By usage and without the necessity of statute, Hebrew servants held property. The old American doctrine—"The slave can own nothing"—had no place in the system of Hebrew servitude. The proof is twofold:——(a) The statutes provided that "if able he might redeem himself" (Lev. 25: 49). This permission would be only a taunting insult if in fact no Hebrew servant could hold property.——(b). The light of history bears witness: Ziba was a servant of the house of Saul; but he had servants under him—a round score; "fifteen sons and *twenty* servants" (2 Sam. 9: 10 and 19: 17), and seems to have had charge of cultivating Saul's estates.

Thus manifold and effective were the humane provisions which softened the severities of slavery, toning them down to a very tolerable system of servitude.

The Slavery that Existed before Moses.

We have spoken of Hebrew servitude as a *modified* system—which raises the question—"modified" *from what?* What was the pre-existing system upon which these modifications were superinduced? A full answer must include (a) The patriarchal system as it appears in the case of Abraham, Isaac, and Jacob: and (b) The system of Egypt and perhaps other contemporary nations.

(a.) In the patriarchal system servitude could not possibly have been compulsory. It must have been voluntary. Force, coercion, was utterly out of the question. Abraham had neither army nor police to hold his slaves in bondage. In fact they were his armed soldiers as against freebooting incursions or any hostile assault whatever. Manifestly they lived with him while they chose—no longer. Some of them rose to bear important responsibilities, *e. g.* Eliezer (Gen. 24); his two young men who went with him and Isaac to Moriah (Gen. 22).——Isaac "had great store of servants (Gen. 26: 14), but there is not the least intimation that they were entailed as part of his estate to either Esau or Jacob; or that he received them by inheritance from Abraham.——Jacob had many servants (Gen. 30: 43), and in fact must have had to help him in the care of his flocks and herds: but the history shows that he did not take them with him into Egypt. Joseph's invitation left out the servants (Gen. 45: 10, 11.), and the record specifies all the family except the servants and gives us the actual enumeration- all servants omitted (Gen. 46: 5-26). Property in servants in the American sense, there was none.

(b.) Of Egyptian slavery enough is known to show that they bought slaves brought in from other nations, holding therefore a property right in them, and that they constituted a menial class in society.

The condition of the Israelites under oppression there was peculiar. Manifestly they were not held by individual Egyptians as their personal property, but rather by the crown. The king of Egypt appears as the great slave-holder of the Hebrew people, making levies upon them for laborers at his pleasure, and exacting the severest tasks with no limitations but his own will on the one hand and their possible endurance on the other. The question of letting the people go was (at least mainly) personal to himself and to his throne. His merciless severity would naturally tend to make slavery in Egypt heartlessly cruel. Laws to restrain masters from severity could not be thought of under such kings. It is easy to see that when, at and after Sinai, the Lord came to legislate for the Hebrew people, fresh from Egyptian usages and laws, there was abundant occasion for statutes to modify the severities of human bondage. With telling force the Lord could say—Never oppress your servants; ye know how oppression feels!

The Jubilee.—(Lev. 25).

In this chapter and here only we have an account of this peculiar institution. The following points in it deserve special attention.

1. Its main scope and purpose were manifestly of the same sort with those of the Sabbatic year—a year of rest from labor, of recuperation for both the laborer and his lands, and of joy in the God of their mercies. Particularly it made provision for restoring lands which had been alienated by any means during the forty-nine intervening years. On this eventful year all lands were to return to the original proprietor and to his estate. The law provided that alienated lands might be redeemed at any time for a price graduated by the years intervening before the Jubilee. But if the poor man was unable to redeem his land and had no relative or friend to redeem it for him before the Jubilee, it then returned to him by the statute with no redemption price.

2. We must note its bearing upon Hebrew servants and its relation to the seventh year emancipation law. ——It treats of two classes of servants of Hebrew blood; those who had sold themselves, because of their poverty, to a fellow Israelite; and those who for the same reason had sold themselves to a wealthy foreigner residing in the land. As to the former class, the law enjoins kind treatment; puts strongly the distinction between the hired and the bond-servant—permitting servants of

Hebrew birth to be held in the former state but not in the latter; and finally gave him and his children freedom at the Jubilee.——Inasmuch as the seventh year emancipation law applied to this very class of servants, if it were enforced there could be no Hebrew servants to go out at the Jubilee except those who had not yet served six full years. This seems to be the bearing of the law of the Jubilee upon Hebrew servants. We can not assume that it superseded the seventh year law and took its place. The historic passage (Jer. 34: 8–17) would quite forbid such a construction.

As to the second class—those who had sold themselves to a foreigner—the law gave the right of redemption to any of his friends or to himself, and fixed the terms, providing for his freedom at the Jubilee.

3. The most difficult point is, the bearing of the Jubilee, if any, *upon servants of foreign birth.* Did it, or did it not, provide for their emancipation?

The passage (Lev. 25: 9, 10) seems very strong in favor of *universal* liberty, not omitting bond-servants of foreign birth. The words are—"*Proclaim liberty through all the land unto all the inhabitants thereof.*" This proclamation was made with sound of trumpet, ringing out its shrill blast over all the land. Now let it be considered: If foreigners were not included, and if the seventh year emancipation law had been duly enforced, there could have been but a meager showing of freedmen—only those few Hebrew servants who had not filled out their six years of service. Is it credible that so much proclamation and so much public display could have meant only the emancipation of say one-tenth or one-twentieth of all the servants in the land?——At any point of their history the number of foreign servants ought to have greatly exceeded the number of Hebrew birth—for two reasons:——(a.) The law encouraged the taking of foreigners into this relation:——and (b.) They continued in it at least till the Jubilee—their maximum service being therefore forty-nine years, while the maximum service of the Hebrew-born was only six. Therefore I urge that a proclamation so high sounding and in terms so absolutely universal can not have left out the great majority of bondmen in the land.

The opponents of this view rely upon the words (v. 46)—"They shall be your bondmen forever"—which they claim must mean *during life.*——But it may be replied—One human life is very much short of *forever.* Also, if the statute had meant during life, why did it not say so?——Again; the order of the Hebrew words favors this construction: "Forever of them shall ye take servants"—or somewhat more literally: Forever among them shall ye serve yourselves, *i. e.* provide yourselves with servants. And this construction harmonizes fully with the drift of the context, the spirit of which is—Go to the heathen about you, or to heathen families living among you for your supply of bond-servants. Let this be the permanent arrangement.

The English phrase—"bond-servant" may perhaps give a stronger sense than the Hebrew will warrant. The Hebrew suggests no sort of "bond"—no obligation of law or justice. It expresses a certain degree of emphasis by means of repeating the words for service and servant, in this way: (v. 39), If thy brother with thee shall become weak "[broken down financially], and shall sell himself to thee, thou shalt not exact of him the service of a servant, [or serve thyself in him with the service of a servant]." This is all that "bond-servant" can mean. It is a somewhat intensified idea of service.——Another prohibition in this passage is sufficiently explicit: "Thou shalt not rule over him *with rigor*" (vs. 43, 46), *i. e.* literally, with crushing; shalt not break him down; or in the American slave-holder's phrase "break him in."

The case of *foreign servants* demands yet a few more words of explication. It can not be denied that the spirit of the Hebrew law favored the choice of foreigners for servants, and the increase of this class of population. This is plainly the doctrine of the passage Lev. 25: 44–46.——In connection with this we may profitably study the law of the Passover in its relation to servants (Ex. 12: 43–49). "There shall no stranger eat thereof, but every man's servant that is bought for money, *when thou hast circumcised him,* then shall he eat thereof."——That this law contemplated Gentile servants is clear on two grounds:——(a.) Only such would need circumcision—all Hebrews being circumcised when eight days old.——(b.) The law (Lev. 25: 44) required them to take their servants from the heathen, and authorized them to "*buy*" such. The buying of a Hebrew servant was a very different thing. The poor Hebrew *sold himself*—*i. e. his services*, and took pay in advance of doing the work. Selling himself is precisely the sense of the Hebrew in Lev. 25: 39, 47, though in the former case (v. 39) our translators made it "be sold" and in the latter "sell himself." The Hebrew verb is equally reflexive in both verses.——Moreover, no man might steal a Hebrew and sell him on pain of death. It does not appear that Hebrew fathers sold their sons. When they took pay for a daughter, it came under the usage of paying for wives. She was betrothed to her purchaser (Ex. 21: 7-11) and of course had the rights of a wife. Hence this "buying a servant for money" (Ex. 12: 44) contemplates a foreigner. ——The law proceeds to say—"A foreigner (one not a servant) and a hired servant shall not eat thereof." ——Furthermore, circumcision was naturalization; it brought the servant within the pale of the Hebrew community. For this law of the Passover declares that "when a stranger sojourning with thee, *i. e.* in thy land, desires to keep the Passover to the Lord, let all his males be circumcised, and then let him come near and keep it; *and he shall be as one that is born in the land;*" *i. e.* his circumcision is equivalent in force to being born in the land; it secures his naturalization. Hence the buying of foreign servants would be a perpetual process of naturalizing them, and bringing them into the Hebrew community. They came to the Passover and were entitled to all the religious privileges of the children of Israel. Abraham himself circumcised, not his sons alone, but "all that were born in his house or bought with money of the stranger" (Gen. 17: 23, 27).——Thus the system reached forth its arms, gathered to its genial bosom and blest with religious nurture thousands of alien birth, some of whom attained renown among the servants of the God of Israel. We have the history of Rahab and Ruth, and to name no more of "Uriah the Hittite," and of "Ittai the Gittite" [of Gath].

VIII. *Judicial Procedure.*

Under this general head the following topics should receive attention.

1. *Judges.* The reorganization suggested by Jethro has been noticed, and also its further modification to adjust it to the fixed residence in Canaan.——Between Joshua and Saul, there was an irregular series of Supreme Judges, closing with Samuel of whose circuit court, taking four cities in rotation, we have a notice in 1 Sam. 7: 15–17. The kings manifestly held this function of Supreme Judge. In the absence of other Judges, the High Priest seems to have served ex-officio. His powers, under the "Judges" above referred to and the kings, are not sharply defined; but probably religious and semi-religious questions came before him and his associates. The Judges between Joshua and Samuel were military men.——A special reorganization of the judiciary under Jehoshaphat (2 Chron. 19: 5–11) will repay a careful reading. It provides subordinate judges in all the fortified cities; solemnly admonishes them to administer justice in the fear of God; establishes a supreme court in Jerusalem, where "he set of the Levites, priests, and chief of the fathers of Israel for the judgment of the Lord and for controversies when they returned to Jerusalem"—the last clause apparently referring to cases carried up for decision before this supreme court.——It should be noted that we read nothing of cases taken up to a higher court by appeal of a dissatisfied party; but only as carried up by the lower court itself when the case seemed too hard or too high for its decision. This principle went into operation in the reorganization by Moses (Ex. 18: 22, 26 and Deut. 1: 17)—"The cause that is too hard for you, bring it to me and I will hear it." It passed into the general law as we may see (Deut. 17: 8–13) which provides for a supreme court at the religious center, the judges being "the priests, the Levites, and the judges that shall be in those days."

The warnings against partiality and bribery were earnest and solemn—the penalty for these offenses being left, it would seem, to be visited upon the offender by the Almighty (Ex. 23: 6–8, and Lev. 19: 15, and Deut.

1: 17, and 16: 18–20). They were not even allowed to favor the poor man in his cause *against justice* (Ex. 23: 3 and Lev. 19: 15)—there being sometimes a temptation to do this out of sympathy with his poverty and his necessities. But God put justice in law above sympathy for even the necessitous poor.——The public anathema fell on him who took a bribe to slay the innocent (Deut 27: 25).

2. The seat of justice—the place for holding court—was "in the gates of the city." Hence this being with all Orientals the place of public resort, the courts were public—open to all.

3. The processes of prosecution are not specially described. In cases of a personal, private character, the aggrieved party brought suit. In cases of a public nature "the elders of the city" bore responsibilities, as we see in the case of murder by an unknown hand. A remarkable case of appeal to the sensibilities of the whole nation is given Judg. 19: 25–30, under which the people woke to a consciousness of horrible wickedness in Israel, and their indignation became irrepressible; yet they carefully sought counsel of the Lord in this terrible case.

4. *Advocates.* We find no notice of professional advocates. The "lawyers" of New Testament history were men versed in the law and were teachers of law, but not by any means the modern advocate. Every man might be his own advocate, and even women were heard before no less a king than Solomon himself (1 Kings 3: 16–18). Noble-hearted, disinterested men seem in Oriental life to have undertaken this service voluntarily for the poor and the fatherless, of which Job gives a touching description (Job 29: 7–17). Isaiah exhorts to this duty: "Plead for the widow" (1: 17). It was the noble doctrine of this system—"Our law judges no man before it hears him and knows what he doeth" (Jn. 7: 51). Moses puts it thus—"Ye shall hear the small as well as the great" (Deut. 1: 17). "If there arise a matter in judgment between blood and blood, *between plea and plea*," etc. (Deut. 17: 8).

5. *Of Witnesses*—the points of chief importance are these:

(1.) They testified under oath—the manner of administration being this: The witness listened to the rehearsal of the words, and gave his oral assent, "Amen," or, "As thou sayest." The passage (Lev. 5: 1) describes the case of one who sins in this way, hearing the voice—*i. e.* the words of the sacred oath, adjuring him to testify whether he has seen or known any thing in this case. Then if he will not make known, "he shall bear his iniquity."——A special statute for the case of a wife suspected of conjugal infidelity shows how she is to be put under this solemn oath (Num. 5: 19–22). She listens to the words of the oath and responds, "Amen, amen." (See also Prov. 29: 24 and Mat. 26: 63).

(2.) That the witnesses were examined separately and in presence of the accused appears probable from a comparison of Mat. 26: 61 with Mk. 14: 55–59. Jesus was present (Mat. 26: 62).

(3.) As to the requisite number of witnesses—a criminal case of capital crime required two besides the accuser (Deut. 17: 6 and 19: 15). Hence the phrase—"In the mouth of two or three witnesses shall every word be established" (Mat. 18: 16).——A supposed case is stated (Ex. 22; 10, 11) in which the complainant and the accused are the only witnesses. Both are put under oath; but the testimony of the accused under oath seems to be accepted as his vindication.

(4.) By another peculiar provision of the Mosaic statutes, the witnesses in certain cases must be first to execute the penalty (Deut. 17: 7, and 13: 9, and Acts 7: 58, and John 8: 7). This provision was doubtless morally wholesome.

IX. *Punishments.*

A few points not already brought to view deserve a brief notice.

1. *Fines.*—Some were fixed by statute. The highest known to the law (one hundred shekels of silver) was laid on the man who falsely accused his wife of previous unchastity (Deut. 22: 19). Another case among violations of the seventh commandment appears (Deut. 22: 28, 29).——In the case of an ox goring some one fatally, the penalty of death upon his owner might be commuted to a fine at the discretion of the judges (Ex. 21: 28–31)—a wise provision because the real culpability of his

owner must vary with circumstances. In another case (Ex. 21: 22), the suffering party and the judge fixed the amount of the fine.

2. The sin and the trespass offerings sustained a slight relation to fines, since the party bore the cost of the animal sacrificed—a young bullock, a kid of goats, etc. These laws may be seen in Lev. 4 and 5 and in Num. 15: 27–29. They pertain to sins of ignorance and of remissness; never to presumptuous sins. In addition to the cost of the sacrifice the penalty included a public confession of the offense, and was well adapted to make a good moral impression.

The special cases which come under this general head of sin and trespass offerings were——(1.) Unintentional transgressions of the Levitical law.——(2.) The rash oath, ill-considered and not conscientiously kept (Lev. 5: 4).——(3.) Perjury in a witness;—not however the case of false swearing to condemn the innocent, which was punished by retaliation; but the offense of *not* testifying what he knew when put under oath (Lev. 5: 1).——(4.) Debts due to the sanctuary—a failure to pay tithes; the penalty being, one-fifth added to the original amount and all paid, coupled with the trespass offering (Lev. 5: 14–16).——(5.) Denying any thing given in trust, or retaining another man's lost property which he may have found, and similar offenses, coupled with false swearing (Lev. 6: 1–7); the penalty being, to restore with one-fifth added and to make his trespass offering.——(6.) Adultery with a slave. The penalty— a sin-offering and the punishment of death commuted to stripes.

3. *Stripes* were made the penalty of certain specified crimes (Lev. 19: 20 and Deut. 22: 18). The law was careful to limit the number of stripes to forty, giving as the reason—"Lest if thou shouldest exceed" [this number] "then thy brother should seem vile unto thee;" *i. e.* not merely lest the man might lose his self-respect, but lest he lose the respect of the community, and be hopelessly degraded. In usage the Hebrews limited the number to thirty-nine—said to have been administered by thirteen strokes of a triple cord.

4. Of retaliation ["lex talionis"] notice has been taken already.

5. *Excommunication;* excision; being cut off from his people. When executed by God himself, it meant destruction by some providential agency. Compare 1 Kings 14: 10 with 15: 29 and 2 Kings 9; 8–10.—— When executed by human agency, it was capital punishment, usually by stoning (Ex. 31: 14, and Lev. 17: 4, and 20: 17, 18).

6. The customary modes of capital punishment were two: *stoning* and *the sword.* (Deut. 13: 9, 10, and 17: 5, and Josh. 7: 25.) The sword appears in later ages.

7. *Disgrace after death* in some cases heightened the penalty, *e. g.* by burning the dead body (Gen. 38: 24, and Lev. 20: 14, and 21: 9). That in these cases the death was by stoning and the burning was only that of the dead body, seems to be sufficiently proved from Josh. 7: 15, 25. "All Israel stoned him" [Achan and his family] "with stones and burned them with fire *after* they had stoned them with stones." Their very bodies seem to have been thought of as polluted and *polluting.*—— Another method of posthumous disgrace was by hanging on a tree (Num. 25: 4, 5 and Deut. 21: 22, 23). The body must not remain suspended over night "that thy land be not defiled; for he that is hanged is accursed of God." See cases of the execution of this law in Josh. 8: 29 and 10: 26, 27.

Several forms of punishment were introduced from other nations in later ages which we may omit as foreign from our subject.

In closing this topic let it be noted that judicial procedure and punishment were summary—both the trial and the execution being carried through with apparently no delay. Compared on these points with the most highly civilized countries of our age, the Hebrews have greatly the advantage, and the efficiency of their law must have been for this very reason surpassingly great. Their methods afforded but the smallest possible hope of escape. Punishment followed close on the heels of detection, and usually, we must presume, of crime.——Furthermore, these punishments, compared with those of other nations in that age were by no means severe. Indeed the modes of capital punishment which come to view in the Scriptures as existing among other nations were terribly barbarous compared with those of the Hebrew code; *e. g.* burning in a fiery furnace; being torn in pieces by lions; being sawn asunder; crucifixion.

The design of punishment is put in the plainest terms. In its severer forms it is not the discipline of the criminal but the good of the public—to deter the evil-minded from crime and so to make society safe from outrage. In the case of presumptuous sins we read—"That man shall die, and thou shalt put away the evil from Israel, and all the people shall hear and fear and do no more presumptuously" (Deut. 17: 12, 13 and 19: 20).

It is worthy of special notice under this head that we find in this code a considerable number of statutes *with no penalty attached* which human hands were to inflict. God reserved the infliction of the penalty to himself. The fear of his displeasure, coupled with his promised rewards for obedience were the only forces coercing obedience to these statutes. They were left upon the conscience of the people, and upon their fears and hopes under a system in which God's hand in providence was often made most palpable. For cases in point I may refer to the laws against usury and requiring favors to be shown to the poor;—as for example (Deut. 15: 9, 10): "Beware that there be not a thought in thy wicked heart, saying—The seventh year, the year of release is at hand, and thine eye be evil against thy poor brother and thou givest him naught, and he cry unto the Lord against thee and it be sin upon thee. Thou shalt surely give him, and thine heart shall not be grieved when thou givest unto him; because that for this thing the Lord thy God will bless thee in all thy works," etc.

The moral power of this invisible force upon the heart and conscience of the people we shall be able to appreciate more justly if we carefully study the words which stand (Ex. 23: 20-25), *i. e.* at the close of the first catalogue of the "statutes and judgments." It seems to come in here legitimately as a moral force to induce a conscientious and careful obedience to these statutes. "Behold" (calling special attention) "behold, I send an angel before thee to keep thee in the way, and to bring thee into the place which I have prepared. Beware of him, and obey his voice; provoke him not, for he will not pardon your transgressions, for my name is in him. But if thou shalt indeed obey his voice and do all that I speak, then I will be an enemy to thine enemies," etc.——This angel, bearing authority to pardon or not pardon sins, and of whom the very God could say—" My name is in him" could be no less than really divine. *Name* in Hebrew usage as applied to God involves and implies his real nature—his essential attributes. Corresponding to this view of "the angel" in this passage is the injunction to "beware of him and to obey his voice"; and also his power to forgive sins—for who can forgive sins but God only"? This passage therefore affords decisive proof that the personage who manifested himself to Israel in the pillar of cloud and of fire; whose presence abode in their tabernacle; whose voice they heard in this holy law—was truly divine, and yet was mysteriously distinct from the speaker—the "I"—of this remarkable passage. Truly he was God, manifest—if not precisely in human flesh—yet in palpable forms, in tangible demonstrations, in voice of power and tongue of flame; in the luminous pillar; in perpetual agencies of protection and of supply as to earthly need; and, not least, as their Ruler and their Lord whose voice in these statutes it behooved them to hear and obey as they would hope to be blessed in their national life and in any desirable prosperity. Hence it was both practicable and wise under this Hebrew system to leave some statutes upon the naked conscience of the people with no attempt to enforce obedience save the appeal to this invisible Presence.

These remarks will naturally suggest to the thoughtful mind a train of inquiries of this sort:——How can we account for it that the books of Moses allude so very rarely to the future state of man's being—to heaven and to hell? Had even the best men of those times any definite belief in the future life and in its retribution for deeds done in this? How happens it that both the law and the rewards or penalties of their civil code, and indeed of their religious code as well, make so much account of present retribution and so little of the future?

These points will be treated more conveniently and in a more satisfactory manner after the religious code shall have been examined and after we have surveyed the history of Israel in the wilderness—*i. e.* at the close of the present volume.

There are two historic questions pertaining to this civil code of the Hebrews which have sufficient interest to justify a few moments' attention; viz.

I. *How far was this system indebted to Egypt?*

II. *How far have the best civil codes of the most civilized nations of all subsequent history been indebted to this Hebrew code?*

I. As to the possible relations of this Hebrew code to Egyptian life and jurisprudence, perhaps the word "indebted" is too strong. It is by no means intended to disparage the divine originality of this law or of any and every feature of the system. I assume two things:——(1.) That Moses, "learned in all the wisdom of the Egyptians," may have had intimate personal acquaintance with very many things in civil jurisprudence which the Lord taught him in and through his Egyptian life rather than by immediate and independent revelation:——and (2.) That the people became familiar with some valuable usages and customs connected with Egyptian law and Egyptian life, and by this means were prepared to receive and adopt them under this new code and in this new style of life in Canaan, when, without this previous culture, these laws and usage could not have gone into operation so readily if at all.

The Hebrew code and its system of jurisprudence—as also the entire Hebrew national life—were benefited by the Egyptian in the following points:

1. The example and silent influence of a full civil, written code of law. That Egypt had such a code admits of no question. The Hebrew patriarchs, prior to the sojourn in Egypt, had nothing of the sort. Their life in Egypt therefore gave them their first lessons—their first ideas, of a complete code of written law. We shall be in small danger of over-estimating the value of these lessons and ideas in their bearings upon a higher civilization.

2. Egypt gave to the Hebrew mind the example of a well digested system of judicial procedure, established courts and forms of trial; laws put in force by the aid of judges, witnesses, and the systematic execution of penalties.——Remarkably the last quarter of a century has brought to light documentary evidence of a judicial trial in Egypt as far back as the age of Moses, develop-

ing the most finished method; well digested forms of procedure; a state trial, conducted with great dignity and decorum; and the whole proceeding put on record so carefully that this original document is before the world in perfect preservation at this day.*

3. Egypt gave to the children of Israel the example of a national life *based on agriculture*, as distinct from and indeed opposed to the wandering, unsettled life of the shepherd. The nomadic mode of life, perpetuated by necessity to this day in the deserts of Arabia, in which individual right to the soil is unknown and no family has a fixed home, each living for the time where its flocks may chance to find herbage and water—this had been the style of the patriarchs before Jacob went to Egypt. It was not the best for social and mental culture. God had a better life for his people prospectively in Canaan, and their residence in Egypt introduced them to it and gave them a preparation for it. It made subsistence less precarious; blended the cultivation of the soil with the care of flocks and herds; provided for a denser population; greatly enhanced the opportunities for social culture and for such a religious system as that of Israel. In a word it provided for a much higher Christian civilization than could have been possible under the strictly nomadic mode of life. To Egypt, the nation was indebted for the example and for the training into this agricultural mode of life.

4. In another important respect, the example of the national life of Egypt was a preordained training for their own national life in Canaan:—it was that of a people providing for their own wants; living within themselves; maintaining substantially non-intercourse with other nations, and for the most part excluding foreign commerce. Such was Egypt during the residence of Israel there, and such God wisely designed Israel to be in her promised land of Canaan. As to Israel in Canaan, the purposes of this policy are obvious— protection from the contaminating influences of idol-

---

* See a "State trial in ancient Egypt," fully reported in Bib. Sacra, July, 1869, p. 577. This is written in the hieratic text; is known as "The Judicial Papyrus"; is now in the museum of Turin and is presumed to be the official record.

atry, not to say also from the contaminations of luxury and wealth.

5. In Egypt, the priests were the learned class of the empire, and held the highest responsibilities in the civil and judicial as well as the religious life of the nation. A system essentially the same was introduced into Israel, the priests and the Levites holding the same place in the nation which they had seen held by the priests in Egypt.

6. It is a very noticeable fact in the history of the legal life in Egypt, that though magic arts were in a sense tolerated and indeed were resorted to by the king in his emergencies, yet their influence in society proved to be so pernicious as to demand legal restraint. We have the record of a man indicted "for many crimes and wickednesses committed through his magic arts and writings, such as paralyzing limbs, empowering a slave to do audacious things," etc. The decision of the court in his case reads—"For his various abominations, the greatest in the world, he is condemned to death."
——It will be remembered that the Mosaic law held *all* practice of magic arts to be a penal offense, punishable with death (Ex. 22: 18 and Lev. 20: 27).

7. In some points the spirit of the Mosaic code was so greatly in advance of the Egyptian as to stand related to it, not in the way of imitation or even modification, but of direct opposition. It held squarely the opposite doctrine and put forth statutes of an opposite character. Thus, the Egyptian code legalized slavery, and had its special law for the reclamation of fugitives. Among the recent discoveries in Egyptian antiquities "A warrant for the arrest of fugitive slaves" has been brought to light. From the tone of this warrant and from other evidence, collateral, it is inferred that slaveholders were obliged by law to register them in a list kept by government and disputes with regard to ownership must be brought before the judges. The rights of the master in his slave were not absolute. It was not by virtue of orders direct from the owner that search was instituted and arrest made, but by the authority of a high functionary of government, to whom the case is reported and who issues his mandate. Thus the government itself put forth its hand to recover a slave who had escaped from any citizen.——It was

therefore specially pertinent that the law of Jehovah to Israel should plant itself on ground precisely the reverse of this:—*no reclamation of fugitives whatsoever*. Thou shalt *not* do what Egyptian slave-holders were authorized by the highest authority of the kingdom to do—force back the escaped fugitive to his unendurable bondage.

In the line of their religious institutions Israel stood related to Egypt in numerous particulars, borrowing some things for the adornment of its tabernacle from Egyptian art; and on the other hand, guarding by stringent prohibitions against many Egyptian usages associated with idolatry. These points will be in place after we have considered the religious institutions of Moses.

II. The second proposed historic question, viz. How far have the best civil codes of all history and how far has the world at large been indebted to this Hebrew code?—opens a field of inquiry quite too wide to be fully canvassed within our prescribed limits. A few hints may be useful perhaps to guide the further inquiries of the reader. The following points are put comprehensively and suggestively:

1. Moses sought to impress it upon his people that this system far surpassed that of any other nation. "Behold, I have taught you statutes and judgments, even as the Lord my God commanded me. . . . Keep, therefore, and do them, for this is your wisdom and understanding in the sight of all the nations who shall hear of all these statutes and shall say, Surely this nation is a wise and understanding people, for what great nation hath their God so nigh to them as the Lord our God is to us in all that we call upon him for? And what great nation hath statutes and judgments so righteous as all this law which I set before you this day"? (Deut. 4: 5–8.)

2. The Hebrew system surpassed all others, especially in this—that *it gave to human government and law the sanction of God's authority*, and enforced them upon the human heart and conscience by this most impressive and benign of all influences.

3. Preparatory to this result it maintained against the whole Pagan world the doctrine of *one God*—perfect in character, supreme in power, righteous in all his ad-

ministration of rewards and punishments. Only so could it make the idea of God a really wholesome power and his authority effective in sustaining civil government.

4. This divinely given code rested upon justice and equity, and determined every thing by this standard. So doing, it ruled out at once a multitude of interests and ends which human laws have often sought to secure. Its example therefore, in so far at least, was simply and supremely beneficent.

5. In yet further detail, it recognized the common and equal rights of all men, irrespective of condition, rank, wealth—holding constantly the doctrine, "*No respect of persons.*"

6. It appreciated at their just value the rights of the poor and of all that large class who look only to God and to human law for protection.

We come now to the question of historic fact: *Did this Hebrew code and government send forth its influence upon the nations of ancient history?* Did it in any perceptible degree leaven the best systems of human law and jurisprudence.——If the proof for the affirmative falls short of positive certainty, what is its amount of probability?

Here we may fitly consider—

(a.) That God chose for Israel the land of Canaan, in the center of the ancient world of mind; immediately between Egypt on the one hand and Babylon, Assyria, Persia—all the great nations of Western Asia—on the other; and closely contiguous to ancient Greece and Rome.

(b.) That David and Solomon became known to all the great powers of the world of their time. Solomon's renown turned largely on the fact that his people were prosperous and happy, his government well ordered, and his own wisdom in all affairs of state unsurpassed. ——It is simply impossible that such examples should drop powerless upon the nations of the earth.

(c.) That at a later period the personal history of Mordecai, of Esther, and especially of Daniel in the courts of Nebuchadnezzar and of Cyrus show that the Jews, their religion, their God, and their law, did impress themselves upon the greatest centers of influence and power in their time.

(d.) This dispersion of the Jews at and after their

captivity planted them in large numbers in the chief seats of human science and learning; in Egypt on the South-West; in Babylon, Persia, and adjacent countries of the East. It is historically certain that in the age of the Ptolemies, a large body of learned Jews lived in Egypt; that the Old Testament was translated into Greek by request of Ptolemy Philadelphus; that the Egypt of that age was the school of wisdom and jurisprudence for Ancient Greece and was herself the pupil of Moses.*——That the best Greek authors knew Moses is matter of history. Longinus quotes from Moses (Gen. 1: 3) in his treatise on Sublimity; Strabo makes honorable mention of him as a law-giver; and Diodorus Siculus acknowledges him to be "the first of legislators from whom all laws had their origin." Numenius a Greek philosopher of the Pythagorean school, speaking of Plato, exclaims—"What is Plato but Moses Atticising"—*i. e.* teaching in Attic Greek? Origen believed that Plato drew largely from Moses.——The list of eminent Grecian authors and savans who went personally to Egypt for wisdom and science is long—such as Thales, Anaximander, Anaxagoras, Pythagoras, Plato, Herodotus. There they came into contact with learned Jews and not improbably with the writings of Moses.† Prof. Wines (p. 335) cites the learned Grotius as saying— "The most ancient Attic laws, whence in aftertimes the Roman were derived, owe their origin to Moses' law. That the Grecians, especially the Attics, took their laws from Moses is credible. This is the reason why the Attic laws and the Roman twelve Tables which sprang from them so much resemble the Hebrew laws."—— This similarity between the Attic laws and those of Moses has been noticed by many other learned men, *e. g.* Josephus, Clement of Alexandria, Augustine, Sir Matthew Hale, Archbishop Potter. The last named in his "Grecian Antiquities" has adduced many points of

---

* Of Ptolemy Philadelphus Prof. Wines says—"He was delighted with the laws of Moses; pronounced his legislation wonderful; was astonished at the depth of his wisdom, and professed to have learned from him the true science of government."—Wines' Commentaries. See also Josephus against Apion, p. 308.

† Prof. Wines' Commentaries on the Laws of the Ancient Hebrews, pp. 312–388, a work which elaborates its theme very fully, substantiating its points by copious authorities.

Grecian law which seem to have been taken from Moses—viz. the laws of divorce; the purgation oath compared with "the oath of jealousy" among the Hebrews; the harvest and vintage festival; the law of first-fruits; the law requiring the best offerings for God; the portion for the priests; protection to the man-slayer at their altars; requiring priests to be unblemished; the agrarian law; laws regulating descent of property, and prohibiting marriage within certain degrees of consanguinity.——Plato in his ideal "Republic" is thought to have drawn largely from Moses.——Clement of Alexandria accosts him (by Apostrophe)—"But as for laws, whatever are true were conveyed to thee from the Hebrews."

These historic facts seem to indicate the definite channel through which the laws of Moses reached the Grecian mind in its earliest stages of culture and thus wrought themselves into the great fountains of Grecian and Roman civilization and jurisprudence.

(e.) There seem to be strong grounds for the general statement that the greatest reformers of all known history have acted upon the ideas of Moses, and have probably drawn their doctrines more or less directly from that fountain. I will venture to place in this category Zoroaster, Plato, Confucius, Buddha, and Mahomet. These men were in their time reformers of society, of morals, and of jurisprudence. Their influence led *toward* if not fully *unto* the doctrine of *one God*, and by natural consequence, to a purer morality and juster views of law and equity; of love to one's neighbor and purity of life.——I regret that my limits forbid any attempt to present the historic evidence which might support more or less fully these broad, comprehensive statements. The historic evidence that Zoroaster, Plato, and Mahomet drew from Moses is very strong. Of the great Indian reformer and of the Chinese comparatively little is known.

(f.) Of Roman law as finally embodied in the great code of Justinian, it has been already suggested that its best things came from Moses and the Septuagint through Greece and the Egypt of the Ptolemies.——I add two other remarks:—(a) That in the age of Justinian (first half of the sixth Christian century) primitive Christianity had quite fully leavened the public sentiment and thus the jurisprudence of the then civilized world.——(b.) That when Justinian created a commission of learned jurists to "collect the scattered monuments of ancient jurisprudence," he recommended them in settling any point to regard neither the number nor the reputation of the jurisconsults who had given opinions on the subject, but to be guided solely by reason and equity.*

(g.) Of Alfred the Great (reigned A. D. 871-901) the central testimony of history is that he was severely *just*. Despite of surroundings almost barbarous, he rose by dint of his irrepressible manliness to become the greatest legislator and scholar of his age, and so was able to lay the foundations for the best and truest glory of the English name. The common law of England and of the English-speaking world began its development under his hand. One fact is of itself a volume of testimony to the spirit of this ancient law. When after a long struggle Wilberforce brought the question before the English bench—Does English law sanction human bondage? the world heard the answer—*Never*. "Slaves can not breathe in England." What moment they take in her pure air, they are free! The spirit of her law from the days of Alfred was justice and righteousness between a man and his neighbor. The laws of Moses were in Alfred's eye; the spirit of those laws filled and fired his noble soul. It is currently said that the telling words which describe the needy as "*God's poor*" are original (for our mother Saxon tongue) with him. Moses had reiterated the sentiment long ages before.——"Sir Matthew Hale has traced the influence of the Bible generally on the laws of England. Sismondi testifies that Alfred, in causing a republication of the Saxon laws, inserted several statutes taken from the code of Moses, to give new strength and cogency to the principles of morality.

"Thus have the principles of the Mosaic code found their way to a greater or less extent into the jurisprudence of all civilized nations." [Wines—p. 337.]

---

* Taylor's Manual of History, p. 335. Moses and the Lord speaking through him (Deut. 1: 16, 17 and 16: 18-20) had announced this doctrine more than two thousand years before. It is fair to presume that the earlier promulgation had sent its influence down the ages to Justinian's time.

It falls within our plan to speak briefly of the civil code of Moses *as a series of progressive revelations of God to man.*

I have spoken of the law of Sinai as a manifestation of God to man at once sublime in its majesty and most benignly practical in its moral bearings. The civil code—"the statutes and judgments"—carry out yet more fully the practical unfoldings of God's wisdom and of his sense of justice and right as between man and man. It is not easy to select the most striking cases to illustrate this point, for the whole code is radiant with divine wisdom and aglow with testimonies of his love, manifesting itself in wisest legislation for human welfare.——Confining our attention to the second table of the law of Sinai—man's relation to his fellow-man—we may consider how much there is here adapted to conserve all the best elements of society—in securing the honor due to parents and rulers; in guarding human life and providing the means for its protection; in making the marriage covenant sacred; on the one hand shielding the sexual relation of the race against abuses most pernicious; and on the other, providing agencies which may enrich man's social life with priceless blessings. So also the statutes in detail respecting rights of property and rights of reputation are replete with fresh testimonies to the wisdom and the love of the Great Father.—— Speaking frankly of the impressions made on my mind by this study of the code of Moses, I must say that no part has seemed to me more deeply imbued with the tenderness and pity of the Lord than the provisions made for the poor, and the restrictions and limitations upon personal servitude. In all his utterances on these points the Lord assumes that no interests of man more need his protection than these, and he comes promptly to the front to give it. He would have us know that over these interests his watchful eye never sleeps; his quick ear is never shut to any cry for help. The rich and the mighty may get on without his special aid; the poor are his own wards and shall never lack his sympathy nor his present hand. Human laws are in great part worthless—at least they miss their most important function——unless they make it their chief endeavor to protect the interests and rights of those who, powerless in themselves, drop upon the strong arm of law for their defence. Society and legislation might as well not be as to forget that they exist as appointed of God mainly for the sake of the poor and the otherwise unprotected and unbefriended. Such needy ones every human society will have for the moral trial of those who control society, and I may add, to draw out the sympathy of the Great Father.

These revelations of himself stand forth in sunlight throughout this Mosaic code. They are a glorious advance upon all that the world had seen before. The true mission of civil law is brought out here with great fullness; for it seems to be every-where assumed that if laws protect and befriend the poor, they protect and befriend *all*. If the spirit of law faithfully guards their interests, it can not well fail to guard all interests that need the guardianship of human legislation. It is a priceless boon to the race to have these ideas so beautifully set forth and so substantially embodied in a code of laws fresh from the hand and from the heart of the Infinite Father.

CHAPTER XIX.

THE RELIGIOUS SYSTEM OF THE HEBREWS.

This system contemplates as its ultimate end the obedience, homage, and worship due from men to God. As a prime means toward this end, it prescribes modes and forms of worship. It proposes to bring God near to men and men near to God; and for this purpose would cultivate in men the spirit of penitence and of faith—impressing them with a sense of their sins and suggesting to them how sin may be forgiven; and how, on the basis of God's own provision for pardon, he can accept the humble, reverent worship of his people.——
These fundamental ideas respecting the sinner's acceptance with God, the system now before us sought especially to develop by means of visible symbols—these symbols constituting the very elaborate and minutely described *religious system of the Hebrews*.——This system, having long since "waxed old and vanished away" is no longer in practice, and therefore can not be useful as a rule of present duty, but is useful for the light it throws on the great and fundamental questions—How shall man—a sinner—become just before God? Is an atonement necessary? What are the fundamental ideas of "atonement"? How were they developed in the Mosaic system, and what light does this development bring to the atonement presented to view in the New Testament?

With superlative wisdom God began to give lessons on this great subject very early in the history of our race. It was wise to give such lessons long and carefully before the Great Atoning Sacrifice came in human flesh. It was also wise to give them largely by visible illustrations—by the aid of a system having so much of the external and the visible that minds not disciplined to abstract thought might see the truth and feel its power by means of sensible manifestations.

The reader will now see readily the purpose of the ensuing examination of this religious system. It is not for historic curiosity—in which case we might select points amusing or strange or sensational; it is not to guide the worshiper (as Moses sought to do) in the minutest details of the system that he might make no mistake in obeying it:—but it is to gather as best we may its designed moral impression, to study its underlying assumptions, and evolve its true doctrine in regard to the great question of the sinner's acceptance before a holy and righteous God.

Briefly and comprehensively we may classify the leading features of this system viewed externally, on this wise:
I. *Its prescribed sacrifices and offerings.*
II. *Its stated times and seasons of worship.*
III. *Its sacred edifices and apparatus for worship.*
IV. *The religious orders—classes designated for sacred service.*

I. The sacrifices and offerings of this system may be classified variously:——*e. g.* (1.) Bloody, or not bloody:— terms which will be readily understood. The former were slain animals, a portion of whose blood was sprinkled. The latter included offerings of flour, oil, wine, etc.——Or (2.) Some were specially required: others were voluntary or free-will offerings.——(3.) They may be classified with reference to the times and seasons when they were to be made; some being daily, as the morning and evening sacrifice; others for the Sabbath; others for the new moons; others on occasion of the three great yearly festivals; and, among the most useful for its suggestive import, those of the great day of atonement.——(4.) Or we might classify them under the somewhat distinctive names given them in the law, of which we find a large number. We have (a.) The generic word sacrifice [Heb. Zebah]—a word which implies slaying, taking life:——(b.) Another quite generic term, "offering," which is used to translate several Hebrew words, and of course with very considerable latitude of meaning:——(c.) "Burnt-offering"—[which is the quite constant translation of the Heb. "Olah"] signifying what *goes up upon the altar* and is consumed there. The phrase "whole burnt-offering" gives according to the Hebrew, the sense of *completeness*—the whole of the animal being burned on the altar:——(d.) "Sin-offering"—in Hebrew, one of the most common words for *sin*—[hatta]. Paul's use of the corresponding Greek word (2 Cor. 5: 21) follows this usage of the word for sin: "God hath made him to be sin" [a sin-offering] "for us who knew no sin," etc.: ——(e.) "Trespass offering";—which is another of the Hebrew words for sin, offense ["asham"]:——(f.) "Meat-offering"; some variety of food or drink other than flesh:——(g.) "Peace-offering"—which seems closely related to the "thank-offering," being an expression of gratitude to God; the animal sacrificed being in large part eaten socially by the offerer and his friends; also by the poor, the widow, servants, etc.: ——(h.) Wave and heave offerings—terms which refer to ceremonies of elevating or waving certain parts of the sacrifice.

(5.) A much more important distinction in the Mosaic sacrifices lies between those which were *expiatory* and those which were not specially so, the former class being slain animals whose fat at least was burned on the altar and whose blood was sprinkled in specified and various ways; the latter class having somewhat various objects, but chiefly that of expressing gratitude for blessings or joy in the God of their salvation.

Two other points in respect to sacrifices are of importance, viz—

(a.) *The choice of animals to be slain in sacrifice.*

(b.) The killing itself, coupled with the use made of the blood, of the fat, and in some cases of the flesh—with the attendant ceremonies.

(a.) It should be carefully noted that animals for sacrifice were not taken up at random. It was not merely life and blood that were sought. They were not the wild, but the tame, domesticated; not the savage, flesh-eating animals, but the docile, grass-eating; not animals mostly or altogether useless to man, but precisely those which were most useful; not animals of the sort nobody loves or cares for, but those most loved and cared for, between whom and the human family there often arises a special intimacy and affection. In a word they were the representatives of utility, docility, and innocence. The ox, patient of toil, in his early years invaluable for food; the goat, useful for flesh and milk; the lamb—the symbol of affection, attachment, innocence:—these three classes of animals formed the staple material for bloody sacrifice. [Of birds, the turtle-dove and young pigeon, being less expensive, were permitted to the poor. As naturally representing innocence and loveliness, they are quite of the same class].——It sometimes escapes notice that the Orientals brought these animals much nearer to their hearts and homes than our Western notions and habits know of. We forget that not infrequently to this day they live under the same roof along with sons and daughters. The prophet Nathan in that touching verse about the "one little ewe lamb" (2 Sam. 12: 3) drew not from his imagination but from Oriental life. "The poor man had nothing save one little ewe lamb which he had bought and nourished up, and it grew up together with him and with his children: it did eat of his own meat" [food] "and drank from his own cup and lay in his bosom, and was to him as his daughter." ——Moreover, the Hebrew might not select for sacrifice the deformed, the torn, the lame, the sickly; but evermore, the unblemished, the perfect—those specially lovable and choice pets around which the hearts of the household, young and old, were wont to cling: of these must the worshiper take for the altar.

Let us think of the scene at that altar of sacrifice. The place is in the front court of the tabernacle, whose inner sanctuary was made glorious with the visible presence of Jehovah. The one all-engrossing thought associated with this sacred spot, was—*God is here.* I go up to meet God. Before his face I bring this prescribed offering. It is one of my sweet lambs of the flock, or as the case may be, a young bullock of one or two years old. I know that the animal must die there. Either in my own person or through the priest, acting in my behalf, I am to lay my hand on the head of the victim and thus confess my sin. From that moment the innocent lamb takes my place and stands before the executioner, as if guilty of capital crime. The sight and the smell of blood; the struggle and the recoil; the outcry of horror—the only awful, horrible sound uttered by these animals—go to make up a scene which, once witnessed, can never be forgotten. We of this age might see it in some of its aspects if we would; we rarely do. We should find it, not in our worshiping sanctuaries

THE SIGNIFICANCE OF SACRIFICE.

but in the secluded slaughter-house whither no one is ever attracted—whither none ever go save those who must. Think of the blood, the death-groans, the struggle, the whole dying scene. Is there any meaning in it? Is there any thing in it appropriate to the sanctuary of God and to his solemn worship?

The transaction is by no means so mysterious as it might be. It would be profoundly mysterious were it not that man is a sinner before the holy law of God—a sinner under condemnation of death. It would be utterly inexplicable if there were not in nature, in thought, in fact, something which we may call substitution, to which we give the name vicarious—something which involves, not indeed an entire exchange of one personality for another, but something which approximates toward it. One being suffers in the place and stead of another. An innocent being steps into the place of a guilty one and takes upon himself the guilty man's doom. We need not pause here to hunt up analogies of this sort in human life; suffice it that God signifies by these striking symbols that he has found a place for this principle in his great scheme for the pardon of sinners condemned to death by his holy law, and that he saw fit to fill this Hebrew religious system absolutely full of illustrative typical representations of this stupendous fact. The elementary facts in this system of sacrifices, considered as illustrating the scheme of pardon are few and simple; thus—

(a). Man has sinned against God and stands condemned by his law to eternal death.

(b). God loves this sinning man and longs to save him—but must not break down his law.——So he finds a Lamb for a sacrifice whose death for sinners will abundantly sustain the majesty of law, and proceeds thereupon to "lay on him the iniquity of us all." This done, it only remains that the sinner repent of his sin, and humbly, thankfully accept the death of this Lamb of sacrifice in place of his own eternal death.——These few and simple elements comprise substantially the essence of this wonderful system.

This system seeks a symbolic representation in these bloody sacrifices. The offerer brings forward his lamb of the flock; he lays his hand upon that innocent head and confesses there his sin: he in a sort transfers his own personality—or more precisely, his own sin and guilt, to that animal victim; he stands by and witnesses the death-scene with a deepened sense that he deserves a death far worse than that himself. But when the fires from heaven descend and consume his offering, and he finds himself not only spared but blessed of God and bidden to go in peace, he gets a sense unknown before, of the peace and joy of pardoned sin. The blood sprinkled upon and around the altar and toward the most holy place and upon himself becomes a memorial of what his salvation cost; the pardon himself receives testifies how much it is worth, "speaking better things than the blood of Abel."

If any special argument should seem called for to prove that this is the true significance of these bloody sacrifices, we shall come to it with better preparation after the main points of the system are more fully before us.

As an illustrative system, there is yet one other point of great significance, viz. that in many of these sacrifices *a portion of the animal was eaten* by the offerer and by his family and friends. This great amount of animal flesh was not all consumed by the fires of the altar. Yet we are not to suppose that public economy—the saving of so much valuable human food—was the prime consideration. We must go deeper than this. Nor was it that the Lord would cultivate the social nature of his worshiping people, and therefore provided these materials for agreeable social feasting. We must go very much deeper than even this. This feasting upon the flesh of the slain animal is in germ what the gospel gives us in full development, viz. that the same Lamb of Calvary who "washed us from our sins in his own blood" "gave us his flesh to eat" as "the bread of life." The memorial supper carries in it the same double symbol—*blood* and *bread*—the blood looking toward pardon; the bread toward sustenance for the spiritual life. So the pious Israelite might on the one hand see the blood of his sacrifice gurgling forth, caught, sprinkled toward the mercy-seat and upon his own person; and on the other hand, might take of the flesh of his slain lamb and sit down, not merely in peace but in joyful thanksgiving that death brings life—that sacrificial blood brings after it the new life of the redeemed, restored sinner, and sustenance therefor from the very animal whose body and blood became symbols of his pardon.

Besides these sacrifices of a general character, the system provided others of a special and personal character for individuals under peculiar circumstances, *e. g.* for the case of vows; of purification from ceremonial uncleanness; for the restored leper, etc. Of these I need say only that they suggest the fitness of recognizing God's hand every-where, in all possible events and under all the various dispensations of providence. These events are never barren of significance. It behooves us to study their meaning and adjust ourselves to God's hand with resignation and with gratitude—with a sense of our unworthiness and of God's great mercy.—— The detailed methods of that ancient system have at this day no vital interest.

Scarcely of the nature of sacrifice, yet intensifying the idea of ceremonial uncleanness was the burning of the "red heifer"—the gathering up of her ashes and the preparation from them of "the water of separation"—a purification from sin in the ceremonial sense. Num. 19 gives the details, specifying the sorts of uncleanness which this purifying water washed away. The writer to the Hebrews (9: 13, 14) gave the great moral inference thus: "For if the blood of bulls and of goats and the ashes of an heifer sprinkling the unclean sanctifieth to the purifying of the flesh, how much more shall the blood of Christ who through the eternal Spirit offered himself unto God, purge your conscience from dead works to serve the living God"?

II. STATED TIMES AND SEASONS OF WORSHIP.

1. *The Morning and Evening Sacrifice.*

Two lambs of one year were offered every day; the one in the morning and the other at evening [Heb. "between the evenings"]; burnt offerings, consumed wholly upon the altar. They were accompanied with a small portion of flour, oil, and wine. This was a perpetual ordinance, never to be omitted. The original institution (Ex. 29: 38–46) is accompanied with God's very gracious promise to meet with his people and dwell among them, sanctifying the place of this meeting by his glory. Nothing could suggest more pertinently and tenderly that God loves to see the face of his worshiping people and to meet them as each day opens in the morning and as it closes with the setting sun. Let this communion between God and his sons and daughters never be in any wise interrupted.——The usage seems to have led pious Jews in later times to adopt these hours for their morning and evening prayer, as we may see in the case of Daniel (9: 21), and in the New Testament history.——The ritual for these sacrifices is given in detail (Num. 28: 3–8).

2. *The Sacrifices for the Sabbath.*

Each Sabbath had an extra service in addition to the continual morning and evening sacrifice—two lambs of the first year without spot; with the attendant meat and drink-offerings (Num. 29: 9, 10).

3. *The sacrifices at each new moon* were on a larger scale than either of the preceding, viz. two young bullocks, one ram, and seven lambs for the burnt-offering; one kid of goats for the sin-offering. As the Hebrew months were lunar (not solar), these sacrifices upon the appearance of the new moon inaugurated the successive months. It was probably for this reason that they were announced with blowing of trumpets (Num. 10: 10). The calendar was thus regulated—a matter of special importance, since it fixed the time of their three great religious festivals as also the great day of atonement.

4. *The Three Great Religious Festivals.*

Of these the first in order (the Passover) has been considered already.

The next in order of time was the *Pentecost*—otherwise called "the feast of weeks, of the first-fruits of wheat-harvest" (Ex. 34: 22); "the feast of harvest, the first-fruits of thy labors which thou hast sown in the field" (Ex. 23: 16); also "the day of first-fruits" (Num. 28: 26). The other passages which treat of it are Lev. 23: 15–21 and Deut. 16: 9–12)——The name *Pentecost* is not from the Hebrew but from the Greek, meaning the *fiftieth* day, *i. e.* after the great Sabbath, which fell during the Passover week (Lev. 23: 15, 16).——On the first day after that Sabbath, the first-fruits of their barley harvest were brought before the Lord. From that point seven full weeks were numbered, and on the fiftieth day the feast of Pentecost occurred.

This festival, unlike the other two in duration, was of one day only—at least this is plainly assumed: "In *the day* of the first-fruits" (Num. 28: 26), also in Lev. 23: 21, only one day is spoken of.——It was specially a day of thanksgiving for the first-fruits of the wheat harvest. Two loaves made of the new wheat flour were waved before the Lord on this hallowed day.——The reference (in Deut. 16: 10–12) gives prominence to the social and joyful character of the day. "Thou shalt keep the feast unto the Lord thy God with a tribute of a free-will offering of thy hand which thou shalt give according as the Lord thy God hath blessed thee, and thou shalt rejoice before the Lord thy God, thou and thy son and thy daughter, and thy man-servant and thy maid-servant, and the Levite that is within thy gates, and the stranger, the fatherless and the widow that are among you."

As a feast of joyful thanksgiving over the first-fruits of their principal grain harvest, it was eminently the appropriate occasion for the Pentecostal scene of the first great Christian ingathering. How suggestive of the gratitude due to God for the shedding forth of the Holy Ghost and the glorious fruitage from this gospel power!

Some have supposed (not without reason) that the Hebrew Pentecost commemorated the completion of the giving of the laws by the hand of Moses, which they suppose was brought within fifty days from the first Passover. Of this however the books of Moses affirm nothing explicitly.

The third and last of the three great festivals was "the *Feast of Tabernacles*," otherwise called "the feast of ingathering at the end of the year when thou hast gathered in thy labors out of the field" (Ex. 23: 16).——The speciality of this feast was the dwelling in booths or tabernacles, made of "boughs of goodly trees, branches of palm trees and the boughs of thick trees and willows of the brook" (Lev. 23: 40). This feast began on the fourteenth day of the seventh month and continued during eight days, the first and the last being days of special solemnity. It had a double purpose, viz. to commemorate the forty years wandering of the fathers in the wilderness, dwelling in tents; and to give thanks to God for the last harvests of the year—the fruits of the olive and the grape—last in order—being now all gathered in.

Thus none of these three great feasts omitted the element of thanksgiving for the fruits of the season, the first barley sheaves being brought with grateful thanks before the Lord during the Passover; the first-fruits of the wheat harvest giving a special thanksgiving character to the Feast of Pentecost; and the latest fruits, the olive and the grape, reminding them of God's crowning blessing upon the labors of the year at the Feast of Tabernacles. What a beautiful training into the service of thanksgiving for the fruits of the earth!

This last of the festivals was pre-eminently one of joyful festivity, and of loud and high praises to the Lord, their Great Benefactor. The Jews have a saying—that "whoever has not seen the rejoicing of the last great day of the Feast of Tabernacles has never seen a day of joy in his life."

The principal passages of Moses that treat of it are Ex. 23: 16, and 34: 22, and Lev. 23: 34–43, and Num. 29: 12–40, and Deut. 16: 13–15.

The celebration of this feast in the age of Nehemiah (8: 14–18) the reader should not fail to notice. At this time the law was read daily in the hearing of the people. The law of Moses provided for this public reading on each seventh, *i. e.* the Sabbatic year, during the Feast of Tabernacles (Deut. 31: 10–13).

The striking allusion (Jn. 7: 37) to the scenes on the last great day of the feast will be readily recalled. A custom unknown to the law of Moses had then come into practice—that of going in vast procession to the fountain of Siloam for water, and bearing it with joyful acclaim to the temple to pour it out there before the Lord. While this procession was passing, Jesus lifted up his voice and cried—"If any man thirst, let him come unto me and drink." May we suppose that possibly the words of Isaiah were before him:—"Ho, every one that thirsteth, come ye to the waters"

THE FEAST OF TABERNACLES.

—to these waters of life which I give for the life of the world!

Upon these three great festivals all the males of Israel were required to appear before the Lord at the one place of his choice—the tabernacle or the temple—ultimately in Jerusalem "whither the tribes go up." The women of Israel manifestly went when they chose and could. According to Oriental usage they traveled in groups—little caravans—several adjacent families, or as the case might be by households, the patriarch with his children and children's children together, moving on with many a song of social cheer and grateful praise till at length they lifted up their eyes to the hills of the goodly city. The so-called "songs of degrees" (Ps. 120–134)—more strictly songs of the stages or up-goings—are specimens of this free and outflowing worship of the traveling companies, bound upward to Jerusalem. The allusion in Luke 2: 41–45, is pleasant to think of.

We must not overlook the fact that the Lord relieved their minds of all fear lest their defenseless homes might be assailed and robbed and perhaps their wives and little ones murdered by foreign enemies while all their able-bodied men were away from their homes in Jerusalem. "Neither shall any man desire thy land when thou shalt go up to appear before the Lord thy God thrice in the year" (Ex. 34: 24). None but a God of universal providence and omnipotent resources could safely make such a promise. In their own Jehovah they might safely trust.

Of sacred seasons, the most peculiar and striking yet remains to be noticed, viz. *the great day of atonement*. This was one day only; was not a feast day but a *fast*—a day "in which ye shall *afflict your souls*," *i. e.* subject yourselves to the discomforts and pains of entire abstinence from food for the whole day, "from even to even." Whoever would not afflict his soul on this day must be "cut off from his people." All labor was forbidden under the same penalty. The passages Lev. 23: 26–32 and Num. 29: 7–11 give these general features of the institution. Only in Lev. 16 do we find a full description. In this chapter it appears that the original appointment of this day stands connected with the sad death of Nadab and Abihu, the two eldest sons of Aaron for their rash unauthorized offering of strange fire before the Lord (Lev. 10: 1–8). That awful scene of death suggested the great necessity of ceremonial purity in the priesthood and of the utmost care and self-control when they came before God. There would be sins in the priesthood and sins among the people of which they might not be aware: hence the propriety of one comprehensive, all-embracing service for atonement.

The points to be specially noted in this service are—That the High Priest washed himself clean; put on white linen garments, symbolic of purity, and then made a special offering for his own sins and for the sin of all the people. The latter had this striking peculiarity—that two goats were taken for a sin-offering, upon whom lots were cast to select one for the Lord and one for Azazel [Eng. "scape-goat"]. Another still more important peculiarity was that on this day only (never on any other) the High Priest went alone into the most holy place, bearing both the blood of the sin-offering and incense. First he bore into the most holy place the blood of a bullock as a sin-offering for himself, and sprinkled it with his finger upon the mercy-seat and in front of the mercy-seat seven times. He also bore a censer full of coals from the great altar and upon it burned incense, the smoke of which enshrouded the mercy-seat. Then the goat upon which the lot fell for the Lord was slain, and the High Priest bore his blood also into the most holy place and sprinkled it there to make atonement for the whole people. No other man save the High Priest might go in at any time on pain of death.

The other goat, called in our English version "the scape-goat" was then disposed of thus: Aaron "laid both his hands upon the head of this goat and confessed over him all the iniquities of the children of Israel and all their transgressions in all their sins, *putting them upon the head of the goat,* and then sent him away by a fit man into the wilderness—the goat bearing upon himself all their iniquities into a land not inhabited." He was then set at liberty in the wilderness (Lev. 16: 20–22).——The precise meaning of the word Azazel ["scape-goat"] and the reason for using this name have been much disputed. Our English Bible fails to give a satisfactory translation of v. 8 where by a most obvious antithesis the sacred lot selects one of the two goats for Jehovah and the other for Azazel. Was it, as many suppose, for Satan, conceived of as "walking through those dry and desolate places, seeking rest but finding none"—to whom this goat, symbolically bearing the sins of the whole people, is sent? If so, what is implied and signified in this sending of the goat to him? I must say I am not wise on these points. If any ideas were current in that age in respect to Satan which might illustrate this transaction, they have not come down to us. It must I think suffice for us to see in these two goats for a sin-offering a sort of double figure to indicate the atonement—the first one slain in the usual way and his blood sprinkled before the mercy-seat—a solemn witness that without the shedding of blood there can be no remission of sin: the other, supplementing the great idea of atonement by a most vivid representation of *sins borne away*—forever away, to be known and remembered no more. The sins of the whole people were transferred to the head of this second goat; he takes them away into the unknown desolate wilderness, never to return. Symbolically, the sins are gone forever!——The prophet Micah (7: 19) gives a turn to the same thought only slightly different—" Thou wilt cast all their sins into the depths of the sea." Jeremiah also (31: 34)—"I will remember their sins no more." No symbol could give more precisely, more unequivocally, more forcibly, the great idea of *taking away sins*. You see them transferred to this second goat by means of hands imposed and formal declaration, "*putting them* [the sins] *upon the head of the goat*"; and then he is driven away, bearing his burden into an unknown, desolate land, never to be heard from again! ——The sacrifice of the first goat for a sin-offering and the sprinkling of his blood before the sacred Presence of Jehovah had the usual significance of an innocent animal substituted for the guilty sinner—the former dying that the latter might not die—thus showing *how* God could safely forgive sin. These two goats therefore represent respectively the two great ideas which make up the atonement—the first signifying *by what means*

God can testify duly against sin while yet he forgives the sinner; and the second certifying that—the innocent victim having been substituted for the sinner and slain in his stead—God does truly *take sins forever away*. In briefest phrase these coupled ideas stand out before us in the New Testament: "Behold the Lamb of God who *taketh away* the sin of the world" (John 1: 29).

III. *Sacred Edifices and Apparatus.*

A system of worship which included altars and sacrifices, and much more, one which had the ark of the covenant and the visible manifestation of Jehovah's presence, demanded an *edifice* for its center and home. It was essential to the proper reverence that this edifice should provide a place of seclusion as well as of safe-keeping for its most sacred things.——Moreover, so long as the people were unsettled—subject to removal any day—this structure must be movable, like the tents of all nomadic people. Hence the first structure was the *Tabernacle* or *Sacred Tent*.——A general idea of it may be presented to the reader thus:— Conceive of an inclosed court, one hundred cubits long by fifty wide [the cubit being eighteen inches]; this inclosure being made by hanging curtains of linen five cubits high, suspended from horizontal rods which were supported by posts. The entrance to this inclosure was always at its eastern end, and the eastern section, forming the outer or first court, was twenty cubits in depth, cut off from the rest of the inclosed area by curtains.——In the center of the rear portion stood the sacred tent proper, thirty cubits in length from east to west, and ten cubits in width. This also was in two principal apartments, the eastern being twenty cubits by ten, known as "the holy place"; the western, "the most holy place," or the "Holy of holies," being ten cubits square. The perpendicular walls of this sacred tent were of boards set on end, ten cubits high, so supported as to be readily set up, taken down, and transported. The covering was four-fold, of cloth and skins, and was manifestly arranged like the roof of a house, the covering passing over a ridge-pole in the center. Such briefly was this sacred structure.

Of its furniture, the important articles were as follows:

(a.) In the open court in front of the tabernacle proper, were the great altar of burnt-offering and a laver—an immense reservoir or tank for water. (b.) In the holy place—the first section of the sacred tent—stood the altar of incense; the table of shew-bread; and the golden candlestick.——(c.) In the most holy place, enshrouded in the thick darkness, stood the ark of the covenant, containing originally the two tables of stone on which the ten commandments were written, the pot of manna, and Aaron's rod that budded. Upon the lid of this ark, known as "the mercy-seat," there reposed the refulgence of the Divine Presence—a visible brightness and glory, called by the later Jews "the shechinah"—itself overshadowed by the wings of cherubic figures which rested upon either end of the ark.

The whole structure might be readily taken down and transported from place to place with all its furniture; parties being designated for this service.

In Num. 10: 35, 36 we have the words customarily used by Moses as a form of prayer, accompanying the order for striking and pitching tents: "When the ark set forward Moses said, Rise up, Lord, and let thine enemies be scattered, and let those that hate thee flee before thee: and when it rested he said, Return, O Lord, unto the ten thousands of Israel."

Of the temple built by Solomon I need not say more than this—that its plan was essentially that of the tabernacle, differing in the following points: Its dimensions were twice as great; and it was built for a permanent, immovable edifice, of the most substantial and costly materials.

IV. *The Sacred Orders.*

The tribe of Levi was chosen and set apart for the services of worship and of religious instruction. Out of this tribe the family of Aaron was selected for the priesthood. The most sacred services devolved upon the priests, the High Priest only being permitted to enter the most holy place once a year, as we have seen. The Levites performed subordinate services, supplying the requisite wood and water for so vast a system of sacrifices and offerings, and serving also in the transportation of the sacred tent and its furniture. At a later period the service of song in the house of the Lord was in their hands.

The law provided a full ritual for the induction of the High Priest into his office and for the consecration of all the priests to their work. Their robes of office, their various dress on all occasions, are detailed with great minuteness.——The law also provided specially for their subsistence. A portion of various sacrifices fell to them as their perquisite. The great expense of the entire ritual service, including the cost of the animals offered for the people at large; the support of the priests, and to some extent of the Levites, was provided for by law in the tithes; the poll-tax of a half-shekel from every man of Israel; and from various other sources.

In the ultimate settlement in Canaan, forty-eight cities with their suburbs were given to the Levites. They were thus distributed among the entire population of Canaan both east and west of the Jordan, and if true to their mission would fill a very important sphere in both the civil and the religious life of the nation. Of their civil and judicial duties I have spoken already. They were also teachers of religion.——Their suburban territory would afford them a small amount of land for cultivation; but the divine plan was that they who served at the altar should live from the altar. While religious services were conscientiously performed and the religious spirit was in due strength, both priests and Levites would be comfortably fed and clad. Idolatry and religious declension would cut their supplies short.

The careful reader of those portions of Exodus, Leviticus, and Numbers which give the plan of the tabernacle, the ritual of the priests and Levites and the minute detail of numerous sacrifices and offerings and purifications, will not need the suggestion that in many respects the interest and the value of these details have mostly passed away. Of prime importance in that age; vital to the proper construction of the tabernacle; vital to the due consecration of priest and Levite and to their instruction in duty; entirely essential to the ends of a ritual system which was to be the religious law of a great people—they were all in place then and were indispensable; but in most respects this interest and value have long since ceased. Whereas in the time of Moses not one word of this minute detail was superfluous, not one point could be safely omitted; now, it may be passed over with only brief notice. Few will care to read all its particulars.

Yet two points deserve remark:

1. That this very minuteness of detail is the strongest evidence of the genuineness and antiquity of these books. They were certainly written at the time of the events they record. They never could have been gotten up in any age subsequent to the events. The specifications for the tabernacle and for all its furniture had a purpose then; but could have had no purpose to justify such minuteness after the construction was finished. It would be the supremest folly to forge such documents ages after the events had passed. No man in his senses ever attempts such a forgery. Men never submit to such labor without an object; and the case precludes the possibility of any object *after* the tent was built and after the ritual was fully understood and wrought into established usage.

2. While these minute details neither require nor reward particular investigation in our day, yet taken in whole *they are pregnant with great moral lessons for all time.*

(1.) There was a perpetual inculcation of cleanliness, external purity; and the most careful avoidance of whatever was defiling. The ceremonial washings and cleansings, the removal from the camp, or as the case may be, the seclusion from the court of the tabernacle for a term of purification, occur frequently. By a natural law of mind, sin is associated with uncleanness; crime is defiling. Hence, with almost infinite pains the Lord was impressing upon his people the great idea that their God who deigned to dwell among them "was of purer eyes than to behold iniquity." He could not abide with them save as they kept themselves clean and pure.

(2.) On every hand we note the most solemn inculcation of care, thoughtfulness, consideration, especially in their religious worship, and the most impressive warnings against a rash and inconsiderate spirit. Hence wine was forbidden to the priests when about to go to the altar (Lev. 10: 8–11). It seemed that God could have no patience with the thoughtless and irreverent. At whatever cost, the fear of the Lord must be impressed upon the people—else all effort for their religious culture would be vain.

(3.) Their great thanksgiving festivals; their numerous thank-offerings; their vows; their required tithes—all concur in this one idea—the recognition of God as the Giver of all blessings, their great personal and national Benefactor. No pains was spared to impress and enforce this great truth. The long course of God's redeeming mercies toward their nation; the rescue from Egyptian bondage; the miraculous supplies of bread and water forty years in the desert; the gift of the goodly land of Canaan;—these were the staple facts of their history which God sought to engrave upon the national heart and to work into the living thought of the thousands of Israel. By every hopeful appliance their religious system was shaped to keep alive and intensify these feelings.

(4.) More important than all the rest were the great moral lessons set forth *by the perpetual presence of atoning blood*. The Israelites were never allowed to forget that they were sinners, and that their approach to God must always be through the blood of atonement. No day might begin, no day might close, without the shedding of animal blood—the sacrifice of an innocent animal's life. The great days were great because of the multiplication of these sacrifices—evermore distinguished and memorable for the rivers of blood that flowed; for the struggles and throes of the dying; for the sprinkling of blood, *blood*, BLOOD, all round about the hallowed altar, toward the unseen Presence within the most holy place, and upon the assembled hosts of Israel.——It may cost us a few moments' effort to reproduce those scenes before our mind's eye so as to take in their full significance; but this effort to comprehend that ancient ritual would bring its reward. What a demonstration it would be in proof that "without the shedding of blood there is no remission"! that God never looks propitiously on guilty sinners save through the bleeding sacrifice of his crucified Son! As bearing upon the great questions—the *fact* and the *nature* of the atonement—this bloody ritual has a most vital and impressive significance. No questions of deeper and more vital import can ever arise than such as these: Was the death of Christ expiatory? Was his blood shed for the sins of men? Did he lay down his life, an innocent victim, that the guilty sinners who place their hands upon his sacred head and there confess their sins may live and never die? In a word, was his death foreshadowed and its true significance pre-intimated by the bloody offerings enjoined in this Hebrew system?

Argumentatively, it would seem that these great questions are decided forever by the following considerations:

1. If the bloody sacrifices of this ancient system do not set forth the atoning death of Christ, they mean nothing; this, or nothing at all.

2. The writer to the Hebrew Christians testifies that they mean this. To give the proof of this statement in full would repeat entire the seventh, eighth, ninth, and tenth chapters of this epistle. It would be idle to say that this writer does not refer to the sacrificial system of ancient Israel; equally idle to claim that he does not speak of the bloody death of Christ; more than idle to deny that in his view that old system sought to illustrate this new one—those bloody scenes were foreshadowing pre-intimations of Christ's death; that those priests were precursors of this greater High Priest; that the blood which Aaron bore once a year into the most holy place meant neither more nor less than that Jesus was in his time to enter once for all into a yet more holy place with his own blood and thus achieve for us eternal redemption. Jesus "needed not daily as did those priests to offer sacrifice, first for his own sins and then for the people's; for this he did once" [for all] "when he offered up himself" (Heb. 7: 27).

3. All the New Testament writers were Jews; men of Jewish education, men of life-long training in religious ideas based on this Hebrew sacrificial system. They never speak of the purpose or results of Christ's death save in terms and phrases taken from this system given through Moses. Jesus never speaks of his own death save in these same words and phrases. When he speaks of "giving his life a ransom for many" (Mat. 20: 28); when he said, "This is my blood

of the New Testament which is shed for many for the remission of sins" (Mat 26: 28); when his great forerunner speaks of him as "the Lamb of God who taketh away the sin of the world" (Jno. 1: 29);—or Peter (1 Eps. 2: 24) as "bearing our sins in his own body on the tree;" or Paul (2 Cor. 5: 21) as being "made a sin-offering for us that we might be made the righteousness of God in him," it is simply impossible to disprove the reference of these terms and phrases to the Mosaic system—impossible to give them any other sense than that which is illustrated in the bloody death of the sin-offerings and burnt-offerings of that ancient law.

Thus with bands which no sophistry can sever, the Old Testament and the New are bound together, and the atonement prefigured in the former is embodied and made perfect in the latter. The almost ceaseless blood-sheddings and blood-sprinklings of the former culminate in the latter in the one great scene of death-agony and blood on Calvary. The grand idea of expiatory suffering—of the vicarious death of the innocent in place of the guilty, which ages of ceremonial sacrifice had been setting forth and working into the minds of all reverent worshipers, had prepared the way for Christ's disciples to understand the mystery of his bloody death and to teach the Christian world in the writings of the New Testament *how* the blood of Jesus "*takes away sin.*"

In closing our notice of this religious system, let us revert for a moment to the fact that all its important features were so many important *steps of progress* in the manifestation of God to man. These were lessons in advance of all that had preceded on that greatest of all questions—How shall man approach his Maker, and how shall he offer acceptable worship?——That God deigned to come down and dwell with his obedient people is the precious truth which underlies all these provisions for his worship. How shall man treat this Heavenly Guest; how adjust himself to this pure and majestic Presence; with what state of heart; with what purity and cleanliness of person; with what offerings and sacrifices and of what significance?——These are the points embraced in these great lessons taught in this religious system. The perpetual inculcation of cleanliness and of conscientious, scrupulous care; the practice of perpetual thanksgiving; but above all, the copious illustrations of the great idea of bloody sacrifice to take away sin;—these have been already named as the salient features in this system, and all (it will be noticed) are *points of progress*. Bloody sacrifices and altars appear in the worship offered by Abraham, Noah, and even Abel. But how much more fully is their true import unfolded here? Here is confession of sin on the part of the worshiper; here is the symbolic transfer of sins by imposition of hands upon the head of the victim brought out to die: here is the sprinkling of his blood all round about the altar; upon the very mercy-seat and immediately in the presence of the Holy One who sat beneath the cherubim; upon the worshipers also gathered round the bloody altar: here are the special solemnities of the great day of atonement in which the whole sacrificial system culminated—all combining their significance to unfold the great idea of the vicarious sufferings of an innocent victim in place of guilty men.

CHAPTER XX.

HISTORIC EVENTS OF HEBREW HISTORY FROM SINAI TO THE JORDAN.

The Golden Calf.

We dropped the thread of this history at Sinai to study with undivided attention the civil code of Moses and also the religious system. We now resume it.

Moses tarried on the Mount forty days to receive from the Lord the civil statutes in detail and also all his instructions in respect to the tabernacle, the priesthood, and the ritual. The time seemed long to the restive people. They became utterly impatient; they lost faith in God and in Moses; fell back upon their previous Egyptian notions; and consequently applied to Aaron, saying: "Up, make us gods which shall go before us; for as for this Moses—the man that brought us out of the land of Egypt—we wot not what has become of him." Aaron replied: "Break off and bring to me your golden ear-rings." Whether he hoped they would withdraw their request when they saw how much it was to cost them does not appear. But it does appear that their enthusiasm for idol gods was equal to this sacrifice of their golden ornaments. They brought them freely as Aaron had proposed, and he made of them a golden calf. Strangely enough, the people greeted this senseless thing with the shout: "These be thy gods, O Israel, which brought thee up out of the land of Egypt." What could this mean? Did they really believe that this calf was the power that brought those plagues on Pharaoh; that rolled away the waters of the Red Sea; bore them safely over, but hurled destruction on Pharaoh's host? Did they see the Power that wrought all these wonders in this powerless calf? Or did they assume that the Invisible Power which achieved this work was well represented by this golden image?——The ineffable folly of idolatry according to either notion staggers us; we know not what to make of it. If the facts were not so patent the world over and through all the ages of the race, it would be our first impulse to assume it all a fiction and to say—Men never could be so supremely silly and foolish as to suppose the Great God to be *like a calf!* or as to suppose that a calf, whether of gold or of flesh and blood, could be a God!

We are tempted to digress, perhaps too much, into a discussion of the *philosophy of idolatry*. On this point it must suffice to say that no philosophy of such a fact can ever be satisfactory save one that assumes and makes large account of human depravity—thus: Some recognition of superhuman power is inevitable; it is in man's deepest convictions, and can not be got out. But men shrink from the near presence of a pure, sin-hating God. Any thing else is more endurable. Give us (they say) some God to worship who will not disturb our sinning, or some way of worshiping the Supreme which will at least put that pure, all-searching Eye farther off. And as to the reasonableness of such notions of God, there is only this to be said: Sin makes men *think* like fools; sin makes men *act* like fools!——This philosophy of idolatry, and this only, touches bottom and must stand.——In the case before us, it is noticeable that the people were charmed with this new worship, for they could sit down to eat and to drink *and rise up to play!* A fine time they had of it. There was no troublesome sense of a pure, sin-hating God there. The question how this calf could be the same God who brought them out of Egypt was of the least possible concern to them.

Aaron is swept along in the current of this mad infatuation. When he saw this calf, he built an altar before it and made proclamation: "To-morrow is a feast to the Lord." Full of heart for such a service "the people rose up early on the morrow and offered burnt-offerings and brought peace-offerings; they sat down to eat and to drink, and rose up to play."

A view of this scene from another stand-point follows next in the narrative. We are shown what transpired on the Mount where the Lord, Moses, and his servant Joshua were still engaged together. The God of Israel whose eyes are in every place, apprised Moses of what the people were doing. In words adapted to make Moses feel his personal responsibility, and perhaps to intimate that for himself he must disown such a people, he said—"Go, get thee down, for *thy people*, whom *thou broughtest* out of the land of Egypt have corrupted themselves." They have made and are now worshiping a golden calf as the God that brought them out of Egypt. ——The Lord closed with a proposal which was in many points of view intensely trying to Moses; viz. that Moses should suffer the Lord to consume this corrupt people. Then he would make the posterity of Moses a great nation, in place of rejected Israel.——Did the Lord say this to prove Moses in the line of personal pride? However this may have been, the result was morally sublime. The temptation (if we may call it such) made no impression. Moses passes it by as a thing not to be thought of. The Lord seemed to anticipate that Moses would pray for the people, and therefore said—"Let me alone that my wrath may wax hot against them and that I may consume them."——Not deterred a moment by this, "Moses besought the Lord his God and said: Why doth thy wrath wax hot against *thy* people [not merely "*my* people"] which Thou [not I] hast brought forth out of the land of Egypt with great power and with a mighty hand"? He boldly argues the case: Why, Lord, shouldest thou give occasion to the Egyptians to say that thou broughtest forth this people only to slay them in the mountains and consume them from the face of the earth? What will be said of thy solemn oath to Abraham to multiply his seed as the stars and to give them Canaan? How will these things bear upon thine own glory before earth and heaven?

This is a most remarkable case of prayer. Was ever mortal more bold and more persistent, despite of all the Lord had said which seemed to shut the door and bar off all entreaty? Yet Moses prevailed, and it does not appear that the Lord rebuked him for his persistence or for his boldness. It is simply said—"The Lord repented of the evil which he thought to do unto his people."——This point being so far gained, Moses must go down to the people. With the two stone tablets of the law in hand and Joshua by his side, he descends the mount. Joshua's ear first caught the sound from the camp. His military antecedents suggest to him a a battle: "There is a noise of war in the camp." With

THE INTERCESSION OF MOSES. 345

juster discrimination Moses replies: "It is not the shout of victors; it is not the outcry of the vanquished; but it is the voice of song that I hear." They come within sight—and true enough—there was the calf-god, and the people were dancing and singing around it with wild, mad enthusiasm. What a scene to Moses! How is his soul fired with holy indignation! He casts to the earth the two tablets and breaks them at the foot of the mount. Next, he demolishes the calf; grinds it to powder; mixes it with water and compels the people to drink it. A million of men are in dismay before him—all powerless to resist.——He turns to Aaron, his elder brother, to rebuke him. Aaron's defense is both tame and lame, as that of a man thoroughly ashamed of himself. "Thou knowest the people, bent on mischief. They beset me to make them a calf; I told them to bring forward their gold; they did so. I threw it into the fire—and the calf made itself!

The more vital movement followed. Moses took his stand in the gate of the camp and cried aloud: "Who is on the Lord's side? Let him come over to me." The sons of Levi, his tribal brethren, responded to the call and came. He bade them take every man his sword and pass to and fro through the camp, cutting down every man they met. There fell that day three thousand. The sin called for some fearful visitation of God's displeasure—something that should impress the whole people with a sense of God's irrepressible indignation.

Thus closed this fearful day. After one night's reflection, Moses convenes the people, brings their great sin before them again, and says—"I will go up before the Lord; perhaps I may make atonement for your sin." His prayer is on record—short, but full of meaning. "Oh, this people have sinned a great sin and have made them gods of gold. Yet now, if thou wilt forgive their sin:—and if not, blot me, I pray thee out of thy book which thou hast written."——To which the Lord answers: "Whosoever hath sinned against me, him will I blot out of my book."

The prayer of Moses (v. 32) should be read with a strong emphasis on the word "*if*," making it equivalent to *O that:* IF thou wilt forgive their sin, all will be well. O that thou wouldest! If not, life is nothing to me; blot me out from the book of the living. Let me rather die than live any longer.——The primary meaning of this "book" of life is a register of living men—with reference to the earthly life, of this world only and not of the next. It is not to be taken here as including the future life. The Lord's final answer spares the national life, but subjects the people yet to visitations of judgment for this terrible sin.

Though the main point seemed to be gained—God could consent to spare the nation—yet a qualifying condition troubled Moses exceedingly. The Lord said—I will send an angel before thee to drive out the Canaanite; but I will not go up in the midst of thee myself, for thou art a stiff-necked people, lest I consume thee in the way. It can not be safe for so wayward a people to have with them the personal presence of a God so pure and so sin-hating.——In the settlement of this grave matter, Moses was permitted to come very near to the God of Israel, to talk with him as a man talks with his friend. Moses said (in substance): Thou hast made me responsible to lead this people onward to Canaan; but thou hast not told me whom thou wilt send with me. Yet thou hast very kindly said, "I know thee by name, and thou hast found grace in my sight." If this be so, show me now thy way that I may know thee; that I may find grace in thy sight; and do not call this people *mine*, but consider them *thine*. Let me know what thy way of dealing with me and with thy people is to be and what I may depend upon in this thing.——The Lord graciously answers:—"My presence shall go with thee, and I will give thee rest:" this rest being probably the promised rest of the nation in Canaan, and not merely rest in the sense of a satisfied mind exempt from harassing vexations.——Moses promptly answers—"If thy presence go not with me, carry us not up hence." If thou art not going with us, let Canaan be given up and this whole enterprise be abandoned, for what can we do unless our own God be with us? How have we ever been distinguished from other peoples on the face of the earth, save in this—that our God, the great, the pure, and the Holy One, has been personally present with us?——The Lord graciously yields this point also.

Moses has still one more request to make—the last

and perhaps the greatest: "I beseech thee, show me thy glory." Moses had seen the pillar of cloud and of fire; more than this, he had been on Mt. Sinai where the August Presence was so grand and awful that he said—"I do exceedingly fear and quake;" and just at this time we are told that the cloudy pillar descended and stood at the very door of Moses' tent, and the Lord talked with Moses, speaking unto him face to face as a man speaketh unto his friend (Ex. 33: 9, 11). But this last request asks for something yet more deep and spiritual. These recent developments have made on the mind of Moses a painful impression that after all he does not yet know God fully—does not really understand him; and therefore needs to know him more thoroughly. Where is the line between his mercy and his wrath? How much can he bear in his covenant people, and at what point will his mercy surely turn to consuming judgment? When and on what grounds will he forgive his sinning people and blot out their iniquities?——These are the points in the character of God which he feels that he must know, and which he expresses under the one most comprehensive word—"thy glory." They belong to the depths of the divine nature.

This inquisitive spirit is prompted by one supreme desire in the heart of Moses, viz. to do faithfully and well the work to which God has called him, and to learn how to bear himself toward God under these responsibilities. Therefore the Lord yields here also, the request being not only reasonable but pleasing to him; for, does not the Lord always delight to meet those who long to see more of his glory, especially when the deepest aim and purpose of this longing culminate in the passion to do the Lord's work more perfectly?——Noticeably, the Lord's answer chooses a new word. He does not say—Yes, my servant Moses, I will show thee my "glory"; but this: "I will make *all my goodness* pass before thee, and I will proclaim the name of the Lord before thee."——This is not by any means an evasion of the main question, for the Lord comes squarely up to the very point that labors in the mind of his servant Moses—the mutual relations in the character and ways of God between his mercies and his justice; his compassion toward his children, and his fearful severity to the guilty whom no mercy can hold to obedience; whom nothing can move but terrific judgments.——It can scarcely be necessary to explain the usage of the word "*name*" as spoken of God: "I will proclaim the *name* of the Lord before thee." We have become familiar with the fact that in the Scriptures, the *name* (usually) does more than merely distinguish one individual from another (as in our common parlance), being significant of nature, of character, of some predominant quality. It is not that God may be called the Lord, the Lord God, but that he *is* the Lord, *i. e.* the real *Jehovah*—forever the same, and forever faithful to his promises. To proclaim his *name* therefore is to proclaim his *nature;* to testify to his real character.

The manner and circumstances of this proclamation in the case before us are altogether unique and striking. The ground idea is that, in human relationships, we learn the character by *seeing* the man. We depend on the eye and the sense of sight above the testimony of any other sense, and we expect to see the character *in the face*. To "see the face" is, therefore, the most complete and satisfactory means of learning the character—of knowing the man—that we can have under the limitations of our present mortal state. The language and the whole transaction before us rest on these simple facts of our present life.——The Lord said to Moses: "Thou canst not see my face; for there shall no man see me and live." To see the very face of God would imply a more full revelation of his ineffable glory than mortal man could bear. A softened manifestation of those unutterable glories is all, therefore, that can be granted even to the man of God, Moses; and this is expressively put by saying: "Thou shalt see my *back parts;* my *face* shall not be seen." This was the Lord's proposal: "Behold, there is a place by me, and thou shalt stand upon a rock; and it shall come to pass while my glory passeth by that I will put thee in a cleft of the rock, and I will cover thee with my hand while I pass by: then I will take away my hand and thou shalt see my back parts, but my face shall not be seen" (Ex. 33: 21-23).

It will be noted that in this narrative Moses makes no attempt to describe the scenes of this visible manifestation, or the impressions it made on his mind.

CONDITIONS FOR THE FUTURE.

Words are too weak for such a service. Those glorious views of God which sight may give, and which we may assume that Moses obtained in this proposed manifestation, each one must have for himself alone and not for another. . They will come to all the Lord's true children in the day when they shall see even as they are seen and know as they are known.——The matters which Moses does record at this point are, that the Lord bade him prepare two other stone tablets to replace the broken and to appear with them the next morning on the top of the mount; that he must come alone and let no other man be seen in all the mount, nor let any animal of the flock or herd feed before the mount; that then the Lord descended in the cloud and stood with him there, and *proclaimed the name of the Lord.* The words of this proclamation are recorded:—"The Lord [the Jehovah], Jehovah God, merciful and gracious; long-suffering and abundant in goodness and truth; keeping mercy for thousands; forgiving iniquity, transgression and sin, and that will by no means clear the guilty; visiting the iniquity of the fathers upon the children and upon children's children unto the third and to the fourth generation."——Profoundly awed by these words and by this impressive manifestation; encouraged by the prominence given in it to the ideas of mercy and loving-kindness, Moses made haste, and bowed his head to the earth and worshiped, and then lifted up his prayer—"If now I have found grace in thy sight, O Lord, let my Lord, I pray thee, go among us (for it is a stiff-necked people) and pardon our iniquity and our sin and take us for thine inheritance." ——The same points are prominent here as before (Ex. 32: 11-13)—that God would forgive the great sin of the people; that he would go among them again, and dwell in the midst of them; and that he would truly take and hold them as his own inheritance. Upon all these points the heart of Moses is intently set, and he brings them before God every time. The Lord responds—I renew my covenant; I shall go on to work marvelously among this people. The revelations of my great name before them and before all the world by means of them, are only begun. I will go before this people to drive out the Canaanite; but this one thing I must insist upon: My people must wash out every stain of idol-worship; they must destroy all idol-altars, break down their images, cut down their groves, have no associations with corrupt idol-worshipers; worship no other than the one true and holy God, for the Lord whose name is Jealous is a jealous God. Other requirements follow as may be seen (Ex. 34); Moses fills out another forty days on the mount; the law is again written on two tablets like the former; Moses comes down with his face (unconsciously to himself) shining as if the reflection of the more shining face of God still lingered upon it. When Aaron and all Israel saw this, they feared to come near him. Moses called to them (*i. e.* to come); Aaron and the rulers (not the people) came and Moses talked with them. Afterward all the people drew near and Moses rehearsed the recently revealed commandments of the Lord, putting a vail on his face while speaking with the people. This glory on his face was the sensible witness that he had been in very deed talking with the all-glorious God, and that it behooved them to accept him as God's authorized messenger.

In tracing thus rapidly the general course of thought in these chapters (Ex. 32–34), I have aimed to bring out the salient points and the spirit of the transactions. Some things have been passed which it were well to return and examine more fully.

This first great apostacy into idol-worship was doubtless born of their Egyptian life. There they had seen the ox, the cow, and the calf made objects of worship. It is supposable that the leaders in this movement were of that "mixed multitude" who came out from Egypt with them (Ex. 12: 38), and who seem to have led off in the lusting and murmuring at Taberah (Num. 11: 4). Neither of these facts—their having seen such worship in Egypt, nor their being seduced by the Egyptians among them—can at all excuse their sin. It admits of no excuse.——Moses recites the main points of this case again (Deut. 9: 8–21), omitting the special manifestation of God's name, but giving prominence to his own anxiety, not to say agony, on their behalf lest the Lord should indeed destroy them. "I fell down before the Lord as at the first forty days and forty nights; I did neither eat bread nor drink water because of all your sin which ye had sinned in doing wickedly in the sight of the Lord to provoke him to anger (for I was afraid of the anger and hot displeasure wherewith the Lord was wroth with you to destroy you)". He also speaks of his prayer for Aaron whose sin in this matter had been great (v. 20).——How much this great apostacy impressed itself upon the nation's history and affected good men in after ages, may be seen in Ps. 106: 19–23, and Acts 7: 39–43, and 1 Cor. 10: 7.

The fact that Moses burnt and pulverized the golden calf so that he might compel the people to drink it, shows him to have been profoundly skilled in the science of metallurgy. He has not told us what solvent he used, other than fire, for it was no part of his object to teach this art or to exhibit his skill therein. Few men have ever lived in any age who could have done it.

The *social and moral influence* of this festival for idol-worship is expressively put by Moses: "The people sat down to eat and to drink, and rose up to play." As the subsequent narrative shows, here was revelry—dancing, shouting, and song. God was forgotten; all true sense of his presence and indeed of his nature was ruled out by the very fact that they had exalted a golden calf into his place. By a law of human nature men become like the object they worship. Calf-worshipers go down to the level of the calf they worship. Alas! would that they did not sink far lower in passion and in crime!

In Ex. 32: 25 we read: "When Moses saw that the people were naked—(for Aaron had made them naked unto their shame among their enemies), then he took his stand in the gate of the camp and said, "Who is on the Lord's side? let him come unto me."——Modern critics for the most part give the Hebrew words the sense, not of being naked, but of being cast loose, demoralized, put into the state of being lawless, *without restraint.* The principal verb occurs rarely; it may of itself bear either sense above indicated. The sense "naked" does not well suit the context; for in what sense did Aaron make them naked? And how could their nakedness be a reason why Moses should send armed men among them to slay three thousand?——The other sense, therefore, should be preferred. Aaron had utterly demoralized them. They were powerless, and only objects of scorn before their enemies. God had in wrath forsaken them.

From Ex. 33: 4–6 it appears that the people were mourning over the sad tidings that God refused to go with them to Canaan, and that they indicated their grief in part by leaving off their usual ornaments, as God had commanded them to do. In v. 6 our translation reads, "Israel stripped themselves of their ornaments *by* the Mount Horeb." The Hebrew favors the sense, "*from* Mt. Horeb"—*i. e.* from that point of their history and onward; signifying that they gave this permanent indication of humility and shame for their great sin. Nothing could be more appropriate, since those ornaments of gold were strongly associated with their awful sin in the matter of the calf. It is pleasant to see that they were so prompt to give this expression of their sorrow and shame.

In that most emphatic announcement of the name of the Lord (34: 6, 7), we must note the reiteration of the ideas of mercy, grace, long-suffering, compassion, goodness, truth—as if the leading purpose were to inspire hope and comfort in souls contrite and humble for sin. Solemn and awful words were indeed spoken of "visiting men for their iniquity;" and not the fathers only but the children also by the laws of inevitable connection between parent and offspring. Nationally and socially, the children in this nation must suffer for the sin of their parents. The smiting dead of three thousand guilty fathers left many thousand children orphans. If for the sins of the fathers God had dropped the nation at Horeb, where would have been their promised Canaan? What could have been the lot of coming generations of Israel but disaster—privation of good; accumulation of evil? That God should put so prominently in the fore-ground this feature in his threatened retribution implies his hope that he might touch the heart of fathers and mothers in this way when they were fearfully insensible to all other considerations.—— As to the bearing of this announcement of God's names upon the then pending question—What may the nation hope for from the God of their covenant? we must suppose that it encouraged Moses greatly. He would say—

Assuredly God would not put his mercies forward so sweetly, so richly, so in the front of all his manifestations, if he had not some blessed thoughts of mercy for us. Let us trust his loving-kindness! While we will listen to his solemn words of warning against sin, we will believe that it is his purpose to forgive this great sin and to grant us still his gracious protecting presence. So he presses his suit once more in prayer.

Among the greatest lessons of this history are those that relate to *prayer*. The whole character of Moses as seen in this transaction is wonderfully pure and true. How unselfishly he casts away, as not to be thought of, the divine suggestion—" I will make of thee a great nation"! With what solid grasp and singular tenacity did he hold fast to the great ideas of God's covenant with Abraham—to make this nation his own peculiar people; to abide among them; to manifest himself in works of power and grace, and get himself a great name in all the earth! Shall God forget this covenant; abandon this people; drop them midway from Egypt to Canaan, and leave all the nations to exult in their ruin and to put it to the caprice or the impotence of Israel's God? Never.——It is wonderful how Moses holds on upon these strong points in his case and the case of Israel; how thoroughly he proves himself to have been raised up of God for the great mission of Israel's Leader and Advocate with God. With what boldness does he debate the case before the Lord and set forth his strong reasons—reasons, not of selfish sort, not looking so much to the human side as to the divine; reasons that entered deeply into the greatest of all considerations—the honor of God before all the nations, and the success of his plans in making Israel his chosen people. As we search the annals of human history in vain to find a stronger case of power with God in prayer, so we must look far to find a case more instructive in regard to the proper attitude for praying souls before God, and the proper arguments to use in prayer. Moses seemed not so much pleading for himself or for his people, as *for God*. Therefore it was that his pleas, based on the revealed counsels of the Almighty and fully in sympathy with his designs and with his glory, took hold of the heart of Jehovah and could not be denied.

The scenes of murmuring and lust; Taberah and Kibroth-hattaavah.

These transactions, recorded Num. 11, seem to have occurred soon after the people moved onward from Sinai. In the official record of the halting stations on their march from Egypt to Canaan (Num. 33), "Kibroth-hattaavah" is next after Sinai.——The name Taberah does not designate a station, but simply indicates the remote quarter of the camp where the fire of the Lord broke forth upon the murmuring people, till in answer to the prayer of Moses it was quenched.—— The particular ground of this murmuring is not stated. Probably it was the general hardships of their wilderness life; a shrinking from the march into the depths of the desert, just then commenced.——In close connection follows an account of a more serious murmuring, begun by the "mixed multitude" of Egyptian and miscellaneous followers of whom we read Ex. 12: 38, but into which the men of Israel were drawn. The ground of complaint was their food. They were tired of their manna and longed for the vegetables and fish of Egypt.——At this point, as if to show how unreasonable their complaints were, Moses gives a full account of the manna, its appearance, the way of preparing it for food, and of its flavor. (See what is said on manna in Ex. 16.)——Moses heard the complaints of the people and was greatly displeased. Naturally he bore the case to God in prayer, but in the spirit of one whose endurance was overtaxed and whose nerves were but too sensitive to his burdens. Noticeably the Lord does not rebuke him, but very kindly provides relief by creating a council of seventy elders who shall help him to bear his responsibilities for the people. They were to be endowed with a measure of the same divine spirit which abode with him. Having received this spirit it is said (v. 25) that they "prophesied," *i. e.* exhorted, spake under the divine influence, but *added no more.* This is obviously the sense of our Hebrew text; and not, as our English version has given it—"prophesied and did not cease." If they did not cease, we might expect to hear more of what they said. But the word used by Moses is decisive. They simply prophesied for once to indicate the presence of the spirit with them, and added no more.——As to the complaining people, God answered their demands with such a supply of flesh that the surfeit, by natural law or otherwise, brought upon the people a fearful plague from which many perished. The vast graveyard which received the dead gave name to this memorable station— *The graves of lust, or the graves of the lustful ones.* The Lord had brought up to them quails to cover the whole region about their camp for a day's journey (twenty miles) on every side to the depth of two cubits (three feet).——The moral of the case is well put by the Psalmist: "He gave them their request, but sent leanness into their soul" (106: 15); or as another has it: "He gave them their own desire. They were not estranged from their lust, for while their meat was yet in their mouth, the wrath of God came upon them and slew the fattest of them and smote down the chosen men of Israel" (Ps. 78: 26–31).——There is danger of being too demanding and persistent for the gratification of any appetite or passion, lest the blessing we demand may prove a curse. Let God's wisdom and not our own impulses be our guide, and rule our life.

Miriam and Aaron jealous of the honor given to Moses.

In Num. 12, we are told that Miriam and Aaron speak disparagingly of Moses because of his Ethiopian wife, jealous of the almost exclusive honor shown him by the Lord. "Hath the Lord indeed spoken by Moses only? Hath he not spoken by *us* also?"—Miriam seems to have been the moving spirit in this. She had no special love or even respect for her sister-in-law; but had more than enough of self-conceit and pride. Perhaps she thought of her prominence in the song on the hither shore of the Red Sea (Ex. 15).——Remarkably we find here this verse interposed: ("Now the man Moses was very meek, above all men who were upon the face of the earth.")——The manner in which this is introduced favors the supposition that it came from some other and later hand, like the account of Moses' death (Deut. 34: 5–12). Yet it is impossible either to prove or disprove this supposition.

It is plain that Moses made no reply to what Miriam

said, but left the whole matter with God. His work was not of his own choosing; his high position came to him unsought. The event showed that it was perfectly safe for him to leave his fair name and his high position with the Lord. For the Lord soon interposed: "Moses is more than a prophet: to the prophet I make myself known in visions or speak in dreams; but with my servant Moses I speak mouth to mouth, and the very similitude of the Lord shall he behold: Wherefore then were ye not afraid to speak against my servant Moses"? ——All suddenly Miriam is leprous, white as snow. The quick and trained eye of Aaron detects it, and he cries out to Moses for pardon and help. Moses, always the man of prayer, calls upon God in her behalf and is heard. After seven days' exclusion from the camp, she returns sound, and hopefully, a wiser and more humble woman.

Kadesh-barnea and the Unbelieving Spies.

In Num. 13 and 14 stands the record of a series of events of exceedingly vital moment to the children of Israel.——By a route not definitely ascertainable at this distance of time, they had come (eleven days' journey Deut. 1: 2) from Sinai to Kadesh-barnea which most critics concur in locating in the northern part of the wilderness of Paran, near "the mountain of the Amorites," and also near the southern border of the land of Canaan. Leaving the wilderness of Sinai (Num. 10: 12, 13) "on the twentieth day of the second month of the second year" [from Egypt]; spending at least one month (Num. 11: 20, 21) at Kibroth-hattaavah, they were supposably about two years out from Egypt when the question came up the second time whether the people were prepared to march into the land of Canaan. On the former occasion, as we have seen (Ex. 13: 17, 18) the Lord decided this question at once, rejecting the short route to Canaan and heading their hosts through the wilderness, because, being then just from bondage in Egypt, they were in no condition, physically or morally, to enter Canaan.——Now at Kadesh the question comes up again. As the case is put by Moses (Deut. 1: 22) it would seem that the people suggested the mission of the spies: "Ye came near unto

me, every one of you, and said—We will send men before us and they shall search us out the land and bring us word again by what way we must go up and into what city we shall come. And the saying pleased me well, and I took twelve men," etc. But the more full account in Num. 13 ascribes the movement to the Lord himself: "The Lord spake unto Moses, saying, Send thou men that they may search the land of Canaan" (vs. 1, 2). This is probably the more exact account. The people however heartily concurred.——Very wisely the explorers designated were thoroughly representative men, "heads of the children of Israel," "every one a ruler among them." Thus selected, they would fairly represent the moral tone of the people on the great point of faith or unbelief; and moreover were men reliable as judges of the country and of the people of Canaan.—— The points which they were to investigate and report were well defined: "To see the land, what it is; whether good or bad; the people, whether strong or weak, few or many; what cities they dwell in; whether in tents or strongholds; and whether the land be fat or lean; and also" (a point of interest to men so long on the desert) "whether there be wood therein or not."
——In a tour of forty days they traversed Canaan to the very northern border and seem so far to have done their work well. It being the time of first ripe grapes, they brought a magnificent specimen cluster from Eshcol, so large as to be borne by two men.——Their report made two strongly marked points—that the land was truly "flowing with milk and honey"—all in this respect that they could desire; but on the other hand, ten of their number concurred in saying that the people were strong; their cities walled and very great, and some of their warriors, men of Anak, giants of stature, in whose sight they were only as grasshoppers. Their conclusion was—"We be not able to go up against that people, for they are stronger than we" (Num. 13: 31).
——Two of the spies—Caleb representing Judah and Joshua of Ephraim—brought in a minority report, differing totally in the one only vital point, viz. whether Israel were able to drive out the Canaanites and take possession of the land. Or, more fundamentally, they based their conviction upon *their faith in God;* while the men of the majority report seem to have made not

the least account of God's help in the case. Caleb and Joshua said—"The land is exceedingly good; and if the Lord delight in us, then he will bring us into this land and give it to us; only rebel not ye against the Lord, neither fear ye the people of the land, for they are bread for us; their defense is departed from them, and the Lord is with us; fear them not."——Sad to say, these considerations fell powerless upon the hearts of the ten unbelieving spies, and also upon the mass of the people. "All the people murmured against Moses and Aaron; the whole congregation said unto them: Would God that we had died in the land of Egypt, or would God we had died in this wilderness"!——They even proposed to "make themselves a captain and return into Egypt"!——It was inevitable that the Lord should feel himself dishonored and even insulted. "How long," said he, "will this people provoke me? How long will it be ere they believe me for all the signs which I have showed among them"? And again, referring to what was most disheartening and cruel of all: "Those men who have seen my glory and my miracles which I did in Egypt and in the wilderness, and have tempted me now these ten times, and have not obeyed my voice—they shall not see the land which I sware unto their fathers to give them." Ah, they had seen all the plagues on Egypt; they had seen Pharaoh's proud host buried in the Red Sea; they had seen Amalek smitten before Israel while the hands of prayer were upstayed before the Lord—and must all this go for nothing? God had promised to give them Canaan; could they not trust him? They had bound themselves by most solemn covenant to follow him as their king; and shall they go back upon this great covenant; make another captain; and return to their old bondage in Egypt? Alas, for such treachery! Alas, that they will not believe in God; that they have no faith in his power to save; and apparently no faith in his readiness to attempt it!

Here again (as after the sin with the golden calf) the Lord proposes to Moses to smite this whole people with pestilence, and then make of his posterity a nation greater and mightier than they (Num. 14: 12). But in this case as in that, Moses listens not a moment to the proposal which might seem flattering to his ambition if he had any; and turns his plea wholly to the point of God's glory before the nations:—What will they say of him if he abandons this whole people as if in despair?——It was well understood that he had promised to bring them into Canaan; what will they say if he fails to do it? How will it bear upon the name and the fame of Almighty God if the nations are left to say—" Because the Lord *was not able* to bring this people into the land which he sware unto them, therefore he hath slain them in the wilderness."——To this, Moses adds an appeal to that blessed *name* which the Lord had given him on the former occasion:—Let the power of my Lord be great according as thou hast spoken, saying: "The Lord is long-suffering and of great mercy, forgiving iniquity and transgression. O pardon thou the iniquity of this people according unto the greatness of thy mercy and as thou hast forgiven this people from Egypt until now."——To this prayer the Lord promptly answers: "I have pardoned according to thy word; but as truly as I live, all the earth shall be filled with the glory of the Lord"—(*i. e.* with the glory of his righteous justice); for of all those men who have seen my glory and my miracles in Egypt and in the wilderness, and yet have not believed in me at all, but have utterly dishonored my name, not one shall enter into the land of promise. March them back into this great and dreary wilderness; let them wander there forty years—as many years as they have spent days in searching out the land of Canaan. So let their judgment perpetually remind them of their sin, till all that unbelieving generation, old enough to bear moral responsibility for this unbelief, have fallen in the wilderness.——Then their children who, they said, would fall before the sword of the Canaanites, shall go into the land, drive out those men of Canaan, and possess the goodly land of promise.

The ten unbelieving spies perish at once by the plague before the wrath of God. The people were sorely distressed by this decision. Some of them rushed at once to the mad extreme of marching unbidden against the Canaanites—only to be smitten before them.

Thus issued this sad case of strange, cruel unbelief. The conquest of Canaan was postponed almost forty years; the generation of twenty years and over when they came out from Egypt were doomed to fruitless wandering and an early death in the wilderness; and that nation and the world had one more lesson on the wisdom of believing God, and on the infinite folly as well as guilt of refusing to believe and trust the Lord.——Moses (in Deut. 1: 19–46) gives a somewhat full recapitulation of these scenes. In Ps. 90 he puts in the form of sacred song his meditation and prayer on this sad yet most instructive event.

The Rebellion of Korah and his Company.

During the period of thirty-seven years intervening between the scenes at Kadesh last noted and the return to Kadesh in the last year of the wandering, one event of most signal and solemn moment occurred, viz. the rebellion of Korah and his company, recorded Num. 16, and referred to Num. 26: 9–11. The leaders were Korah of the tribe of Levi, a near relative of Moses, and Dathan, Abiram, and On, of the tribe of Reuben;—the former ambitious of the distinction enjoyed by Moses and Aaron, and doubtless believing himself at least equally capable and worthy; the latter probably restive under the loss of that pre-eminence which was normally conceded to the first-born. Associated with them were two hundred and fifty leading men of the tribes, not otherwise distinctly designated. The movement thus assumed formidable proportions in the outset. They seem to have demanded that Moses and Aaron should retire from office and give place to themselves; or at least that they should resign and open the way for another election by the people.——Moses wisely referred this matter at once to the Lord. Let him say who shall be the Leader of this people, and who shall come near before him as High Priest. Take you, said he, every man his censer and put fire therein, and come before the Lord. Let him pass upon this great question.——Expostulating with Korah, he said, Should it not suffice you that God has given the whole tribe of Levi special responsibilities and honors? Why should ye murmur against Aaron because the Lord hath chosen him to lead in the most holy services?——The Reubenite faction, resisting the summons of Moses, stood off obstinately. With falsehood and insult they arraign Moses upon two grave charges: (a.) that he had brought them out of a land of plenty to kill them in the wilderness; and (b.) had utterly failed to bring them into a land of plenty as he had promised. And now, said they, "wilt thou put out the eyes of these men"? Wilt thou dupe them and lead them on blind-fold to their utter ruin?——These were cutting charges. Moses was indignant. Appealing to God he said, "Respect not thou their offering. I have not taken one ass from them, neither have I hurt one of them."——Again Moses refers the decision of the great question to God. "The glory of the Lord appeared (we read) unto all the congregation." Inasmuch as the pillar of cloud and of fire was always visible to the people, we must suppose that on this occasion these words imply an unusual brilliancy—a blaze of glory.——The first words from the August Presence indicated the divine purpose: "Stand ye aloof from those rebels; separate yourselves from that whole congregation that I may consume them in a moment"! Suddenly Moses and Aaron are on their faces in supplication that God would stay his hand; for they seem to have feared a most sweeping judgment. "Shall one man sin" (said they) "and wilt thou be wroth with all the congregation"? Promptly the Lord replied: Give orders to the people to withdraw from the tents of those leading rebels as they would escape their doom. They did so, leaving only the leaders and their households in their tents, awaiting the result—with what feelings and anticipations we know not. Whether their impudent hardihood failed them and terror seized upon them, or whether they stood boldly or stupidly, awaiting the issue, nothing is said to show.——With words inspired of God, Moses put the great question of God's choice of Leader upon its decision: "If those men die only the common death of mortals, the Lord hath not sent me; but if the Lord create a new creation [Heb.], *i. e.* work a miracle; do something outside the course of nature; if the earth open and swallow up those men alive and all that appertain to them, then ye shall understand that these men have provoked the Lord."——With not one moment's delay, as the last word fell from his lips, the earth opened her mouth beneath their feet and they went down into that awful grave, and the earth closed over them! They perished from among the congregation. Their place was thenceforth vacant forever!——

Significantly it is added "all Israel that were round about them fled at the cry of them"—those shrieks of awful horror as they went down thrilled the whole people with terror and they fled from the scene; for they said, "Lest the earth swallow up *us* also."

It seems almost incredible that after such a scene of holy judgment on guilty rebels and of such consternation upon the whole people, we read that on the morrow all the congregation murmured against Moses and Aaron, saying, "Ye have killed the people of the Lord." This, although their prayer had saved the masses of the people (v. 22); this, although the hand of God only and of no mortal man had wrought their destruction; this, although they had seen the whole transaction and fled in horror lest God swallow them up also!——It should not surprise us that the wrath of the Lord broke forth against them and the plague began. Moses cried to Aaron to take a censer with incense (the symbol of prayer) and run in among the people, waving his censer between the living and the dead. Only so was the plague stayed. Yet fourteen thousand seven hundred fell in that fearful judgment.——We are simply amazed at the perverseness and folly of many of that Hebrew people. "How often" and with what strange infatuation "did they provoke their God in the wilderness and grieve him in the desert"! (Ps. 78: 40.)

The next chapter (Num. 17) records a special test to show which of the twelve tribes the Lord had chosen for the priesthood. Each tribe brought forward its several rod; Aaron's among them for the tribe of Levi. All were laid up before the Lord for one night only. In the morning Aaron's rod had blossomed and was bearing fruit; all the others were still dry sticks! Aaron's was thenceforth laid up in the most holy place—a perpetual memorial of God's choice of Aaron and his family for the priesthood.

If it be asked *by what means* were Korah and his company destroyed? Were the common agencies of earthquake employed in this case? Or was the effect produced by the divine fiat with no intervening force of imprisoned steam or explosive gases? All I can reply is that the record says nothing on this point whatever. The agencies common in earthquakes have produced similar results often in the world's history. If the Lord saw fit he could have brought those agencies into action at precisely that moment; or he might have produced the result miraculously with no intervening physical agency. It would be the Lord's hand in either case. The question which method God employed in this case is of no practical consequence whatever, and can never be decided save by a special revelation from himself.

The events of history beginning with Num. 20 fall within the last of the forty years of wandering. This date is obtained indirectly from the death of Aaron which is recorded at the close of this chapter (vs. 22-29) and was connected with its events. It is definitely dated (Num. 33: 38) in the fortieth year from Egypt on the first day of the fifth month.

Of the murmuring for water during this sojourn in Kadesh and the sad rebuke of the Lord upon Moses, I have spoken in connection with the scenes at Rephidim (Ex. 17: 1-7).

The Fiery Serpents and the Brazen One.

On the journey from Mt. Hor, compassing the land of Edom, the people became "much discouraged because of the way." Travelers represent this route as abounding unusually in the discomforts of the desert. So Israel, weary, foot-sore, often suffering for water, not satisfied with their manna—murmured both against Moses and against God. The Lord sent fiery serpents among them: many were bitten and died. *Burning* serpents, the original calls them, with reference to the virulent poison of their bite and the fiery inflammation which ensued. When Moses cried to the Lord for help, he was told to make a brazen serpent and suspend it high upon a pole, with the promise that any man, bitten of a serpent and looking up to this brazen one, should live. Thus relief required as its condition this act of obedience and of faith toward God.

The chief interest in this scene turns upon its acknowledged and undeniable character as a type of Christ. The type (resemblance) includes two distinct points: the *lifting up;* and the *looking* with its results of salvation. The evangelist John (3: 14, 15) has them both: "As Moses *lifted up* the serpent in the wilderness, even so must the Son of man be *lifted up;* that whosoever believeth in him should not perish, but have eternal life." In two several cases Jesus spake of himself as being "*lifted up*," with manifest reference to this historic scene in the wilderness. "When ye have *lifted up* the Son of man, then shall ye know that I am he" (John 8: 28). "And I, if I be *lifted up* from the earth will draw all men unto me." That his readers might not miss his meaning, the Evangelist explains: "This he said, signifying what death he should die" (Jn. 12: 32). Hence it is plain that Christ recognized the brazen serpent as a special type of himself to the point of the manner of his death.——It is not less so in the second point—*looking,* the condition of living. Nothing can better represent the simple act of faith than looking. In looking, there is a turning of the mind toward the object; and there is some degree of expectation. There *may be* inexpressible longings. We must assume such longings in the case of the bitten, suffering, dying Israelite in the desert.——So let sinners, stung with a terrible consciousness of guilt, borne down with a sense of want and woe and ruin, look with longing heart to the uplifted Lamb of God; yea to Jesus considered as lifted up in the agonies of a vicarious death—dying for us that we might live. There is life in such looking!

Balak and Balaam.

In Num. 22-24 stands a very unique history. The two prominent characters are Balak, king of Moab, and Balaam, a renowned diviner, magician from the East. ——Moab, descended genealogically from Lot, was not among the doomed nations of Canaan, and had nothing to fear from the Israelites, provided only that she neither blocked their march nor seduced them into idol-worship. But Moab, both people and king, were "sore afraid of Israel because they were many," and because they had smitten Sihon of the Amorites and Og of Bashan, and had taken possession of their respective countries. The near proximity of such a host, marching and encamping with military precision, fed as no other people in that wilderness were ever fed; invincible in arms when their God was with them, and bearing the prestige of victory over Pharaoh and Amalek and the Amorites, was very naturally the occasion of no small alarm. Balak had seen and heard enough to convince him that the unseen power of some God was in these strange facts of their history. Unfortunately he did not know enough of the true God—the real God of Israel—to see that he could be none other than the One Infinite God, and therefore that resistance against him and his people was necessarily and utterly vain. His theology was doubtless of the type common among all the nations of antiquity, not blessed with the light of revelation, viz. polytheism—gods in unknown numbers; each nation having its own, one or many—so that the contest for mastery between hostile nations was supposed to turn on the question which had the mightiest gods for their help.——With this theology, Balak's policy was soon determined upon, viz. to send for the most renowned diviner of the ancient East, and match the prestige of his divination and of his curse against the blessings which the God of Israel was conferring upon his people. He understood well that the strength of Israel lay in the strength of her God. There was miracle there—superhuman aid coming in from a higher Power; and he had no idea of any thing which he could bring into the field against this save the most potent divination and magic. So he sent for Balaam to come and curse Israel.

Concerning Balaam; his residence, his previous and subsequent history, and his personal character, we have (outside of Num. 22-24) three references in the Old Testament and the same number in the New; viz. Num. 31: 8, and Deut. 23: 4, and Josh. 13: 22 :—2 Pet. 2: 15, 16, and Jude 11, and Rev. 2: 14. [The reference to both Balak and Balaam in Micah 6: 5 adds nothing to their history.] These passages locate Balaam among the Midianites (Num. 31: 8); in Pethor (Num. 22: 5); in Aram (Num. 23: 7); and in Mesopotamia (Deut. 23: 4). The Old Testament passages describe him as a soothsayer, practicing divination for reward. The New Testament writers go to the bottom of his character and represent him as "loving the wages of unrighteousness; rebuked for his iniquity, the dumb ass, speaking with man's voice forbade the madness of the prophet" (2 Pet. 2: 15, 16). They speak of "going after the error of Balaam for reward" (Jude 11), and of him as one who "taught Balak to cast a stumbling-block before the children of Israel, to eat things sacrificed to idols, and to commit fornication" (Rev. 2: 14).——Further, we are told (Num. 31: 8 and Josh. 13: 22) that he was found among the Midianites—enemies of God's people, and slain with the sword.

The narrative by Moses (Num. 22–24) informs us very minutely how Balak sent and brought Balaam to curse Israel, but failed in every endeavor; how he plied him with munificent rewards and royal honors, but God would not let Balaam curse Israel, much as he might have wished to do so; how Balak took his man to one mountain summit and another and another to show him this strange people, superstitiously hoping to break the spell of his purpose to bless; but all in vain.

The history taken in whole shows that Balaam was a godless man; that he exceedingly desired to please Balak and get his money, but that God would not let him. His is perhaps a solitary case to show that the Lord can (when he pleases) give some really prophetic visions to an ungodly man, and yet hold him so firmly under control that no harm can come of a wicked prophet.

Some points in this case deserve special examination. ——In the passage (Num. 22: 9–35) it appears that God positively forbade Balaam's going at all, yet that the second embassy, greater in number and of nobler rank and offering richer pay (v. 15) touched Balaam in his most sensitive point and made him long to go. So he told the men to tarry and he would see if he could get permission. According to the record (v. 20) the Lord said to him that night: "If the men come to call thee, rise up and go with them"; yet the real meaning must be—If you *will* go, and if my prohibition avails nothing, go; but do when there according to my word. Balaam was glad to go; but "God's anger was kindled because he went" (v. 22)—a fact which shows very clearly what sort of permission God had given him. It can not well be doubted that Balaam knew he was going, contrary to the real mind of the Lord; for when did the Lord ever give a real permission, and then kindle into anger because his permission was accepted? Or when did he ever leave an honest inquirer after the way of duty to follow his supposed permission and then take such offense as in this case at what was in its purpose true obedience?——Yet while God always deals honestly with the honest inquirer after his will, he may sometimes, both in word and in providence, let men who love their own will better than his take their course and bear their own responsibilities. Such I take to have been the Lord's policy in this case.

The record sets forth that God used the ass on which Balaam rode to "rebuke with man's voice the madness of the prophet." The ass saw what Balaam's dull eye saw not—the angel of the Lord with drawn sword, heading him in his way—a fact strikingly suggestive of his dull vision in regard to comprehending the spirit of that apparent permission which the Lord gave him to go. Why did he not see that he was led on, not by God's will, but by his own cupidity, his own intense and over-mastering covetousness? Alas for him; the eye of his ass could see what his cultured intellect could not discern—that God was squarely against him. It was moreover fully the Lord's purpose, if Balaam *would* go, to hold him back from Balak's influence and compel him to bless Israel. This renewed, special charge on this point seems to have been one object in this remarkable meeting of the angel, Balaam and his ass.

Does any one ask—*How* could an ass speak with man's voice? Were real words uttered, words which any other ears within hearing could have heard as well as Balaam's? Or was it simply a miraculous sensation upon his ear, having no cause whatever in the mouth of the ass?——I answer: It is of small avail to push such inquiries. We can say wisely but two things:—(a.) That God could work a miracle as easily in one of these ways as in the other:—and (b.) Therefore the method which the description most naturally suggests is the most probable; viz. that the ass spake audible words, and Balaam heard them as men are wont to hear words audibly spoken.

The points of real prophecy in Balaam's visions should be noticed.

Observe that in each case, before Balaam inquired of God he directed Balak to prepare seven altars and to offer upon each one bullock and one ram. The object in this seems to have been to propitiate the Lord and secure his favorable consideration. It is remarkable that Balaam, coming from the region of the Euphrates, should have these ideas as to the sacrifice of clean animals. The fact seems to show that the idea of animal sacrifices was revealed to the race in its infancy and that it prevailed extensively over the Eastern world.

The offerings having been made, Balaam retired to "an high place" (23: 3) as our version puts it, but really to a hill of bare, naked summit to await the Lord's presence and word there. [Such a summit was chosen for its range of view]. The Lord came and gave him his word for Balak, put thus: "Balak, the king of Moab, hath brought me from Aram, out of the mountains of the East, saying: 'Come, curse me, Jacob; come, defy [in the sense only of curse, maledict] Israel. How shall I curse whom God hath not cursed? Or how shall I defy whom God hath not defied"? [How can I gainsay the Almighty; how put my word against his? Balak asks this of me: I have no power to do it].
——"From the top of the rocks I see him, and from the hills I behold him: lo! the people shall dwell alone and shall not be reckoned among the nations."——
From his naked mountain top Balaam saw their encampment spread out before him; there they were, a peculiar, secluded people, having neither political, social, or religious connection with any other nation under heaven. In this most salient feature of their case Balaam saw a symbol of their whole future history—dwelling alone, a scattered people, never reckoned as being of or like any other nation of the earth.
——Their great numbers also were prophetic of their prosperous future: "Who can count the dust of Jacob, and the number of the fourth part of Israel"?—the reference to a "fourth part" coming of the fact that their encampment was in four parts, three tribes to each.——
His closing words are weighty: "Let me die the death of the righteous, and let my last end be like his."——
In interpreting these words I can by no means assent to the view of many commentators (largely German) who suppose Balaam had no ideas of a happy future life, it being as they maintain far too early in the progress of religious thought for any such ideas. They therefore restrict his meaning to a happy earthly life,

prosperous even to its natural end in death.——I have no faith in such interpretations. They do not come by any fair construction from the text. What Balaam said was: "Let my soul die the death of the righteous, and let my after destiny be like his." After destiny—the afterpart of my existence, is the legitimate sense of the word here used.——Besides, to pray that I may die of the same disease, at the same age, amid the same surroundings, as the righteous, is very tame, is a very insignificant blessing at best, and no sensible man could put his soul very earnestly into such a prayer. I see no reason why we should emasculate the prayer even of a Balaam in this style. Let us rather say that he prayed like one "whose eyes were open; who had heard the words of God and knew the knowledge of the most High and saw the vision of the Almighty" (24: 15, 16) as he himself said.——As to toning down the sense of his words because their Christian construction would be so far in advance of the age, I can not accept the assumed fact that they were in advance of the age. I can not believe that Enoch, "walking with God" and translated to heaven knew nothing of heaven until he found himself there; or that Noah whose faith and whose preaching of righteousness breasted the wickedness of that whole generation had no thoughts as to the blessed world to come; nor that Abraham's faith was limited to the hills and to the corn and wine of Canaan and had never an outlook of longing desire and assured hope of a "better country even an heavenly one" (Heb. 11: 16); nor that Moses, "esteeming reproach for Christ greater riches than the treasures of Egypt," had no "*respect to* the [future] recompense of reward." The writer to the Hebrews reasons far better than the Neological critics as to the faith and the hopes of those glorious patriarchs. I find my sense of fitness and my convictions of truth far better met in his reasoning than in their speculations.

Let it be noted that Balaam spake as one versed in moral distinctions. He understood that the blessed future life falls to the lot, not of the wicked but of the righteous. When a man comes so near to God as he seems to have done in these hours, this distinction must be seen and felt.——That this most appropriate prayer should have proved in his case utterly unavailing is a sad and mournful fact to which we must give some attention in its place.

Balak was by no means pleased with Balaam's "parable." Indeed he retorts sharply: "What hast thou done to me? I sent for thee and was to pay thee to curse that people, and now thou hast blessed them altogether"—with blessings and nothing else.——But Balak proposes to try again. Perhaps if the great soothsayer shall see them from the top of Pisgah, he may get a different view and may utter the much desired imprecation upon them. The same process is gone through, of burnt-offerings and of withdrawing for a private interview with God; after which Balak eagerly inquires: "What has the Lord spoken" now? Has he changed his mind? Has he given you leave to curse the Hebrew people?——The answer is pertinent and very decided, but not any more to his mind than the former:—"God is not a man that he should lie, nor the son of man that he should repent. Hath he said, and shall he not do it? or hath he spoken, and shall he not make it good? Behold, I have received commandment to bless; and he hath blessed, and I can not reverse it. He hath not beheld iniquity in Jacob, neither hath he seen perverseness in Israel; the Lord his God *is* with him, and the shout of a king *is* among them. God brought them out of Egypt; he has as it were the strength of a unicorn. Surely *there* is no enchantment against Jacob, neither is *there* any divination against Israel; according to this time it shall be said of Jacob and of Israel, What hath God wrought? Behold, the people shall rise up as a great lion, and lift up himself as a young lion; he shall not lie down until he eat *of* the prey, and drink the blood of the slain" (Num. 23: 19–24).

At this point of time Israel was on the threshold of Canaan. Sihon and Og had fallen. The spirit of a pure and vigorous faith in God was never more thoroughly national than in this generation. As between Moab and Israel, the contrast was never greater. God's people as seen by his prophetic eye were on the eve of sublime victories. No enchantment or divination could have force against them. That was the era in their history when it might fitly become a standing exclamation:—"What hath God wrought"?

Worse and worse for Balak. Curiously his next effort is to shut Balaam's mouth altogether. Since he can not get from him curses against Israel, he begs him to hold still and not bless them. "Neither curse them at all, nor bless them at all."——Balaam replied: "Did I not say to thee, All that the Lord speaketh, that I must do"?——But Balak has not yet lost all hope. Perhaps it was of the Lord rather than of his hope however that he is in for another trial—this time "on the top of Peor that looketh toward Jeshimon." Great faith he must have had in the prestige of new points of vision—of other mountain tops.——The altars are set up; the bullocks and rams are offered as before. But in one respect the course of events changes. "When Balaam saw that it pleased the Lord to bless Israel, he went not as at other times to seek for enchantments, but set his face toward the wilderness;"—which seems to imply that on the two former occasions he had pursued his usual methods of divination to obtain messages from the spirit-world, but now changed his course, and simply turned his face toward the wilderness where the camp of Israel lay in full view before him. Now we read, not that the Lord "met him" and "put a word into his mouth" (Num. 23: 4, 5, 16), but that "the Spirit of God came upon him," giving him prophetic visions in manner quite different from the preceding. His spiritual eye was now opened; what his natural eye had just seen as he set his face toward the wilderness (the camp of Israel), led his thought in these spiritual visions of Israel's glorious future, and his imagery naturally came from the scenes still fresh in his mind. "How goodly are thy tents, O Jacob, and thy tabernacles, O Israel"! Exalted be thy kingdom; glorious thy king! His own great God brought him up from Egypt; befriends him still; will give him assured victory over all enemies in his own time! Blessed be all who bless thee; cursed be all who curse thee!

Balak is terribly enraged and bids Balaam flee and begone. Balaam with apparent mildness and undisturbed equanimity proposes to give Balak some further prophetic views of what Israel should do to Moab in the coming days. Again "he takes up his parable:" "I shall see him, but not now; I shall behold him, but not nigh: there shall come a star out of Jacob and a scepter shall rise out of Israel, and shall smite the corners of Moab, and destroy all the children of Sheth" (v. 17).

Who is "the star" and "the scepter" of this prophecy?——The leading thought of the passage (vs. 17-19) and indeed of the entire prophecy to the end of verse 24 is *the supremacy of Israel*, and the fall of all powers hostile to Israel and to Israel's God. The key-note is in the words: "*Out of Jacob shall come he that shall have dominion.*" The prophetic future (as usual) is built upon the visible present, or perhaps more precisely, springs out of it—is suggested by it, and takes its phraseology and costume from it. The Lord forces the truth upon Balaam's soul that this Israel whom he was called out from his Eastern home to curse could not be cursed to any purpose by any earthly divination or power because they were God's own people, and it was his fixed purpose to bless them. To impress this great truth the more deeply, the Lord reveals to him in prophetic vision that this present fact is not transient but destined to reach into the remote future; that it is indeed only a *beginning* of their supremacy—a pledge of a far more sovereign ascendency, to be manifested in future ages.——With this view of the spirit of the prophecy, we must find here, not merely David in whom as the first conqueror of Moab and of Edom (2 Sam. 8: 2, 12, 14) these words receive the first palpable installment of their meaning; but yet more surely that greater Son of David whose scepter is to rule the nations with a rod of iron.

That this broad construction is the true one will appear yet more fully when we compare the use of the word "scepter" here with Jacob's use of it (Gen. 49: 10); the "star" here with the "star in the East" (Matt. 2: 1) seen by other wise men [magicians] from Balaam's own country; and not least, the fact that Edom and Seir became in the usage of later prophets symbolic names for the declared and malign enemies of Christ's kingdom (See Isa. 34).——"He shall smite the corners;" better the two sides of Moab, *i. e.* Moab from side to side, through and through, laying waste her whole country.——The word "Sheth" ("all the children of *Sheth*") seems to be used as a common, not a proper noun, the sense being—all the sons of tumult—

all the men of war and strife. Her war-power he shall utterly break down. Edom and Seir—two names for one and the same kingdom, often affiliated with Moab, shall become the possession of their enemies and Israel shall outmaster them through her valor, and yet more through the might of her God—first fulfilled by David (2 Sam. 8: 14).

Of Amalek he said: Amalek was first among the nations to assail Israel (Ex. 17: 8–16); her end shall be utter annihilation. (See the notice of Amalek on Ex. 17).

Verses 21, 22, spoken of the Kenites, of whom Jethro and Hobab were the earliest representatives, are not without difficulties, yet their history places them in marked contrast with Amalek—friends, not enemies of Israel; and therefore suggests—not to say demands, a contrasted prophetic destiny. Placing themselves on the side of Israel, their dwelling-place was strong; their nest in the rocks. Keil translates the passage—"Durable is thy dwelling-place, and thy nest laid upon the rock; for should Kain [the Kenite] be destroyed until Asshur shall carry thee captive"?—the question in his view having the force of a negative: The Kenite *shall not* be destroyed, etc. But it is not quite clear that the original words will bear this construction. It is however certain that the prophecy assures the Kenites, as friends of Israel, of long-continued prosperity.

Again Balaam "takes up his parable," forcibly impressed with the fearful judgments God would send upon the enemies of Israel: "Who shall endure the day of such judgments on the guilty foes of God? Great powers from the West [ships of Chittim] shall sweep over the ancient Eastern empires and level them with the dust; and God will stand before the nations far down the ages as one mighty to protect his people and to overwhelm their enemies."

Balaam's oracles are expressed in the purest style of Hebrew poetry—such as few can read without a sense of its beauty and majesty. If read with a present sense of the moral status of this prince of diviners—of the conflict in his soul between the love of riches and honor on the one hand and some regard to the high behests of the Almighty on the other, we can not well suppress a feeling of sadness that one so gifted by nature and so favored of God with prophetic revelations, should, despite of all, have yet succumbed to the dominion of the baser impulses of his soul. His final record is dark and distressing. "He taught Balak to cast a stumbling-block before Israel" and drew them into idolatry and fornication (Rev. 2: 14 and Num. 25). He cast in his lot with the Midianites, and (apparently) counseled them into the same infernal policy. Hence when the Lord in self-defense hurled down the sword of his people upon Midian and five of her kings fell, Balaam the son of Beor also was slain (Num. 31: 1–8). Thus he who so plaintively yet so pertinently prayed—"Let me die the death of the righteous," met the death of the wicked. He had seen reason enough for the prayer: "Let my last end be like his"; and yet he "died as the fool dieth"—in arms against Almighty God. While in imagination and intellect he might have taken rank with the noblest of earth's sons, yet through the baseness of his impulses and the greed of a covetous soul, he chose his rank among the meanest and utterly missed the immortality which seemed at one moment so nearly in his grasp! For awhile God held him to the utterance of lofty thought, and apparently of pure and resolute purpose. But no sooner was the Lord's restraining hand lifted off than Balaam slumped into the mire of his selfish, covetous nature and went fast "to his own place"!

The question has been raised (more curious than useful) how Moses and the archives of Israel came into possession of these prophecies of Balaam. In answer it has been suggested that, failing to get the pay he expected from Balak, Balaam went to Moses and laid before him the contents of these chapters (Num. 22–24) with the hope of ample reward (which his covetous heart was loth to forego); but failing here also, left in disgust; threw himself into the arms of Moab and Midian; retaliated with selfish malignity upon Israel and Israel's God, and of course hurried himself swiftly to his final doom.——Let his example never cease to be a warning!

CHAPTER XXI.

THE LAST FOUR BOOKS OF THE PENTATEUCH: THEIR METHOD OF ARRANGEMENT AND SUBJECT-MATTER.

THE manner in which the last four of the five books of Moses are made up is peculiar and should have a moment's special attention. Their striking peculiarity is the blending of matters pertaining to the religious system, to the civil code, and to the national history with no well defined order or method—the historic facts taking their place probably as they occurred and came before the writer, and the other topics being arranged quite miscellaneously. This method obviously indicates that the writer was not an author by profession—a mere writer and nothing else; but one who was pressed with the cares and burdens of public office; bearing the chief responsibilities for the constitution of the religious system with its elaborate ritual observances; for the civil code—its exact record and its judicial administration; and for the general government of the people—quelling disturbances; answering their complaints; supplying their wants; guiding their desert march, and directing their wars in defense against assailants. These books answer so perfectly to the circumstances of Moses as to leave no rational doubt that he was their author. Incidentally and most inadvertently they write out his daily history, showing us how he was occupied during those years when the events he narrates were transpiring. For the most part the record in these four books pertains to the first two years after Moses entered upon his great mission and the last two years before his death. There was a long interval between these periods of which nothing special is said.

Passing the first twenty chapters of Exodus which are history and follow the natural order of the events; and passing also the thrilling and solemn scenes of Sinai—the great work of Moses was to receive and record the statutes of the civil code, and the directions respecting their religious system, including the construction of the tabernacle; the services of the priests and Levites; the sacred festivals, and the whole ritual of worship. We are told how the long sessions of Moses with the Lord on the Mount were interrupted (Ex. 32–34) by the sin of the people in the matter of the golden calf; after which the record of the tabernacle—its construction, etc., is resumed and continued to the close of Exodus.

Leviticus, takes its name from Levi whose tribe furnished the line of priests and the servants for all the religious ritual. The first nine chapters record ritual observances and sacrifices; then the death of Nadab and Abihu, occurring, is recorded in its chronological place (chap. 10); after which the author resumes his main subject—things clean and unclean; purifications; the case of leprosy, etc. In connection with the consecration of the High Priest and his duties, we have (chap. 16) the very interesting description of the great day of atonement. Statutes of a civil character are interspersed with those which are religious (chap. 19, and 20, and 24); the great feasts are described (chap. 23); the Sabbatic year and the Jubilee (chap. 25); a chapter of moral warnings and admonitions (26); closing with one on special vows and consecrations (27).

The book of Numbers is named from the theme of its first two chapters—the census of the tribes. Another census was made during the last year of their wandering, viz. on the plains of Moab (chap. 26). It has also an *itinerary* of the journeyings of the people during their entire wilderness life (33). Several chapters are devoted to the religious ritual (none to the civil code); and several (more than in Leviticus) to historic events; *e. g.* the murmuring and the consequent plague at Taberah and Kibroth-hattaavah (chap. 11); the envy and sedition of Miriam (chap. 12); the case of the spies and the doom of the unbelieving (13 and 14); Korah and his doom (16). Then passing over to the last year of the wandering, we have the scenes at Kadesh—the murmuring for water and the sin of Moses for which God forbade his entering Canaan (20); a conflict of arms with Arad the Canaanite; the fiery serpents; the overthrow of Sihon and Og (21); Balaam and his prophecies

(22–24); and other matters of miscellaneous character (25–36).

Deuteronomy—the name meaning the second law, i. e. the law repeated—takes this name from the fact that the book repeats portions of the civil code and also of the religious system. It also gives a resume (a brief summary) of the leading historical events of the Exodus, of Sinai, of the golden calf, and of the murmurings of the fathers in the early years of their wanderings. This book was manifestly written within the last one or two years of Moses' life, when the scenes of the desert wandering were drawing to a close. Moses stood before the people, almost the only old man of the nation at the age of one hundred and twenty years, while all the rest (Caleb and Joshua excepted) were under twenty when they came out of Egypt, and not exceeding sixty at the writing of this book. "The fathers—where were they"! Fallen in death; smitten with the swift judgments of the Almighty for their murmurings or cut off in middle life during their wanderings, to which they were doomed for their unbelief upon the report of the spies. The nation, as they stood before Moses, were truly his children. How had he borne them on his parental heart for forty years; given them line upon line of statute and of ritual; shaping their civil life and their religious life; watching with the interest of a patriarch every development of their character; devoted with the deepest love of his heart to their moral culture.—— Such was Moses and such were the people whom he addressed on the plains of Moab, with the words of sublime moral power, recorded in this book.

It is not my purpose to repeat the points of this history from Egypt and Sinai onward to that hour, which form the staple of Deut. 1–11. Let it suffice to say that Moses brings them forward here with more or less expansion of the details for the sole purpose of *enforcing their moral application.* He makes those historic facts the text for this most impressive sermon—the basis of a series of exhortations to holy living which well up from the depths of his parental, loving heart, and testify how deeply he sympathized with God and with the true interests of his covenant people. Most solemnly does he exhort them against the great sin of their times—

idolatry; and implore them to remember the God of their fathers; the Giver of all their mercies; the God of their national salvation. As a specimen of the historic sermon, nothing can be more admirable, complete, and effective. Coming from such a patriarch, from one who had done and suffered so much for his countrymen; who had been admitted so freely into the deep counsels and sympathies of Israel's God; who had been honored of God not only as the great law-giver, but also as the Savior and Deliverer of his nation—these words ought to have been listened to with profoundest attention. Let us hope they were truly wrought into the very souls of this generation. No one can read them attentively at this day without a quickened sense of the solemn relations which God establishes between himself and his covenant people in every age of time.

Of the statutes, mostly civil, in small part religious, which chiefly fill chap. 12–26, there is little occasion for special remark here. They have chiefly come under consideration in my treatment of the civil code of Israel. Some points are much more fully expanded here than in the previous books, *e. g.* the year of release (chap. 15: 1–11), the case of female captives (21: 10–14). There is some new matter; *e. g.* the war-law (20); the expiation for murder by unknown hands (21: 1–9); the case of partiality toward sons (21: 15–17) and to mention no more, the form of announcement and consecration with which the Hebrew worshiper was to bring before the Lord the first-fruits of his land, and also his tithes of the third year (chap. 26). These forms are instructive as giving us a just idea of the solemnities of Hebrew worship. Let us think of the Israelite coming up to Shiloh or to Jerusalem, say from the mountains of Ephraim or the pasture lands of Gilead, after the conquest and possession of Canaan, in obedience to the law here recorded, thus:

"That thou shalt take of the first of all the fruit of the earth, which thou shalt bring of thy land that the LORD thy God giveth thee, and shalt put *it* in a basket, and shall go unto the place which the LORD thy God shall choose to place his name there. And thou shalt go unto the priest that shall be in those days, and say unto him, I profess this day unto the LORD thy God, that I am come unto the country which the LORD sware unto our fathers for to give us. And the priest shall take the basket out of thine hand, and set it down before the altar of the LORD thy God. And thou shalt speak and say before the LORD thy God, A Syrian* ready to perish *was* my father; and he went down into Egypt, and sojourned there with a few, and became there a nation, great, mighty, and populous: and the Egyptians evil-entreated us, and afflicted us, and laid upon us hard bondage: and when we cried unto the LORD God of our fathers, the LORD heard our voice, and looked on our affliction, and our labor, and our oppression: and the LORD brought us forth out of Egypt with a mighty hand, and with an out-stretched arm, and with great terribleness, and with signs, and with wonders: and he hath brought us into this place, and hath given us this land, even a land that floweth with milk and honey. And now, behold, I have brought the first-fruits of the land, which thou, O LORD, hast given me. And thou shalt set it before the LORD thy God, and worship before the LORD thy God: and thou shalt rejoice in every good *thing* which the LORD thy God hath given unto thee, and unto thine house, thou, and the Levite, and the stranger that *is* among you" (vs. 2–11).

This offering, put so impressively upon its great historic grounds—the preservations and mercies with which God had crowned their nation in fulfilling the promises made to the national fathers, became no unmeaning service. All is instinct with life. Those children of the old patriarchs reposing under their vine and fig-tree in the land flowing with milk and honey had a wonderful history, and God meant to have their ritual of worship link itself continually with that history and take quickening impulses from those impressive associations.

Not less pertinent and impressive is the form of announcement and protestation for the service of "tithing the tithes of their increase the third year"—on this wise:

"When thou hast made an end of tithing all the tithes of thine increase the third year, which *is* the year of tithing, and hast given *it* unto the Levite, the stranger, the fatherless, and the widow, that they may eat within thy gates, and be filled; then thou shalt say before the Lord thy God, I have brought away the hallowed things out of *mine* house, and also have given them unto the Levite, and unto the stranger, to the fatherless, and to the widow, according to all thy commandments which thou hast commanded me: I have not transgressed thy commandments, neither have I forgotten *them:* I have not eaten thereof in my mourning, neither have I taken

---

* Jacob might properly be called a "Syrian" as having lived full twenty years with Laban the Syrian in the great *Aram* of the East. The point of his history where he was "ready to perish" was that of the great famine in Canaan which drove him and his household into Egypt for bread.

away *aught* thereof for *any* unclean *use*, nor given *aught* thereof for the dead: *but* I have hearkened to the voice of the Lord my God, and have done according to all that thou hast commanded me." (Deut. 26: 12–15).

——We must note with pleasure the fraternal and liberal spirit which this service cherished so effectively, remembering kindly the Levite, the stranger, the fatherless, and the widow: the Levite as the religious servant of the nation; the stranger as one but too often neglected and forsaken according to the impulses of man's selfish nature, but one whom God remembered out of the depths of his fatherly care for the neglected and forlorn; the fatherless and the widow as those whose cup of affliction is sore and should commend them to every humane sympathy of the heart. Such treatment of the stranger would naturally bring most of them into the Hebrew communion as proselytes. Where else in all the earth could they expect such kindness and such inducements to build their family home?——This inside view of the institutions and usages of Hebrew thanksgiving worship remind us that God's religion has a social side; forgets not man's social nature, but provides for fraternal sympathy and for the ministrations of kindness and relief to all the children of want and sorrow.

This chapter (26) closes appropriately with the mutual relations between God and his people—they having solemnly declared ["avouched"] the Lord to be their God, and he on his part having in like manner declared them to be his people.

"*The Prophet like unto Moses.*"

From this point we turn back to consider a special prophecy (Deut. 18: 15–22), passed without notice in the rapid and general view taken of those chapters.

Moses is contemplating the state of the people located in Canaan; frequently brought into contact there with diviners, soothsayers, and magicians. The devoted nations of Canaan, he tells them, were rotten with those abominations; and for these sins the Lord drove them out before Israel. Addressing the Israelites, he tells them they shall not have the least occasion to resort to magic arts for superhuman knowledge or help.

THE PROPHET LIKE MOSES.

"The Lord thy God will raise up unto thee a Prophet from the midst of thee, of thy brethren, like unto me; unto him ye shall hearken; according to all that thou desiredst of the Lord thy God in Horeb in the day of the assembly, saying, Let me not hear again the voice of the Lord my God, neither let me see this great fire any more, that I die not. And the Lord said unto me, They have well *spoken that* which they have spoken. I will raise them up a Prophet from among their brethren, like unto thee, and will put my words in his mouth; and he shall speak unto them all that I shall command him. And it shall come to pass, *that* whosoever will not hearken unto my words which he shall speak in my name, I will require *it* of him. But the prophet, which shall presume to speak a word in my name, which I have not commanded him to speak, or that shall speak in the name of other gods, even that prophet shall die" (Deut. 18: 15-20).

Here the great question will be—*Is Jesus the Messiah predicted here?*

The supposable theories are three:

1. That the passage treats of the Hebrew prophets only, and not of the Messiah;
2. Of the Messiah only, and not of the Hebrew prophets;
3. Of the Messiah primarily, yet not excluding the Hebrew prophets.

The reasons for including the Hebrew prophets lie in the connection of thought in which the passage stands; its relation to the magicians of Canaan, and to false prophets. The Lord says to the people through Moses. I do not leave you dependent on magicians; I give you prophets as I have given you Moses; they shall teach you my words from time to time as ye may need words from your God. Moreover, there will be counterfeit prophets coming up; but I will give you tests of their character, take heed to prove and reject them.——This close connection of thought demands some reference to the succession of Hebrew prophets.

On the other hand, the reasons for including the Messiah, and in fact for assuming a primary reference to him, lie in the use of the singular—"a prophet; one great Prophet;" and in his being compared to Moses—"like unto me." Moses stood in many respects quite above the grade of the future Hebrew prophets, having none like him in the obvious sense of this comparison except Jesus.——This construction is greatly strengthened by the authority of the New Testament writers and of Jesus himself, who manifestly found here the real

Messiah. See his words (Jn. 5: 46). "He [Moses] wrote of me." (Compare Luke 24: 44.) Christ's allusion to his words as having authority (Jn. 12: 48, 49) seem to refer to this passage (vs. 18, 19). "He that receiveth not my words hath one that judgeth him; the word that I have spoken, the same shall judge him in the last day. For I have not spoken of myself, but the Father who hath sent me, he gave me a commandment what I should say," etc.——The Lord said unto Moses—"I will put my words into his mouth, and he shall speak unto them all that I shall command him, and whosoever shall not hearken unto my words which he shall speak in my name, I will require it of him."——The current opinion of the men taught by Christ finds in these words a prophecy of him. Philip (Jn. 1: 45) said: "We have found him of whom Moses in the law did write—Jesus of Nazareth." Peter (Acts 3: 22, 23) cites this very passage as having been spoken truly by Moses and as being fulfilled in Christ. So also does Stephen (Acts 7: 37). The Samaritans also (as appears from Jn. 4: 25) found the Messiah here, since they received of the Old Testament scriptures the Pentateuch only. The circumstance that the Christ whom they expected would "*teach them all things*" points certainly to this prophecy rather than to prophecies from Genesis (e.g. 3: 15 or 49: 10).——Finally, the voice from the cloud at Christ's transfiguration—"Hear ye him" (Mat. 17: 5) corresponds to the prominent point of this prophecy—"Unto him shall ye hearken" (v. 15). Moses (present at the transfiguration) must have recognized this identity.——These considerations compel us to find here a primary reference to the Messiah.

The full answer to the question: How can these words cover both the one great Prophet—the Messiah; and also the succession of Hebrew prophets?—will be found in these facts: That the spirit of Jesus was in all the old prophets; that they were his servants, bearing his messages; that he and they were parts of the same great system of divine revelation to men; and that Christ's mission was at once the guaranty and pledge of theirs—their work being linked in with his as the natural consequent and adjunct. Comprehensively spoken of, the one great prophet included all the lesser prophets; the promise of the one embracing and implying the promise of all.

Chapter 27 provides for a special service to be performed after they are located in Canaan. The record of its fulfillment appears in Josh. 8: 30–35. The service was two-fold: first the writing of the law on large plastered stones: second, the proclamation of a series of blessings and also of curses in the presence of the whole people.

As to the first, it does not appear definitely how much was to be written upon these stones. Somewhat more probably than the ten commandments as written originally on two stone tablets; yet probably not all the statutes and judgments which appear in the last four books of Moses. Perhaps the writing included the curses and blessings proclaimed from Mounts Ebal and Gerizim.——The stones were great; the number is not given. The writing was done while the plaster was yet fresh and soft. When hardened it would stand for a considerable time. The purpose was rather present effect than permanent record—a solemn testimony that the people who had now taken possession of Canaan were in covenant with their God to obey this law.

Moses records in full the manner of the rehearsal of blessings and of curses: the blessings from Mt. Gerizim; the curses from Mt. Ebal: six tribes standing on the former and six on the latter: the Levites solemnly and in concert pronouncing the words, and the people in concert responding, Amen. Here may be seen the words of these blessings and curses (Deut. 27: 14–26, and 28: 1–6). The "curses" specify the sins, but the announcement of blessings, assuming in general obedience to God, simply enumerates the various good which the Lord will bestow.——The curses do not enumerate *all* the sins which might be committed nor all upon which curses would fall, but only some heinous crimes as specimens.——This service, performed with due solemnity, must have been impressive. The gathered thousands of Israel overspreading the contiguous mountains; the priests and Levites rehearsing with loud voice these fearful curses, and the people responding to each curse their expressive Amen:—how must every thoughtful heart have been thrilled, and every sensitive conscience recoiled from the sins thus terribly denounced!

Moses proceeds to expatiate through chapter 28 upon the blessings which should reward obedience, but especially upon the curses that must come upon disobedience. It would seem that this catalogue of curses has well-nigh exhausted the possibilities of calamity—personal, social, national—that can befall the children of men. Alas! this catalogue was fearfully prophetic of that avalanche of woes which came upon this same people in the destruction of their city and country, first by the Chaldeans; last and most fearfully, by the Romans. How were the vials of wrath through those agencies of God poured out upon the guilty people for their great iniquities!

In the two next chapters (29 and 30) Moses seems to gather up all the moral forces of the nation's history into one fervent appeal to induce obedience and to press the people to most earnest consecration to the Lord their God. The great mercies of God upon them and their fathers on the one hand coupled with largest promises of good hereafter; on the other hand, the fearful curses impending over disobedience, are spread out to their view: life on the one hand, death on the other, awaiting their choice, pending upon their decision, sure to come according to their free election of the one course or the other:—How are these moral forces made to culminate and press upon the conscience of the whole people!

It is a solemn act for even one so holy as Moses to gather a nation of children about him to say to them his last words and prepare to die (chapter 31). There are some last words to be said; some last things to be done. Fully conscious that his days are numbered and that his end is near he must make the public transfer of his responsibilities to Joshua. The written law upon which he has spent so much thought and labor must be properly committed to the priests the sons of Levi (31: 9–13), and provision made not only for its preservation, but for its public rehearsal in each Sabbatic year at the feast of tabernacles.——Not the least important of these last things was the putting of farewell thoughts into the form of *song* which might be committed to memory, impressed with all the power of music (perhaps), and embalmed in the hearts of the people with the fragrance and impressiveness of its poetic power. There are properly two songs, one of a general character (chapter 32); the other specific, in the form of blessing or benediction upon the several tribes (chapter 33). The latter follows the patriarchal usage which we have seen in the case of Jacob (Gen. 49).——As to the first which is distinctively styled "this song," Moses received from the Lord special directions to write it out and "teach it to the children of Israel" (31: 19); to "put it in their mouths that it might be a witness for God against the children of Israel," and "not be forgotten out of the mouths of their seed" (v. 21). In this chapter (31: 16–30) the Lord not only directed Moses to write out this song but gave him its subject-matter almost entire—the whole current of its thought—the facts in the future history of the people upon which it is built:—in substance, thus:

The Lord said to Moses—Thou shalt sleep with thy fathers; other generations of this people will arise who will depart from me in grievous apostasy—going after the strange gods of the nations; they will break my covenant with them. My anger will kindle against them in that day; I will forsake them and hide my face from them and bring upon them sore judgments—until they say: "Are not these evils upon us because our God is not among us"?——Yet more definitely the Lord gave Moses some of the inducing causes of this apostasy; viz. fullness of bread; the absence of want and trial; coming into a land flowing with milk and honey. Filling themselves and waxing fat, they will become sensual, pleasure-loving, and lost to the fear of God. So they will turn to other gods (v. 20). Hence the occasion for this witnessing song, of solemn forewarning, pregnant with moral forces against apostasy and rich in suggestions of untold value for those apostate generations to whom it would specially apply.

I place this song before the reader with explanations of its dark points and some suggestions as to its line of thought and its moral application.

1. Give ear, O ye heavens, and I will speak; and hear, O earth, the words of my mouth.
2. My doctrine shall drop as the rain, my speech shall distil as the dew, as the small rain upon the tender herb, and as the showers upon the grass:
3. Because I will publish the name of the Lord; ascribe ye greatness unto our God.
4. *He is* the Rock, his work *is* perfect: for all his ways *are* judgment: a God of truth and without iniquity, just and right *is* he.

This call upon the heavens and the earth to hear the words of this song must be construed not as a call upon the intelligent beings of heaven to listen to it; much less, upon the material sun, moon, and stars, and this globe of ours; but rather as poetic usage, due to the lofty inspiration of the poet's soul who feels that the message which burns in his heart is so momentous to his people that all nature—above and beneath—may fitly be summoned to hear. It is his strongest way of saying—Let all people of this and future generations give ear and heart to these messages from the God of heaven and earth.——The poet-prophets of Israel in later days adopt the same form of address (Isa. 1: 2, and Jer. 2: 12, and 6: 19).——" My doctrine "—the truths I teach—" shall drop as the rain"; good for the soul as rain for the grass; refreshing, fraught with real life and the beauty of holiness:—the reason of its great value being, "Because I am to proclaim the *name* of the Lord"—*i. e.* his name as significant of his nature.—— Appreciating this sacred name, ye will testify to his greatness; your heart will be impressed with a sense of his excellent glory.

"Their *Rock* is he"—the writer placing this forcible word first in order. The great elements of his character are stable, solid, enduring, changeless: every thing in his nature and work is perfect; all his ways are righteous; a God of truth is he, whose words of promise or of threatening can never fail. "Without iniquity" moreover; there is nothing in him morally tortuous; all is on the right line of equity and justice. Such is the Great God of our fathers—the God of our national covenant. It was pertinent to place these views of God at the head of this song because they set the guilt of forsaking God in its true light, and would also vindicate his justice in sending even great calamities upon his apostate people.——In later ages David uses this figure—(the "Rock")—of God with exquisite beauty and force (Ps. 18: 2, and 28: 1, and 42: 9).

5. They have corrupted themselves, their spot *is* not *the spot* of his children; *they are* a perverse and crooked generation.

The poet turns suddenly to the great fact of the future apostasy of God's people.—"Their spot"—moral defilement—the dark pollution of their souls. That does not indicate my children. My dutiful sons and daughters never carry such stains; never give their hearts to other gods; never turn their backs upon their loving and glorious Father!

6. Do ye thus requite the Lord, O foolish people and unwise? *is* not he thy Father *that* has bought thee? hath he not made thee and established thee?
7. Remember the days of old, consider the years of many generations: ask thy father, and he will shew thee; thy elders, and they will tell thee.

Is it possible that ye can thus requite your own Jehovah? Is this fair treatment of such a Father? Is not the God whom ye have forsaken the very same who hath bought thee from bondage; redeemed thee for himself; made thee a prosperous and happy nation, and established thee in permanent strength? Go back over the grand ages of your national history; ask the fathers for their testimony to the great works of your God in your behalf.

8. When the Most High divided to the nations their inheritance, when he separated the sons of Adam, he set the bounds of the people according to the number of the children of Israel.
9. For the Lord's portion *is* his people; Jacob *is* the lot of his inheritance.

In the original planting of the nations the Lord reserved Canaan—best and fairest of all lands—for his people. This refers to those providential agencies by which God assigned to the nations descended from Noah's sons their geographical localities and national home. In this arrangement he reserved sufficient territory for Israel—"according to their numbers"; and in the best locality for their residence. The Lord accounted them his own people and gave them his own reserved "lot."

10. He found him in a desert land, and in the waste howling wilderness; he led him about, he instructed him, he kept him as the apple of his eye.
11. As an eagle stirreth up her nest, fluttereth over her young, spreadeth abroad her wings, taketh them, beareth them on her wings:
12. *So* the LORD alone did lead him, and *there was* no strange god with him.

"He found him in a desert land." With poetic license the writer touches Hebrew history where he will—in this case at Sinai where God met Israel visibly, and called them into special covenant with himself. All through that wilderness he led Israel about by his guiding pillar of cloud and of fire; instructed him by precepts and statutes; kept him from danger even as a man guards the apple of his eye (which the more poetic Hebrew called the *little man* of the eye—that diminutive picture of yourself).——The next figure—at once exquisite in beauty and forcible for illustration—comes from the eagle training his young to fly. When he sees that the time has come for this training, he stirs up his nestlings—waking them as the father does his sons at the morning hour; flutters over them as if to show them the exercise; spreads abroad his wings; takes them up aloft, casts them off upon their flying power—coming swift to the rescue if their strength should fail;—all to train them into courage, and strength of wing, and steadiness of stroke. So the Lord alone—he and none other—did lead Israel. There was no strange god there. In all his wilderness training of forty most eventful years—that tender youth-time of Israel, there was not the least help from Baal or Ashtoreth. But the hand of his own God was every-where; in his daily bread; in his rock-gushing waters; in his pillar of cloud and of fire; in his victories over Amalek, Arad, and Midian. This high hand and uplifted arm, strong as the eagle's pinions, bore the younglings taken from his nest over and through the roughnesses of that waste howling wilderness, until at length he set them down in the promised Canaan.

13. He made him ride on the high places of the earth, that he

might eat the increase of the fields; and he made him to suck honey out of the rock, and oil out of the flinty rock;

14. Butter of kine, and milk of sheep, with fat of lambs, and rams of the breed of Bashan, and goats, with the fat of kidneys of wheat; and thou didst drink the pure blood of the grape.

The fatness of this fertile land calls out the richest poetic imagery.——"He made him ride on the high places of the earth"—letting him down just a little yet but a little from the symbol of the eagle's lofty flight. "Riding on the high places of the land"—as if his were a railway path, stretched from summit to summit, resting only on mountain peaks, commanding every magnificent prospect; or with an eye to his conquest of Canaan, the poet sees him sweeping through with the tread of a conquerer, for the phrase seems to conceive of the hill-tops as the strategic points in war, commanding the whole country. As we might expect, Isaiah admired and adopted this gem of poetry (Isa. 58:14).

The richest luxuries of oriental climes lie at the nation's feet; honey and oil; butter and milk; rams and goats; "with the fat of the kidneys of wheat" which curiously draws its terms for the best of wheat from the favorite qualities of animal food.——In v. 14 the Heb. word for "pure" ["*pure* blood of the grape"], means by its etymology—effervescing, bubbling up, in the process of fermentation. Our translators probably supposed it to have worked itself "pure" by this process. The word seems to describe the process—not the subsequent state.

15. But Jeshurun waxed fat, and kicked: thou art waxen fat, thou art grown thick, thou art covered *with fatness;* then he forsook God *which* made him, and lightly esteemed the Rock of his salvation.

16. They provoked him to jealousy with strange *gods*, with abominations provoked they him to anger.

17. They sacrificed unto devils, not to God; to gods whom they knew not, to new *gods that* came newly up, whom your fathers feared not.

18. Of the Rock *that* begat thee thou art unmindful, and hast forgotten God that formed thee.

Here is the sad moral result of being over-fed, over-tempted.——"Jeshurun," the upright one; he who had bound himself by covenant to walk uprightly with God.
——The Hebrews constantly associate fatness with moral obtuseness, insensibility, and consequent ob-

liquity. The ceremonial distinctions of things clean and unclean assumed this—swine being utterly unclean, and the fatty portions of sacrificed animals being accounted good only for burning on the altar. Hence the figure—Jeshurun, too fat for self-control and self-denial; too fat for the worship of the pure and holy One; and consequently he forsook the God who made and blessed him.——The verb for "lightly esteemed" means to regard as dried up; withered; of faded beauty. So Israel thought of their God though he had been to them the Rock of their salvation. The sad fact of their fall into idol-worship is reiterated and made impressively emphatic. They provoked God to jealousy; for how could he be otherwise than jealous when they cast him off and gave their hearts' homage to devils; to new gods, unknown to their fathers; gods that were no gods at all!——The Hebrew word here for "devils" means primarily *lords*—mighty ones. The Septuagint and Vulgate give it *demons*—true to the ultimate idea, for all idol-worship is equivalent to the worship of the devil, being real obedience to his will.——The blackness of this guilt lies in its forgetting, disowning God, our Great Benefactor; our only real Friend.

19. And when the LORD saw *it*, he abhorred *them*, because of the provoking of his sons, and of his daughters.
20. And he said, I will hide my face from them, I will see what their end *shall be:* for they *are* a very froward generation, children in whom *is* no faith.
21. They have moved me to jealousy with *that which is* not God; they have provoked me to anger with their vanities: and I will move them to jealousy with *those which are* not a people; I will provoke them to anger with a foolish nation.

The most cruel point as to God was that this insult came from his own "*sons and daughters.*" From them he might expect better treatment.——What shall he do? What can he do, less than to hide his face from them and to leave them to try the friendship of the new gods they had so madly chosen? "I will see what their end shall be." They will see in due time!——In v. 21 there is a play upon the words—the same verbs, "move to jealousy" and "provoke," being used first of their ways toward God; next, of God's ways in retribution toward them. Paul (Rom. 10: 14) assumes that this passage at least applies well if indeed it does not refer primarily to God's judgments on Israel by casting her off, and taking into her place of privilege the Gentiles whom Israel had been wont to regard as nobody.

22. For a fire is kindled in my anger, and shall burn unto the lowest hell, and shall consume the earth with her increase, and set on fire the foundations of the mountains.
23. I will heap mischiefs upon them; I will spend mine arrows upon them.
24. *They shall be* burnt with hunger, and devoured with burning heat, and with bitter destruction: I will also send the teeth of beasts upon them, with the poison of serpents of the dust.
25. The sword without, and terror within, shall destroy both the young man and the virgin, the suckling *also* with the man of gray hairs.

These are the vials of retributive judgment poured out on Israel, first for her persistent idolatries; last for her murder of her King Messiah. The fire is thought of as burning *deep;* not merely skimming the surface but penetrating to the deep foundations of her mountains. "Hell" here is not to be taken in its modern usage—the place of future punishment—but in the early Hebrew sense as lying below the earth's surface—the "pit" into which Korah and his company went down.——"Burnt with hunger" (v. 24) is more literally exhausted, their vitality sucked out of them by famine—a fearful doom!——The sword abroad and terror at home (literally, "in the chambers"), shall bereave [Heb.] both the young man and the virgin—a calamity well compared to bereavement of most loved offspring.

26. I said, I would scatter them into corners, I would make the remembrance of them to cease from among men:
27. Were it not that I feared the wrath of the enemy, lest their adversaries should behave themselves strangely, *and* lest they should say, Our hand *is* high, and the LORD hath not done all this.
28. For they *are* a nation void of counsel, neither *is there any* understanding in them.

The thought is that for these great sins the Lord would have utterly annihilated Israel were it not for the honor of his name before the nations as their recognized God.——The word for "scatter into corners" means rather, *to blow away* as with his powerful breath. ——It is not precisely the "*wrath*" of the enemy, but rather the *reproaches,* or the underlying spirit which would manifest itself in insult and haughty exultation.

The context shows the true idea. Lest they should say "Israel is down because *our* hand is high and *our* power resistless. *We* have done it. *Their God* is far enough from being Almighty."——"Behave themselves strangely" should rather be—should *reason* strangely; should make this strange inference, that the fall of Israel was due to their own great power, rather than to God's forsaking them for their great sin.

29. O that they were wise, *that* they understood this, *that* they would consider their latter end!
30. How should one chase a thousand, and two put ten thousand to flight, except their Rock had sold them, and the LORD had shut them up?
31. For their rock *is* not as our Rock, even our enemies themselves *being* judges.

How does the tenderness of a loving Father's heart pour itself out in these matchless words! O if my people were only wise; wise to know and appreciate their Great Benefactor! Wise to render him the homage, the trust, and the love of their heart! How would one of them chase a thousand of their foes if only their God were on their side; if he who is their Rock and Strength had not sold and disowned them!——Expressively Moses adds—For as they very well know—we have it on their own admission—their Rock is not as our Rock; their gods were never like our God. Moses did not say this without authority. He remembered how the Egyptian hosts in the Red Sea cried out, "Let us flee from the face of Israel, for the Lord fighteth for them against the Egyptians" (Ex. 14: 25). The testimony of Balaam was still fresh: "God hath blessed; I can not reverse it. The Lord his God is with him, and the shout of a king is among them. God brought them out of Egypt; he hath as it were the strength of a unicorn. Surely there is no enchantment against Jacob, nor any divination against Israel. Behold, the people shall rise up as a great lion," etc. (Num. 23: 20–24). The fame of God's wonders for Israel was already abroad among all the adjacent nations, as may be seen in the words of Rahab (Josh. 2: 9–11).

32. For their vine *is* of the vine of Sodom, and the fields of Gomorrah: their grapes *are* grapes of gall, their clusters *are* bitter:
33. Their wine *is* the poison of dragons, and the cruel venom of asps.

34. *Is* not this laid up in store with me, *and* sealed up among my treasures?

35. To me *belongeth* vengeance, and recompense; their foot shall slide in *due* time: for the day of their calamity *is* at hand, and the things that shall come upon them make haste.

By a somewhat sudden transition of thought, "for" [first word of v. 32] answers the implied question—Why then, if Israel's Rock is so mighty, does not Israel live and triumph in perpetual victory and prosperity? Do ye ask, *Why not?* Because they are corrupt like Sodom; their "vine" being put poetically for themselves morally considered. Their heart and life are altogether rotten.——In v. 34 I take the sense to be—Do I not remember all their sin? Is it not laid up before me, awaiting its time for a fearful retribution, sealed up as securely as one keeps his choice treasures? "Vengeance belongeth to me"—is my sole prerogative, and can not fail of its due execution.

36. For the LORD shall judge his people, and repent himself for his servants, when he seeth that *their* power is gone, and *there is* none shut up, or left.

37. And he shall say, Where *are* their gods, *their* rock in whom they trusted,

38. Which did eat the fat of their sacrifices, *and* drank the wine of their drink offerings? let them rise up and help you, *and* be your protection.

God will arise for judgment and retribution. Calamities must scourge the guilty; mercy will spare the innocent and ultimately save his Zion. In the latter portion of this song (vs. 36–42), the divine agency seems to be of a twofold character; exterminating the hopelessly guilty, but sparing and restoring the penitent, and ultimately retrieving the fortunes of his kingdom.——When God seeth that his people are powerless and none remain, either bond or free, shut up or let go [the sense of the Heb. words translated "shut up or left"], he will ask, What has become of the gods to whom my people have apostatized, with whom they ate their sacrifices in common? Since those gods have utterly failed them, let me call their attention to myself. Perhaps now it will not be in vain.

39. See now that I, *even* I, *am* he, and *there is* no god with me: I kill, and I make alive; I wound, and I heal: neither *is there any* that can deliver out of my hand.

40. For I lift up my hand to heaven, and say, I live forever.
41. If I whet my glittering sword, and mine hand take hold on judgment; I will render vengeance to mine enemies, and will reward them that hate me.
42. I will make mine arrows drunk with blood, and my sword shall devour flesh; *and that* with the blood of the slain and of the captives from the beginning of revenges upon the enemy.

They shall know the power of their God. When I lift up my awful hand to bring down retribution on the guilty apostates among my people, shall not my arrows be drunk with blood and my sword devour flesh? The guilty must fall; yet through the fires of these sore judgments Zion shall be purified and so redeemed.——The last clause of v. 42 were better read—"From the head of the princes of the enemy."

43. Rejoice, O ye nations, *with* his people: for he will avenge the blood of his servants, and will render vengeance to his adversaries, and will be merciful unto his land, *and* to his people.

This closing strain brings out in unmistakable terms the idea which seems to have been implied since v. 36, viz. that these great judgments on Israel will not ultimately break down God's cause and kingdom, but will only cut off the hopelessly reprobate and really bring deliverance, purity, salvation, to Zion. Therefore let all the nations rejoice with his people. They have a deeper interest than they are yet aware of in this purifying process for the ultimate redemption of Zion. The prophetic eye of Moses sees through to the glorious ingathering of the Gentiles to Christ, and seems to trace the connection of this ingathering with the judgments sent on apostate Israel in the first Christian age.—— The outcome of this song is therefore ultimately hopeful to the real Zion. It gives a fearfully dark view of the guilty apostasies of Israel—those which culminated first in the captivity to Babylon; last in the fall of their city before the Romans. In the result God vindicates his great name; purifies his people, and spreads the glory of his name far abroad among the nations.

Deut. 33.

The blessing of Moses upon the tribes shortly before his death.

This blessing of Moses follows in general the usage of patriarchal times, as seen in Noah, but especially in

Jacob, the great tribe-father (Gen. 49). It also follows the impulses of the great heart of Moses, now a patriarch of one hundred and twenty years, who had long outlived the associates of his earlier days; who had suffered and borne every thing for his people and had labored for them more than a father for his sons and daughters. In this parting hour he has some last blessings to bequeathe before his eyes shall close in death. Let us listen to his dying benedictions.

The first five verses apply generally to all the tribes. The last four also are general rather than special; while the intervening portion of the chapter (vs. 6-25) is made up of special benedictions upon the several tribes.—— Note also that while the "Song" [chap. 32] is largely in the minor strain—a sad prophetic vision of the nation's future apostasies and consequent calamities, this chapter is *pure benediction*—the outpouring of hopeful prayers and heartfelt good wishes, with no shade of anticipated disaster, no foreseen calamities.

1. And this *is* the blessing, wherewith Moses the man of God blessed the children of Israel before his death.
2. And he said, The LORD came from Sinai, and rose up from Seir unto them; he shined forth from Mount Paran, and he came with ten thousands of saints: from his right hand *went* a fiery law for them.
3 Yea, he loved the people; and all his saints *are* in thy hand: and they sat down at thy feet; *every one* shall receive of thy words.
4. Moses commanded us a law, *even* the inheritance of the congregation of Jacob.
5. And he was king in Jeshurun, when the heads of the people *and* the tribes of Israel were gathered together.

The first thing to be noticed was that greatest fact, equally of the life of Moses and of the life of all Israel, viz. the coming forth of the glorious God in majesty so sublime from the mountains of Sinai. How did the blaze of his glory illumine her towering summits and flash forth from all her hill-tops! Such a coming—when had the world ever seen before?——"Rose up from Seir" would suggest to a Hebrew the rising of the sun in his glory.——"He came *with* ten thousands of saints," says our English version; but the Hebrew has it *from*—the same preposition which is used before Sinai, Seir, and Paran—certainly implying therefore that God came forth *from* the midst of those ten thousand holy ones in a sense analogous to that in which he shone forth from Sinai, Seir, and Paran. He must refer to holy angels to whom in great numbers Jacob was introduced at Bethel and Mahanaim. But whether the Lord came forth *from* them, leaving them in heaven, or shone forth *from among* them, attending him on Sinai, can not be certainly determined from the words used here. Other scriptures however speak of the law as given by the ministration of angels, and therefore fully imply their presence on Sinai at the giving of the law. See Ps. 68: 17, and Acts 7: 53, and Gal. 3: 19, and Heb. 2: 2.——The last clause of v. 1—"from his right hand went forth a fiery law for them"—involves grave difficulties of a sort which can not well be put before the English reader. The word translated "law" is unknown to the ancient Hebrew—is not the word used for law in v. 4 and in the Pentateuch generally. The best critical authorities would unite these two words which our translators supposed to mean "fire" and "law," into one word of quite different signification, referring perhaps to the pillar of fire [Gesenius]; or to some geographical point [Fuerst]; or to flashes of lightning [Keil].——V. 3 is singularly abrupt, and consequently the course of thought is obscure. God was loving the people [continuous action]—*i. e.* all the nations and not the Hebrews only—showing that God shone forth from Sinai *in love to the race.* All his holy ones are his wards, upheld by his arm. They lie humbly at his feet; in filial loving obedience they receive his words—indicating most beautifully the spirit with which all true souls welcome God's uttered words as to moral duty. It is perhaps possible that [as Keil suggests] the "holy ones" here are holy angels; yet I incline to apply the phrase without restriction to all holy beings, man certainly not excluded.——Moses gave us a law, as a legacy, inheritance, for the whole congregation of Jacob. He [God] was King in Jeshurun [over the *upright people*], even over all that great nation with its congregated tribes and their tribal leaders.

6. Let Reuben live, and not die; and let *not* his men be few.

As to Reuben, let his tribe be perpetuated and not become extinct; for some fear on this point might have sprung from the scenes of Num. 16; the fearful death of Dathan, Abiram, and On, all sons of Reuben (Num. 16: 1, 27).

7. And this *is the blessing* of Judah: and he said, Hear, Lord, the voice of Judah, and bring him unto his people: let his hands be sufficient for him; and be thou a help *to him* from his enemies.

Judah is thought of as leading the tribes in battle, going forth in advance of all others to war. Hence the prayer—Bring him back safely to his people from the scenes of battle. Let his hand [military power] be equal to any emergency.

8. And of Levi he said, *Let* thy Thummim and thy Urim *be* with thy holy one, whom thou didst prove at Massah, *and with* whom thou didst strive at the waters of Meribah;
9. Who said unto his father and to his mother, I have not seen him; neither did he acknowledge his brethren, nor knew his own children: for they have observed thy word, and kept thy covenant.
10. They shall teach Jacob thy judgments, and Israel thy law; they shall put incense before thee, and whole burnt sacrifice upon thine altar.
11. Bless, Lord, his substance, and accept the work of his hands: smite through the loins of them that rise against him, and of them that hate him, that they rise not again.

The blessing on Levi suggested the insignia on Aaron's breast-plate, known as the *"Urim and Thummim"* [described somewhat in Ex. 28: 29, 30]—the words signifying *Light and Right*. These breast-plate insignia were used in some way, not altogether clear at this day, in obtaining special directions from the Lord. ——The tribe of Levi as a whole became in a sense God's "Holy One," bearing in the person of Aaron these insignia. God had proved them at Massah and Meribah where the people murmured against Moses and Aaron. It was especially in the scenes of the calf-worship (Ex. 32) and of the Midianites (Num. 25) that the tribe of Levi, and particularly Phineas, proved themselves true to God, with higher regard for him and his honor than for father, mother, brethren, or children; for they remembered and honored God's word and covenant. Let them therefore have the functions of the priesthood, to teach Jacob thy law and to minister at the national altar.

12. *And* of Benjamin he said, The beloved of the Lord shall dwell in safety by him; *and the* Lord shall cover him all the day long, and he shall dwell between his shoulders.

Let Benjamin, the beloved of the Lord, dwell safely by the side of the Lord, his protector, abiding between his shoulders—*i. e.* upon his back where fathers are wont to place their children to bear them long distances. This tribe is thought of as God's child, to be borne upon his shoulder.

13. And of Joseph he said, Blessed of the Lord *be* his land, for the precious things of heaven, for the dew, and for the deep that croucheth beneath,
14. And for the precious fruits *brought forth* by the sun, and for the precious things put forth by the moon,
15. And for the chief things of the ancient mountains, and for the precious things of the lasting hills,
16. And for the precious things of the earth and fulness thereof, and *for* the good will of him that dwelt in the bush: let *the blessing* come upon the head of Joseph, and upon the top of the head of him that was separated from his brethren.
17. His glory *is like* the firstling of his bullock, and his horns *are like* the horns of unicorns: with them he shall push the people together to the ends of the earth: and they *are* the ten thousands of Ephraim, and they *are* the thousands of Manasseh.

The blessings on Joseph comprise all good upon his land; the dew and the shower, the sunshine and the moonbeams; all the products of the mountains and of the deep;—let all come upon the head of him who was *prince* among his brethren [in Egypt]—this being the sense, rather than "separated" from his brethren.

18. And of Zebulun he said, Rejoice, Zebulun, in thy going out; and, Issachar, in thy tents.
19. They shall call the people unto the mountain; there they shall offer sacrifices of righteousness: for they shall suck *of* the abundance of the seas, and *of* treasures hid in the sand.

Let Zebulun and Issachar rejoice both in their going forth and in their tents; equally in their labor and in their repose. Living on the shore of the great sea, let their influence go forth upon and beyond the great waters, calling the nations to the mountain of the Lord's house for worship with sacrifices of righteousness to the God of the whole earth; and let Zion under their hand become enriched with the abundance of the seas—of all countries beyond the seas—bringing their gold and their treasures to the God of Israel. Isaiah has the same thought often; *e. g.* chapters 49, 60, and 66.

20. And of Gad he said, Blessed *be* he that enlargeth Gad: he dwelleth as a lion, and teareth the arm with the crown of the head.
21. And he provided the first part for himself, because there, *in a* portion of the lawgiver, *was he* seated; and he came with the heads of the people, he executed the justice of the Lord, and his judgments with Israel.

The allusion to Gad seems to be built upon his then recent history—leading the movement for locating the two and a half tribes on the East of Jordan and foremost in battle and in victory over the national enemy; prompt also to go over Jordan to execute God's righteous judgments on the devoted nations of Canaan.

22. And of Dan he said, Dan *is* a lion's whelp: he shall leap from Bashan.

Dan is fierce and formidable in war, to which his border locality on the extreme North may have conduced. Jacob touches the same tribal characteristic (Gen. 49: 16, 17).

23. And of Naphtali he said, O Naphtali, satisfied with favor, and full with the blessing of the Lord, possess thou the west and the south.
24. And of Asher he said, *Let* Asher *be* blessed with children; let him be acceptable to his brethren, and let him dip his foot in oil.
25. Thy shoes *shall be* iron and brass; and as thy days, *so shall* thy strength *be*.

Let Asher be blessed *above* the sons—may be the sense—the favored one among his brethren. May thy castle-bars [not "shoes"] be of iron and brass. But the best authorities on the word "strength" prefer *rest* [Gesenius], or affluence [Fuerst]. The prayer is that this rest or affluence may be life-long.

26. *There is* none like unto the God of Jeshurun, *who* rideth upon the heaven in thy help, and in his excellency on the sky.
27. The eternal God *is thy* refuge, and underneath *are* the everlasting arms: and he shall thrust out the enemy from before thee; and shall say, Destroy *them*.
28. Israel then shall dwell in safety alone; the fountain of Jacob

shall be upon a land of corn and wine; also his heavens shall drop down dew.

29. Happy *art* thou, O Israel: who *is* like unto thee, O people saved by the Lord, the shield of thy help, and who *is* the sword of thy excellency! and thine enemies shall be found liars unto thee; and thou shalt tread upon their high places.

These words of unsurpassed sublimity and most exquisite poetry set forth the glories of the God of Israel and the blessedness of the people who enjoy such a Father and live under such a Protector. Perhaps we can not give them higher praise than to say they are worthy of the pen of Moses—worthy even to be his last words—the noblest utterances of one who above any other mere man had communed with God face to face as man does with his dearest friend.——The English translation is almost faultless, constituting one of the grandest passages to be found in English literature. In the last clause of v. 27, I prefer to follow the Hebrew more closely and say simply *Destroy!* The high behest of Jehovah, hurling the enemy forth from the land of his people is best expressed in the emphatic word, *Destroy!*——In the last verse, the clause, "Thine enemies shall be found liars unto thee," means that they shall cringe, fawn, and flatter with false and lying pretenses to gain if but a little favor from a people so terrible in arms as Israel with God on her side. The case of the Gibeonites is mostly in point.

It was due to the stand-point of Moses, looking forth across the Jordan upon the earthly Canaan, beholding the earthly Israel just then entering there; Jehovah the shield of their help, the sword of their excellency, the scourge of their foes—this mighty God riding sublimely upon the heavens for their help, his everlasting arms underneath them forevermore—that this view should be primarily of scenes in the present life and not in the future; of earthly and material relations rather than of spiritual. Yet let us not forget that the manifestations of God in blessings of earthly sort foreshadow like manifestations in the spiritual life. The God who saves his people here in things of earth, in ways so grand, with power so transcendant, in a spirit so parental and so tender, may surely be trusted to save and shield and bless with his own Godlike wisdom and power against spiritual foes and for the other world no less than for this. Surely there is none like the God of Jeshurun who comes in the tenderness of infinite pity to wipe away the penitent tear; to bind up hearts broken for sin; to place underneath all feeble souls his own everlasting arms; to bid away every spiritual foe with the mandate *Destroy;* and to gather home his redeemed in his own best time to his Canaan above, of which that ancient land of promise gives us only some poetic images and some illustrations of God's faithfulness and love. It is quite well, therefore, to exchange the earthly sense of this sublime passage for its spiritual significance and transfer its imagery to that world whose glories are worthy of sublimer strains than even these.

The death and character of Moses.

These benedictions having been uttered, it remained for Moses to see the goodly land with his eyes and then close them in death. The record is that his vision from the top of Pisgah swept the whole country of Palestine even to the Mediterranean—a statement which implies miraculous power. We must either tone down the statement in extent, or admit a superhuman extension of sight—the latter being by far most probable.

The record assumes that at his death Moses had no attendant save the Lord himself—a circumstance which throws a shade of doubt over the ultimate disposition of his body. According to the narrative the Lord buried him in a valley in the land of Moab; yet the place of his burial remained unknown to mortals. Was the fact of his being buried at all revealed to some Hebrew prophet by special inspiration; or was it merely assumed as the common course of events; or was his body really translated, as in the case of Enoch and Elijah? In favor of the latter supposition are two circumstances; viz. the allusion by Jude (v. 9) to a dispute over his body between Michael the archangel and the devil; and his appearance together with Elijah at the transfiguration of Jesus (Mat. 17: 3). These hints comprise all that is known on the point or can be known at present; or as we may say, all that the Lord thought it important to let us know.

Altogether in keeping with the masterly vigor of mind manifested in the last exhortation of Moses (chap.

27–31); in the "Song" (chap. 32), and in the tribal blessings (chap. 33)—is the statement that although at the age of one hundred and twenty, "his eye was not dim nor his natural force abated." The Hebrew word suggests, instead of natural force, the idea of freshness, youthful vigor. How wonderfully were his powers of both mind and body preserved till his great work was done!——The historian who wrote this last chapter says: "There arose not a prophet since in Israel like unto Moses"—which raises the question, How long a period of time is embraced in this comparison? Was this remark made in the time of Samuel, or in the time of Ezra, or at some point between? Or was it based upon the belief or the special revelation that the divine policy included but one Moses—all later prophets down to the coming of the Great Anointed being of a subordinate grade? I do not see that the choice between these several alternatives can be made with absolute certainty, and it is not specially important that we attempt to balance nicely the mere probabilities.

We think of Moses (as of Paul, Isaiah, Daniel) as a sublime illustration of God's marvelous resources for raising up great men for great occasions. Where shall we set the limit to these resources? True, these great men die (unless they may be translated), but their names die not; their work does not die; their influence travels onward down the ages, and will, long as men live on the earth. They are the world's really *great men*, belonging to a totally different order from the Cæsars, the Alexanders, and the Napoleons, or the Platos and the Aristotles of the race. It may not be unprofitable to note that all these were *modest men;* meek above most other men; of unaspiring spirit; true to their divine mission, and little caring to give their thought to any thing else. The fact in the recorded history of Moses which seems to me the very gem of his life was that God's proposal, twice made to him, to cut off all Israel and make of him a great nation (Ex. 32: 10 and Num. 14: 12) did not get from him a moment's attention. He never even alluded to it. But as the Lord seemed to overlook the glory of his own name before the nations, Moses took the responsibility (boldly, shall we say?) of reminding him as to this point. Apparently his soul was so much absorbed in this line of considerations—the glory of God as before the nations of the earth—that he could not let it drop from his range of view. Hence Moses was mighty (almost omnipotent we may say) in prayer. It would seem to have been the Lord's special purpose to bring out this prime quality of his religious character and set it in sunlight before all future ages—an illustration of the fact that *the great men of all time are mighty with God in prayer.* They know the secret of communion with God. They have easy, unrestricted access to his throne.—— One blemish—nay rather, one sin, stands on the record of his life in his own hand-writing; one sad, humiliating fact mars his history—viz. that at Kadesh his sensibilities to himself were too keen; that for the moment, self threw even his God into the shade, and he cried out: "Ye rebels; must *we* fetch you water from this rock"? True, the complaints of Israel were severely cruel as against Moses; but how much more so against God! And if Moses had thought and felt much less as to himself and much more of God, he had passed through this stern ordeal unhurt. From that point onward this sin could not pass altogether out of his mind. It had been the aspiration of his life to see the goodly land of Canaan and to plant his children—the great Hebrew nation—there with his own hand and see them with his own eyes in their glorious home! We sympathize in his disappointment and trial in that he must die short of Canaan. But this is not quite a sinless world. The painful experiences of imperfection force themselves into the best Christian lives. There is a better life beyond!

The Mosaic system and the future life.

The question often comes up in even the most candid and honest minds: Why is the Pentateuch silent, or at least, *so nearly* silent as to the rewards and punishments of the future life?——Moreover, there is a class of critics who are fain to decry the Hebrew people as almost contemptibly low in point of knowledge, culture, and civilization, and who are wont to deny that the Mosaic system, civil or religious, has any allusion to the future life or even assumes its existence.——From this supposed fact, they infer that the Hebrew people and even Moses himself *had no knowledge of the future life.*

In briefly discussing this subject, I propose,

1. To qualify somewhat the absolute statement—*No allusion to the future life or assumption of its existence.*

2. To give some reasons for placing the Theocracy mainly on the basis of temporal rewards and punishments.

3. To maintain that Moses and the patriarchs knew and believed in the future life as one of rewards and punishments.

1. I propose to qualify somewhat the absolute statement—"No allusion to the future life and no assumption of its existence."

Here I call attention to the remarkable fact that there are several statutes *without penalties*—left simply upon the consciences of men and upon their sense of the fear of God.——As to those who violate the third of the ten commandments, it is simply said, "The Lord will not hold him guiltless"; but it is not intimated that any due punishment should befall him in the present life. The statutes touching this sin stand also without penalties. Correspondingly the statutes forbid perjury; but they seem to leave the sanctity of the solemn oath upon the conscience and upon men's fear of God. So of the precept, "Thou shalt not revile the judges, nor curse the rulers of thy people" (Ex. 22: 28).

Now it scarcely need be suggested that human laws without penalties are mere puerilities—virtually no laws at all. Suppose under any human government, sundry statutes were left without penalties, the law saying only, "he shall bear his iniquity"; "his sin shall be upon him": Would not the whole body of lawless, law-breaking men say in their heart, What of that? What then? Every violator of human law knows well enough that there is nothing to fear *from it* beyond the grave. If human law will only let them have their way in this world, they would scoff at the thought of *its penalties* in the next.——Now my point is that the Hebrew statutes did not leave the law-breaker's conscience in this attitude. The man who scorned those statutes because they stood without penalties in this world *had something to think of for the world to come.*

Those statutes, left without penalties for this life were not by any means for that reason powerless. So far from being powerless, they were in many minds more terrible than any other statutes. Was it of no account to them that God had said—"His sin shall be *upon him*" and "he shall bear his iniquity"? Did they not know that "it is a fearful thing to fall into the hands of the living God"—fearful, moreover, not because he might bring trouble on them in time, but because there is an after-life and the same dreadful God is there—terrible to those who have defied his authority and scorned his law?——Therefore the statement that this Hebrew code did in no manner assume the existence of an after-life and of a God terrible to the sinner there, must be somewhat modified.

2. *I am to assign some reasons for putting this Theocracy mainly on the basis of temporal rewards and punishments.*

(1.) It was to be administered chiefly by human agents. Human judges sat upon offenses against it, and human hands executed their decisions.——I qualify these statements with the words "mainly," "chiefly," stating this as being the case *for the most part*.——The fact as to human agents being admitted, there is no need of further reasons for placing the administration of this government mainly on the basis of earthly rewards and punishments—penalties in this world, not in the next. How could human judges award judgments for the world to come, and human hands execute them there?

(2.) God governed Israel *as a nation, not as an individual man*. Now since nations as such exist in this life only, it follows of necessity that all retribution that is truly *national* must be in time, not in eternity. The nation as such is not known in the eternal world. The individuals that compose the nation have their own personal account to settle with God in the world to come; but this has no bearing upon the government of God over the nation. This national government must be complete in time, else it remains incomplete forever. It may run on through many human generations; national life may outlast scores of individual human lives; but God's retribution as to nations must be administered in this world, no part lying over to the next. Hence when God made himself king in Jeshurun over the Hebrew nation, he of necessity established a government to be administered mainly in time, not in eternity; by the rewards and penalties of this world—not of the next.——This again would be in itself a sufficient reason for the fact we are accounting for, even if there were no other.

(3.) This national system of government was intended to be a moral lesson for all other nations of all time. Hence the government must be put on the same basis as that of all other nations *in the point of providential retribution*. As God holds every nation on earth to a positive retribution in time, giving them prosperity for their righteousness, and adversity for their violation of the common laws of humanity; and as he would fain make his administration over Israel a cogent moral lesson to every other nation on this great point, he must needs govern Israel in this respect *as* he governs them—*i. e.* administering his retributions *in time*.

(4.) Yet one reason more. Distinguishing carefully between God's providential government and his moral—the former being of time only; the latter of both time and eternity; the former being (for our present purpose) over nations as such; the latter over individuals only and not over nations—it remains to say that God manifestly designed his providential government over Israel to be suggestive, perhaps we might say typical—certainly illustrative of his moral government over all men which is not of time only, but which reaches into the eternal world. In the early ages of the world men needed some proof that God would punish sin in the world to come. They needed some illustrations of God's character as a righteous, moral governor. Therefore the Lord planned to put himself at the head of the Hebrew nation, and then in that position, to give to mankind some illustrations in this world of what all sinners are to believe and expect for themselves, not in this world only or chiefly, but in the world to come. He would make this limited government illustrate that universal one. He would show in the case of the Hebrew people under his law what all men have to expect from their righteous God when his moral government shall have had full scope and shall have administered its perfect retribution in the world to come. This divine policy is well set forth by Peter (2 Pet. 2: 4-9); "For if God spared not the angels that sinned but cast them down to hell"; and "spared not the old world, but saved Noah"; if he "turned Sodom and Gomorrah into ashes, but delivered just Lot";—then (we may infer), "the *Lord knoweth how* to deliver the godly out of temptation, and to reserve the unjust unto the day of judgment to be punished." Yes, the Lord *knoweth how* to do this, and he means to let all living men see that he knoweth how; and see also that being a holy moral Governor, he can not fail to do it. He will give them occasion to see in his ruling over nations in time that his ruling over individual sinners can not be less righteous—can not be less retributive according to deeds done; and since equal and perfect justice calls for more time than one human life on earth, there must be an after part to it, to come in when death has located men in the eternal world.——This designed use of a theocratic government over Israel to illustrate God's moral relations to every individual man, required an administration mainly in this world, in time, before human eyes; and is therefore another reason for working this theocracy mainly with temporal rewards and punishments.—— I do not see that further reasons can be rationally called for.

3. I am to rebut the inference made from the fact of a theocracy administered mostly in time, viz. *that Moses and the patriarchs did not believe in or even know of a future life.*

(1.) The inference is utterly illogical. The rewards and penalties of the Hebrew system were of time and not of eternity, *for other good and sufficient reasons*, and not necessarily for the reason that the Hebrew law-giver and his people knew of no future life. To be of any force the argument must assume that if Moses had known of a future life he would have built this system upon it. But what is the proof of that? By what right is that assumed?——On the contrary there are reasons in abundance, not to say in excess—far more than would be sufficient—why the theocracy should be temporal in its penalties, whether Moses knew or did not know of a future life.

(2.) That Moses and the patriarchs assumed and believed in a future life is apparent from *their words*.

Moses wrote of Enoch (Gen. 5: 24); "And Enoch walked with God; and he was not, for God *took* him." "Took him" *where?* Did not Moses know where? "*Took* him"—in what sense? Is it even supposable that Moses thought this was annihilation—taking a godly man out of existence? Extinguishing his being because he walked with God! Is this a credible construction? Shall it be assumed that Moses was so ignorant, or so misinformed, or so little versed in logic, as this?——If the Lord had made this problem a special study—how best to teach and impress the doctrine of a future blessed life for the righteous who walk with God on earth, we can not see how he could have improved upon the method he actually adopted, viz. to take the godly Enoch from earth to heaven without dying.

Again, Moses constantly spoke of the death of the godly patriarchs as a being "gathered to their people." He said this of Abraham (Gen. 25: 8); of Ishmael (25: 17); of Isaac (35: 29); of Jacob (49: 33). And he records these as Jacob's words when he supposed Joseph to have died: "I will go down into Sheol *to my son* mourning" (37: 35).——In the face of these facts can it be said that Moses knew nothing of the future life? Did he think the fathers—the righteous people—had passed by death into non-existence—into what was *not life* in any sense whatever?——Again, when at the bush the Lord said to Moses so solemnly: "I am the God of thy fathers; the God of Abraham, the God of Isaac, and the God of Jacob (Ex. 3: 6), is it credible that Moses was so obtuse as not to see that this implied that Abraham, Isaac, and Jacob were yet living, since the Lord could not be the God of dead things, but only of living souls?——A sensible view of the case may be obtained thus: Suppose that Moses had replied—"Lord, I see not how that can be, for Abraham has been dead and out of existence more than two hundred years"! If really Moses had no knowledge of a future life, he ought frankly to have made substantially this reply at the bush.

(3.) In proof of their faith in the future life, is another argument, of greater force if possible than their words; viz. their *lives.* For men sometimes say more than they mean, or perhaps something other than what they think; but their lives testify truthfully to their real beliefs.——Here we might expand the argument already suggested by the writer to the Hebrews (11: 8–16), calling up to review the actual lives of the patriarchs; how Abraham tore himself away from home and kindred, and went, obeying a call believed to be from God, to a land before unknown; how he and his family sojourned as strangers there, dwelling only in tents but "looking for a city on beyond which hath foundations whose builder and maker is God"; how they lived in the faith of promises to be fulfilled far in the future ages of time; and how by such a life they "declared plainly that they were seeking another and better country, even an heavenly" one.——But waiving this, the argument will be more directly in point if made on the case of the man Moses himself.——Born a slave, it was little of earth that he had at his birth save the faith and consequent heroism of a godly mother. In the providence of God it fell to him to be taken—a beautiful babe of three months—into the family of the reigning Pharaoh. There he lived, trained in all the wisdom of Egypt, till he was full forty years old. Of prepossessing person and splendid talents; of capacities equal to any responsibility, the honors of all Egypt lay before him—we might probably say—were pressing upon his acceptance. What did he do?——The writer to the Hebrews answers our question on this wise: "When he was come to years, he refused to be called the son of Pharaoh's daughter, choosing rather to suffer affliction with the people of God than to enjoy the pleasures of sin for a season: esteeming reproach for Christ greater riches than the treasures of Egypt."—— Was not this choice and all this course of conduct unaccountably strange? Did any man in his senses, *knowing nothing of the future life*, ever make such a choice before or since? What! choose affliction before pleasure; reproach before the highest of earthly honors? What could be in the man to make such a choice and even carry it out in his actual life?

The writer of this Epistle has an explanation to suggest. He says in the outset that Moses *had faith*—a sort of faith described by himself as "the evidence of things not seen." Quite unlike the doctrine of the critics above referred to—nay squarely in the face of their assumptions, he holds up this Moses as a special and illustrious example of real faith in the future life. "*By faith* Moses refused to be called the son of Pharaoh's daughter"; "*by faith* he esteemed reproach for Christ greater riches than Egypt's treasures—for he had respect to the recompense of the reward." Aye, he had his eye onward upon that glorious recompense of reward which God gives his people when the joys that are transient have all faded out—when the life that is immortal dawns on the human soul. In his view the pleasures of Egypt were only *for a season*—too short to be matched against the joys before him—fully believed in—that endure forever.

Of this explanation, say what else men may of it, they must admit that it answers the purpose. It accounts for the choice Moses made of affliction before pleasure; of shame before the highest of Egypt's honors. This explanation represents Moses to be a man of sense, and not a fool. Neological criticism holds him up to the world as void of all sense—as playing the part of supreme folly. Paul said—"If in this life only we have hope in Christ, we are of all men most miserable" (1 Cor. 15:19). He would have said of Moses, If his hope and belief as to God were of this life only—if he had no belief in the future life and no knowledge of it, then he was of all men most foolish—most void of that judgment and good sense which are common to sensible men.——Therefore I claim that the *life of Moses*—the whole choice and purpose and labor of a life of one hundred and twenty years, witness to his full and glorious faith in the future life. The men who deny to him this faith stultify not Moses, but themselves.

(4.) It can scarcely be necessary to suggest that over and above the logical merits of the facts themselves, we have the current traditions of Jewish history and the authority of the inspired New Testament writers. He who wrote the Epistle to the Hebrews—a man of sense as his writings show and of surpassing eloquence and power—must have spoken the current voice of Hebrew tradition—to say nothing (in an argument with Neologist critics) of his unquestionable inspiration from God.

(5.) Still further, we have collateral proofs that the future life was known in the age of Moses.——Job gave a grand declaration of his faith that after the perishing of his body he should see God (Job 19: 25–27). Balaam, representing the thought of the ancient East, saw and believed in the blessedness of the righteous dead.——And to mention no more—the wise men of Egypt, even before the age of Moses, believed in the future life of man. With scarcely a doubt they built their pyramids in the faith of man's immortality. Sepulchers with them had a special and grander significance because they thought of man, not as dropping at death into annihilation, but as having even then a future nobler life before him. It is more than supposable that the art and practice of embalming the body—thus providing for it a sort of immortality—was really an outgrowth of their belief in the immortality of the soul and of its returning again to its former bodily home.——That the Egyptians held the doctrine of a future life and of future rewards and punishments according to the deeds of this earthly life, is not questioned at all by those who are familiar with her ancient mythology. Symbolic representations are found which are affirmed to be nothing else but the personification of the grand principle of the immortality of the soul and the necessity of leading a virtuous life.* Also a picture "representing the trial and judgment which the Egyptians supposed the soul of a man to undergo before he was allowed to enter the regions of rest and happiness."†——R. S. Poole (in Smith's Bible Dictionary on "Egypt," p. 675) says: "The great doctrines of the immortality of the soul, man's responsibility, and future rewards and punishments were taught" [in Egypt]. "The Egyptian religion in its reference to man was a system of responsibility, mainly depending on future rewards and punishments." "Every Israelite who came out of Egypt must have been fully acquainted with the universally recognized doctrines of the immortality of the soul, man's responsibility, and future rewards and punishments."——Dr. J. P. Thompson, in supplementing this article on "Egypt," refers to Dr. Lepsius as having given the earliest known text of the [Egyptian] "Book of the Dead" "which contains the

---

* Greppo's Essay, p. 235.
† Greppo's Essay, p. 237.

important doctrines of the immortality of the soul, the rehabilitation of the body, the judgment of both good and bad, the punishment of the wicked, the justification of the righteous and their admission to the blessed state of the gods" (p. 688). See also Bib. Sacra. Oct. 1867, p. 775, and Jany. 1869, p. 190.

Hence we must conclude that even if it were possible that the Hebrews had no knowledge of the future life before they went to Egypt, they must have learned it there. Really however, the fact that this doctrine appears in the oldest records of Egyptian antiquity proves that it came down from Noah—not to say from Adam. It was not indigenous and original with Egypt. It was there because Egypt had retained the primitive beliefs of the race.

In concluding this argument, I refer to the allusions which appear in the Psalms to the future life (*e. g.* Ps. 17, and 37, and 49, and 73),—which speak of it not as being then a new revelation, just sprung upon the universal darkness of all foregoing ages, but distinctly as an old doctrine, to be learned by "going into the sanctuary of God" and there hearing the old Hebrew scriptures publicly read; and also to be seen as illustrated and assumed in the records of God's judgments in time on such sinners as those of the old world, and of Sodom, and as Egypt's hardened king. Let it suffice here to specify Ps. 73, whose author says of himself: "I was envious at the foolish when I saw the prosperity of the wicked. It was too painful for me until I went into the sactuary of God; then I understood *their end*. Surely thou didst set them in slippery places; thou castedst them down into destruction."—"But [all unlike *their* doom] thou wilt guide me with thy counsel and afterward receive me to glory. Whom have I in heaven but thee? And there is none upon earth that I desire besides thee. My flesh and my heart faileth; but thou art the strength of my heart and my portion forever."——The good men who wrote thus, and the worshiping congregations who sung these rapturous strains in their temple worship were not in utter darkness as to the final doom of the wicked, or as to the glorious future life of the righteous.

In closing this volume it only remains to refer in a

word to the progressive developments of God's truth as manifest in these closing portions of the Pentateuch. Of previous points and periods in this history as developing progress I have spoken when the scenes were fresh in our reading and thought;—particularly of the age before the flood; of the scenes in the life of Jacob and Joseph; of the scenes of the Exodus and at Sinai; of the civil code and also of the religious Institutes.——
The few incidents of history during the forty years of wilderness life bring us new lessons, some exceedingly instructive in regard to the intercessory prayers of Moses; many sadly painful, touching the unbelief, the murmuring, the sensuality, and the idolatrous tendencies of Israel. If it were not that apostasies from God occur in our own age, not at all less guilty considering the light sinned against, though less revolting perhaps to the current religious sentiments of the age, we might perhaps afford to pass these historic developments with little notice. Alas, that they should reveal sins of the human heart which it so much behooves us to study for our own admonition!

The book of Deuteronomy is an acquisition to the moral forces of the Pentateuch. Speaking now specially of its first eleven chapters and of its last nine; *i. e.* of the review which Moses gives of the scenes of Sinai and of his accumulation of predicted woes and of appeals at once tender and terrible in the last chapters, it is not easy to over-estimate their moral power. Let us hope that they thrilled the very heart of that generation and toned up their religious life with impulses not only deep and strong but abiding. That generation, then about to enter Canaan under Joshua, was unquestionably the best, morally, which appears throughout the entire history of Israel. For proof of this estimate of them it must suffice to refer to the spirit manifested in Josh. 1: 16–18 and in the entire scenes of Josh. 22, and indeed in the history throughout this book of Joshua.
— —Leaving Egypt while yet young or wilderness born; mostly uncontaminated with her idolatries and pollutions of moral life, looking upon the scenes of the Exodus and of Sinai with young eyes and susceptible souls; trained under Moses forty years; taking the ritual of religious worship in its freshness, with hearts, let us hope in a good measure tender to its first strong im-

pressions—they give us certainly the best fruits of this wonderful moral and religious training. So many fearers of God—so large a host imbued with the spirit of obedience to God's authority—the world had never seen before. They were prepared of God for the conquest of Canaan. They are living witnesses that the discipline of those desert wanderings was not in vain—witnesses also to the moral and spiritual forces of the new revelations which God made of himself during those forty years from Egypt to Canaan.

www.ingramcontent.com/pod-product-compliance
Lightning Source LLC
Chambersburg PA
CBHW052138300426
44115CB00011B/1429